Flying Down to Rio

NUMBER TEN:

Centennial of Flight Series

Roger D. Launius, General Editor

FLYING DOWN TO RIO

Hollywood, Tourists, and Yankee Clippers

by Rosalie Schwartz

Texas A&M University Press
College Station

Library of Congress Cataloging-in-Publication Data

Schwartz, Rosalie
Flying down to Rio : Hollywood, tourists, and Yankee Clippers /
by Rosalie Schwartz.—1st ed.
p. cm. — (Centennial of flight series; no. 10)
Includes bibliographical references and index.
ISBN 1-58544-382-4 (cloth : alk. paper)
ISBN 1-58544-421-9 (pbk : alk. paper)
1. United States—Civilization—20th century. 2. Popular culture—United
States—History—20th century. 3. Technological innovations—Social
aspects—United States—History—20th century. 4. Motion picture
industry—Social aspects—United States—History—20th century. 5. Flying
Down to Rio (Motion picture) 6. Aeronautics—Social aspects—United
States—History—20th century. 7. Tourism—Social aspects—United
States—History—20th century. 8. United States—Territorial expansion.
9. United States—Relations—Latin America. 10. Latin America—
Relations—United States. I. Title. II. Series.
E169.1.S385 2004   303.48′32—dc22
2004003678

For
Yoshiye, Trevor, Lilyan,
and Elizabeth

Contents

Illustrations

Acknowledgments

FAMILY, friends, and colleagues offered timely encouragement and useful suggestions as an intriguing array of serendipitous historical connections jelled into a readable narrative. The knowledge and generosity of the dedicated staff at the San Diego Aerospace Museum, particularly assistant archivist Alan Renga and librarian Pam Gay, guided me through an abundance of treasures to useful gems. As always, Paul Vanderwood carved time from his own scholarly pursuits to read, comment, regenerate, and inspire.

Flying Down to Rio

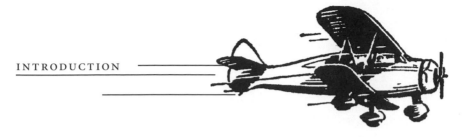

An Entertainment Century

W HO COULD have imagined the degree to which airplane antics, a passion for motion pictures, and an appetite for pleasure travel would shape a century?

Inauspicious Seeds, Powerful Fruit

In December, 1903, a motor-driven, heavier-than-air flying machine—built by Orville and Wilbur Wright and flown first by Orville—remained aloft for twelve seconds and traveled 120 feet. A handful of helpers observed the historic flight at Kill Devil Hills in Kitty Hawk, North Carolina. Most people ignored the achievement, even if they heard about it. In general, disbelief and an inexplicable lack of curiosity marked the debut of the delicate aircraft.

For the next few years the Wright brothers worked in relative obscurity at their home factory in Dayton, Ohio, while they improved their machine's capabilities. When the brothers formed an exhibition team of fliers who followed the circuit of country fairs, the Wright Flyer finally established itself in the consciousness of the country as entertainment. Races and tricks excited the cheering crowds, who accepted the flying machine as one more thrill in their expanding world of commercial amusements. The ticket

buyers purchased seats in the grandstands and watched this fragile, often-unreliable machine climb and dive and loop. Few imagined themselves ever using an airplane for transportation.

While the Wright brothers experimented at Kitty Hawk in
1903, Edwin S. Porter projected an action-packed motion picture,
The Great Train Robbery, before an audience unaccustomed to
such sustained filmed energy, scene after scene, for twelve long
minutes. The perplexed audience watched a theft at gun point,
pursuit of criminals by lawmen on horseback, and the capture of
lawbreakers as they struggled to piece the scripted segments into a
story.

Before long, audiences understood the relationship of the
scenes and integrated them into the intended narrative. They
threw themselves wholeheartedly into the experience and paid
hard-earned money to satisfy an unquenchable thirst for entertainment. Within a few years millions of people in many parts of
the world were enjoying a great variety of silent film comedies and
dramas. As a consequence, an international business complex of
film producers, distributors, and exhibitors blossomed along with
the novel entertainment medium.

In December, 1933, thousands of dedicated moviegoers
trudged through huge snowdrifts and lined up in record-breaking
cold weather to see the much-heralded Christmas show at New
York's Radio City Music Hall, featuring *Flying Down to Rio,* a motion picture romance with spoken dialog and music. At the end of
an elaborately plotted, boy-meets-girl story, in a breathtaking
show-business climax, chorus girls danced on the wings of airplanes high above the heads of tourists at a resort hotel on Copacabana Beach near Rio de Janeiro, Brazil.

A Hollywood studio, RKO-Radio Pictures, produced the film,
and movie stars played the main characters in the story. This statement, commonplace to our ears and perfectly ordinary even in
1933, would have been unintelligible in 1903. The world had leaped
beyond the agricultural rhythms of the nineteenth century, an era
in which farmers and peasants had gradually conformed to the demands of an industrialized society. In the twentieth century, enter-

tainment gained ascendancy as a shaper of people's behavior and expectations and as a determinant of social and cultural values.

At the turn of the last century such a transformation would have been beyond imagining. In only three decades, air travel, tourism, and Hollywood, with its production facilities, movies, and movie stars, staked their claims on the global consciousness.

Global Networks

Mass tourism, air travel, and movies, separately and in conjunction, exert a profound influence on the nature of daily life for a significant proportion of the earth's populace. As international businesses, they provide work and recreation for a worldwide population and engender aspirations, expectations, and behaviors that transcend national borders. Fledgling enterprises at the start of the twentieth century, they achieved global stature as economically and culturally powerful industries, with film companies inaugurating the expansion process.

The motion picture created a global community of shared interests. Over the course of the last century, hundreds of millions of people in numerous countries went to movie theaters, but they watched many of the same films. Tens of thousands of producers, directors, actors, animators, set designers, and so on made movies in any number of locations. They gathered at international film festivals, which, incidentally, evolved into tourist attractions for tens of thousands of fans. Moreover, those fans and aspiring actors and directors read about films and movie stars in newspapers and magazines and watched them on television.

The same—or other—multitudes took pleasure trips and served people who traveled. Increasingly, and most notably in the second half of the century, tourists traveled by airplane to their destinations, particularly to those locations beyond the borders of their own homelands. International travelers confronted unfamiliar and culturally diverse societies within hours of leaving home. Their encounters—variously engaging, voyeuristic, or negative— contributed to a sense of a shrinking world. The networks they wove enmeshed a substantial portion of the world's people in shared or similar experiences, though unequal and often contrived.

The thrill of awesome inventions such as motion pictures and airplanes and the challenge of unaccustomed actions and transactions swept people along the paths of discovery. Twentieth-century culture pioneers adopted new behaviors when they attended movie theaters, boarded passenger airplanes, or traveled for pleasure. They also invented or learned the vocabulary required to communicate in and about this unaccustomed universe. Their life choices became agents of change. Consider this thought-provoking possibility: Entertainment preferences, including which movies to see and what travel destinations to visit, exert an influence on one's circle of friends and potential marriage partners. Thus, we might conjecture that these new lifestyle options help to determine the genetic makeup of subsequent generations.

On the other hand, more hesitant or isolated population segments perhaps shied away from the changes that accompanied the early-twentieth-century emergence and expansion of aviation, movies, and tourism. If these powerful historical forces swept past them at first, the lag dissipated with time, and the world at large has encompassed many formerly self-contained societies.

As an example of the altered consciousness of global citizens fashioned by an entertainment century and the inclusion of remote populations into the entertainment mainstream, consider this contemporary news story. In May, 2002, an Irish musician accompanied a high-ranking U.S. government official (the rocker and the Republican, as the media termed the odd couple) on a ten-day, fact-finding trip to Africa. Bono (Paul Hewson), head of the popular Irish band U2, hoped to influence then–U.S. Treasury Secretary Paul H. O'Neill in the formulation of economic policy concerning the impoverished populations of the African continent.

More "world theater" than diplomacy, the trip fostered Bono's continued efforts to shape global development policy. The well-known, widely traveled musician intended to educate the less-recognizable cabinet official. When the two men met to plan the trip, Secretary O'Neill interrupted Bono to ask a question, prompting Bono's shocked companion to marvel, "The secretary cut right in, which people often don't have the guts to do with a rock star."[1]

That single sentence, hardly a profound statement of cultural or social history, nevertheless gives voice to a twentieth-century transposition in human relations and political status. That is, entertainment and entertainers achieved a stature unimaginable in 1900. Even conceding Bono's familiarity with Africa, the extent of his knowledge, and the sincerity of his concern for Africans, should O'Neill have hesitated to disrupt his train of thought? As treasury secretary of the United States, O'Neill's decisions dramatically affected the global economy. Yet, the cachet of celebrity elevated a rock musician to the position of mentor to a cabinet official of the world's most powerful country.

Rock stars, air travel, movies, and international tourism all represent milestones in twentieth-century cultural history and transformations of consciousness. Within a decade of Porter's *Great Train Robbery,* a visit to the cinema became a ritual. Within several decades of the Wright brothers' flight, people considered international air travel a right. Within a century we have become creatures of entertainment.

Entertainment and Historical Curiosity: The Film as Artifact

The movie *Flying Down to Rio,* product of an entertainment industry, affords the social and cultural historian an interpretive key to the twentieth century, much as historians of antiquity examine the details of coins to trace the paths of commerce. In 1933 an airplane trip from Miami to Rio represented a triumph of aeronautics, as well as a milestone in international travel. That year, RKO-Radio Pictures, with Pan American Airways board member Merian Cooper as production chief, planted Rio as a travel destination in the imaginations of millions of moviegoers. Cheerful chorus girls who performed on the wings of airplanes high above the Brazilian city conveyed a confidence in the reliability of the equipment that provided the thrill of flying. Moreover, the film's tourists were ordinary folk, not the elegant elites who traveled abroad by luxury liner. With an abundance of money and time, affluent tourists had boarded steamships in Europe or in North and South America and had enjoyed Rio de Janeiro's entertainment potential long before RKO-Radio Pictures and Pan American Airways joined forces to extend an invitation to travel by plane.

The beauty of the city alone attracted visitors; the liveliness of the Carnival season enhanced its appeal. As Rio's population doubled between 1900 and 1920, from one-half to one million people, the city's leaders followed the direction of numerous other urban modernizers. They replaced neglected, crumbling, colonial-era houses, churches, and narrow streets with broad boulevards and public buildings—including the impressive Municipal Theater, National Library, and Fine Arts Museum. The first grandly dramatic movie theaters opened in the same area in the mid-1920s. By then, tunnels through the mountains connected the beautiful beaches at Copacabana and Ipanema to central Rio.

By the 1930s many people identified Rio de Janeiro with tropical sensuality, the samba, and the excitement of Carnival revelries. European and African traditions mingled and gave Rio's carnival its distinctive culture. During the pre-Lenten season, neighborhoods formed street dance groups accompanied by their own percussion bands. They began to meet regularly and formed samba schools. By 1933 more than thirty costumed groups built floats, paraded, danced, and competed in the pageantry. The rhythms of the Carnival samba, like the Cuban rumba and Argentinean tango, moved beyond native shores and found new favor with musicians and dancers in far-flung locales.

RKO expended considerable resources to bring Rio de Janeiro to moviegoers. Photographers spent a month capturing the city's mood and attractions on film and then edited a location-setting montage of palm trees, seashore, exclusive shops, horse races, street peddlers, modern buildings, and nighttime city lights, all backed by lively Latin rhythms.

Flying Down to Rio, the musical comedy with a tourism-related plot, caught my attention and piqued my curiosity when I wrote *Pleasure Island: Tourism and Temptation in Cuba.* Working backward from 1933, I explored the history of its production and, as the pieces fell into place, assessed its significance. This probe

into the movie turned up a fascinating story, less a history of aviation or film or tourism per se than their interaction within the
context of the evolving entertainment culture. That is, the sciences
of aerodynamics and optics yielded the technologies that underpinned the development of airplanes and motion pictures. As a
global phenomenon, people in crowded urban centers or in scattered communities integrated the new technologies into their lives
as forms of art and commercial entertainment. In varying degrees
they gradually devoted greater time and energy to the pursuit of diversion. The multitude of new amusements included planned trips
to attractive destinations (i.e., tourism). Thus, a collage of episodes, experiences, and ideas unveiled connections among technology, art, and twentieth-century cultural change.

Studying the film's production also widened my frame of reference on the Depression-era business climate and the interplay between culture and corporate profits. RKO-Radio Pictures expected
the movie to deliver financial rewards, of course, with long lines of
eager moviegoers lined up at the box office. Pan American Airways
anticipated enhanced revenues from airline ticket purchases stimulated by the film. The airline operated profitably, thanks to U.S.
government airmail contracts but sought passengers to fill the
seats in its newer, bigger planes.

Pan Am, the only international airline operating from the
United States in the 1930s, carried North Americans to Rio and
other destinations in the Caribbean and Central and South America aboard comfortable, four-motor passenger planes that bore
no resemblance to the Wrights' flying machine. The airline called
its planes "Clippers," after the swift, ocean-crossing commercial
ships of the nineteenth century. To lure prospective travelers, Pan
Am circulated seductively illustrated brochures that offered the romance and excitement of foreign travel along with the safety and
speed of flying.

Air Travel and the Promise of Romance

The plot and action of *Flying Down to Rio* reinforced the airline's sales messages. Gene Raymond, fair haired and pleasant

faced, not unlike aviation hero Charles Lindbergh, played happy-go-lucky Roger Bond. The character more than filled audience expectations for a romantic fantasy hero. Endowed with good looks and wealth, Bond flies his own plane. He also writes music and leads a dance band called the Yankee Clippers, an obvious reminder of Pan Am's planes. Impetuous and supremely confident and an irrepressible playboy, Bond aggressively pursues his romantic inclinations, even though his dalliances sometimes interfere with band schedules. Fred Astaire plays Bond's witty, ironic, loyal sidekick, Fred Ayres, the band's accordionist.

The action begins when Bond and Ayres rush into a nightclub, having arrived in Miami in Bond's plane, just in time for the Yankee Clipper band's weekly radio show. The musical troupe plays in (and broadcasts on the radio from) the lavishly decorated Date Grove at the Hotel Hibiscus in the tropical tourist mecca of Miami, Florida.

If Bond is at all apologetic about his tardy arrival, he gives no hint of it but picks up his baton and starts the music. The first number communicates a mischievous nonconformity to both the nightclub audience and the movie viewer. Honey Hale (Ginger Rogers), glamorously dressed in an alluring, translucent outfit, sings the suggestive song lyrics: "In me you see a sinner, and music is my crime. . . . Music makes me do the things I never should do."

Indeed, the film's musical numbers stir romantic thoughts, rouse a desire to dance new dances with new partners, and tempt viewers to fly to Brazil—things that people might hesitate to undertake under ordinary circumstances.

Even as Honey Hale sings the playful words, Roger Bond's attention wanders. While he directs the musicians, he also assesses his romantic prospects in the nightclub. His roving eye falls on a lovely, regal Brazilian, Belinha de Rezende, seductively portrayed by Dolores Del Rio. The flirtation that follows sets up the plot and, more importantly, moves the story's location to Brazil.

Belinha has come to the Date Grove with several young North American girlfriends and her ever-watchful aunt and chaperone. Hale, the scrappy, liberated, working-girl vocalist contrasts in class, manner, and style with Belinha, but Hale's musical confession reaches Belinha. Contrary to the restraints her cultural background imposes but encouraged by her friends, she turns on the charm to entice Bond. He responds eagerly, hands the baton to Ayres, and moves from bandstand to Belinha's table and then to the dance floor. One of Belinha's female companions wisecracks, "What have you South Americans got below the equator that we haven't?"

Bond once again has breached a limit of professional conduct. An officious hotel manager who has forbidden employees to fraternize with the guests fires the entire band. "Here we go again," groans Ayres, as he, Hale, and the other musicians worry about their sudden unemployment. Reversals of fortune certainly played to the sympathies of the depression-era movie audience, but unlike the real-life viewers, the musical comedy plot rescued the actors. Belinha's father falls ill; the resort hotel he plans to open loses its orchestra; and Roger Bond receives a radiogram from old college friend Julio Rubeiro (Raoul Roulien) to bring the band to Rio, where a job awaits.

Unfortunately for Belinha, she has learned of her father's illness too late in the day to catch the scheduled Pan American Airways flight bound from Miami for Rio. Bond offers to fly her to Port au Prince, Haiti, to catch up with the plane on the airline's first overnight stop. (The absence of beacon lights precluded nighttime operations in 1933. The trip therefore took a week, with multiple overnight stops.) Belinha's aunt would follow on the next scheduled flight, along with the band. A hesitant Belinha, anxious about her father, accepts the offer.

Bond's instinct for conquest overcomes his gallantry. A pretense of engine trouble sets up an opportunity for both a romantic interlude and a pitch for Haiti as a tourist destination (via Pan American, of course). His plane conveniently carries its own piano, and on the lonely stretch of beach where he has made an emergency landing, the romantic lyrics and sensuous music of "Orchids in the Moonlight" almost make Belinha do things she should not even consider. She finally breaks the romantic spell and explains her reticence: Her life is arranged; she is promised to another man. That's the way of life in Brazil, and she cannot break with convention. Belinha goes to sleep—alone.

In the morning a man carrying a golf bag informs her that the seemingly wild natives who frightened her into startled wakefulness are in fact energetic employees of the Haitian hotel on whose beach she has slept. They are headed for their morning swim. The helpful caddy, who inexplicably speaks British-accented English rather than French patois, also reveals that the Rio-bound plane is on the runway. Her reputation unsullied, Belinha flies Pan Am to Rio, while Bond continues the air journey solo.

Once Belinha, Bond, and the band are reunited in Rio, romantic wire-crossing moves the plot forward. Bond's old friend Julio is, of course, Belinha's betrothed, and the band's engagement is at her father's hotel. So, Bond's wooing of Belinha will be considered the betrayal of a friend when Julio learns of the relationship; moreover, Bond's aggressive pursuit of romance could cost the band another gig.

The move to Rio adds a political dimension to the otherwise customary Hollywood romantic triangle. Three unsavory Europeans, colluding with bankers to cause the financial failure of the new hotel so that they can take it over, plot against Belinha's father.

The villains' skullduggery hinges on the issuance of an entertainment permit without which the band cannot play at the hotel. If disappointed guests disparage the Hotel Atlántico's management and discourage future reservations, the loss of income will result in nonpayment of loans, foreclosure by the bank, and seizure of the property by the conspiratorial Europeans.

The menacing characters show up as shadows of men wearing top hats and carrying walking sticks. As their silhouettes fall across a poster announcing the hotel's opening, a workman comments solemnly, "The shadows of the buzzards." Moviegoers in December, 1933, understandably might have connected the Europeans who cast shadows on Brazil with the threat of fascist expansion into Latin America.

With the subplot of a threat to Belinha's father's business established, the story returns to lively Rio. The hotel has not yet opened, so the band members check out the musical competition at a Brazilian nightclub. The maître d' at the Carioca Casino warmly welcomes the band members as honored guests from a sister continent. ("Carioca" is the nickname for Rio's residents.)

The nightclub visit sets up the movie's spirited centerpiece, an eighteen-minute, lavishly costumed, and intricately choreographed musical extravaganza. The scene starts slowly, almost comically, and then gains momentum. Musicians and then the singers and dancers arrive on the bandstand a few at a time. The camera pulls back to capture the entire elaborate scene and to incorporate the movie audience into the nightclub setting. The tempo picks up. Singers warn the audience about the effects of the Brazilian dance called the carioca—"It's not a fox-trot or a polka; when you dance it, you find love." Then dozens of costumed dancers take up the beat while the camera moves in and out, alternating close-ups of feet and bodies with wide shots of the whole stage area. Singers and dancers fill the club and the screen.

The Yankee Clipper band players respond to the musical beat, and Fred Ayres says to Honey Hale, "Let's try it." They dance the captivating carioca, easily picking up the steps, of course, to the appreciative applause of the Brazilians, and the band members confess, "Our music can't top this."

Meanwhile, a welcome-home party for Belinha is underway at the Aviators' Club—an elaborate, multitiered banquet hall where uniformed attendants keep out the rabble and the orchestra plays from a large platform hung from the ceiling, simulating the basket of a hot-air balloon. Roger and Julio unhappily discover each other's involvement with Belinha. Moreover, Julio has sensed an aloofness in Belinha's behavior. He suspects Bond is the cause because his old friend has related his pursuit of a new Brazilian love, and Belinha has just returned from the United States.

Eventually they resolve their romantic rivalry through mutual self-sacrifice. Roger develops an understanding of and appreciation for Brazilian traditions and steps aside so that Julio and Belinha can marry. Then, when Julio realizes that Belinha really loves Roger, he pushes them into each other's arms and arranges for their marriage by the captain of a Pan American plane headed back to the United States.

While the love story pairs the appropriate partners, Yankee ingenuity and a little rule bending save the Hotel Atlántico. Unable to obtain the proper entertainment permit for the hotel, Fred Ayres stages the opening-day show, with its contingent of beautiful girls, on the wings of airplanes *above* the hotel, rather than *in* it. The ingenious Yankee Clippers save Belinha's father's hotel from the scheming "buzzards," and Roger Bond marries Belinha. Thus, the film has reassured audiences that North and South America can live in harmony, with mutual respect and well-intentioned assistance when needed.

Flying Down to Rio's breathtaking finale dazzled moviegoers and film critics. Although the words on the screen proclaimed, "Hotel Atlántico presents the Yankee Clippers," with scenes of Rio behind the planes, RKO filmed the dance sequence in southern California with rear-projection technology. Hollywood beauties moved their torsos in choreographed syncopation on the wings of airplanes while wind machines plastered costumes against curvaceous bodies and hair flared backward behind lovely faces.

Dozens of chorus girls, strapped into safety harnesses, sang the title song, with its exuberant message of modernity: "An old sailor in old times would sing an old song, 'Rolling Down to Rio by the Sea.' A young sailor in these times would sing a new song, 'Flying Down to Rio.' Come with me. Got to get to Rio and got to make time. You'll love it, high above it."

Inspiration for the song's lyrics came from the pen of the romantic, nineteenth-century imperialist, intrepid traveler, and spinner of stories Rudyard Kipling. The poem at the end of *The Beginning of the Armadilloes*, one of Kipling's *Just So Stories* for children—this one set along the Amazon River—expresses a longing to roll down to Rio on one of the great white-and-gold steamers that left Southampton, England, each week. Kipling finally visited Rio in 1927, twenty-five years after he wrote the story and the poem and five years before he might have joined the modern travelers who flew to the grand city.

Old times, new times; sea voyages, air travel. Actors portrayed North American tourists, described stereotypically in script directions—women wear Sears Roebuck hats and men in horn-rimmed glasses, shorts, and sun helmets smoke cigars. They watch the pageantry from the terrace of a Rio seaside resort hotel and respond with appropriate expressions of awe and excitement. For moviegoers who longed to visit Rio, camera magic created a fantasy trip. Whatever the reality, the illusion thrilled audiences.

In 1933 RKO Radio Pictures connected tourism to air travel in *Flying Down to Rio*. By 1953 post–World War II prosperity, coupled with bigger, faster, and safer airplanes, extended the parameters of international tourism. By 2003—a century after the Wright brothers' flight—an international economic sector developed around tourist revenue, and the mass tourism industry depended in large measure on people's desires to be entertained, on sufficiently high levels of disposable income, and on a relatively peaceful world.

Flying Down to Rio stirred thoughts of air travel in 1933. Since then, significant segments of the world's population have incorporated practices, rituals, and values into their lives based on the development of aviation and the motion picture and tourist industries. They pass these behavior patterns and expectations on to new generations while understanding little of their origins. Meanwhile, the industries have achieved global proportions and exert exceptional social, political, and economic power. How might a book about movies, air travel, and tourism shed light on this process?

This book begins with those educational and exhilarating tourist attractions, the turn-of-the-century world's fairs. The wondrous Chicago World's Columbian Exposition of 1893 and the Louisiana Purchase Exposition held in St. Louis in 1904 set lofty standards for visual impact and intense activity. Only slightly less dramatic and ambitious, trade and commemorative fairs at New Orleans, Omaha, and Buffalo made their own contributions to the development of event tourism.[2]

The short-lived expositions exploded on the urban landscape, energized people's consciousness for a number of months, and then ceased operations. However, we might compare the inventive and instructive impacts of their ephemeral existence to the phenomenon of beautiful objects dropped into a river. Although the objects themselves quickly disappear beneath the surface, they generate expanding ripples that intersect with other interruptions in the flow of life. At those fairs, the past collided with the future in unpredictable ripples.

The colossal exhibitions whetted appetites for novel and exotic entertainment and satisfied a growing thirst for travel. Along with the latest machinery, fair operators paraded tribal peoples from around the world before curious onlookers. Like the Paris exposition of 1889, Chicago's fair also assembled scholarly conclaves. Aeronautical pioneers exchanged visions and findings as part of Chicago's series of scientific and philosophical meetings. Frederick Jackson Turner presented his seminal essay on the closing of the frontier at the annual meeting of the American Historical Association, held in Chicago in 1893 at the invitation of the fair's promoters. Edison's Kinetoscope—that early example of a motion-picture machine—made an appearance as well.

The St. Louis Fair devoted considerable space to a field for flight demonstrations, used new techniques of photographed visual effects in its displays, and brought the modern Olympics to the United States. New Orleans and Buffalo both focused on commercial ties to Latin America. Omaha integrated the conquest of the trans-Mississippi West into a larger, worldwide mission for the United States. Visitors to these fairs, numbering in the tens of millions, rewarded the visions of promoters and the confidence of investors, took their memories and impressions home with them, and spread the joys of pleasure travel to fellow Americans through postcards.

Airplanes and motion pictures added their own ripples to international cross-currents. Two chapters in this book track the evolution of scientific invention into spectator amusements like nickelodeons and barnstorming air circuses, which then became life-altering, economically powerful industries—film studios and commercial airlines. The interplay between them is embedded in the wider history of U.S. commercial and territorial expansion and international competition.

Experimenters, engineers, and entrepreneurs dominated aviation in the decades between 1893 and 1913. The Wright brothers' plane unleashed a fierce competition on both sides of the Atlantic

Ocean that advanced the viability of flying machines and placed pilots in the vanguard of technology's heroes. Air meets drew tourists eager to see speed, distance, and altitude records broken or perhaps hoping to be taken aloft as passengers. By 1913 aerial competitors flew from city to city for prizes, an early indication that airplanes might develop commercial significance as transportation.

Also by 1913, established motion picture studios engaged in the international trade in multireel narratives. They created film stars and promoted them through movie magazines in order to ensure audience loyalty. They also incorporated airplanes into action films that featured breathtaking aerial stunts.

The loops and dives of stunt flying became real maneuvers in World War I, after which people and governments took the possibilities of commercial aviation more seriously. Airline companies formed in the 1920s and competed for investment capital, but airplane crashes took a tremendous toll on pilots and equipment. While movie plots based on midair robberies, chases, and crashes did little to assure audiences that planes were safe, Charles A. Lindbergh's 1927 trans-Atlantic solo flight drew attention to improvements in aircraft design that made sustained flight feasible.

Tourists formed a pioneering contingent in the nineteenth-century movement to explore the western United States, although few historians recognized their contributions to conservation and population growth. Forerunners of eco-, health-, and ethno-tourism, they rode the railroads to national parks and the lands of Native Americans and went to California for winter warmth. In the 1920s some tourists traveled west by plane, while others traveled to Mexico and Cuba to outwit the agents of Prohibition.

The next chapter traces the histories of two companies that flourished in the period of air-mindedness and movie madness and became linked briefly in 1933. As market potential and improved production techniques turned the technological innovations of the 1910s into the airline and movie industries of the 1920s, Pan American Airways and RKO Radio Pictures rode an exhilarating, but risky, wave.

The politics and personalities entangled in their rise to prominence reflect the business optimism of a roaring decade. A generation steeped in technological utopianism overlay their financial ambitions with social purpose; that is, both airplanes and movies promised to bring people together in peace. On the other hand, the companies also represented the cutting edges of transportation and communications sectors that relentlessly contended for market domination, both domestically and internationally.

Given the connection between the companies, RKO's movies about airplanes are particularly revealing. Five films released in 1932 and 1933 suggest an attempt to redirect the public's attitude toward airplanes and air travel. At a time when increased passenger traffic required confidence in air safety, RKO's production chief, Merian C. Cooper, also sat on Pan American Airways' board of directors.

In 1932 Cooper brought to RKO a long-standing love of flying, experience in film production, and an idea for a project that imagined an epic battle between civilization and nature. In Cooper's *King Kong,* airplanes defeat the beast that threatens both fair womanhood and the metropolis that embodies modern society. RKO released *King Kong* in 1933.

The Lost Squadron, another film made under Cooper's aegis, criticized Hollywood's callousness toward the safety of stunt pilots. Thus, if planes crashed in movie thrillers, egotistical directors who fed the audience's desire for thrills could be blamed, not the planes themselves. *Christopher Strong* placed a beautiful woman in the cockpit, demonstrating how tame flying machines had become. *Flying Devils* transformed stunt fliers into contented airline pilots who protected passengers' lives and guarded their own. Finally, *Flying Down to Rio* combined safety, convenience, romance, and good times and wrapped them all in a tourism-driven musical fantasy.

Pan American Airways flew to Rio and all around Latin America in 1933, an area of the world—and a market—very much in the forefront of U.S. interests. Since the movie's themes reflect the larger world of commercial competition in the hemisphere, the next chapter embeds air commerce and tourism in the complexity of Depression-era international relations and then briefly addresses the ties among airplanes, movies, and international tourism on the eve of World War II. Even President Franklin D. Roosevelt wanted people to fly to Rio in 1933. This last chapter confirms the unusual perspective on U.S. foreign policy that *Flying Down to Rio,* with its airplanes and tourism, imparts to the curious historian.

CHAPTER 1

Reflections on Wonderlands

THE UNDULATING mirrors elicited chuckles from curious gawkers, whose altered reflections flashed back at them. Bemused fairgoers in the Temple of Mirth at the 1904 Louisiana Purchase Exposition watched themselves grow fat and thin, short and tall—or disappear altogether—as they approached the mirrors, backed away, or moved from side to side. Every direction they turned, their reflection changed. People laughed at the distorted images and left the fun house to enjoy the excitement of a mile-long amusement zone that exploded with noise and color and movement. Barkers and pitchmen coaxed them to one inviting location or another to enjoy the mechanical and human diversions, the technological marvels, and the educational exhibits of the sensation-filled St. Louis fair.

The fun-house mirrors, in which each angle of one's gaze offered a new and different perception, represented the marvel of the great, turn-of-the-century world's fairs. The fairs reflected a complex and changing world from different and sometimes contradictory perspectives—self-reflective yet conscious of others; serious yet frivolous; cosmopolitan yet provincial; industrial yet agricultural; intellectual yet practical.

In the United States, expositions in Philadelphia, Chicago, Atlanta, Omaha, Buffalo, and St. Louis celebrated a machine age and ushered in an entertainment century. They revealed the excitement of a young country confident in its achievements, eager to take on greater challenges, and anxious to be accepted as a powerful force among the world's nations. Convinced of the progress of human history, fair organizers typically commemorated past events in order to celebrate the future. They staged a world and imparted their vision to visitors. Moviemakers and tourism promoters would do the same.

The world's fairs functioned in part as giant collections of curiosities and wonders. Cabinets of curiosities, or *Wunderkamern,* became popular in Europe in the sixteenth and seventeenth centuries, around the time that explorers ventured into new lands. Collectors accumulated, documented, and organized unusual or rare items that demonstrated the marvels of the natural world, as well as artifacts and devices fashioned by humans. They created a microcosm of the world as they knew it and presented that world to others to enjoy.

The multifaceted, ambitious fairs similarly opened windows onto the world for those fortunate enough to attend. Fair organizers distilled representations of a world that they hoped to share with millions of people within a limited extension of time and space. However, even as they prepared their displays of technology, art, and culture, the world changed. The achievements the fairs highlighted—whether steam engines, electric lights, or automobiles—reconfigured economic and social relationships even as people walked among the exhibits.

The expositions attracted tourists, whose admission fees repaid the underwriters and investors. Exhibits aroused curiosity and suggested destinations for future adventures, while the amusement zones mixed information, fun, fakery, and visions of the future. With their diverse missions, the fairs expanded a consciousness of the world, promoted education and scholarship, and bestowed legitimacy on commercial entertainment.

The serious, self-reflective aspect of these fairs celebrated the tremendous economic growth the United States enjoyed in the last quarter of the nineteenth century. Led by the industrial sector, the gross national product quadrupled; the value of manufactured goods increased by a factor of ten; and railroad track mileage increased ninefold. Mechanical processes and the factory system generated unprecedented leaps in productivity; accumulated profits turned over as investment capital.

From time to time, however, productive capacity outpaced the need for goods and caused an economic downturn. Then the expositions served as great trade fairs. Philadelphia's Centennial Exhibition of 1876, for example, celebrated a century of national history but shared the country's attention with an acute and lingering depression. To everyone's satisfaction, the successful exhibition garnered credit for increased domestic and foreign commerce.

A decade later the necessity to find new markets to absorb surplus production instigated the effort behind the 1885 World's Industrial and Cotton Exposition in New Orleans. Exposition directors set their sights on the Latin American market, which they perceived would benefit the city's shipping interests, as well as improve the export potential for the entire Mississippi Valley.

The opening of the Chicago World's Fair coincided with a particularly severe economic slump, characterized by financial panic, cuts in wage rates, a drop in farm prices that precipitated a high rate of mortgage foreclosures, and layoffs in every industry. The distress of hard-hit farmers and wage earners, set off by the "Panic of 1893," contrasted sharply with the fair's optimistic gaiety. Whereas the fair lasted only six months, the economic depression continued for four years.

Columbus himself had launched his fifteenth-century voyage in the interest of international trade, a precedent well appreciated by the business leaders whose vision and money impelled the Columbian exposition. Economic necessity, in fact, reinforced the strategy of the organizers, who aggressively courted Latin American participation. Two years before the fair opened and before the Panic inflicted its hardships, a ten-man delegation had traveled to various Latin American capitals with a message that combined good will and good business. In establishing their credentials as alternative trading partners to the more favored Europeans, the delegates affirmed a common hemispheric history, since Columbus had opened all of the Americas to European contact. In response to this Pan-American spirit, six Latin American nations built representative pavilions at the fair, while others organized displays for inclusion in larger buildings.

The United States, in fact, assumed a larger posture in world commercial and political circles between 1893, the year the world's Columbian exposition opened in Chicago, and 1904, when St. Louis hosted the Louisiana Purchase Exposition. Both fairs commemorated territorial expansion by established nations into acquired territory (Spain in 1492 and the United States in 1803). Not without debate and fierce opposition, the United States had joined another scramble for colonial possessions in the late nineteenth century and gained Hawaii, Puerto Rico, and the Philippines. Moreover, President Theodore Roosevelt precipitated the separation of Panama from the sovereign nation of Colombia in 1903 and wrested a strip of land from the newly independent Panamanians on which to build a trans-isthmian canal.

By 1904, a decade of well-attended fairs had invoked the material abundance conferred by technological advances. Grandiose architecture and the statuary of the expositions—imitative of classical Greece and Rome, Renaissance Europe, and Golden Age Spain—embodied the ideals, aspirations, and self-satisfaction of the nation.

Ironically, two remarkable technological innovations of the turn of the last century, airplanes and motion pictures, prefigured a world prominence for the United States far beyond the imaginations of the manufacturers, merchants, expansionists, and empire builders of the time.

Wonderlands of Entertainment

The promoters and designers of expositions located myriad displays of civilization's accomplishments in intentionally lofty settings, expressive of the grandeur of human capabilities. The stupefying array of new and experimental technologies (electricity, wireless telegraphy, automobiles, and indoor plumbing among them) became ordinary conveniences in the twentieth century.

The mainly upper-class proponents of Chicago's Columbian exposition had no significant reputation as seekers of unaccustomed and uncontrolled revelry. Exposition organizers, mainly civic leaders from business and financial circles able to pledge funds to the enterprise or principals of the stature required to persuade others to invest, generally agreed on the criteria for acceptable activities and behavior among their peers. They formed the city's establishment, with the power and authority to shape the destinies of their communities and to determine who could gain access to the social power structure.

In keeping with their status as patrons of progress, the backers authorized stately settings for their exposition and entrusted the conceptualization and implementation of their multipurpose visions to a considerable contingent of urban planners, architects, sculptors, muralists, landscapers, and scientists. However, at the same time that they extolled the achievements of innovation, work, and intellect, the investors kept an eye on the public's increasing inclination toward travel, recreation, and play. The mostly middle and upper strata of society filled the ranks of an excursion market that the backers hoped to tap as assurance of profit on their investment.

In recounting the history of vacations in the United States, Cindy S. Aron relates the post–Civil War growth of vacation tourism to increased disposable income, railroad building, and the advent of travel agents who both apprised people of desirable trips and facilitated their access to travel and lodging facilities.[1]

Most late-nineteenth-century tourists traveled to resorts and recreational areas that permitted them to maintain the proprieties established at home. They visited natural attractions such as Niagara Falls and Yellowstone Park, historically significant locations in the United States, and Europe's sedate health spas and culturally rich cities. A small percentage of tourists followed the advance of the railroads into the Southwest and Mexico or capitulated to the enticement of steamship travel to the Caribbean.

With the transcontinental railroad completed in 1869, the more rigorous touring vacation, that is, a visit to several locations of a healthful or instructionally beneficial nature, gained favor over stays at a convenient seaside or mountain resort where fresh air, space to move about freely, and minimal exertion were the objectives. Because critics warned of the dangers of resort-engendered idleness—leading to dissipation and moral ruin—sightseers "who toured from place to place could persuade themselves that they were engaged in purposeful activity," given the "educational, spiritual, or patriotic benefits of their 'jaunts.'" When they visited places that "glorified American achievement, industriousness, ingenuity, perseverance, and heroism," their travels gained acceptance as self-improvement rather than indulgence.[2]

The transcontinental railroad also sent the moneyed classes of the Gilded Age to the West to explore the open spaces, enjoy the scenery, experience its cities, and meet the indigenous populations. Luxurious hotels opened in the 1880s to cater to the newly rich residents of an urbanized and industrialized East and Middle West. Leisure time and money expanded the market for natural wonders and human oddities, and railroad companies linked Pullman's elegant "palace cars" onto excursion trains that permitted comfort-loving passengers to alight, experience the promised attraction, and reboard without undue distress.[3]

When railroads connected the United States to Mexico in the 1880s, promotional materials encouraged North Americans to make their tours even more educational, as well as adventurous. The Mexican Central and National Railways connected the U.S. border to Mexico City, thus creating possibilities for train trips from the northern heartland to the very center of Mexico. In the effort to increase the demand for their services, railroad promoters offered the scenery, history, and historic ruins of Mexico as an alternative to Europe and promised friendly people and sunshine in the package. Not unlike today's government tourist boards, railroad owners provided journalists with free excursions, expecting, of course, that subsequent articles would laud the beauties of Mexico and spread the message to readers. Promotional materials also enticed privileged travelers with the prospect of fine dining and contented rest in the luxury of well-appointed palace cars while Mexico's unique scenery passed their train windows.[4]

Increased business and tourist travel to Mexico justified publication of *Appleton's Guide to Mexico* in 1884. Some of author Alfred R. Conkling's hints to potential visitors probably encouraged them to remain within the confines of their train cars, since his advice contrasted sharply with promoters' portrayals of a benign, relaxing journey among friendly natives. Although tourists had little to fear from train robberies, Conkling affirmed, travelers should go armed and keep their firearms in sight. He also warned them that villages where tourists might obtain food and lodging were few and far between. Without some familiarity with the Spanish language, moreover, they should not attempt to travel alone. Conversely, he discouraged large parties since most hotels had only a few rooms.

While Conkling provided useful tips, his admonitions could hardly be considered encouraging. The public officials or businessmen who hoped to transform a location into a tourist destination might have found his recommendations less than satisfactory. For example, Conkling warned that lack of transportation might force a visitor to spend two or three days in some uninteresting town. Winter months were the best time to visit Mexico, he promised, because yellow fever rarely broke out then. During the rainy months of June to September, the fortunate tourist would avoid the clouds of dust that often covered the central Mexican plateau, and the air would be delightful. However, the rainy season often made the roads impassable. When the stage coaches sank into the muddy highways, travel came to a halt altogether.[5]

No doubt, many vacationers passed up Conkling's invitation to visit Mexico and instead chose to explore a pseudo-Mexican village installed at one of the world's fairs held in the United States.

By the turn of the twentieth century, perceptions of the good life included leisure travel and commercial entertainment. World's fairs encouraged both. The advent of mass tourism reflected the confluence of three forces: destination, motivation, and transportation. The potential pleasure traveler had to be made aware of a location, find it attractive, and be able to reach it in relative safety and comfort. Promotional materials for world's fairs communicated those attributes to potential attendees. Travelers to expositions looked forward to unaccustomed cultural encounters; they experienced extravagant concentrations of sensual stimuli. In this way, the fairs set the stage for the twentieth-century's mass tourist industry and an addiction to amusement.

World's Fair Enchantments

Christopher Columbus had opened a process of cultural transference when his ships unintentionally encountered uncharted lands. Spain subsequently took physical possession of the lands he claimed and founded cities for Spanish colonists. England and France carved their own colonies out of American territory. Four hundred years after Columbus, the promoters of the World Columbian Exposition brought classical and Renaissance Europe to the banks of Lake Michigan, created the majestic, though temporary, White City, and invited everyone to celebrate.

Civilization—urban life—represented as splendid, inspiring, and uplifting, expressed the exposition's concept of civic culture. Human beings had advanced the totality of knowledge in the service of social improvement. The artifacts of an industrial age, on display in impressive profusion in grand exhibition halls, reinforced the commanding impression created by the Court of Honor, with its vistas of elongated palacelike structures facing each other across a wide pool of water. Faux marble arcades, multicolumn façades, and rooftop domes shone in the sunlight or basked in artificial illumination at night. Tenements, slums, poverty, and disease found no representation in this urban arena.

Teams of designers translated the ideas behind the exposition into structures. Foreign participants put the best, or best-known, achievements of their societies on exhibit. Smithsonian Institution associates lent their expertise to science and technology displays. Ethnologists and anthropologists arranged for representative groups of other cultures to transfer their daily activities to the fairgrounds. In carrying out their work, they acted as agents of the exposition's educational mission. More than simply a showplace, the fair communicated information visually and transmitted knowledge through personal interaction with objects and people. This exceptional opportunity fostered awareness of, and experience with, the world beyond one's own limited geography.[6]

More than twenty-seven million adults and children paid their admissions to the Chicago fair, at a time when the U.S. census recorded some sixty-three million people, and the entire labor force counted little more than twenty-eight million. With industrial workers earning some $480 a year and clerical personnel averaging about $840, a round-trip ticket to Chicago might represent a considerable sacrifice, even when the railroads offered special excursion fares and a modest hotel cost $1 a night.

The cost of transportation, admission, and incidental expenses meant that most fairgoers came from the middle-to-upper social sectors, although special-rate days afforded access to a wider spectrum of the local population. Certainly, visitors from abroad came from the upper classes. Since the electric tramway cost only a nickel, no doubt some Chicago residents went more than once to the fairgrounds. Photos of crowds at the fair show men with open-neck shirts and caps amid the velvet-trimmed jackets, celluloid collars, and occasional top hat of more affluent attendees. Most people dressed up for the occasion, despite Chicago's summer heat, and the fanciful decorations of women's hats appear throughout the crowd.[7]

A day at the fair could be an exhausting pursuit. Awed by the charm of the lakeside setting, the harmonious beauty of the structures, and the excitement of the crowds, visitors traversed the grounds and then trod miles of walkways through exhibits of machinery and technology. Views of the fairgrounds from electric-powered elevated railroads and gondola rides on the water competed with daily concerts. Free in the daytime and subject to admission fees at night, the musical entertainment included both popular and classical pieces to cover a wide range in tastes.

Festive though they surely were, the fair's official activities tended more toward expanding knowledge than inducing laughter. As for amusements, the upper social strata demonstrated a preference for the familiar, staid, and structured presentations of legitimate theater and for the concert hall over vaudeville and bur-

Tourists "saw the world" at the St. Louis Fair. Some sampled Egyptian food and rode camels at the Streets of Cairo exhibit. *Courtesy of the Missouri Historical Society.*

lesque, where both the performance and the audience's decorum might prove less than predictable. Thus, fair operators contracted private concessionaires to provide the livelier attractions and consigned their offerings to an area deliberately separated from the achievements of civilization.

Despite the best intentions of cultural guardians, the circuslike atmosphere of the Midway Plaisance, with its noise and bustle and smells of unfamiliar food, proved the primary attraction for a significant portion of Chicago's twenty-seven million paid attendees. Their admission fees helped to cover the expenses and contributed to the profits that investors enjoyed, a reality not overlooked by subsequent fair promoters and entrepreneurs who invested in amusement parks.

The appeal of exotic entertainment and the promise of an opportunity to satisfy curiosity about foreign cultures still find their way into tourist brochures, and those who respond still generate profits for investors.

Each of the world's fairs boasted its unique attractions. Chicago launched what became a classic midway attraction—the sinuous belly dance of "Little Egypt." Although the suggestive muscular gyrations of the bare-midriffed Fahreda Mahzar may have scandalized some viewers, no one who saw the legendary young dancer forgot the performance.

What the French termed a *danse du ventre,* Americans translated into hootchy-kootchy, and the word made its way into the dictionary. Expositions that followed, whether in Atlanta, Nashville, Omaha, Buffalo, or St. Louis, generally found room for a belly dancer or two. As visual shorthand for the exotic Middle East, movie directors often included belly dancers to establish the atmosphere and location of their films, and the sinuous sirens have functioned as representative cultural performers for thousands of tour participants.

The Columbian exposition and subsequent fairs bequeathed an entertainment legacy of successful attractions to generations of amusement park operators and tourism promoters, including museum displays, historical reproductions, and battle reenactments. Chicago's respected Field Museum, for example, originally housed industrial and commercial collections from the fair, as well as anthropological exhibits that illustrated the technological achievements and lifestyles of a variety of the world's societies.[8] Similarly, the fine arts exhibit in St. Louis's Forest Park contributed to the cultural uplift mission of Louisiana Purchase Exposition promoters before it became a public museum.

Millions of people munched Cracker Jack and ate ice cream cones (introduced to the public in 1893 and 1904 at the Chicago and St. Louis fairs, respectively) as they wandered through a temporary world—a fascinating, exhilarating, exaggerated, wavy-mirrored cosmos—created by civic leaders and exhibition professionals to enlighten, amuse, and amaze them.

The directors of both Atlanta's 1895 Cotton States and International Exposition and Nashville's 1897 Tennessee Centennial Exposition paid tribute to the antebellum South and contracted with concessionaires who produced fanciful, self-serving representations of plantation life; that is, they hired African Americans to play contented slaves who sang to fiddle and banjo accompaniment and danced old-time dances. While Georgia and Tennessee together counted about four million in population at the time of their respective fairs, some three million entrants—most undoubtedly born after the Civil War—had an opportunity to "visit" a sanitized version of their history. Like most tourists, they satisfied their curiosity without questioning the authenticity of the presentation.

Concessionaires sold miniature cotton bales as souvenirs at the Old Plantation exhibit in Buffalo in 1901. They also reminded visitors to Buffalo's Pan-American Exposition that slaves had suffered hardships that only a contented nature permitted them to endure. However, the cheerfulness that the selected southern African Americans displayed on the "plantation" had been carefully rehearsed at a performance school operated by a midway impresario.[9] If the performance proved entertaining, the history lesson remained suspect.

The same complaint could be directed at the Native American encampment arranged by an agent of the Bureau of Indian Affairs for the 1898 Trans-Mississippi and International Exposition in Omaha, Nebraska. Fairgoers wandered among tents and tepees to observe the everyday life of various tribes that occupied the land before the settlers arrived. Family groups prepared meals and carried out religious ceremonies under the watchful gaze of paying customers.[10]

However, battle reenactments contradicted this peaceful pageantry. Omaha's contribution to theatrical excitement pitted settlers against hostile Native Americans. Accompanied by war whoops, the charges and countercharges resulted in torture, mutilation, murder, and scalpings. The U.S. army rescued white settlers captured by Native Americans; the Native Americans either died in battle or surrendered to the troops to be led off to a reservation.

Thousands of spectators watched the frequent repetition of that sham battle during the summer of 1898. Six years later, reenactors playing the parts of British and Boer troops held simulated fights against real Zulus twice a day to entertain visitors on the Pike at St. Louis.[11]

In the course of the twentieth century, the diversions grew more elaborate, the mechanical rides more sophisticated and physically challenging, and the reenactments more diverse. Benchmarks in the new world of commercial entertainment, the three- or six-months' world's-fair midways of the turn of the century evolved into permanently located amusement and theme parks. The revitalizing release from everyday cares inspired by the fairs' recreational wonderlands—the "magic," if you will—carried over to their successors.

Even though not consciously promotional, the world's fairs also prefigured the earliest phases of flying machine development and introduced motion picture peep shows to mass audiences. Now, a century later, theme parks sponsored by movie studios (e.g., Disney and Universal) depend on airlines to transport their patrons.

In the current competitive tourist world—as at the fairs of the past—history and culture represent powerful attractions. The publicists for Las Vegas, Nevada, boast of cosmopolitanism, not just casinos and theatrical extravaganzas. The recreated visual delights of Paris, Rome, Venice, New York, Luxor, Mandalay, and Rio are on display in appropriately decorated, themed hotels. Every day pirates victimize sailors at predetermined hours, as tourists gather to watch. If the twenty-first-century desert gambling mecca brags that it brings the world to one tourist location, the world's fairs attempted no less. A hundred million people visited the dozen international exhibitions held in the United States between 1893 and 1916 and enjoyed pseudotouring vacations within the confines of the fairgrounds.

Even the most jaded world traveler must share the anticipation of a visitor to the 1893 Japanese Ho-o-den Palace in Chicago, with its screened walls and upturned corners on the peaked roof. The German village surrounded a typical town hall. An Irish village and a replica of St. Peter's Basilica stood within walking distance of Lapland reindeer, a Brazilian music hall, and a Hungarian theater. Farther along, Persians congregated alongside Algerians,

Tunisians, and Turks. The Ceylonese (now Sri Lankans) constructed a temple; the Moroccans, a mosque; the Chinese, a teahouse and theater.

The educational function of various villages extended beyond cultural acquaintance, however. Smithsonian Institution ethnologists with impressive scientific credentials used the midway to convey a social hierarchy. Thus, in contrast to villages filled with recognizable residential, religious, and cultural structures, that is, familiarly constructed buildings that signaled the relative technological sophistication of their exhibitors, the African-style Dahomey village housed several dozen warriors, whose fierce appearance and animated dances stereotyped them as "savages." By contrast, Samoan Islanders who sang and played Yankee Doodle on their drums demonstrated a capacity for progress. After all, the program described the group as recent practitioners of cannibalism, now reformed.[12]

The villages appeared at fair after fair because they fascinated the crowds. They also reflected the prevalent social Darwinism of the times and the pseudoscientific racial categorization of Smithsonian Institution ethnologists.

Concessionaires and ethnologists developed the expertise and the personal contacts necessary to provide exposition directors with the types of participants they desired. Recognizing a high level of public curiosity, backers of Buffalo's 1901 Pan-American Exposition contracted with a veteran concessionaire to bring Filipinos from the newly conquered islands. One hundred "somewhat reluctant" new Americans lived in thatched huts in the Filipino village. Transported around the village in carts pulled by water buffalo, visitors passed a Catholic church, a theater, a museum, and a lake displaying war canoes. The short journey demonstrated the cultural background and the development potential of Philippine Islanders under U.S. tutelage—not unlike the cannibalistic Samoans turned *Yankee Doodle* singers.

Ninety-eight Africans, selected to conform to the show business preferences of the exposition's directors, lived in an African village complete with monkeys and parrots. Farther along the midway and up the evolutionary scale, the Mexican peons could replicate typical village street life, complete with burros, as they demonstrated commercial skills in the marketplace. The contract called for entertainment, interpreted by the concessionaire as typical folk dances, augmented by archeological displays.[13]

Thus displayed, the fair's villages illustrated the powers of human ingenuity to manipulate the natural world. That process continued in the collections and demonstrations exhibited in the halls of modernity.

Wonderlands of Science and Technology

The 1893 Columbian exposition celebrated one explorer's successful rebuttal to a flat-world, fifteenth-century geography. Four centuries after sailors first traveled around the world, aviators flew above it. Technologies of navigation and propulsion made both feats possible, and displays of new technologies at the great fairs demonstrated the creative imagination and scientific principles that turned ideas into realities.

In 1893 few people understood the latest advances in aeronautics. Like the Europeans who expected Christopher Columbus to fall off the edge of the earth, nineteenth-century skeptics assigned the idea of a motorized, piloted airplane to the category of science fiction. They might visualize a person aloft, sustained by an apparatus that resembled a bird with its wings spread. They could even draw pictures of the flight, whereas they denied the possibility of its achievement.

One's imagination forms thoughts and images that may or may not conform to reality or experience. Belief, on the other hand, goes beyond imagination and suggests confidence in the truth or reliability of something, even without proof.

Columbus believed in a round world, sailed west to reach Japan, and found America instead. Four centuries later, the confidence of belief and a reasoned, analytical process turned an imagined flying machine into an airplane.

The application of scientific knowledge to real-world goals underlay an extraordinary burst of inventiveness. As a measure of the significance of the phenomenon, the U.S. Patent Office issued more than 400,000 patents between 1860 and 1890—more than ten times the number issued in the nation's history before the Civil War. Scientists, engineers, mechanics, and laborers applied a disciplined, problem-solving process—experiment, observe, conceptualize, rework, and refine. They attacked one technical problem after another and devised useful products.

Steelmaker Alexander L. Holley, who relied on the interaction between science and technology in his business, articulated the process of invention as a synergy of human brain power. First, driven by knowledge and ideas, investigators undertook basic research. Then scholars studied the research and conclusions of the scientists who worked in the laboratories. They speculated on the probable results of various physical and chemical combinations. Third, practical innovators applied their experience to determine the hidden pitfalls the academics had overlooked and solved the engineering problems that escaped the theoreticians.[14]

Confronted with voluminous proof of new processes and materials, more powerful machinery, and innovation and invention, thoughtful observers speculated on the accelerated pace of technological advances. Mathematician and philosopher Alfred North Whitehead, for example, extolled scientific research methodology itself as the greatest invention of the nineteenth century, far overshadowing railways, telegraphy, radio, spinning machines, or synthetic dyes. Scientific method, he noted, had transformed a "slow, unconscious, and unexpected" process of innovation into one that was deliberate and conscious and thus had fostered the rapid development of technology.[15]

Evidence of the machine power produced by the rapid advance of technology dominated the self-congratulatory 1876 U.S. centennial celebration. President of a young and scrappy nation, Ulysses S. Grant opened the Philadelphia Centennial International Exhibition and led a huge contingent of invited dignitaries past the representations of a hundred years of material progress in the main hall to the spot where they could pay homage to the steam engine. Steam-powered machines increased industrial output, and steam engines drove the trains and ships that carried raw materials to factories and finished goods to markets. The majestic Corliss engine, a steel-and-iron giant, powered the exhibits in Machinery Hall, a fitting aesthetic and functional symbol of a technical age.

The hundreds of technological innovations on display at the exhibition signaled profound alterations in American life. Machines mass-produced and processed items formerly made at home, such as textiles, clothing, food, and furniture. Gadgets and equipment increased the productivity of a pair of hands. (They would also foster leisure time and enable people to travel and enjoy various forms of entertainment.) An optimistic cadre of civic leaders, businesspeople, scientists, and engineers welcomed those changes as the underpinnings of a prosperous United States.

The Centennial Exposition captured a tumultuous United States, and the image of steam power fit the rapid pace of change. "The pot was boiling briskly," Vernon L. Parrington enthused a half-century later, and he continued an exuberant outpouring of mixed metaphors: "All over the land a spider web of iron rails was being spun." The rise of science had unleashed a revolutionary force that "enthroned the machine." Science and the machine ruled "a new civilization, of which the technologist and the industrialist were the high priests." [16]

Parrington's extravagant prose reflects the hyperbolic symbolism of the international expositions at Chicago and St. Louis, where elaborately designed exhibit halls, devoted to machinery, electricity, transportation, and communication, filled otherworldly temporary cities. These utopias of material abundance confirmed a strongly held faith in machines as instruments to improve the quality of human life. If the belief required substantiation, the fairs provided it. Alongside the displays of a machine-ruled civilization lived subsistence societies still dependent on human labor and hand tools, which graphically illustrated the disparities in material comfort and achievement.

Audacious engineers, empowered by trusting investors, launched wondrous projects for the fairs. Alexandre Gustave Eiffel, a builder of bridges, had designed a 984-foot tower for the 1889 Paris exposition. Its construction placed engineers in the forefront of public consciousness, and the whole city watched as its iron framework rose from four masonry piers. Four columns came together at a height of 620 feet to form one shaft that pointed heavenward. The tower became the symbol of the city after the exposition closed.

With people still in awe over Eiffel's soaring artistry, an element of competition undoubtedly motivated civic boosters as they developed grandiose plans for the Chicago fair. Financial considerations and a desire to showcase Chicago motivated fair promoters to attempt to surpass predecessor expositions in spectacle and novelty.

Four years after Paris, George G. W. Ferris, an engineer from Galesburg, Illinois, built a colossal steel wheel for the Chicago Exposition. Two hundred fifty feet across, the wheel hung by tension rods from a shaft resting on two 140-foot-high towers. Between the two rims of the wheel, thirty-six cars—with a seating capacity of forty passengers each—lifted riders high above the fairgrounds. Fifty cents paid for two revolutions of the wheel, and we can presume that some people paid again for another chance to experience the breathtaking ride.[17] As both an impressive engineering feat and a successful mechanical amusement, the Ferris wheel embodied the spirit of the fair and its era. Admittedly, the Eiffel Tower was taller, but it did not move.

Ferris's wheel offered Chicago's ticket buyers a bird's-eye view of the world, but the wheel did not fly. Still, the 1893 fair spurred devotees of human flight toward their goal. Although technological utopianism encouraged belief in the ability of machines to create a better world, only a handful of dreamers, scientists, and engineers had the imagination to consider air travel as a contributor to that aspiration.

The Chicago organizers, following the precedent set by earlier European gatherings, formed the World Congress Auxiliary to host a series of scholarly meetings with topics of interest to "enlightened and progressive" participants. Perhaps competition for recognition and stature prompted the auxiliary to call for an International Conference on Aerial Navigation, patterned after the Congress of Aeronauts and Aviators that met in conjunction with the 1889 Paris Exposition.[18]

The Chicago meeting that opened on August 1, 1893, consolidated the knowledge base that had accumulated over several decades of experimentation and encouraged a sense of community among aviation enthusiasts. The competitive urge to develop the first flying machine, as well as the advancement of science and its community of scholars, encouraged many of the scientists, engineers, and mechanics who struggled in their laboratories and at their workbenches. They studied the reports of colleagues and competitors, refined their designs, and risked their lives attempting to defy gravity.

The application of scientific methodology to fantasies of flight planted the first footsteps on the path to a successful motorized, mechanical airplane. If birds flew, the aeronauts asked, could humans don simulated wings and rise on air currents? If so, what knowledge did a designer of such an apparatus require? If flight required wings, what shape and weight would they be, and how large a surface would be required to support the weight? What mechanisms would facilitate ascent, descent, and forward motion? The consideration of motorized propulsion and mechanically controlled wings added tremendous complications. Unless experimenters built on the technical knowledge of others, the task would require multiple lifetimes. Not even a genius could read the scientific tomes, perform the experiments, and resolve the technical problems of materials, construction, propulsion, and wing and engine design in one life span.

To mitigate against the constraints of human life expectancy, aviation enthusiasts came together to share the results of their efforts. Around the middle of the nineteenth century, professional and amateur aeronautical scientists, engineers, and technicians formalized their relationships. Their organizations offered lectures and sponsored technical meetings, published annual reports and aeronautical journals, and, in general, encouraged a dialogue about problems encountered and potential solutions. Amateur experimenters and professional engineers from various fields joined the Aeronautical Society of Great Britain after its founding in 1866. Members approached aeronautics not as a fantasy, but as another scientific and technical challenge to be overcome through the application of knowledge and experience, and they underwrote the first public exhibit of aeronautical technology.[19]

The career of Paris-born, U.S.-reared, civil engineer Octave Chanute, who later befriended Wilbur and Orville Wright, exemplifies the cross-discipline, transnational intellectual currents of this scientific development. Born in 1832, Chanute reached maturity amid the hurly-burly of railroad construction. The ambitious young man worked as a railroad engineer, but he also used his expertise in building materials and stress analysis in the design and construction of other large projects, including a bridge over the Missouri River near St. Louis.

The world of civil engineers transcended national boundaries, and Chanute traveled extensively in the role of consulting engineer. He became interested in aviation during an extended stay in Europe in the late 1870s. A small but growing body of airship devotees convinced him that persistence would produce a flying machine.

Over the next decade Chanute studied the scientific and technical papers on aeronautics published in various journals, most of them based on work done in Europe. He also attended conferences in France, England, and the United States and acted as a compiler of information and catalyst in the fledgling field. Chanute engaged in some experiments himself, but mostly he tried to communicate his interest in and the value of working on the problem to other, more skeptical, engineers.[20]

Chanute lectured to organizations about aviation and arranged conference sessions on aeronautics. He threw his support behind an unproved field of endeavor and addressed professional audiences of analytical scientists and engineers, where even the most dedicated designer of gadgets and machinery might not credit the possibility of airplanes.

The accomplished engineer's first major conference effort suggests the risk that his pursuit of human flight inflicted on his professional credibility. Many skeptical attendees at the 1886 meeting of the American Association for the Advancement of Science (AAAS) went home confirmed in their disbelief. In fact, Chanute's session on aeronautics, intended to entice Americans to engage in investigations that had already captivated their counterparts in Europe for a decade, had the opposite effect.

At Chanute's invitation, amateur naturalist Israel Lancaster presented a lecture based on his conviction that the flight of birds offered insight into the potential for humans to fly. Lancaster's observations and experiments—undertaken as a serious contribution to understanding aerodynamics—resulted in a series of models that, when presented to the scientists, produced laughter and derision for the most part, rather than inquisitiveness and inspiration.[21]

In the often serendipitous unfolding of aeronautics history, however, Lancaster's ridiculed presentation provoked self-trained astronomer Samuel Pierpont Langley to pursue the amateur experimenter's proposition. Perhaps his studies of planets, stars, moons, and asteroids moving through the void above the earth predisposed him to consider the possibility that objects fabricated by humans might one day course through the sky. Whatever his motivation, curiosity, or conviction, Langley researched the literature and then embarked on a course of critical experiments in aerodynamics. After four years of laboratory work, he concluded that motorized, mechanical flight was possible and affirmed the value of continued experimentation.[22]

When Langley took his work outside the laboratory (about the time that the Wright brothers opened their bicycle shop), he joined an international brigade of experimental fliers who devoted their energies to building flying machines. They based their work on data accumulated through years of technical trial and error. Avoiding the added complication of motors for the time being, many of the early flight pioneers built winged gliders, embarked from high ground or elevated structures, and rode air currents until they landed—smoothly or in a heap—at a lower elevation. Each flight, they calculated, would yield information to improve the stability and duration of the next.

Langley worked at the Smithsonian Institution. Across the continent, San Diego physicist John Joseph Montgomery returned time and again to his barn-loft laboratory on the family ranch, undeterred in his efforts by occasional mishaps. After two flying machines failed in 1883, he built a glider in 1884 and sailed it into the sea breeze from an elevation south of the city. Montgomery traveled some six hundred feet in a few seconds, but when he tried to repeat his triumph, the glider collapsed.

Montgomery worked in relative isolation, thousands of miles from the scientists and engineers who, like Samuel Langley, attended the 1886 AAAS meeting or who maintained contact through east-coast academic networks and the Smithsonian Institution. Nevertheless, he continued to experiment and build his gliders and finally enjoyed an opportunity to engage other aeronauts and exchange information and experiences at the 1893 Chicago Conference on Aerial Navigation.[23]

Unlike the isolated Montgomery, German glider pioneer Otto Lilienthal lived and worked in Europe, where the great interest in aeronautical experimentation ensured that his achievements did not go unnoticed. By 1891 he gained international renown for his aviation prowess, hanging from a horizontal crossbrace in a biplane glider with a thirty-foot wing span and six feet of space between the upper and lower wings. For many followers of aviation developments, Lilienthal represented the inventive engineer of the period. Like Montgomery, he had studied the physics of flight and conducted his own laboratory tests before subjecting his experiments to field proof. Lilienthal continued to improve his glider until 1896, when a fall from an altitude of fifty feet cost him his life.

Photographers sometimes captured a triumphant "birdman" dangling from his glider and guiding it toward the ground or recorded a calamitous heap of wood and cloth sent smashing to the earth by a sudden wind gust. Miscalculations, as well as successes, contributed to aviation advances and sent determined would-be fliers back to their fields, barns, garages, shops, or wherever they toiled at the task of constructing a machine that could take them aloft. On the other hand, pictures of successfully soaring, heavier-than-air craft convinced potential experimenters that they chased a reality and not a fantasy.

The 1893 Chicago aeronautics conference showcased the accumulated knowledge and tangible accomplishments of Langley,

Montgomery, Lilienthal, and others and stimulated new efforts. This gathering of scientists and engineers conferred legitimacy on the experimenters and laid the groundwork for further serious study and practical advances.

The conference agenda linked the researchers of scientific principles—that is, questions of lift, air resistance, and air currents—with designers of components (propellers, aeronautical motors) and entire machines (materials for airframes). Balloon enthusiasts mixed with glider builders. Geographically isolated scientists like Montgomery were afforded the opportunity to exchange ideas and experiences with engineers who communicated frequently with colleagues like Langley at the Smithsonian Institution. They offered papers on their findings or listened to others who hailed successes and lamented failures. At the end of the conference, the published proceedings provided a benchmark in aeronautics.[24]

The importance of this data sharing to the progress of aviation engineering—for inspiration as well as information—cannot be overemphasized. Moreover, individuals or aviation pioneers from any one country could not claim sole credit for successful human flight. Conferences of various scientific and technical associations, as well as aeronautical conclaves at the 1889 Paris exposition and Chicago's 1893 World Congress Auxiliary gathered participants from the old world and the new, generated interest among newcomers, and reinforced the commitment of those already at work in the field.

Furthermore, most participants in the pursuit of flight consulted the published findings of predecessors and contemporaries. Newspaper and magazine articles on aviation, written for laypeople, joined annual reports of professional organizations and regularly published journals. Octave Chanute played a critical role in this process by gathering information from numerous sources, writing articles on aviation's history and current status, and then publishing the series in 1894 as the highly acclaimed book *Progress in Flying Machines.*

In the preface to his book, Chanute expressed his hope that, given the extent of mechanical knowledge then available, scientists

and engineers soon might solve the problems that thwarted aviation. In addition, he wrote, an understanding of the principles involved in flight would encourage further experiments. By consulting his book, experimenters might learn from the mistakes as well
as the successes of others and avoid duplication of effort.

Chanute must have drawn great satisfaction from the realiza-
tion that his role as catalyst and disseminator of information facilitated his goal. He began to correspond with Orville and Wilbur
Wright and traveled to personally witness many of their early
glider flights. His lectures to French flight enthusiasts on the
Wrights' glider experiments inspired the competitive Europeans
to advance their own work.

Perhaps the overall technological triumphalism that pervaded
Chicago spurred the increased interest in aviation among experimenters. Certainly the fair's representations of hemispheric
achievements and the country's awakening sense of world importance fed American enthusiasm. Whatever the impetus, the tempo
and scope of aeronautical study, the design and construction of
machines, and attempts at flight intensified in the decade from
1893 to 1903. An aeronautical society sprang up in Boston in 1895,
and a glider club in Schenectady, New York, started up the following year. Individuals worked on inventions or taught the principles
of aerodynamics to receptive college students. When newspapers
covered exploits and events, awareness of the interest in potential
flight extended to a wider population.[25]

The net cast by media attention undoubtedly snared Orville
and Wilbur Wright, young men whose lives reflect the trends and
temper of their times. Wilbur, the older of the two, was born on an
Indiana farm just after the Civil War ended; Orville, the younger,
was born in Dayton, Ohio, two years after the family—like so
many others—had moved from rural to urban America. The
brothers grew up in this era of rapid industrialization and unparalleled inventiveness. They opened their bicycle shop in 1892—
barely a year before the Chicago fair—when the bicycle-riding fad
had taken hold in the United States and Europe; they showed little
interest in flying, however, until the middle of the decade.

Imaginative as well as entrepreneurial, the Wrights moved

from sales to the design and manufacture of their own bicycles in 1896. By the middle of the 1890s, Orville and Wilbur not only imagined but also firmly believed they could produce a workable flying machine. Americans had already joined Europeans in attempts to perfect a flying machine. Perhaps Lilienthal's well-publicized crash and death in 1896 directed the Wrights' attention to a technology as yet unmastered. Intellectually and creatively restless, the brothers began to study the problems of flight.

We might aptly describe the Wrights' piloted, motorized flight more as a breakthrough in the ongoing process of technological innovation than as an invention. In May, 1899, Wilbur Wright requested that the Smithsonian Institution send information appropriate to aeronautical inquiry and then ordered a copy of Samuel P. Langley's *Experiments in Aerodynamics.*

Within two months, the brothers had built and tested a biplane kite. In methodical fashion they consulted the U.S. Weather Bureau about a suitable location for further tests and established a link with information collector and disseminator Octave Chanute. Shortly thereafter they went to Kitty Hawk, North Carolina, and tested a biplane kite-glider.

Then, in 1901, tests of a larger glider convinced them that they needed to learn more about aerodynamics. Following the familiar and accepted reiterative practices of technology development, they performed laboratory tests, designed a new machine that incorporated their findings, and returned to field tests. They also reported the results of their glider experiments to the Western Society of Engineers.

However, the Wrights' real interest lay in motorized flight, not gliders. They refined and modified the glider until they could sufficiently control vertical and lateral motion to maintain stability, then they tackled the problem of propulsion. The brothers incorporated available knowledge into their glider designs and used their own experiments to advance the technology. They carefully researched earlier propeller development in order to design their own, and when they built a four-cylinder piston engine to drive two wooden pusher propellers, they benefited from the work of engineers on both sides of the Atlantic Ocean.

In 1859 French engineer J. J. Etienne Lenoir had built an internal combustion engine that ran on gas, and in 1862 French scientist Alphonse Beau de Rocha patented a four-stroke, gas-powered engine. Bostonian George Brayton produced a liquid-fuel engine in 1873 and exhibited a two-stroke kerosene engine at the 1876 Philadelphia Centennial Exposition. Then, in 1889, Gottlieb Daimler produced a four-stroke gasoline engine with a high power-to-weight ratio.

Most aviation people understandably questioned the suitability of the internal combustion engine to the risky nature of flying. Again, the Wrights adapted available technology to their needs and built their own engine. In December, 1903, a decade after the Chicago Exposition and half a decade after they undertook a serious study of aviation, they piloted a mechanical flying machine of their own design: a biplane that took off from a monorail launch track placed on level ground.

> A spider web of struts and wires held the forty-foot wings in place. The pilot lay on a "cradle" amidships, working with his hips the wires that warped the wings. In front was a horizontal elevator, in the rear a vertical tail with the new movable rudder. The engine nestled ominously alongside the pilot. It drove the two pusher-propellers by means of a clanking chain drive that reminded people of the builders' background in the bicycle business.[26]

The millions of fairgoers who marveled at the White City and gazed in wonder at the abundance of gadgetry on display in Chicago most likely paid little attention to the aeronautical developments gathering force not far from the diversions of the Midway Plaisance—if they knew about the meeting at all. Yet, the mastery of aviation technology, an accomplishment of profound consequence for the twentieth century, followed directly on the interaction of a relative handful of people who had assembled in a serious, intellectual subsidiary of a vibrant, entertaining, and sometimes awesome spectacle.

A Visually Moving Experience

Curiosity about gadgets no doubt motivated strollers at the Chicago fair to halt before a three-foot-high, nondescript brown cabinet, bend slightly forward, and peer through the black eye-piece at the mechanical wizardry of a "peep show." Thomas A. Edison, well known for his incandescent light bulb and the phonograph and for his contributions to the telegraph and microphone, had dedicated his technical knowledge and inventive talent to the field of moving pictures and devised the "Kinetoscope."

As with the Wrights and aeronautics, Edison advanced an existing field of scientific and technical inquiry into the mechanics of vision. Research had indicated that the brain retains a perceived image slightly longer than the eye does, a phenomenon that makes objects in a sequence of still photographs appear to move when seen in rapid succession. In this optical illusion, the brain interprets an instantaneous overlap of images as fluid motion. This property of human vision encouraged the development of devices that captured the image and amused viewers.

More than a decade before Edison's birth, Joseph Plateau, a Belgian, successfully combined rotating disks, a mirror, and drawings and produced images that appeared to move. Two years later William G. Horner attached images to a revolving drum, called the device the Zoetrope, and sold it as a toy. While Edison occupied himself with a host of other inventions, Eadweard Muybridge and Etienne-Jules Marey developed equipment capable of taking photographs in rapid succession, and George Eastman introduced celluloid roll film on which to capture multiple images.

With a young man named William Dickson, Edison began to experiment with moving picture technology, intending to devise a commercially profitable, visual accompaniment to the phonograph. The partners took the celluloid film strip and perforated the edge at equidistant intervals. Thus, the photographer could control the speed at which the film advanced past the camera shutter.

By the early 1890s Edison and Dickson had built a camera that moved the film fast enough to photograph moving subjects lit by sunlight. The bulky, one-ton "Kinetograph" produced moving picture negatives that could be turned into positive film strips and exhibited in the Kinetoscope. Inside the cabinet, batteries powered a motor and a light. The motor turned sprocketed spools that moved the perforated strips past the light at a speed sufficient to create the illusion of movement.

One of Edison's first motion picture efforts captured a man name Fred Ott as he sneezed. The film made history less for the interest in its subject than for the simple reality of its existence. It became the first motion picture copyrighted by the Library of Congress. Although not yet obvious to curious viewers at the fair, moving pictures were not to be sneezed at. Moviemakers soon introduced audiences to places they had never seen, characters they had not met, and life experiences far removed from their own.

Edison's peep show gave way to projected motion pictures. The motion picture frontier advanced from cabinet-constricted individual viewing to images projected for multiperson audiences and from real-life subjects to fictional narratives. Edwin Porter evoked cheers, yells, and shouts with *The Great Train Robbery,* his twelve-minute-long action tale of suspense and gunplay. Although made in New Jersey and first shown in Manhattan, the story featured bandits who robbed a train out West.

Porter, who worked for Edison as a cameraman and then took charge of Edison's film production company, heightened the dramatic tension of his film by editing the footage he shot. That is, he filmed fourteen different scenes, including one in a saloon, and then cut between indoor and outdoor locations. The viewer had to connect and interpret images presented as separate scenes and from different perspectives. Carried out at a rapid pace, villains tied up a telegrapher at a railroad station, stopped a train, shot a guard, and robbed the train. Good guys chased the villains and defeated them in a shootout. Porter's scenario became a standard for the Western genre: fast pace, villains, saloon, open territory, a chase, shootout, victorious good guys. His Westerners wore broad-brimmed hats and bandannas, rode horses, and carried revolvers.

The story line and style proved a great success with audiences and an inspiration for other filmmakers.

During the lifetimes of many fairgoers who stopped to investigate Edison's peep show, movie newsreels would provide millions of people their first glimpse of an airplane, and airplanes would enliven feature film narratives with daring stunts. Movie locations would tempt viewers to travel, and airplanes would fly them to their destinations. Even before air transport, railroads opened enchanting vistas to travelers in the U.S. West.

Wonderland of the West

At the turn of the last century, most people in the United States could imagine, but had not seen, the 60 percent of the continental United States that lay beyond the north-south line that defines the western edges of Minnesota, Iowa, Missouri, Arkansas, and Louisiana. In 1860 only 4 percent of some thirty million European Americans lived in the vast territory that had been home to a million or so inhabitants before the Caucasians arrived. The process by which settlers made their way to the West to build new farms and ranches came to most Americans secondhand—through newspapers, letters, contact with transplanted family members, travelers, and the novels that filled the frontier with cattle rustlers and rampaging natives—or from assertions disseminated by historians such as Frederick Jackson Turner.

The American Historical Association agreed to hold its 1893 annual meeting in Chicago, one of the numerous auxiliary activities at the World Columbian Exposition intended to demonstrate the country's intellectual progress. No one could have imagined the spark that would inflame and transform the consciousness of the history profession.

At the meeting Turner delivered a scholarly paper whose central idea refocused the very history and social theory that the exposition celebrated. The young historian turned his back on the imposing representations of European culture and artistry embodied in the White City, challenged the idea that the United States owed its success as a democracy to European antecedents, questioned the evolutionary "upward" process of civilization, and designated the settlement of the western territories as the most critical feature in American development.

In the thesis that Turner presented to the historians, the simplicity of primitive conditions on the frontier transformed the complexity of European life, offered openness and opportunity, refreshed and invigorated the waves of settlers, and forged a uniquely American society. The availability of free land, converted from open space to populated areas over three hundred years, had produced an exceptional people.

At the end of his presentation Turner pronounced this era of American history at an end, since the superintendent of the 1890 census had reported that settlement had intruded into the open spaces of the West to such a degree that a frontier no longer existed. By implication, if the democratizing frontier had closed, what did the mechanized world of the exposition hold for America?

Turner offered his startlingly revisionist assessment of American history at the extravagant homage to Columbus and, by extension, to Europe's achievements and legacy. Rather than express gratitude for institutions transferred to American shores by explorers and colonists, Turner downplayed the influence of the very process the exposition celebrated and elevated the materially deprived frontier experience to explain the cause of U.S. success.

Turner, in fact, reversed the lesson constructed by ethnologists at the Chicago fair. That is, the White City exalted European civilization and industrial society, while displays of Native Americans consigned Sioux, Navajos, Apaches, and other Indian tribes to living examples of less productive societies displayed near the Midway Plaisance. In Turner's historical narrative, Europeans advanced in egalitarianism as they returned to a primitive existence on the frontier. To survive, they modified old cultural patterns, often with the Native American as facilitator or instigator of the transformation. The process of change—not retention—nurtured a democratic America.

Thus, Turner relocated the Native American groups—at least in historical value—from Midway attractions to the central core of the nation's development. Conversely, the fair lauded the world of commerce and technology as "civilized" and exhibited Native American as "savages" who "suffered" from the absence of European culture and politics.

Despite the contradiction, the persuasive force of Turner's argument swept beyond the conference and the midway and the White City. A generation of scholars, public officials, and writers in the popular media reiterated Turner's frontier thesis and propelled its central tenet to the forefront of American historical thought.

Turner enthusiastically invited other historians to join his investigations into the significance of the frontier in American history. The coterie of colleagues and graduate students who pursued Turner's provocation perhaps found in the struggles of pioneers an antidote to the crass materialism of the Gilded Age, the aggressive tactics of financiers and monopolists, and the corruption of urban political bosses. However, when they trained their mirrors on "the West," the reflections revealed numerous "wests," a historical Temple of Mirth that defied a single vision.

Distinguished by climate, geography, soil quality, and resources, the variety of frontiers engendered a multiplicity of experiences. Grassland, desert, subtropical coastal areas, mountains, forests, fertile valleys, and river basins lent themselves to exploitation for cattle grazing, farming, logging, the trapping of fur-bearing animals, or the mining of mineral resources that ranged from gold and silver to arsenic and salt. These enterprises attracted people with different skills and expectations and required various levels of capital investment. Dishonest schemers, as well as hard-working settlers, participated in the great trek—and sometimes the hectic scramble—westward. Moreover, the area was not empty of population.

In many cases markets—rather than hunger for open land—drove development. For example, the Texas cattle industry that fueled so much western lore (and movie scenarios) grew in response to population growth and market demand. Settlers from eastern states who populated Mexico's northern province of Coahuila y Texas in the 1820s encountered herds of cattle tended by Mexican vaqueros, or cowboys. When the Anglos wrested Texas from Mexico in 1836, they took over a great deal of land and stock as Mexicans fled south or found themselves displaced. With neither transportation nor market, the cattle had limited value and were allowed to roam.

By the 1870s the number of Texas longhorn cattle had increased one thousand percent. Cattle herds had spread as far north as the Dakotas and west to New Mexico, Colorado, and Wyoming. By then the United States had completed the transcontinental railroad. With population growing in eastern cities, slaughterhouse owners established holding pens near the railroad, and cowboys rounded up the cattle and drove them to the new cow towns of Abilene and Dodge City.

Thus, as much as a pioneering spirit, eastern population growth produced the western mythology spread by dime novels and movies. The roundup and the cattle drive, as well as the commercial cow town with its saloon and entertainment, represented incorporation in—not a retreat from—the industrial society east of the Mississippi River. With money to be made, property rights took on importance, so cowboys branded their cows and chased cattle thieves—ready-made plots for adventure stories. The stockmen resented the farmers who cut up the open range and put up fences. Eventually, the cattlemen put up their own fences and became ranchers, and the more land they owned, the less democratic their society became.

Many of the settlers who wanted land obtained their parcels in ways that echoed the federal government's policies toward Native Americans and thus did not reflect well on American democracy. Ironically, concessionaires for the various world's fairs exhibited tribal representatives as savages in need of civilization, when, in fact, the government's civilizing agents had robbed them of their self-reliance and dignity, their culture, and their land.

By 1885 the government had placed some 300,000 Native Americans on 171 reservations scattered over twenty-one states and territories, with a total area about the size of Texas. The scandalous consequences—ill health, disorientation, and exploitation by government agents—generated a reform movement intended to address these wrongs. Under the 1887 Dawes General Allotment

Act, the government moved to parcel out reservation land to individual owners who would farm it and thus integrate into the dominant culture. The government could purchase nonallotted land, sell it to settlers, and put the proceeds in trust to educate Native Americans. When four-fifths of their lands became government property, the former reservation dwellers benefited far less than did the prospective settlers.

Miners did not brave the hardships of the West in order to farm; rather, they broke the earth to gain immediate wealth. If their brush with primitive conditions modified hierarchical social patterns that had originated in Europe, few people would have recognized the outcome. Many of the lucky ones who fulfilled their ambitions wanted to live like aristocrats and acquired the accoutrements of their new status as quickly as possible.

By the 1880s some 200,000 optimistic prospectors had rushed to various areas in the West. News of a strike drew fortune hunters, merchants, service providers, gamblers, and prostitutes. The semblance of towns sprang up. When the mines—or their luck—played out, the people moved on, from California's gold fields to Nevada, Colorado, Arizona, Idaho, Montana, and Wyoming.

Hardly areas of entrepreneurial individualism, mining areas in Colorado and Montana came under the sway of heavily capitalized corporate interests. As early as the 1860s, Denver counted 8,500 people and $10 million in annual business transactions.

Hotels, restaurants, theaters, churches, and schools followed the saloons and gambling halls as the mining frontier filled up with urban populations. Washoe, which served Nevada's Comstock Lode, counted 20,000 people by 1860, including con men and entertainers. Because Nevada mines required considerable capital outlay, mining companies sold shares. Unscrupulous speculators manipulated securities in Nevada, just as they had in New York. California provided many of the goods required for the mining towns, creating a commercial elite on the coast and a frontier that moved west to east. Freight haulers carried machinery and merchandise for daily living from west-coast ports inland, along with luxury goods for those who had struck it rich.

The tourist industry also did its share to "tame" the West. Even as farmers, ranchers, merchants, and miners relocated, affluent members of the Gilded Age society trekked to the American West, where they found an adventurous alternative to the familiar European foray.

By the 1870s California's Yosemite Valley and Wyoming's Yellowstone National Park existed as tourist destinations. Denver attracted a trickle of East Coast tourists who could afford the round-trip fare of $100 from New York. Once they had taken in the Rocky Mountain commercial metropolis, seekers of scenery could set out by train to view Colorado's breathtaking forests and peaks from the windows of the Colorado Central Railroad.

Aside from naturalists who sought escape from urban crowding, most pleasure travelers from the East avoided primitive living conditions. To satisfy their clients' preferences for refinement, tourist entrepreneurs developed an appropriate infrastructure— comfortable transportation by railroad touring car, well-appointed hotel and restaurant accommodations, tasteful retail establishments, trained guides, and so on. Like visitors to the fairs, these tourists wanted to observe Native Americans and even meet them, but in controlled situations.

By the time Turner gave his talk, the closing frontier had already opened to new and exciting possibilities. Organized excursions took advantage of trains, stage coaches, wagons, and horses to expose visitors to the imposing immensity of the territory. Sales agents printed and disseminated brochures that advertised sightseeing and entertainment as well as food and lodging. As the tourist infrastructure expanded to accommodate a more financially modest clientele, tent cities and lake and beach cottages joined the great resort hotels.

The Reel West

For two generations after Frederick Jackson Turner and the 1890 census declared its end, motion pictures breathed life into the frontier experience. The popular Western film fired viewers' imaginations with its own representation of the frontier as the meeting point between savagery and civilization. Like the fun-house mirrors, they exaggerated and distorted the reflected image, even as they served as a textbook for an increasingly city-based America. Many youngsters whose education ended at elementary school, as well as immigrant workers who frequented silent-movie theaters before they could read English, learned about the frontier and the triumph of good over evil through the heroes and villains of Western action films. The genre also spread the myth of the American West to diverse cinema fans around the world.

The reassuring predictability of the Western movie plot became part of its appeal, and repetition induced credibility. Because moviegoers saw the pattern so often, the West, they believed, must be a place of action, violence, chases, and gunfights. Cowboys drove cattle to market and fought rustlers. They resented farmers and fences. Wagon trains took farm families to new homes and kept a lookout for hostile American Indians. Stagecoaches took eastern city folks to new lives in western hamlets, each of which had a tavern.

In contrast to the crowded, complicated world of great steam engines, telephones, wireless communication, automobiles, flying machines, and prospects for international commerce, Western movie plots reenacted the Turner thesis. Hazardous pioneering, material deprivation, separation from family and neighbors, encounters with American Indians, and tenuous communications created a society distinct from Europe. The films reiterated an east-west tension that pitted a crowded, corporate, artificial, urban, industrial society where wealth determined status against an open, natural, struggling, pragmatic frontier society where rugged individuals earned their places according to ability.

The Western film genre sustained the contrapuntal ideal of open land and pioneer spirit while formal commercial empires took shape. Filmmakers gave the audiences what they wanted. Movies about the West exploited obvious lifestyle differences between the older, populated, structured sections of the country and the newer, scattered settlements of the frontier. The sedate parlor contrasted with the boisterous saloon, but the two areas existed in economic symbiosis. Railroads made money hauling goods and passengers, including tourists; farmers, ranchers, and miners in western lands sent products to eastern markets and purchased manufactured merchandise from eastern suppliers. The completion of the transcontinental railroad, the expansion of U.S. industrial production, and western settlements forged an interdependence despite the differences.

At a time when bicycles, cars, trolleys, trains, and then airplanes changed the nature of transportation, horses remained critical to the Western movie. And the horseman with a shady past found a new life as a force for good, a lover of freedom, and an enemy of corruption in the dry, dusty, open spaces. At a later date filmmakers began to attribute many of the cowboys' characteristics to the aviator—a pioneer looking for freedom and combating villains in the endless sky instead of on the empty plains.

Western movies lost favor at about the same time that historians turned their backs on the simplicity of Turner's thesis. As the Great Depression deepened in the early 1930s, the grim world of urban poverty and the cynical gangster illustrated the dark side of civilization. The complex technological innovations and internationalism exhibited at the world's fairs once more overshadowed the focus on frontier development as a paradigm for understanding America's past and future.

Chicago's fair celebrated exploration and population expansion at the service of fifteenth-century commerce. It also provided a forum for historians to ponder the profound contradictions in the development of American institutions and culture.

Wonderlands of Commerce

The public figures who advocated U.S. overseas expansion in the 1890s and sponsored expositions to demonstrate the nation's production capabilities counted on exports of agricultural and manufactured goods—not on movies, airplanes, and tourists—to promote prosperity. Nevertheless, the three incipient industries accompanied the United States in its transition to world commercial power.

An overseas expansionist sentiment overtook the settlement of the western territory. By 1893, when Turner described the character of American life and the unbounded energy that drove the western migration, the United States had already purchased Alaska, annexed the Midway Islands in the Pacific, and signed commercial treaties with Hawaii and Samoa. The United States vied with British and German merchants for influence over native leaders in Samoa and with Spain for trade supremacy with Cuba. American missionaries, traders, and sugar planters pressured the U.S. government to annex the Hawaiian Islands. Even as late-nineteenth-century tourists took in the splendor of the western landscape, satisfied their curiosity about Native American cultures, and basked in the coastal sunshine, the United States had broken through its continental limits.

The desire for Asian trade required the United States to develop a Pacific policy. Increasingly vocal public figures talked about a larger navy, overseas bases for refueling and to protect access to new markets, and a canal to link the Atlantic and Pacific Oceans.

In 1881 Colombia granted a concession to the French Interoceanic Canal Company to cut through the narrow neck of land in its northern province of Panama. French entrepreneur and promoter Ferdinand de Lesseps had planned, supervised, and completed the construction of the hundred-mile-long Suez Canal, which connected the Mediterranean and Red Seas. The commercial advantage in shortened time between Europe and Asia weighed heavily on competitive American industrialists.

Then de Lesseps won the canal-building contract from the Colombian government, an understandable recognition of his Suez achievement and a continuation of traditionally strong ties between Latin America and Europe. The Monroe Doctrine, aimed at limiting European power in the Americas, did not apply to a French company, of course. Private interests gaining a toehold in the hemisphere in the 1880s differed from the French government's invasion and domination of Mexico in the 1860s. The canal concession and contract nevertheless escalated a lobbying effort in Washington by U.S. manufacturers and New Orleans port officials for a rival U.S.-built canal.

While procanal advocates encouraged a competing channel

across Nicaragua, the reality of Panama caught up with an overly optimistic de Lesseps. The flat, arid landscape of Suez had little in common with the isthmus. Digging crews encountered seventeen different types of rock in the mountainous terrain of Panama. Annual rainfall of 105 inches sent rivers coursing through the dense jungle and increased the potential for disease in the tropical heat. An estimated twenty thousand workers died. Between 1881 and 1888 the canal company spent more than $280 million and had not nearly completed the project. The company went broke.

The failure of the French Interoceanic Canal Company heightened the expansionist mood of the United States. Pressure to improve U.S. relations with Latin America and to build a canal intensified. Secretary of State James G. Blaine's encouragement of hemispheric solidarity culminated in the first Pan American conference, convened in Washington in 1890. Faced with the specter of limited domestic growth, signaled by the statistical closing of the frontier, the United States sought relief in trade beyond its own borders. The government offered its southern neighbors a reciprocal tariff policy in an effort to reorient trade patterns away from Europe and toward the United States. Lack of an enthusiastic response in some capitals reflected Latin America's concerns over the growing economic strength of the United States and its publicly expressed desires for enhanced military power.

Two years after the 1893 Chicago fair, when businesspeople courted Latin American participation, Atlanta hosted the Cotton States and International Exposition. Southern agricultural interests pursued new markets to absorb overproduction and investors to develop its untapped resources. Atlanta fair officials took great pains to solicit Latin American involvement. They traveled thousands of miles to make personal presentations and to express a solidarity of American interests, with an eye to mutual economic benefits. If the Atlantans saw Latin America as a market for North American products, Latin Americans similarly regarded the United States and responded to the invitation with extensive displays of their own resources.

In this era of intensified overseas commerce, when ocean-crossing steamships gained speed and safety and reduced spoilage losses, U.S. public debates increasingly focused on international economic and strategic issues. As European nations engaged in a scramble for foreign markets, colonies, and investment opportunities, some Americans expressed the competition as a Darwinian struggle for survival: Nations that failed to adapt would fall behind.

Ethnologists at the Chicago fair had structured a Darwinian world and encouraged an industrialized United States to integrate the less fortunate into the international economy. The country indeed entered the global competition for trade and colonies. After considerable, often rancorous, debate, the United States succumbed to imperial temptations. Its armed conflicts moved from frontier clashes to full-scale warfare of worldwide proportions, and the nation acquired more territory.

In 1898 the United States overpowered Spanish military forces. The Treaty of Paris acknowledged the victory, and Spain ceded Puerto Rico, Guam, and the Philippine Islands to the United States. Cuba gained its independence from Spain, but the United States took upon itself the responsibility for the island's economic well-being and political stability. Hawaii became a part of the United States by legislative act.

Possessions in both the Caribbean and the Pacific Ocean enhanced the arguments for an interoceanic canal, although the location—Panama or Nicaragua—remained in dispute. Nicaragua would prove less costly, while technical experts favored Panama. Meanwhile, the New Panama Canal Company had taken over the Colombian concession, which had been extended to 1904.

The canal remained unfinished in 1901, when Theodore Roosevelt assumed the presidency upon President William McKinley's assassination at the Pan-American Exposition in Buffalo. Roosevelt, with committed congressional backing, undertook negotiations with the Colombian government to rescue the faltering French performance. The United States offered to buy the rights and property of the French company and asked for perpetual control of a strip of land on either side of the canal.

The Colombians regarded the United States warily. Its citizens in the Panamanian province had demonstrated defiance of the central authority. Elements of the local population coveted the canal and its potential revenue, and talk of Panamanian independence circulated in the province and in the Colombian capital. Roosevelt enraged Colombian officials with his aggressive dispatch of U.S. Marines to quell a disturbance in Panama without the consent of the Colombian government. When the two countries finally signed a canal treaty, the U.S. Senate ratified it, but the Colombians did not. A furious Roosevelt spoke of the Colombians in very undiplomatic terms.

Political tensions crackled around the unhappy Panamanians, and on November 3, 1903, they rebelled. The United States gave military assistance and recognized their independence on November 5. A canal agreement, favorable to the United States, took a mere two weeks to reach. Panama ceded legal jurisdiction in a ten-mile-wide canal zone and gave the United States the right to acquire other lands as needed. In return, the newly established government gained $10 million and $250,000 in annual rent. The U.S. Senate approved the arrangement the following February, a mere six months after Colombia had rejected the negotiated treaty and just in time for the opening of the St. Louis fair.

The 1904 fair stamped its approval on U.S. territorial ambitions and the adventurism of the late-nineteenth century as well as the expansionist Louisiana Purchase. The country had entered the dazzling arena of world power.

Wonderland of Wonderlands

The well-known chorus of the Andrew B. Sterling-Kerry Mills song, *Meet Me in St. Louis, Louis,* suggests the irresistible attractions of bright lights and an abundance of entertainment. The seldom-heard verse reflects a characteristically restless society in pursuit of excitement and novelty.

In the narrative lyric Louis comes home one day to find a note from his wife, Flossie, with a message that moves him to tears. "Louis, dear, it's too slow for me here, so I think I will go for a ride." The dissatisfied Flossie had cleaned out the apartment and left Louis and his pedestrian existence behind. In the chorus, however, Flossie offers a remedy, an alternative to separation. She invites him to meet her at the St. Louis fair, where they can dance the hootchy-kootchy and continue their romance.

As the distraught Louis complains to the janitor when he shows him the note, what good is the flat without Flossie? If Louis wants to salvage his marriage, he has to learn to play as well as work.[27]

I missed the astonishing "Pike," as they called the Louisiana Purchase Exposition amusement zone, by several decades. But I grew up in St. Louis and lived within walking distance of Forest Park—site of the memorable event—while in my early teens. Unmindful of the historical significance, my sister and friends and I trod the pathways that millions of fair visitors had followed across the lawns, past the fountains, and up the hill to the museum, where exposition promoters had introduced art masterpieces from foreign lands to an eager public.

We meandered through the Jefferson Memorial Building, built to mark the entrance to the fairgrounds after workers dismantled more than fifteen hundred exhibition palaces, foreign pavilions, and amusement structures. Named for the U.S. president who had authorized the Louisiana Purchase, the Thomas Jefferson Memorial later housed another symbol of local pride, Charles A. Lindbergh's plane, *Spirit of St. Louis,* in which the famed aviator had flown alone across the Atlantic Ocean.

Not until I began to investigate the connection between the turn-of-the-century fairs and twentieth-century tourism, aviation, and movies did I learn that my house actually stood on ground formerly occupied by some attraction on the Pike, the most-visited part of the grandest exposition of the era. Perhaps hip-swinging dancers of the make-believe Cairo had performed where our dining room later stood. Had the high peaks of reproduced Tyrolean Alps marched down the alleyway and pointed the direction to the enchanting stagecraft at the Irish theater? Where was the Temple of Mirth, with its irregular, laugh-provoking mirrors?

The imprint of a much-different world existed beneath my street, an earlier reality made accessible through a movie musical comedy, *Meet Me in St. Louis.* Behind my high school stood Kensington Avenue, where, song lyrics tell us, a certain boy lived next door to a family that took the clanging trolley to the fairgrounds.

A characteristically spirited *St. Louis World* headline bragged, "To See the Pike Is to See the Entire World." Dozens of countries sent skillfully prepared replicas of iconic buildings to St. Louis. A model Bastille and guillotine represented French political history, while the Moulin Rouge—surrounded by an imitation Montmartre—transported viewers to Henri de Toulouse Lautrec's Gay Paree. Ornate furniture and tapestries greeted visitors to the reproduction of the Grand Trianon at Versailles, and the more historically aware viewer perhaps connected its luxurious interior to the Bastille and the guillotine. The entire display may have reminded visitors why the French had to sell the Louisiana Territory.

The English displayed pride in British accomplishments with recollections of palace architecture and appropriately elaborate decorations in a replica of the Orangery, the banquet hall of Kensington Palace, designed by Sir Christopher Wren. China simulated the summer palace of Prince Pu Lun and filled it with jade, porcelain, bronze, and ceramic artifacts. The Siamese constructed a building similar to the temples located at the Imperial Palace in Bangkok and displayed musical instruments and ancient weapons inside. Geishas entertained and served at Japanese tea houses, surrounded by lakes and gardens filled with two hundred bonsai trees. The beautiful girls in kimonos competed for customers with traditionally costumed and coifed Sinhalese men who served up various brews in Ceylon's temple of teas.[28]

In keeping with its ambitious scale—nearly double the acreage of the Chicago fair—the Louisiana Purchase Exposition outdid the former in offering its patrons a comprehensive lesson in evolution, again using the yardsticks of technology and cultural sophistication. At one end of the scale, elaborately decorated palaces of transportation, electricity, manufactured goods, and machinery, located alongside the fountains and gardens of the Grand Basin, housed the latest mechanical marvels. An awed public inspected 160 models of automobiles and sent messages to destinations as far away as Chicago through wireless telegraphy.

Stunned by the technological achievements they had already witnessed, enthusiastic observers arrived day after day at the eleven-
acre Aeronautics Field, where they were confronted with a vast array of competing balloons, kites, gliders, and airships. What might
they have thought had they only known about Orville and Wilbur
Wright's flying machine?

People who could not afford to travel abroad, lacked the time,
or were not sufficiently adventuresome immersed themselves in
multiple foreign cultures in the space of only a day or two. From
a tramcar through the pseudo–Tyrolean Alps they could spy
Mozart's birthplace among the Alpine villages tucked in the
mountain folds. A facsimile of the Irish House of Parliament
adorned the entrance to the Irish village, where actors performed
Irish plays in the theater and then greeted the audience as they
worked the crowds between shows.

The fair familiarized visitors with the world's manners and
customs through representative national and ethnic villages incorporated into the honky-tonk midway setting, where foreign
people, food, and music joined the sideshow excitement of wild
animal acts, sword swallowers, jugglers, and sensational mechanical amusements. Professed educational benefits notwithstanding,
people flocked to the villages for entertainment.[29]

Awestruck visitors not already overwhelmed by the magnitude
of sensual stimuli wandered from the enticements of Cairo in the
midst of the Pike across a street to Great Britain, then along a
pathway to France. Recrossing Skinker Road they encountered Japan and then traipsed up the hillside to discover the labyrinth-like
narrow passageways, markets, and reproduced holy places in a
thirteen-acre city of Jerusalem. If not overcome by physical ex-
haustion, they might have continued up the hill to the Fine Arts
Building, which displayed treasured art works on loan to the fair
from around the world.

Among the millions of attendees, many may have faltered on a
map quiz (as would most people a century later), but they no
doubt had some awareness of most of the countries whose displays
they visited. Many probably could connect the distinctive styles of
artifacts with the countries that produced them. In fact, affluent

consumerist Americans had incorporated foreign furniture and accessories into their home decorations for years.

Furnishings from around the world, displayed in numerous national buildings at the fair, had grown familiar to readers of magazines devoted to interior decoration. The widely distributed periodicals encouraged a self-congratulatory sense of sophistication and fostered eclectic settings for fashionable families.

While immigrants and their descendants might not consider their own transported items "foreign," parlor furnishings and bric-a-brac became objets d'art in the vocabulary of the experts who contributed to the newspapers and magazines of the day. The style-conscious householder, whether owner of a mansion or dweller in a modest house or urban apartment, might mix "German tankards with French chairs and Persian embroideries and Moorish grille work" or combine "Turkish brass, Japanese tables, a Chinese cabinet, carved gourds from Central America, a Mexican fan, a Breton vase, a Bohemian chalice, and posters from Paris and London."[30]

The internationally traded items evident in American homes at the turn of the century mostly represented the output of technically advanced peoples. On the other hand, most fairgoers had little or no knowledge of the cultural artifacts and practices of the various ethnic peoples, some two thousand of them, displayed at the St. Louis fair as exemplars of the lower end of the social evolution scale. Anthropologists who selected the representative peoples and commissioned concessionaires to transport entire villages desired to illustrate the premise that less technically developed humans could climb toward modern civilization.[31]

As with earlier fairs, the ethnic villages hosted in St. Louis figured among the most popular attractions. The reality of contact with the world beyond the U.S. boundaries must have imparted a heady self-satisfaction to those who invested in the price of admission. Villagers brought or were provided with the necessities to construct dwellings and create a habitat sufficient to allow them to carry on their daily routines. For the seven-month duration of the fair, they cooked, ate, bathed, slept, created artifacts, performed housekeeping chores, enacted rituals and dances, and carried out the ordinary responsibilities of their lives to the best of their abilities, interrupted occasionally for obligatory appearances in parades and planned activities.

Preserving the essential quality of native life in this artificial and alien setting understandably required a steadfast dedication on the part of the supervising anthropologists and some compromises by authorities. For example, members of the St. Louis Women's Humane Society objected to the city dog pound's arrangement to accommodate the eating habits of the Filipino Igorots. When rumors circulated that residents on the perimeter of the fair reported missing pets, the courts intervened. Over the objections of the animal protectionists, the city issued vouchers for unwanted dogs, and fair employees brought the animals as food supplies to the fairgrounds.

Even the least perceptive fairgoer who walked through the exposition must have agreed that the United States had acquired a well-deserved stature in a remarkable world. If the country envisioned itself engaged in the "white man's burden," an Igorot chieftain signaled a certain receptivity to the message when he requested a telephone in his thatched hut as a designation of his elevated rank.[32]

Whether repelled by Igorot eating habits or impressed by their acceptance of technology, the people of St. Louis remembered the Filipino villagers. The Wydown School, built on land once included in the fairgrounds, still called its football team the Igorots long after the city had forgotten the dog-eating controversy.[33]

We can expect that the various villagers must have found themselves bewildered by the appearance and practices of other ethnic groups. What did they observe that challenged their own notions of proper conduct? How did the slender, under-five-foot Pygmies, renowned for their prowess with poisoned arrows, react to the towering, six-foot-tall Patagonians, who hunted by hurling bolas (three stone balls attached to leather thongs)?

In fact, some of the Filipino Samal Moros demonstrated great enthusiasm when confronted with unaccustomed behaviors. The Moros lived in houses built over water on stilts, from which they fished for food. Taken on a visit to the Pike, a group of Moro boys

Spectators arrived at the fair by train and trolley, while Igorot tribespeople came by ship from the recently acquired Philippine Islands. Today's tourists travel by air, still attracted by the promise of exotic, indigenous peoples. *Courtesy of the Missouri Historical Society.*

saw the ride called "shoot the chutes" for the first time. Passengers in flat-bottomed boats descended a steep incline, and then the boats plunged into the water. After a leap and a bone-shaking heave, the shallow craft glided to a stop with the riders clinging to the sides of the boat or to each other.

The curious Moros jumped into the water and scrambled up the incline. The next day they attempted to build a bamboo "chute" in their water-filled village. After it collapsed, helpful fair personnel acquired some boards and built a suitably secure incline, which the boys happily descended in their dugout canoes.[34]

From the vantage point of the high-tech, twenty-first century, when electronic equipment brings the everyday experiences of myriad remote peoples into our presence, we must stretch our imaginative capacity to appreciate the wonderment of an average

Posing for photographs with the "natives" is as prevalent among tourists in 2004 as it was in 1904. However, the fair reversed the roles; exotic visitors traveled long distances to satisfy the curiosity of those who remained in their own country. *Courtesy of the Missouri Historical Society.*

tourist confronted by loin-cloth-clad, drum-beating, dog-eating representatives of far-off lands. What comments would the strait-laced, proper, mostly middle-class strollers make as they traipsed from display to display, watching nearly naked women cook over open fires outside thatch-roofed huts or bathing children in open pools of water? Did they turn away from the Igorot men, who roasted dogs over an open fire for the evening meal, or flinch when headhunters posed with their shields and spears?

The human exhibits undoubtedly communicated potent messages about relative developmental levels to an audience that had just seen the mechanical wonders located in the transportation, electricity, and machinery palaces and several dozen elaborate, artifact-filled architectural representations on the Terrace of Nations. Although world's fair visitors most likely had little awareness that they followed a scheme laid out by purposeful organizers bent on education, they probably came to the intended conclusion. That is, the United States had an obligation to bring the benefits of twentieth-century technology to peoples dependent on primitive weaponry and inferior tools.

In fact, historian Robert W. Rydell's exhaustively researched and persuasively argued study, *All the World's a Fair,* draws a critical picture of the period's opinions, theories, and attitudes as expressed through the fairs. His close interpretive reading of the records and activities of backers and promoters of a dozen trans-century exhibitions recounts a racially based, Darwinian justification of U.S. territorial expansion incorporated with scant subtlety into both the material and human exhibits and the entertainment.

On the one hand, Rydell explains, the fairs highlighted the benefit of goods made available through agricultural and industrial production and extolled the commerce that expanded access to the overflowing cornucopia. The tools and their produce represented human domination over nature and the resultant well-being of civilized societies. On the other hand, various exhibits cast the coerced transformations of less technologically advantaged peoples and the places they lived as positive steps in the march of progress.

We know from a variety of written sources—letters, post-cards, diaries, and media reports—that the fairs awed, titillated, entertained, educated, thrilled, and satiated the curiosity of millions of paying customers. In addition, we can expect that the thousands of foreign persons put on exhibit reacted in similar fashion. No doubt the encounters between transient fairgoers and displayed temporary residents changed both groups in incalculable ways. That encounter continues; in fact, it repeats on a daily basis all around the world, thanks to the development of air travel and tourism.

Wonderland Villages Made Real

The expositions opened a simulated world to those people willing and able to venture out and spend their money for a new

REFLECTIONS ON WONDERLANDS / 69

experience. The fairs also demonstrated the educational value and self-satisfaction of viewing the achievements of the world's societies. At a time when the middle classes awakened to the benefits and pleasures of travel, the displays must have stirred desires in some individuals to board a ship or a train in order to observe the world firsthand.

St. Louis cherished its reputation as the gateway to the West, which included the territory of the Louisiana Purchase, whose centennial the fair celebrated. The city bade farewell to many nineteenth-century pioneers, trappers, adventurers, and merchants headed for the Santa Fe Trail and other western destinations. In 1904 concessionaires brought Native American tribal people to St. Louis: Pawnee from Kansas and Nebraska; Wichita and Kickapoo from Kansas and Oklahoma; Cheyenne from the western plains; Arapaho from New Mexico; Pima, Papago, Maricopa, Navajo, and Hopi from Arizona; and Sioux from North and South Dakota.

The *Scientific American* reporter who covered the fair found the southwestern cliff-dwelling Mokis and Zunis "the most interesting of the aboriginal tribes of North America." Several hundred of the "strange people" had reproduced their multistory homes with considerable fidelity, he wrote. Fairgoers could observe their rug weaving and their skills in sewing moccasins and creating silver jewelry. "Among their daily performances, one that naturally attracts the most attention is the snake dance, which has been described by a well-known ethnological student as an 'unparalleled dramatic pagan ceremony.'"

Scientific American reprinted a photograph of dancers with live snakes in their mouths and noted that hundreds of Americans "make the long journey over a rough and inhospitable country" to view an extraordinary ceremony only recently opened to outsiders. At the fair

> They dance the snake dance on the stage of their small theater, dressed in their full savage regalia. Armed with strange implements and chanting wild themes to the rhythm of their drums, they go through their uncanny dance apparently charming into quiescence or stupor

dozens of the deadliest snakes in which their region abounds, until they place the reptiles in their mouths and carry the dance to its climax. The sight is one of the strangest and most weird to be seen at the St. Louis Exposition.[35]

A century after the Louisiana Purchase Exposition recorded the last entrant, such yearnings fuel an industry. Airplanes transport millions of international tourists, encouraged by travel brochures and enticed by articles in newspapers and magazines, to foreign countries. (In 2002 the number of international tourists declined for the first time since 1945, due no doubt to fears of politically motivated violence.)

Once at their destinations, most tourists mimic the behavior of the curious fairgoers. They admire artifacts and architecture, experiment with unfamiliar foods, and observe and comment on the unique practices and peculiar rituals of native peoples.

Twenty-first-century tourists who travel to learn about other cultures and to experience places they have known only through reading probably would feel an affinity with their early- twentieth-century counterparts at the fair. In both cases their travels combine entertainment and learning and open them up to other people's lifestyles. In both cases the experience may be manufactured, that is, purposefully produced by a businessperson to generate profits.

A few examples of international tourist connections, fostered by a powerful industry, barely hint at the great human tide that sweeps across the globe and brings people together in mutual exploitation. The creative promoters of today's tourism industry remind us of the Smithsonian Institution anthropologists and concessionaires who brought entire villages face to face with tourists in the industrial world. Ironically, the pioneers of an air travel industry have reversed and expanded the human flow. Now, rather than concessionaires who brought villagers to the fairs, airlines carry tourists to distant villages.

In the "tourism-speak" of countless contemporary promotional materials, creative itineraries mix adventure and culture in extraordinary settings. The sirens' songs woo the tempted reader as they promise opportunities to observe or engage the preindustrial inhabitants of some distant destination, people perceived as "closer to nature," who maintain traditional values and techniques despite the intrusion of contemporary travelers.

Consider the travel writer who reported his visit to Tanna, a remote island in the South Pacific, part of the Republic of Vanuatu between Australia and Fiji, where village people practice "*kastom,* the strict adherence to traditional life.*" In an area where tourism is relatively new, a guide led the way along a muddy path through the forest to see Tanna's villagers, who live in mud-walled, thatched huts; they cook over open fires and hunt for food with bow and arrow. At a village celebration women in grass skirts and men clad only in raffia penis sheaths dance and sing a song that warns against the "overtures of western missionaries."[36]

How does this twenty-first-century gawker differ from the gaping fairgoer of yesteryear? Both approach the observed society as a privileged, technologically endowed evaluator. The experience satisfies a desire to travel, adds to the writer's knowledge of the world, and possibly fuels a sense of superiority. However, while fairgoers traveled on their own account and paid for the trip, the travel writer supports—and is supported by—a global industry that appeals to an identified market for ethnic tourism. When brochures assure tourists that they will see primitive natives, villagers in developing areas often remove western-style clothes, paint their bodies, and don minimal garb to accommodate lucrative photo opportunities.

Tourists leave home to absorb human and natural history, to relax and enjoy warm climates, or to pursue sexual conquest, among other motivations. Travel literature stirs curiosity and fuels imagination, and many enticing descriptions contain seductive spiels that seem transferable from continent to continent.

For example, one well-known tour planner offers a trip to Papua New Guinea, where "ancient cultures beckon us to join them." Tour participants are invited to observe the daily life of the Huli clan and learn about their traditions. Then they can participate in daily activities and reenactments of traditional rituals in a small village in the Sepik River basin.[37]

On its Copper Canyon (northern Mexico) "adventure," the San Diego Natural History Museum promised personal contact with Tarahumara and Mayo natives and "a visit to an Indian village whose inhabitants live much as their ancestors did—living in enlarged caves, tending fields, making baskets, and celebrating with long-distance running games."[38]

Across the Pacific Ocean again, in a village in Thailand, tour operators assure visitors that they will experience the rural life of hill tribes, who live in Chinese-style houses and transport goods on pack horses to the colorful market, where the "locals" shop among crowded stalls. Then, at night, the market merchants turn into entertainers and perform their traditional dances for the tourists.

Most likely, many of Thailand's hill people live in their own villages and contract with tour operators for performances. However, Thai tourism also supports made-to-order villages. In northwestern Thailand about one hundred "giraffe women" live in groupings conveniently organized for tourist purposes. Brass coils elongate their necks, considered a sign of beauty, and identify them as members of the Kayan tribe. Refugees from neighboring Myanmar's repressive authorities, they live as attractions in villages where they enjoy safety in exchange for a life of confinement as cultural performers:

> Some people describe the villages as a human zoo. . . .
> Nothing here seems private. As they go about their lives—
> feeding their children, washing at the village pump—they
> are on display to all comers. . . . [F]or Mada, 20, who grew
> up here, tourists are a way of life. "I'm glad when the
> tourists come because then we can make money."[39]

Did the residents in world's fair villages also become accustomed to their exposed existence and learn to regard tourists as people with bizarre and shocking customs? In this age of mass tourism, the encounter of privileged observer and villager seems to repeat endlessly.

Few people stopped at the small island of Nias, west of Sumatra, before 1940. Headhunters before the twentieth century, the rather unfriendly Niha people frequently waged war among themselves. Their isolation ended when a cruise line arranged for villagers to perform a few of their dances for several hundred passengers docked in a nearby harbor. Niha rituals and initiation dances proved an irresistible tourist attraction, and cruise ships soon scheduled two stops a month to satisfy the augmented demand.[40]

As Indonesian tourism expanded, a trickle of tourists who arrived by boat in the 1930s, attracted by Bali's spectacular feasts, grew to some 3,500 foreign guests in 1960 and then to 150,000 by 1974. Balinese culture, its art and artisan work, and its way of life became a commodity to be exchanged for foreign currency. Half a century after the first boatload of tourists, some 400,000 arrived each year, as airport expansion accommodated increased international traffic.[41]

(In 2003 terrorists bombed a Balinese resort where young travelers enacted rituals that they themselves had devised in an international, beach-going subculture.)

Less-developed countries lure tourists to exotic villages or beautiful beaches to gain revenue. Profits also motivated world's fair organizers. Pakistan attracted international tourists in pursuit of villages untouched by modernity, although the destination fell out of favor once terrorists' attacks altered attitudes toward its ethnic tribes and the safety of the area. The most concentrated tourism in northern Pakistan focused on the Valley of Kalash, where tour agencies in the 1990s boasted that a "recently discovered" people had maintained a centuries-long isolation by resisting Muslim invaders. The Kalash villagers made Pakistan's list of tourist stops because "impervious to Islam, [they] have preserved their religion, their dress and their rules."

Pakistan understandably exploited assets (i.e., timelessness and tradition) that gained value in a fast-paced, stressful, industrialized world. In an unintentional paradox, Pakistani development agents risked destroying their lure when they attracted harried first-world tourists to the Hunza Valley. The valley's villagers, a reputedly contented people, lived at a subsistence level, did not use money, had not adopted the wheel, deliberately rejected mechanization, ignored illness, and enjoyed exceptionally long lives.[42]

Ethnologists at the world's fairs would have ranked the Kayans, Nihas, Kalashes, and self-satisfied Hunzas at the low end of the evolutionary scale, in need of civilization's blessings. To the contemporary tourist who regards people living "closer to nature" with a certain romantic nostalgia, more traditional societies may represent a cultural authenticity and unharried way of life that eludes the globe-trotting adventurer. At either end of the twentieth century, entrepreneurs found ways to exploit villagers as curiosities and tourists as consumers.

CHAPTER 2

Inventors and Entertainers: Aviation

AS THE PUBLICISTS promised and journalists reported, the Louisiana Purchase Exposition brought the world to St. Louis. From the palaces of technology to the Terrace of Nations to the Pike, fairgoers dipped into storehouses of history and artistry, of cultural diversity and mechanical achievements. The totality of the fair overwhelmed the crowds; the exhibits astounded and educated, titillated and provoked, aroused curiosity, and even encouraged visitors to abandon themselves to merriment.

The unfolding era of world's fairs that crossed the century divide both fostered mass commercial entertainment and contributed to its growing respectability. The upstanding citizens who organized Chicago's fair expressed misgivings about "cheap entertainment" and located the Midway Plaisance at a distance from the "magnificence of the White City." [1] As civic leaders, they preferred that exhibitors educate as they entertained, but as businesspersons, they conceded the financial value of frivolous amusement. Over time, antagonism toward unruly popular diversions gave way to practical necessity, that is, concerns about profit. Thus, the St. Louis fair's backers moved the Pike to an easily accessible location next to the grand entrance. The Pike's acres and acres of displays and attractions combined to stimulate and satisfy visitors' appetites for both knowledge and commercial entertainment.

The Louisiana Purchase Exposition, the largest and arguably the most excessive of the international fairs, fostered an expansive outlook for the new century. Inspired commentators marveled at the new technologies and lauded inventors as the handmaidens of cultural progress. When Irish-Italian inventor Guglielmo Marconi began the century with messages transmitted "through the air," *Popular Science Monthly* predicted a wonderful world in which wireless telegraphy would put an end to isolation and loneliness. How many of the people who stood around the wireless telegraph tower at the St. Louis fair, as it transmitted radio messages to a receiving tower hundreds of miles away in Kansas City, recognized the degree to which new forms of communication would affect their lives in the near future?[2]

However, the twenty million bedazzled consumers of novelty and excitement at the fair saw neither the Wright brothers' flying machine, which had flown for the first time the previous year, nor the seminal French and American moving picture narratives, *A Trip to the Moon* and *The Great Train Robbery,* released in 1902 and 1903, respectively. The Wrights balked at the rules laid out for aviation participants, and Pike concessionaires still operated in the world of nineteenth-century amusements.

Though the path-breaking aviation achievement and the icons of motion picture history bypassed the great gathering, the fair foreshadowed a transformative entertainment decade. Within five years crowds of people gathered at makeshift airfields and county fairs, where they exulted as aviators competed and risked their lives to fly the fastest airplane in the sky. In even less time, an international array of silent movies filled the flickering screens of thousands of hastily outfitted storefronts and theaters and fascinated millions of viewers on any given day.

After decades of laboratory experiments and of technical and practical calculations to translate theories and hypotheses into operational equipment, the general public applauded the airplanes and motion pictures more for their ability to entertain than for their inventors' contributions to the advancement of science.

The airplane, like the motion picture camera, facilitated leisure-time enjoyment, and Wilbur Wright, who devoted years of back-breaking and mind-bending labor to the development of a successful flying machine, acknowledged that reality. Most people appreciated his achievement not out of scientific interest, he lamented, but as a "sport," like boating, cycling, or automobiling. The sense of exhilaration while flying appealed to the aviator, while the element of danger attracted both the flier and the spectator.[3]

By 1904, when messages actually traveled the airwaves and humans had flown short distances, the prospect of human flight also inspired optimistic observations of social progress. Prominent aviation enthusiast Octave Chanute declared that "when man is flying through the air the ultimate effect will be to diminish greatly the frequency of wars and to substitute some more rational meth ods of settling international misunderstandings." Technological utopians offered communication and air travel as antidotes to nineteenth-century romantic nationalism that separated people and at times turned them against each other. They idealized aviators as freely moving agents of connectedness who overturned the barriers raised by nations and inspired a universal culture. When people overcame boundaries, they encouraged peace and harmony and deterred violence. Because airplanes brought people closer together, the idealists argued, nations would be less likely to go to war.[4]

Other observers preferred blinders to rose-colored glasses. They simply decided that humans could not fly and should not even try. Amused skeptics derided experimenters with scientific- and religious-based jibes. Perhaps we could repeal the laws of gravity, they sneered. God would have given humans wings, they taunted, if they had been meant to fly. Some critics pointed to the imaginative theorist who built an elaborate winged apparatus and attempted to emulate birds, which the doubters saw as proof that inventors of flying machines were ridiculous cranks who rushed unworkable contraptions into public trials without ever studying aerodynamics.

Cynical dismissal and laughter often replaced encouragement as the general public misunderstood the importance of failures that necessarily preceded success in the process of invention, and no less so with the first heavier-than-air (as opposed to balloons) flying machine.

Unlike the Wright brothers, who conducted their flight experiments on the little-used beach at Kill Devil Hills, Smithsonian Institution scientist Samuel Langley launched his Aerodrome by catapult from a houseboat in the busy Potomac River, only to watch the gasoline-engine-powered craft collapse into the water. If the well-respected Langley could not fly, critics ventured, why continue? Langley's 1903 misfortune cast doubt on the potential of piloted flight in a heavier-than-air machine and contributed to the dismissive attitude that plagued the Wrights.

Orville and Wilbur did fly, of course, but the patent disputes and rivalries prompted by their flying machine's profit potential challenged utopian visions of a peaceful transcendence of conflict through air travel. In addition, twentieth-century warfare highlighted the destructive capacity of humans in airplanes.

Success and Silence

The world came to St. Louis, but the Wright brothers did not. Wilbur and Orville had made aviation history four months before the fair opened. They should have reveled in admiration at the aeronautics field or in a hall of technology devoted to invention. They missed an obvious opportunity to seize the media spotlight, ignite the public's imagination, confirm the feasibility of flying machines, and perhaps take home some prize money.

With six years to organize, the fair's founders enjoyed sufficient time to publicize their aeronautics prizes: "We have $100,000 for each contestant who can build anything that can fly with at least one person," Dorothy Birk paraphrased the organizers' challenge. "We don't care what it is—a flying kite, a dirigible, or a balloon—just so it can get airborne." [5] By 1904 the Wright brothers had been airborne more than once.

The spectators who cheered balloonists and glider fliers at the aeronautics field most likely did not understand or appreciate the drama and excitement that had been denied them. They might have beheld a biplane, equipped with two propellers and a four-cylinder engine, elevator in front and rudder behind, and watched it roll down launching rails and rise into the air. Wilbur or Orville, lying prone in the hip cradle on the lower wing and manipulating the various cables, wires, and handles, would have controlled the lift, direction, and banking mechanisms in a struggle to keep the unwieldy machine aloft. They might have held their breath as the machine soared several hundred feet and applauded with relief when it landed—or gasped as it hit the sand with a bounce or a crunch.

Astoundingly, the audiences didn't even know what they had missed, for the few newspapers that had reported the Wrights' December triumph rarely had the facts right. For the most part the media had dismissed the story without investigation, perhaps predisposed by Langley's failure to discount the Wrights' claims of success. Even their hometown Dayton newspaper downplayed their efforts as a mere pastime of no consequence. Until they personally saw the machine fly, most people remained unconvinced that humans piloted airplanes. Even reports by firsthand observers carried no weight.

The *New York Times* devoted almost twenty paragraphs to its September 4, 1904, coverage of "air battles" at St. Louis but overlooked Dayton, where Wilbur and Orville flew in a circle around a nearby airfield on September 20 and landed, without any media attention at all. The paper reported the participation of prize-driven "flying machine men" but never mentioned the Wright brothers. Instead, the *Times* named Samuel Langley as America's foremost aeronaut. The excitement generated by ninety entrants in a contest to "eclipse all previous efforts to solve the problem of aerial navigation" ignored the fact that a great advance in the field had already been achieved.[6]

Although difficult to imagine, a *Scientific American* reporter also avoided crediting the Wright brothers' flights when he wrote "the first attempt in the history of aeroplanes to operate a flying machine of that type carrying a man through the air was made on Thursday, the 6th instant, in the stadium at the World's Fair . . . and was considered . . . a remarkably successful venture." The "impressive" machine was a biplane glider, lifted into the air by means of a wire attached to a motor and then propelled by air currents and the force of gravity to a landing. As the reporter described the flight, "The entire operation is based upon exactly the same principle as the flying of a kite."[7] Clearly, the glider had none of the technical sophistication of the 1903 Wright Flyer.

How could months have passed without recognition? Why the public and private silence? Indeed, the Wrights had anticipated success at Kitty Hawk on December 17 and prepared to publicize the dramatic event. The planned press releases included a description of the machine and sketches of Orville and Wilbur. The telegram that carried the news to the family in Dayton prompted family members to inform the press.[8]

The local representative of the Associated Press in Dayton, contacted by the family as instructed, accorded the minute-long flight that followed the first twelve-second effort no news value—perhaps he could find merit only in an hour's flight. The version that finally appeared in several newspapers reflected the exaggerated excitement of the telegraph operator who relayed Wilbur and Orville's message to the family through Western Union. His fanciful account heightened the drama to the point of disbelief and served only to confirm public skepticism.

At Kitty Hawk, before the brothers packed up to return home, newspapers and magazines had begun to request pictures and interviews. The media contacted the family at home in Dayton, also. However, by the time the aviators arrived home on December 23, they had decided to give no interviews.

The brothers had immediately informed their friend and supporter Octave Chanute, who responded from Chicago the following day (December 18) to offer congratulations and to ask when they would be ready to go public. He suggested that they present a report of their experiences to the American Association for the Advancement of Science (AAAS), which would meet in St. Louis in ten days, but the brothers responded negatively. Chanute nonetheless lauded the aerial achievement in his own talk to the association and explained that the Wrights wished to delay revealing either the construction of their machine or the method of its operation.

In January the Wrights felt compelled to issue press releases to correct the original, overstated, newspaper accounts. To set the record straight, they gave the particulars of the events at Kill Devil Hills, which were then picked up across the nation and in Europe. The French responded with disbelief, even though Captain Ferdinand Ferber, a prominent member of the Aero-Club de France and a follower of the Wrights' glider experiments, had published an article in February, 1903, warning that Americans had captured the lead in aeronautics.[9]

Indeed, with a few exceptions, the French had neglected heavier-than-air experiments in favor of promising advances in dirigibles. The affluent members of the Aero-Club had demonstrated a passion for ballooning when they founded the organization in 1898, and the club gradually evolved into a support group for aviation development. Hot-air balloons, pleasurable but unreliable as transportation, depended on the vagaries of air currents for speed and direction. In the last quarter of the nineteenth century, the desire to create a powered airship with directional control had resulted in several dirigible models. The nonrigid "blimp," simple in construction and lightweight, used the internal pressure of a gas-filled bag to hold the structure in form, while the rigid-framed, gas-filled airship invented by Ferdinand von Zeppelin used an internal aluminum, latticework skeleton to maintain its elongated oval shape.

Both von Zeppelin and Alberto Santos-Dumont gained the premier positions in European airship development about the same time that the Wright brothers turned their attention to flight. Zeppelin retired from the German army in 1891 to devote his time to building a motor-driven airship. In July, 1900, he completed a three-and-one-half mile, eighteen-minute flight in his 430-foot-long dirigible airship.

Although Zeppelin's technology gained admirers in France, the expense of building rigid dirigibles and the uncertainty of their utility limited the number of potential imitators. Brothers Paul and Pierre Lebaudy built several, and their name appears among the notable entrants in the St. Louis airship contest.

The outstanding developer of French nonrigid airships in this

Brazilian-born aviation pioneer Alberto Santos-Dumont experimented with various airship designs and became a hero of French aeronautics and Brazilian history. *Courtesy of the San Diego Aerospace Museum.*

period, Alberto Santos-Dumont, was in fact a wealthy, transplanted Brazilian who attracted as much attention for his personal eccentricities as for his fierce dedication to flying. Among the honors accorded him by admiring Brazilians, the title of "father of modern flight" reflects more nationalist sentiment than the significance of his contribution to twentieth-century aviation.

Just over five feet tall and weighing less than one hundred pounds, Santos-Dumont left Brazil for France in 1891. The eighteen-year-old son of a wealthy coffee planter took an apartment on the Champs Elysées. He began building airships in 1898 and gained notoriety for skirting the Paris rooftops and landing in populated areas, like the sidewalk near his apartment. By the time Henri Deutsch de la Meurthe offered 100,000 francs to the first person to pilot an airship from the Aero-Club's ballooning field at St. Cloud to the Eiffel Tower and back in less than half an hour,

Santos-Dumont had improved on his original model. He completed the required journey in October, 1901, and donated 75,000 francs of the prize money to poor Parisians and the rest to his crew.[10] He intended to compete for prizes in the aeronautical races at St. Louis, but someone slashed his airship beyond the point of repair and eliminated him from contention.

Even as Santos-Dumont demonstrated his vehicle's technological capabilities with the Eiffel Tower flight, Ferdinand Ferber expanded his interest in the Wrights' glider and worked to move the Aero-Club in the direction of heavier-than-air machines. He wanted to fly and wanted the French to lead the aviation world. Despite Ferber's correspondence with Octave Chanute and the Wright brothers, his attempts to construct a glider based on the Wrights' machines failed. Chanute's 1903 report to the Aero-Club, in which he described the Wright brothers' experiments, had pushed French aeronauts to greater efforts, but they neglected to replicate the Americans' deliberate, problem-solving approach to flight.

That is, the Wrights assumed the aircraft's instability, based on three years of work with gliders, starting with the tethered, kitelike machine they flew in the coastal winds at Kitty Hawk in 1900. Their 1901 glider traveled almost four hundred feet, but dissatisfaction with its performance sent them back to Dayton for wind-tunnel research and tests. The 1902 biplane glider incorporated mechanisms determined by previous experience and research results—elevator in the front for lift, pilot-controlled single rudder for stability during turns, and the all-important technique of wing-warping.

Once in the air, the pilot had to accommodate to wind changes, be able to turn, and direct the landing in some way. So, fliers were required to control three operations: move up or down, turn right or left in a flat plane, and raise one wing while lowering the other in a rolling motion around an imaginary line through the center of the fuselage. For this lateral control the Wrights devised a way to twist, or "warp," the wings—patterned after the way birds flex their wingtips. The pilot controlled the outer portions of the wing's trailing edge by simultaneously twisting cords in equal and opposite directions to produce a "roll," or banking motion, to maintain lateral balance during turns.

A tremendous effort marked the 1902–1903 design and construction year. The Wrights built the motor and propellers needed to transform the glider into a machine for powered, sustained, and controlled flight. They designed the rail-guided launch system that replaced the glider's dependence on a gravity-assisted takeoff. They engineered the cables and wires by which the pilot manipulated the elevator, rudder, and critical wing-warping mechanism.

Confident in the uniqueness of their design, Wilbur and Orville steadfastly protected the properties of their wing-warping technology from public knowledge. Later, when the world of aeronautics evolved from scientific cooperation to business rivalry, the technique became the focus of contention in multiple patent fights.

While the St. Louis competition attracted numerous contestants willing to pay the $250 entrance fee in order to claim prizes for altitude, length, and duration of flight, with few exceptions the entrants flew lighter-than-air balloons or dirigibles. Some balloonists competed for the $5,000 prize offered to the first piloted craft to reach the Washington Monument, in the District of Columbia, from St. Louis. The $100,000-prize contestants competed within the confines of a complicated set of rules over a course shaped like the letter L, with the short leg in view of the exposition grounds and a total length of between ten and fifteen miles. To win, a contestant needed to record the best average time in three revolutions of the course. No wonder the *Times* called this race the exposition's most spectacular offering.

Even the failures inspired admiration. As St. Louis citizen Dorothy Birk recalled, a young balloonist named Roy Knabenshue took off from the aeronautics field and landed way off course at some distance, near a restaurant. The excited diners rushed out, and several men hoisted the flier on their shoulders and carried him inside, where the bartender created a new drink in his honor.[11] The intrepid Knabenshue returned to the aeronautical field another day and steered the dirigible *California Arrow* in a figure eight over the fairgrounds.

Since the Wright brothers declined to participate in the aeronautics competition at the 1904 St. Louis World's Fair, the spectators understandably may have considered dirigibles, like Thomas Scott Baldwin's *California Arrow*, piloted successfully by A. Roy Knabenshue, as the air transportation mode of the future. *Courtesy of the Missouri Historical Society.*

Thomas Scott Baldwin had built the *California Arrow*, a 95-foot-long, cigar-shaped airship, filled with hydrogen and powered by a lightweight motorcycle engine. Knabenshue had never piloted a dirigible, but for him it was love at first flight. After the fair closed he raced the *Arrow* against automobiles between Los Angeles and neighboring Pasadena. The next year he built his own airship and flew it from New York's Central Park around the *New York Times* building. That first airship flight over Manhattan earned him $10,000 from the owner of the *Times*. Several years later the air show veteran managed Wilbur and Orville Wright's aerial exhibition company.

The Wrights had contemplated entering the competition in

St. Louis, but their predicament lay in the temptation to demonstrate their invention—a heavier-than-air, powered machine capable of sustained flight under the control of a pilot that took off and landed at the same level (unlike the gravity-dependent glider). Perhaps they could challenge the bias toward lighter-than-air craft evident in the race entries. On the other hand, they desired to protect the unique features of their machine from potential competitors. Though they had sought publicity immediately after the flights of December 17, media distortions of their work had made them wary. Their newly hired patent lawyer advised them to say as little as possible about their machine during the time-consuming patent process.

The brothers had known about the exposition and its prizes for at least two years. Chanute had encouraged them to enter as early as 1902, and wherever he had gone, he had told people about the Wrights' advances with the glider. After December, 1903, he urged them to go public and to claim their rightful place in the aeronautics world. In January, they sent their clarification statement to the Associated Press, told Chanute they would say no more, and then went to work on modifications to the machine.

Nevertheless, in the middle of January they wrote for a copy of the revised rules and regulations for the race at St. Louis. Objections to the original rules had disposed them against participation, and they even discussed exhibiting the machine somewhere outside the fairgrounds. In February, they went to St. Louis to inspect the terrain over which the contest would take place. The firsthand view left them less certain than ever, since the uneven ground along the flight course could seriously damage the machine in the event of a forced landing.[12]

The revised rules did not prove reassuring. Contestants for the $100,000 grand prize still had to fly three trials around the course, with the best average speed winning—no rewards for less-than-complete efforts.

Wilbur wrote to Willard A. Smith, a member of the committee that framed the rules, to complain that the smaller prizes offered seemed especially adapted to dirigible balloons, kites, and gliding machines. Indignant, he chastised the committee for ignoring the pilot-carrying flyer. "A flight of even one mile by such a machine would be an event of great importance in aeronautical history," he correctly asserted, "yet your rules would give it no recognition even to the extent of a brass medal."[13]

Wilbur had a point, of course. When he wrote the letter, the fair had not yet opened and would run for six months—more than sufficient time to accommodate an exhibition flight with appropriate recognition that would add revenue at the gate. The lack of positive consideration indicates the degree of apathy and disbelief that greeted the Kitty Hawk flight.

The Wrights' ambivalence about the fair's competition continued throughout 1904. Meanwhile, they gained permission to work at Huffman Prairie, a 100-acre field surrounded by farms eight miles outside of Dayton. They built a shed for their components and other equipment and took the local trolley from their home to the site. Hundreds of people used that trolley every day, so many curious eyes followed their labors. Still, newspapers and magazines carried distorted stories of their flights rather than actually investigate the ongoing effort.

The brothers assembled a new machine in April, incorporating structural changes meant to improve the flyer. Then they invited various Ohio newspapers to send observers for a trial run set for May 23. About a dozen reporters and perhaps thirty locals stood around on the field, waiting to see the flying machine in action. The Wrights had built a new, one-hundred-foot launch rail, designed to gain more speed before takeoff. Unlike Kitty Hawk's dependable ocean breezes, the deficiency of wind at Huffman Prairie made it difficult to get aloft and, once airborne, to stay there.

The winds did not blow at all on May 23. Despite the dead calm, they attempted a late-afternoon flight, but engine trouble— not lack of wind—thwarted the effort. The plane moved down the rails but never left the ground. After two days of rain Orville tried again for the handful of reporters still there. This time the machine lifted off the rails, not for a convincing flight of hundreds of feet, but a hop of twenty-five.[14]

In fact, the strain of continued—and disappointing— experimentation probably underlay the brothers' ambivalence over a public competition. Because the Wrights had invited the press to watch the May flight attempts, secrecy could no longer have been the deciding factor. In June, after a few more flights, they considered entering the race but held back, unsure whether the restructured 1904 machine would be ready in time. In July, they saw the prospect "vanishing into thin air." Entrants had to have flown at least a mile and return in order to qualify, and they had been experiencing discouragingly short hops of 100 to 200 feet and many damaging crashes that required them to replace components. They were running out of time. In mid-August, they finally flew more than the 852 feet achieved at Kitty Hawk the previous December.[15]

Clearly, the lengthened launch rail had not solved the wind problem. To gain sufficient thrust to overcome resistance, they devised a complex system of ropes and pulleys, with a weight dropped from a twenty-foot tower to pull the flying machine down shortened rails and launch it into the air. The system produced the necessary speed, and the flying distances lengthened. On September 20, Orville flew more than four thousand feet in a circle—demonstrating control as well as flight—but still not a qualifying distance for the $100,000 prize at St. Louis.

Because a number of potential contenders had failed to appear or had succumbed to injuries, the entrance deadline had been extended to October 1. The contest officials softened and offered prizes for more achievable feats, like $500 for a flight of one mile from the aeronautical concourse and return. While this came as good news to those who had already paid the $250 entry fee, it hardly sufficed as an inducement for the Wrights. Besides, their machine's performance proved inconsistent, plagued by frequent accidents; long flights only infrequently punctuated the more usual, shorter hops.

By the time Wilbur flew four complete turns around the Huffman Prairie field on November 9, the brothers had given up any notion of participation at St. Louis. Roy Knabenshue had piloted the fifty-three-foot-long *California Arrow* to win the $500 prize on October 31. Balloonist Knabenshue had thrilled some St. Louisans with his off-course first ride, and he fared little better in his first airship performance. He had no experience when he took the *Arrow* up for the first time on October 25. The *Arrow*'s secondhand motorcycle motor quit, and he drifted across the Mississippi River to land some fifteen miles away in Illinois.

Although Knabenshue and *Arrow*'s owner, Thomas Baldwin, won acclaim and the admiration of the spectators, they could not collect their $500. Despite the rave reviews, the St. Louis Exposition lost money. Creditors impounded available funds including the aeronautical prizes. Disconcertingly, the exposition confirmed for many people that flying machines, though entertaining, offered little practical purpose. For the time being, automobiles occupied the transportation spotlight.

The disappointments of 1904 did not deter dedicated aviators who were anxious to conclude a history of mixed success and failure with a lasting triumph. If anything, the aeronautical contests had shown the Wright brothers that no one had superseded their technology or could demonstrate a better, heavier-than-air machine.

Rivalries and Redesigns

How could the leadership in mechanical flight have fallen to the Americans? That reality penetrated the consciousness of French aviation circles and spurred Aero-Club members to intensify their activities. More than a hint of resentment pervaded the atmosphere.

A self-conscious superiority marked the French refusal to cede mastery of the air to the Wright brothers. France gloried in a past that covered centuries; the United States counted scarcely more than one. At the time when thirteen weak colonies had struggled to separate from England and managed to succeed only with the aid of France, French balloonists had already experimented with aerial navigation. The Marquis de Lafayette, who had assisted the colonists militarily and diplomatically, became a lasting symbol of the bond between France and the newly establish United States. While the fledgling nation wrote its Constitution, Joseph Michel and Jacques Etienne Montgolfier inflated a large linen bag with hot air, rose above the village of Annonay, near Lyons, and traveled more than a mile through the air.

Even as reports of the work at Kitty Hawk and Huffman Prairie crossed the Atlantic Ocean, the Louisiana Purchase Exposition commemorated the French cession of territory that contributed to the growth of the United States and to its expanding power. The city of St. Louis had been nothing more than a French fur-trading post while France's monarchs guided the destinies of territorial possessions around the world. By the vagaries of fortune, President Thomas Jefferson purchased the Louisiana territory from a financially strapped France forty years later. St. Louis became the gateway to the newly acquired land beyond the Mississippi River and increased its population from 1,000 to 300,000 in three generations.

Subsequently, the nationalistic French watched as the United States took over the construction of the Panama Canal from a failed French company, entered Europe's imperialist competition, and threatened to achieve primacy in the significant scientific field of aeronautics.

Untouched by the technological contest and mostly unaware of the potential opening of a new transportation era, the social elite of the United States maintained their strong affiliations with, and affection for, France. They traveled by luxury liner—those steam-powered, floating hotels—to Paris as early as April, but certainly by June for the racing season at Longchamps, and enjoyed the northern French seaside resorts in the summer and those on the Riviera in the winter.

A scant 100,000 Americans (out of 75 million) traveled abroad at the turn of the century, but a steady stream of the wealthy, worldly, and restless—the jet-setters of their day—entertained themselves on foreign shores.[16]

Despite French determination to wrest the crown of aviation science from the Americans, they failed to overtake the Wright brothers. The next two years saw steady improvement in the machines under production in Dayton. After a series of redesigns, setbacks, and recoveries, the Wrights piloted their improved machine for more than half an hour at a time and traveled more than twenty miles. Gaining in confidence, they resolved to find a buyer for what appeared in October, 1905, to be a truly functional airplane.

The Wrights recognized that the most likely, immediate use of the airplane lay in military reconnaissance. Photographers had taken cameras along on balloon rides since the middle of the nineteenth century, although the earliest results suggested that an element of nervousness, added to the vagaries of air currents, produced less than the clearest reproductions of surface features. By the early twentieth century, aerial photography pioneer George Lawrence used a balloon to successfully capture American landscapes, which were appreciated mostly for their aesthetic value. Illinois-born Chester Melvin Vaniman recorded spectacular aerial panoramas in New Zealand, Australia, Austria, Germany, and France. The quality of these photographs left no doubt about the useful information that aerial reconnaissance could provide.

Thus, the Wrights hoped to demonstrate the Wright Flyer's potential to the United States government. They stopped flying and would reveal no details until then. Once again they rejected Chanute's advice to gain the widest publicity possible. They had no inclination to be aerial showmen, they declared, or to offer their plane as a gift to the world. No longer in the experimental mode, the inventors had a proven product to sell and adopted a business mentality. There would be no photos of flights or technical drawings, they stated, until they negotiated a contract.

However, U.S. government officials proved less certain than the inventors about the practical value of flying machines. They wanted to see drawings and descriptions and proof of flight. Wilbur and Orville maintained their stance. Finally, government representatives communicated that the nation had no need of flying machines, even with their potential military capabilities.

Although somewhat interested in the airplane, British and French military leaders balked at what they considered an excessively high price. Granted patent protection in 1906, the Wrights still declined to fly or to reveal any details of the machine to a potential buyer without a contract. In fact, two years would pass before the Wright Flyer made its public debut, years in which the brothers concentrated on business, not on flight.

In the meantime, the French worked unsuccessfully to unravel the mystery of the Wright airplane. Anglo-French Aero-Club member Ernest Archdeacon shared Ferdinand Ferber's conviction regarding France's destined leadership in aviation. Archdeacon backed his commitment to French superiority with prize money offered for a very modest achievement in powered flight. When the Wrights flew twenty-four miles (thirty-nine kilometers) late in 1905, the Archdeacon prize for a one-kilometer flight remained unclaimed. Rather than concede American preeminence, Archdeacon rejected the authenticity of reports crediting the Wrights with aviation advances. He even debated the issue at the Paris Aero-Club in January, 1906. Then he challenged the brothers to fly their plane in France and claim the prize he offered, but the growing rivalry failed to move them.

Although French aircraft designers tried to discern the workable elements of the Wright Flyer, they did not abandon airships. Ferdinand von Zeppelin's 1900 flight of three and one-half miles in eighteen minutes had proved the dirigible's air worthiness. While Wilbur and Orville improved their design in 1905, Santos-Dumont combined his previous dirigible work with an innovative, if awkward, heavier-than-air machine. After the disastrous slashing of his airship at St. Louis, he experimented with gliders and also produced a helicopter, which did not fly, however.

Back in his workshop once again, Santos-Dumont devised a flying machine whose appearance observers compared to a duck. The combined elevator and rudder, in box-kite form, protruded far enough in front to resemble the head and neck, while the machine's upwardly angled wings and the stubby rear completed the image. A dirigible first carried the motorized, pusher-propeller craft into the air and then separated, leaving the pilot to fly alone.[17]

After several trials Santos-Dumont managed to stay in the air for a twenty-one-second, 722-foot flight, a longer time but shorter distance than the Wright brothers' first flight had accomplished three years earlier. Nevertheless, the exasperated Europeans, eager for some evidence of progress, elevated the flamboyant flier to hero status.

Even a quarter of a century later, the contest between airplanes and dirigibles had not reached a definitive conclusion as to the safest way to travel, with the most comfortable accommodations for passengers and the greatest capacity for carrying freight.

Meanwhile, Gabriel Voisin and Louis Blériot worked on gliders of various configurations. Voisin built a boxlike machine with a forward elevator and towed it behind a motorboat. It rose above the river Seine and landed gracefully but represented no threat to the Wright brothers. A Voisin-Blériot collaboration came apart while taxiing on a grassy field in Paris's Bois de Boulogne, and eventually the designers also went their own ways. Voisin opened a small factory with his brother, Charles. France's first aircraft manufacturers built machines to customer specification and fabricated their own box-kite-winged airplane with front elevator, rear rudder motor, and metal propeller. Blériot continued to build and test his own designs.[18]

On January 13, 1908, the Anglo-French sportsman-aviator Henry Farman finally won the Archdeacon prize for a one-kilometer flight. His modified Voisin plane had no capacity for banked turns, but he traveled forward for 500 meters, made a wide, flat, somewhat clumsy turn, flew the necessary 500-meter return, and landed softly, thus satisfying the requirements.

Almost four years had passed since Archdeacon had announced the prize. Two years had passed since the Wrights had rejected his challenge to fly publicly in France and take home the $10,000 that a French citizen had now won. The Europeans filled the continued silence from Dayton with raucous self-congratulation. A confident Farman issued his own daring invitation—to a speed-and-distance contest between himself in a Voisin and either Wilbur or Orville in their Wright Flyer. The competition would be held in France and offered a prize of $5,000.

Business, not aerial showmanship, motivated the Wrights, and their steadfastness finally showed signs of promise. The U.S. Army Signal Corps approached the brothers to inquire about their flying machine and the price. When Wilbur suggested $25,000, the government issued specifications for a heavier-than-air craft, one whose features closely resembled those of the Wright machine.

The U.S. War Department had finally taken a step that a hesitant Congress had refused. In April, 1908, *Scientific American* had chastised the military committee of the U.S. House of Representatives for voting against a bill that would have appropriated $200,000 for the development of military aeronautics. When the "enterprise of American inventors and experimentalists has carried the development of the aeroplane to a point which has placed America far in the lead among the nations of the earth," the magazine's editors commented, the "time is fully ripe for substantial government recognition." Since the government had already authorized the formation of an aeronautic corps, the denial of funds appeared inexcusable. By contrast, European governments had embraced the military potential of aviation and backed their commitment with substantial financial resources.[19]

A month after Farman's one-kilometer flight in France, the Wright brothers went to work on the project they had waited years to arrange. Orville would demonstrate a plane for the army that could fly forty miles per hour, with an improved thirty-horsepower engine. The pilot controlled the Model A from an upright—not a prone—position, using control sticks to maneuver the wing-warping system, the elevator, and the rudder. They had designed this Flyer with a second seat and dual controls for instruction purposes and expected no difficulty satisfying the U.S. Army's evaluation team. Meanwhile, a French business group had agreed to manufacture the Wright plane—on license—with the French war department as their target market.

Wilbur sailed for France, not to compete against Farman, but to demonstrate the Flyer in a business proposition. On Saturday morning, August 8, a crowd began to gather at Les Hunaudières racetrack near Le Mans, about 115 miles southwest of Paris. Archdeacon and Blériot joined other curious onlookers who stood around all day until, in the late afternoon, the weight in the launching derrick dropped, and Wilbur Wright flew the machine they had all waited to see. One minute and forty-five seconds of flight dispelled the doubts that had clouded the Wrights' reputation. On September 21 Wilbur stayed in the air for a spectacular and record-setting hour and a half.

The Wrights prevailed as the world's top-ranked aeronauts in

1908, but the accolades obscured the very rapid consequences of the demonstration. The French, who had not caught on to the technology of lateral control even with the published patent documents, saw wing-warping in action. They quickly adapted the mechanism to their own planes and experienced the exhilaration of true flight.

Wilbur's demonstration flights released a burst of creative energy inspired by personal and nationalistic competitiveness. The Voisins improved their machines and opened a sales office in Paris. Blériot incorporated a wing-warping control and a dependable engine capable of hour-long operation into the *Blériot XI*. Leon Levavasseur built an innovative, graceful monoplane and named it for his daughter. The 38-foot-long *Antoinette IV* had a 42-foot wingspan and a lightweight aluminum engine. The pilot sat behind the wing, rather than in front, as in the Wright plane, and used wheels on either side of the fuselage—instead of handles and cables—to manipulate the rudder and the ailerons that replaced the wing-warping.[20]

Meanwhile, Orville successfully demonstrated the Model A on several flights above the Fort Myer, Virginia, parade ground. Four days before Wilbur set the endurance record in France, however, Orville, with Lieutenant Thomas Selfridge as a passenger, crashed the plane before a crowd of two thousand spectators. A cracked propeller set in motion a sequence of mechanical failures that led to a tragedy. Selfridge died of head injuries, and Orville smashed his left leg and hip. The army had to postpone further trials.[21]

Orville recovered from his injuries at home in Dayton while Europe lionized Wilbur. Having ended the long silence and absence from the public arena, Wilbur entered competitions and set new distance, duration, and altitude records in exchange for cash, gold medals, and trophies. While European aviators acquired technological knowledge, European investors sought out Wilbur with offers to build and sell Wright Flyers.[22]

Orville finally joined his brother in the spotlight after Christmas. Photographers—both still and motion picture—recorded the pilgrimages of the European elite to Pau in southern France, where the Wrights had set up a flying school. England's King Edward VII and Spain's Alfonso XIII arrived to share the moment in aviation history with its premier fliers.

The demonstration flights had turned aviation into a spectator sport and pilots into celebrities. As business and promotion superseded research, advances in aircraft design increasingly responded to the temptations of prize money rather than the desire to advance aeronautical science. The media neglect of the Huffman Prairie days had vanished, and the bond between plane and the camera began. From Pau, the Wrights went to Italy and stayed for a month, flying from a field outside Rome. On April 24, 1909, a newsreel camera operator accompanied Wilbur as a passenger and shot the first motion picture footage taken from an airplane in flight.[23]

Life in Europe became a whirlwind for the brothers as they gained both fame and financial reward. Orville and Wilbur sailed home to prepare for the June army trials, and when they arrived in May, 1909, parades, fireworks, and a presidential welcome at the White House awaited them.

The army tests proved disheartening at first but ended in success. Engine troubles and forced landings bedeviled the Flyer's performance. The Wrights finally satisfied the endurance requirement in July and then exceeded the forty miles per hour required to fulfill the contract agreement. Enjoying great personal satisfaction, they left Fort Myer $30,000 richer ($25,000 plus a bonus for flying two and one-half miles per hour over the contractual minimum speed).

If twentieth-century aviation began with a series of starts and stops from 1903 to 1908, a jubilant 1909 flooded the public consciousness with the names and faces of triumphant aviators on both sides of the Atlantic. Despite their honors and renown, however, a nagging irritant dogged the Wrights. Once other aviators understood the efficacy of the wing-warping, lateral control system, they built rival planes and won contest prizes. Competitors used the patented technology—or remarkably similar elements— with neither acknowledgment nor payment. Resentment of the infringement fueled discontent and diminished the pleasure of the brothers' accomplishments. Their repeated attempts to gain clari-

fication and satisfaction through court actions angered other aviators and eventually cast shadows on their own reputations.

The Spur of Competition

Interest in aviation had certainly not disappeared or even declined during the years of the Wright brothers' silence. In fact, the
young American flier and airplane builder who would challenge
their domination in the explosive resurgence of flying activity in
1909 built his reputation while they retreated from public scrutiny.
Ambitious and not the least publicity shy, Glenn Hammond Curtiss practically dared the Wright brothers to file a patent suit.

In the years when Wilbur and Orville experimented with gliders at Kitty Hawk, the mechanically gifted and daring Curtiss built
a gasoline engine adaptable for bicycles and then manufactured
and raced his own motorcycles. He consistently broke speed
records and gained a second distinction as a builder of superior
motors. The cycle motors, necessarily small and lightweight,
caught the attention of the aeronautical world. When Knabenshue
piloted the *California Arrow* at the St. Louis World's Fair, a Curtiss
engine powered the big dirigible, and Curtiss himself tried to sell
one of his engines to the Wrights in 1906.[24]

Wilbur and Orville rejected Curtiss's overtures, but telephone
inventor and visionary scientist Alexander Graham Bell sought
him out. Bell had assembled a number of bright, enthusiastic experimenters at his summer home in Nova Scotia, and he invited
Curtiss to join them. They formalized the group under the name
Aerial Experiment Association (AEA) and began to work on gliders and motorized airplanes. At Bell's request the U.S. War Department sent U.S. Army Lieutenant Thomas Selfridge to observe
the experiments. (As mentioned earlier, Selfridge died in August,
1908, when Orville's plane crashed during army trials.)

On March 12, 1908, the AEA tested a curved-wing biplane on
a frozen lake near Curtiss's home in Hammondsport, New York.
The *Red Wing* flew above the ice for little more than a thousand
feet before it crash-landed. Two months later its improved successor, *White Wing,* soared more than a thousand feet and landed

safely. While Orville prepared for the 1908 army trial and Wilbur assembled the Wright Flyer for demonstrations in France, the AEA tested a Curtiss-designed biplane, the *June Bug*. Then on July 4, before a large crowd of spectators, including reporters and photographers invited to witness the flight, Curtiss flew the requisite kilometer to win a $2,500 prize offered by the aviation-conscious journal *Scientific American*.[25]

Because of time constraints and commitments for demonstrations, the Wrights had decided against competing for the prize, which left the field to Curtiss. After Curtiss's success, Orville contacted the prize winner and advised him against any unlicensed use of Wright-patented designs for commercial or exhibition purposes. The *Scientific American* contest rules had not specified any turns, and Curtiss had flown a straight course of about a mile and then landed. Although he had not demonstrated any banked turns, he had incorporated ailerons in the *June Bug*. Curtiss denied intentions of entering the exhibition business; nevertheless, the legal battle had begun.

The AEA disbanded after Selfridge's death and Curtiss's defection to become Augustus Herring's partner in the first commercial aircraft manufacturing business in the United States. The Herring-Curtiss Company incorporated in March, 1909, and sold its first plane, the *Golden Flyer,* for $5,000 in June, shortly after the Wrights' triumphant return from Europe.

The Wright brothers' public demonstration in 1908 had catapulted American aviators into the rarified air of international celebrity and had stimulated a year of accelerated aviation activity. The U.S. government bought a Wright Flyer; Curtiss built and sold his airplane. Several French manufacturers experimented with alternative mechanisms and motors, and a steady stream of flying machines—biplanes and monoplanes, clumsy and sleek—left the ground for trial runs. Some remained aloft and actually flew; others barely left the ground and returned to the workshops for repairs and redesign.

To circumvent the Wrights' objections regarding patent infringements, Curtiss had moved the lateral-control mechanism from the wingtip, as on the *June Bug,* to a position between the wings. The *Golden Flyer*'s ailerons afforded the same tight turning capacity that the Wright Flyer's wing-warping system achieved. Two months after the sale, the Wrights filed lawsuits to prevent either Curtiss or his company from making profitable use of Wright patents, through either the sale or exhibition of Herring-Curtiss planes. Even though Wilbur and Orville had been willing to share information for research purposes, they refused to afford Curtiss the means to become wealthy without some monetary compensation for themselves.

Thus, flying contests and business competition put the Wrights at odds with their closest U.S. rival and soon plagued them in Europe, too. When the *London Daily Mail* originally announced a $5,000 prize for the first pilot of a heavier-than-air machine to fly across the English Channel, only Orville or Wilbur Wright had the plane and experience to win. Wilbur, already in Europe, declined the unnecessary risk in favor of other, more easily won, European prizes.

Between the October 1908 *Daily Mail* proposal and the summer of 1909, however, a number of French aviators had adapted the lessons learned from Wilbur's European demonstrations. They had flown substantial distances and were ready to take up the challenge. Well-known sportsman, big-game hunter, and motorboat racer Hubert Latham, a cosmopolitan Frenchman with both English and German ancestry, entered the competition with supporters on both sides of the channel. Count Charles de Lambert, an expatriate Russian who had taken flying lessons from the Wrights at Pau, responded to the challenge and brought two Wright planes to the channel coast. Louis Blériot had confidence in his latest design, the *Blériot XI* monoplane, and scraped together the funds needed to prepare for the flight.

On July 19, Latham made an unsuccessful attempt in one of Levavasseur's Antoinettes. The airplane's engine lost power, and Latham landed in the channel's rough waters. The crew of the destroyer escort that was standing by for just such a rescue fished him out. Latham decided to try again. When Lambert suffered a test-flight crash and dropped out, the contest narrowed to just Blériot and Latham.

Anticipation, apprehension, or competitive zeal? Any of these thoughts might be read into Frenchman Louis Blériot's expression as he prepared to take off on his history-making flight across the English Channel. *Courtesy of the San Diego Aerospace Museum.*

The two contestants watched apprehensively for several days, as prohibitive winds blew across the channel. Latham checked out his *Antoinette VII,* the replacement plane for the *Antoinette IV,* which had ditched on July 19. He had not previously flown this latest model, on which Levavasseur had replaced the ailerons with a wing-warping system. Unfavorable weather precluded an opportunity for a test flight.

Early on Sunday morning July 25, the winds slackened. Under a clear sky Blériot's crew began preparations. Shortly after 2 A.M. they awakened the pilot. Blériot ate breakfast and then accompanied his wife to the escort ship, which she boarded. He went on to the airfield, donned his coveralls and leather helmet, warmed up the engine, took a short trial flight, and proclaimed everything in working order. Aided by binoculars, he discerned a surprising absence of activity in the Latham camp. With understandable anxiety Blériot waited for sunrise. At his signal the crew released their hold on the plane, and he took off. A dozen or so spectators watched his progress from the dunes at Calais until—even with binoculars—they could no longer see his plane through the haze.

Blériot passed the escort ship, where his wife monitored his progress. He flew toward the faint gray line that he perceived to be the English coast. As he came closer, the cliffs rose to the front and then slid beneath him.

Flying was one challenge, but landing on unfamiliar territory was another. The winds that had bedeviled the fliers for days became Blériot's enemy again. Even when he found a place to land, unpredictable air currents threatened to smash him into the ground.

In fact, Blériot damaged his landing gear and the propeller while landing, but he had crossed the English Channel. A triumphant thirty-eight-kilometer flight, accomplished in thirty-seven minutes of uncertainty and danger, demonstrated that air-planes could travel over water as well as land. Moreover, the now-undeniable reality of air travel across a national boundary initiated serious discussions about protecting a country's sovereignty and security.

Meanwhile, the winds that had risen after Blériot's takeoff had kept Latham earthbound. While characteristically cordial in his congratulations to the victor, the competitive Latham agonized over his defeat. Two days later he tried again but encountered engine failure once more, this time within sight of Dover. As before, a quick rescue saved him from drowning.[26]

At the end of July, 1909, Blériot's successful channel crossing overshadowed the Wrights' impressive army trials, and Blériot took his turn in the media spotlight. Thousands of Londoners lined up to view Blériot's plane, which had been put on display at a major department store. His return to France had all the pomp and circumstance of a royal welcome, as the French feted both the airplane and their hero of air travel.

Blériot had redeemed French honor and returned the leadership in aviation to France's shores. The feat of traveling by flying machine from one country to another appeared even more astounding than new speed and distance records established by aviators who took off from and returned safely to the same airfield. After a rousing parade through Paris, with crowds estimated at

100,000, the Aero-Club acclaimed Blériot and awarded him a gold medal at a banquet held in his honor.

Sounding a discordant note in the hymn to French aeronautics, pioneer balloonist Santos-Dumont congratulated Blériot on his accomplishment and retired from flying. Only thirty-six years old at the time, Santos-Dumont traveled from country to country for a time and then returned to his native Brazil.[27]

Europe Forges Ahead

The European air crackled with an intensified competition in the wake of Blériot's flight. Not to be eclipsed by heavier-than-air machines, Joseph Brucker, president of the Europe-America Aero Navigation Society of New York, announced arrangements for a 1910 dirigible flight across the Atlantic Ocean. The big airship would take advantage of northeast trade winds to fly from Lisbon or Cadiz to New York by way of Puerto Rico, Havana, and New Orleans, for a total distance of more than six thousand miles. Brucker declared his intentions while attending an aeronautics exhibition in Frankfurt am Main, Germany. As an indication of escalating European excitement over aviation, the exhibition drew impressive crowds that wanted to see aircraft models and machinery, even without the attraction of flying demonstrations.[28]

Orville Wright launched his own salvo from Germany, arguing from Berlin that aviation's future lay with the airplane and not the dirigible. With the German Wright Company prepared to sell his airplanes for $5,000 each, Orville may have expressed a self-interested bias, as well as a technical opinion. Declaring himself "charmed with the personality and character of Count Zeppelin," he nevertheless unfavorably compared the dirigible to the airplane, as the steam engine to the gas engine—one an "exhausted" mechanism of the past, the other a machine whose potential lay in an "undreamed of" future.[29]

The French lost no time taking advantage of the international spotlight that Blériot's well-publicized flight had garnered. Within weeks the media turned its attention to Europe's first organized, aviation-centered tourist holiday. The Marquis de Polignac, with the aid of local champagne industry leaders, arranged a competition among the small, but growing, group of aviators—most of whom were French. The backers floated stock on the Paris exchange to fund the aviation extravaganza, called the Grande Semaine d'Aviation de la Champagne, and inaugurated a new type of business enterprise. With the revenue obtained from stock sales, they laid a railroad track from the renowned cathedral city of Reims to the plain of Bethany, three miles to the north. They built grandstands and outfitted boxes for affluent patrons, complete with buffet restaurant, bars, cooks, and waiters.[30]

The Reims Air Meet of 1909 joined airplanes, tourism, and even motion pictures in a highly visible attraction. The week-long air meet would be "an event of whose magnitude only those who know the tremendous French interest in aviation dream." The country had gone

stark, raving mad on the subject of navigation of the air. Cabinet ministers, school boys, sedate matrons, boulevardiers, university professors, and sportsmen talk, think and dream of nothing else. The sidewalks are blocked by vendors demonstrating and selling toy flying machines. . . . The post card craze has been revived beyond the previous magnitude through the enterprise of photographers with pictures of machines in flight. Hundreds of cinematograph shows all over the city are thronged day and night by crowds eager to see representations of Blériot, Latham, and Farman in the air. . . . Hundreds of thousands of Frenchmen are preparing to go. . . . Not a room is to be had in the Cathedral City. Temporary shelters are beginning to be erected.[31]

The excitement and anticipation surged in the week before the August 22 start date, as the airfield, grandstands, scoreboard, tents, and other facilities rose from the plain and replaced thousands of acres of agriculture. The rectangular flying course alone had a circuit of more than six miles. Crews erected nearly forty large sheds for airplanes and several larger enclosures for dirigibles around the site. They built a special railroad station, installed a telephone system to connect the city with the airfield, and linked the telegraph offices to various European capitals via direct lines. The *New York Times* representative sent special cable dispatches and photos of planes and fliers to the newspaper.

Affluent spectators, eager to watch daring aviators vie for thousands of dollars in prizes, snapped up all the grandstand loges, which rented for the considerable sum of $50 to $200 for the week. A six-hundred-seat terrace buffet in the covered grandstand prepared elegant meals for privileged diners, who had access to beauty, barber, and florist shops as well. Workers also constructed an immense enclosure to hold forty thousand people, who would pay a modest daily entrance fee.[32]

Most of the avid onlookers had never seen an airplane in person but were anxious to be a part of this new aeronautical world. For a year, newspapers had carried reports of aviation adventures: The Wright brothers had flown in France; Farman had captured the Archdeacon prize; Blériot had crossed the English Channel; and Glenn Curtiss had won prizes in the United States.

No doubt the crowds at Reims would have welcomed the famous Wright brothers with great delight and wanted them to personally match their skills against the best that Europe had to offer. Although other pilots would fly Wright planes, Orville and Wilbur once again declined to compete. Instead, Orville demonstrated the Wright Flyer to the Germans, setting altitude and duration records before thousands of onlookers while Wilbur took care of business at home. Representation from the United States fell to the Wrights' rival, Glenn Curtiss, and two thousand Americans arrived to watch him fly his new *Reims Racer*.

As expected, French aviators numerically dominated the field of twenty-two contestants. Among the best known, Louis Blériot brought an improved model of his *Blériot XI*. Charles de Lambert, who dropped out of the channel-crossing competition, planned to fly a Wright plane, as did Eugène Lefebvre. Hubert Latham again chose the Antoinette as he had for the channel crossing. Farman built the pusher biplane, *Farman III,* and Louis Paulhan preferred the Voisins' machine—he had taught himself to fly in a Voisin.

Only France and the United States could claim an aircraft industry in August, 1909. The first German Wright Flyer would not be ready for sale until after October 1. A total of nine Voisins, four Blériots, four Antoinettes, and four Farmans joined several Wright Flyers and Curtiss's *Reims Racer* in this great pageant of flight.

Nearly half a million people showed up at Reims during the aviation week. Hotels and rooming houses overflowed as three thousand Britons came by special excursion and Parisians flocked to the city by railroad and touring car. Locals arrived by cart, carriage, and bicycle or on foot. As with any tourist event, concessionaires, peddlers, restaurateurs, and hoteliers took advantage of the daily increase in numbers, and prices soared.

The Marquis de Polignac and his aviation committee could command the work crews, arrange for prizes, disseminate publicity, but, alas, they could not control the weather. Pounding rain turned the flying field into a soggy mess, and the black flag flew from the signal post on opening day, August 22, to communicate to the disappointed crowds—and aviators—the impossibility of trials or competitions. (A system of colored pennants indicated the names of pilots, prizes, etc., as well as weather conditions.) Anything on wheels sank into the rain-soaked earth. Stylish women in elaborate picture hats and ground-sweeping skirts took shelter where they could find it as the mud conquered everything.[33]

Rain and sunshine alternated for the next few days. During one of the clear periods, packed crowds thrilled to the spectacle of seven planes in the air at one time over the great Reims cathedral and against a vivid rainbow.

On the fifth day Latham took the lead in the distance trials. This time the Antoinette's engine performed well. Latham's 150-kilometer flight earned a ten-minute ovation, but not the prize money. The following day Farman brought out his biplane, with its reliable fifty-horsepower rotary engine. An early series of laps around the course caused little stir among the spectators after Latham's performance. Farman just kept going, however, and when he finally came down after more than three hours in the air, he had set new distance and duration records. He had flown 180 kilometers (more than one hundred miles) and won the

$10,000 offered by France's best-known champagne makers. Since this was the biggest prize, Farman won more money than any other competitor during the week of flying.[34]

For the speed prize, James Gordon Bennett, publisher of the Paris *Herald* and son of the multimillionaire founder of the *New York Herald,* offered $5,000 in cash and an elaborate silver trophy in the form of a winged figure supporting a model of the Wright Flyer. The day of the race—the last of the meet—brought blue skies and around 150,000 spectators to cheer the contestants in the climactic competition of an awesome week. The irrepressible crowds jammed the grandstands and overflowed onto restricted grassy areas. With Blériot a predictable favorite among the French spectators and Curtiss a respectable second choice, the sporting crowds arranged numerous private bets.

Agreed-upon rules allowed each contestant one two-lap try around the ten-kilometer (six-mile) course. Glenn Curtiss, known since his teen-age years for his love of speed, took the first turn and landed after fifteen minutes and fifty seconds, with an excellent score of 46.5 miles per hour. The tension mounted as Eugène Lefebvre took his Wright Flyer into the air. The winds had picked up since Curtiss had made his try, and Lefebvre fought them much of the way. He flew no faster than forty miles per hour. The same winds blew Latham to the wrong side of a pylon and away from the prize.

The French fans now pinned their hopes on Blériot. He had spent most of the day tinkering with his plane and signaled his readiness to the judges a scant twenty minutes before the scheduled racing time ended. When he cut four seconds off Curtiss's time in his first circuit, he seemed a sure winner. The crowd went wild as Blériot blazed around again and landed. The shouts, cheers, and standing ovation came to a sudden, throat-catching halt at the judges' signal, however. Glenn Curtiss had won—by just six seconds, and the band played the *Star-Spangled Banner.* The stunned spectators overcame their disbelief and joined in the applause for the lone American in the competition.[35]

If the sporting throngs demonstrated elation at Blériot's sensational performance and chagrin at his loss of the race to Curtiss, they were horrified by the subsequent aerial drama. Competing in a three-lap race, Blériot landed suddenly and just short of tragically. An overheated fuel pipe had spilled gasoline on the exhaust, and as the shaken pilot wobbled away from the *Blériot XII,* it burst into flame and burned to the skeletal framework.

On the last day of a sensational week at Reims, Blériot's experience encapsulated the world of aviation in 1909. Flying machines had passed the experimentation stage and exhibited undeniable speed and duration capabilities—but clearly they could also be dangerous. Furthermore, competition among the world's best planes and pilots provided hours of exhilarating entertainment because of the speed and the danger.

The rivalries evident at Reims proved a tremendous stimulus to further aviation development. For example, the altitude record of 508 feet set at Reims in August, 1909, reached 8,500 feet the following year. A dozen or so subsequent air meets offered thousands of dollars in prize money and spurred airplane and motor designers to improve the capabilities of their machines. "Bird men" took greater risks, both to please the crowds and to reap the rewards.[36]

Support of the first air meet by the town leaders and the great vintners of France's Champagne province gave legitimacy to airplane manufacture and flying as enterprises. The Reims air meet also established a challenging new spectator sport: the activity of watching, cheering, and applauding air races.

Moreover, the first assembly of the world's best planes facilitated a mental transition. Human flight left the category of fantasy, as flying machines sliced through the air above people's heads, circled, dipped, and landed—or sputtered, stalled, and crashed. News of aviation exploits appeared in daily newspapers and in the newsreels at the local movie house. A series of competitive national and international air meets between 1909 and 1912 attracted heads of state, representatives of royal families, local public officials and civic leaders, industrialists, diplomats, artists, writers, and tourists.

Races and record breaking understandably generated excitement among thousands of enthusiastic curiosity seekers. After Reims, other entrepreneurs turned open spaces into flying fields, filled grandstands with paying customers, and packed exhibition halls with airplanes. French workers had barely dismantled the Bethany Plain grandstands when the aviators packed their airplane parts in crates and boarded the train for Italy.

Brescia, northern Italy's third largest city after Milan and Turin, had acquired a reputation and the logistical expertise for racing sponsorships, starting with bicycles and moving on to automobiles. A highly successful Automobile Week in 1904 had attracted large crowds to the city and encouraged civic leaders to repeat the triumph. The committee organized in 1907 developed the racecourse and worked on issues of security, publicity, rules, accommodations, and transportation. When financial support for the project lagged, the city of Brescia switched from automobiles to airplanes and garnered for itself the honor of hosting Italy's first air show.

Competing auto races in Milan and Bologna might have been responsible for the paucity of sponsors, but the switch benefited from fortuitous timing. In February, 1909, a delegation inspected several possible locations for the airfield and chose an area of flat land to the southeast of Brescia, on the way to Montichiari. In April, Wilbur Wright arrived in Rome, unpacked the newest Wright Flyer that he had shipped from Ohio, demonstrated the plane, and took some passengers for rides. The Rome Club of Aviators bought the plane and paid Wright for flight-training sessions, all of which contributed to a climate of anticipation for the air show.[37]

Posters for the Circuit of Brescia showed a winged classical figure, illustrative of Italy's past glories and the long history of mythological flight, with her arms outstretched to welcome the modern aeronauts. A multinational contingent of fliers, including Blériot and Curtiss, answered the call. French-built planes and aviators dominated the Brescia festivities, as they had at Reims, but Curtiss again won the grand prize for speed. Italian naval academy graduate Mario Calderara, whom Wilbur Wright had taught to fly during his stint in Rome the previous spring, came in second.

Not even the promoters realized just how powerful an attraction the air meet might be. Italy's King Vittorio Emmanuelle III visited the airfield even before the show began and circulated among the aviators, who were assembling their machines, asking them questions about the event and their planes. A fascination with flight drew composer Giacomo Puccini and poet Gabriele d'Annunzio to Brescia.

The young Franz Kafka, having earned eight days of vacation after two years of toil at an insurance company, interrupted his stay at Riva on Lake Garda and went by train with friends Max and Otto Brod to see their first airplane. Brescia overflowed with people; prices for food and lodging escalated accordingly. The adventure-seeking, less-than-affluent friends from Prague found lodging at an inn they later described as a robber's den, not notable for its cleanliness. Max Brod also related the excitement and confusion—a great contrast to the quiet of the Garda shore. They stayed only a day, mostly spent wandering among the hangars while the aviators worked on their planes. They witnessed some flying, but no contests, and then had to leave.[38]

On the first racing day some forty thousand sports fans clogged the road from Brescia to the airfield. As in France the previous month, they traveled by car, carriage, cart, and bicycle. They also crammed themselves aboard the newly constructed, steam-powered tram that followed the road from the city to the show grounds. Traffic bottlenecks and dust marred an otherwise high-spirited journey.

Once at the field the throng spilled out on an open space, dominated by a grandstand that was divided into an upper level for wealthier attendees and a lower level with less costly seats. The restaurant accommodated two thousand diners. Ordinary folk paid a small entry fee and wandered the grounds around the observation tower and the hangars.

The first official day of the show—September 8 —offered no aerial thrills despite the feverish preparations. Signal flags indicated by their colors the likelihood of competitive activity, and the first-day crowds waited all morning and most of the afternoon before any of the aviator-heroes felt confident enough in the sufficiency of the winds and in their planes to try some test flights. When they did, the spectators applauded wildly.

Day after day the crowds returned to watch vulnerable humans climb into fragile machines amid the palpable tension of anticipation and discernible waves of admiration. Some planes taxied across the field or bounced along and could not get airborne. Sometimes the mechanics failed to get the engines to work at all. People milled around and waited for aviators to attempt speed, altitude, and endurance records. Just as likely they watched a pilot take off, reach an altitude of fifty feet, and drop suddenly, smashing airplane parts—often beyond repair. Motors stalled in midair, and inexperienced pilots failed to negotiate air currents.

The intoxication of risk permeated the atmosphere, and the heightened tension added to the restlessness of crowds waiting for action. The rough terrain discouraged some pilots who anticipated severe damage to their craft should they have to land unexpectedly, so fewer planes than advertised actually flew. At one point the authorities called in the local militia to quiet dissatisfied spectators and to protect the buffet feasts from elements in the crowd who were determined to get their money's worth.

Travel agents could not have devised a better scheme than air meets to rouse and inspire Europe's touring crowds. The official poster for the late-September Berlin meet stacked airplanes as far as the horizon against a red sunset, a picture of promise that Latham fulfilled with a six-mile flight across the countryside. The French Compagnie Aerienne filled its poster for a meet in Heliopolis, Egypt, with recognizable iconography: A camel stands on a shadowy hilltop while its rider looks out over sun-lit pyramids beneath a sky filled with airplanes. The winter traveler to Egypt could combine the enrichment of ancient history with the excitement of the most modern diversion. In fact, the Baroness de Laroche, the first woman to earn a pilot's license, made her debut public flight at Heliopolis in February of 1910.

Rouen similarly added an air meet to its familiar tourist attractions. To advertise the aerial contest, the familiar figure of Blériot appears in flight over the city, its cathedral, and the Seine, against a dreamy pastel sky—all the romance—and danger—of Emma Bovary.

Blériot's unmistakable aviator's hat and handlebar mustache graced the poster for the "Meeting d'Aviation" held in Nice two months later. Perhaps the linguistic intermingling suggested the internationally competitive nature of aviation as a sport, or it may have signaled that Blériot had overcome the geographical barrier between France and England. There can be little doubt that Nice also welcomed its traditional winter-season visitors, regardless of whether they enjoyed air races. The poster's perspective is from sky to earth, with the city's tourist-beckoning coastline spread out below the aviator in his plane.[39]

England, in fact, had had no flier with a machine capable of flying the English Channel and had no planes to enter at Reims. British interest in aerial balloons had prompted the war office to send an observer to the St. Louis fair in 1904, and the representative also visited the Wright brothers in Dayton. The war office maintained contact with the Wrights but would not fulfill the brothers' requirement of a contract before presentation of documents. In 1906, two years before its English Channel challenge, the London Daily Mail had offered a financial reward for the first plane to fly from London to Manchester. No plane flew the 185-mile distance at the time, nor did an English experimenter come forward with a design for a machine that could fly any distance at all.

Although the British continued to play catch-up in design, they took quickly to aviation as a sport. Shortly after Reims the British held two meets, one at the seaside resort at Blackpool (after the tourist season) and another in the midlands manufacturing downs of Doncaster. In November, a flying exhibition by Louis Paulhan at Brooklands motor raceway, twenty miles southwest of London, helped to turn that field into a lively center of British airplane experimentation.

By the end of 1910 Brooklands vibrated with activity. Weekend air races attracted thousands of Britons on Saturday afternoons, and by 1913 the crowds swelled to nearly thirty thousand weekly paying attendees. At the same time, several British companies— Avro, Vickers, Sopwith, and Bristol—began to build planes. With the national consciousness awakened to the capabilities of airplanes and aware of the attention paid by the French and German military establishments to the Wright brothers' demonstrations, the British government bought a few of the domestic planes.[40]

Meanwhile, France insisted on and promoted its domination of the aviation industry. An international exposition at Paris, devoted to "aerial locomotion," drew 100,000 people in three days, without any flying exhibitions. People simply walked among the planes displayed in a gaudily festooned exhibition hall, in which France accounted for 318 of the 333 exhibitors. Aerial balloons filled the upper reaches of an *Arabian Nights* fantasy, where colorful banners hung from the domed and girdered glass ceiling.

More than thirty flying machines occupied the main floor. The sturdy channel-crossing *Blériot XI* occupied the place of honor in a gardenlike setting, surrounded by well-known French Voisins, Antoinettes, and Farmans. Other domestic planes occupied lesser positions, but visitors had to climb a staircase to see the French-built Wright Flyer. Various manufacturers displayed aircraft parts and accessories among arcades and draperied balconies, their names prominent on elaborately festooned, decorative backdrops.[41]

The heart-thumping excitement of air races kindled a passion to fly among adventure seekers who heard about—or saw for themselves—the risks, the money, and the admiration of the crowds. Some affluent, hopeful fliers bought or built planes; the less financially independent, but equally ambitious, sought sponsors. Together they composed a market for flying machines that responded to their entertainment value, rather than military utility. According to the New York *World,* not only did air meets account for a boom in businesses catering to a budding corps of novice and experienced fliers, but advertisements for air meet locations also stimulated the real estate market in the areas surrounding the airfields.[42]

As reluctant as the Wrights had been to extend their aviation involvement to showmanship, Wilbur played to the crowds in a well-paid and well-publicized New York exhibition in October, 1909. The organizers of a celebration to commemorate pioneering feats of exploration and invention—Henry Hudson's voyage of discovery and Robert Fulton's steamboat—offered Wilbur $15,000 for a flight of at least ten miles in length or one hour in duration. A public relations firm could not have given better advice for a route than Wilbur's own sense of public sentiment provided. He took off from Governors Island, in the Upper Bay below Manhattan, flew around the Statue of Liberty with all of its patriotic symbolism, and returned. Delighted onlookers aboard hundreds of ships in the harbor cheered him on.

A few days later Wilbur returned to Governors Island and flew ten miles up the Hudson River to Grant's tomb and back. An estimated one million Hudson-Fulton celebrants cheered Wright at some point in his half-hour flight, and a handful of prominent investors—including Cornelius Vanderbilt and August Belmont—acknowledged the performance and the profit potential of airplanes. They backed the Wright Company, which incorporated in November, 1909, and located corporate headquarters in New York and a factory in Dayton capable of producing four planes a month.[43]

That winter many Easterners crossed the continent to watch monoplanes, biplanes, and dirigibles establish new aviation records and compete for prizes at a field outside Los Angeles. The January, 1910, Dominguez Air Meet not only launched another exhilarating round of contests but also afforded thousands of people in the western United States their first look at flying machines.

While Wilbur Wright startled New Yorkers with his Hudson River flight, Glenn Curtiss, Charles Willard (whom Curtiss had taught to fly just months before), and dirigible veteran Roy Knabenshue had met in Los Angeles with Richard Ferris, a local businessman and civic promoter. Willard had encountered Knabenshue at an exhibition while Curtiss flew at Reims. They agreed that Los Angeles would be a good location for winter operations, talked about the possibility of arranging an air show, and then enlisted Curtiss in the effort.

Ferris, a balloon enthusiast, recognized the significance of the interest in aviation that had been initiated at Reims and approached the Los Angeles Merchants and Manufacturers Association with a proposition. If they raised the money, he would mount an even bigger international air show than the champagne makers had promoted at Reims.

Alert to the attendant favorable publicity, the business leaders agreed to act as midwives to the birth of California aviation. This would be the first time that airplanes would fly in the territory west of the Rocky Mountains. Ferris then approached the owners of the Dominguez Rancho property south of the city, a site clear of obstructions and close to a railroad line for transport of both flying machines and patrons. (Aviators traveled by ship and train with their machines in crates and assembled the aircraft at the site.)

With less than two months to complete the entire project, Ferris hired an engineer to lay out the field, construct a grandstand, and build the pylon towers that would mark the course. A committee set the rules and established prizes at a level intended to challenge potential participants and push aircraft capability. The Dominguez Air Meet offered $10,000 for a two-person, heavier-than-air machine that could break world records for duration, altitude, distance, and speed and $5,000 each for new height and endurance records.[44]

Although Wilbur Wright had flown the celebratory Hudson-Fulton exhibition for money, the Wright brothers reiterated their distaste for air meets. They refused to participate in Los Angeles and attempted to prohibit others from showing off airplanes that used their patented inventions. When Paulhan arrived in New York from France on his way to Los Angeles, the Wrights' lawyers met him. A court injunction precluded his flying a plane into the United States whose control system infringed on patents for their wing-warping mechanism. With no time to hold hearings prior to the meet, the Wrights sued to gain control over any profits resulting from Paulhan's flights (such as prizes or sales of planes) and demanded triple damages. They also filed an injunction request against Curtiss, which a federal judge granted. Curtiss responded legalistically and practically: He appealed the ruling, posted bond, and left with his planes for Los Angeles.

Ten airplanes, seven balloons, and three dirigibles entered the competition. The air meet poster featured all three types of aircraft, viewed from a hillside overlooking Los Angeles, from its harbor to snow-topped mountains behind the city—all framed by palm trees. Souvenir folders featuring photographs of airships and aviators sold for fifteen cents. On the cover, airplanes, dirigibles, and balloons soared above palm trees and oranges. For two cents one could mail it to a friend. Daily programs explained the rules and regulations, listed the prizes, and provided the previous day's achievements, information on the current day's participants, and a scorecard for recording times and distances. The booklet also bragged that the Dominguez Meet was America's first.

Los Angeles counted more than 300,000 residents in 1910, and the Angelenos worked themselves into a frenzy over the opportunity to see flying machines in person. Some 30,000 to 40,000 people attended the meet on any given day. They packed themselves into Pacific Electric Railway cars to reach the Dominguez Rancho, or they came by auto. When they arrived, they walked to the viewing areas past ventriloquists and hootchy-kootchy dancers; Trixie, the world's fattest girl; Cora-Etta, a version of the original Siamese twins; and a motley array of other sideshow attractions that Ferris had added to the main event. Suited to the carnival atmosphere, the aircraft hangars resembled circus tents.

Even before the meet began, thousands of people trekked out to the airfield, where aviators and mechanics assembled airplanes and inflated dirigibles, while a thousand workers put finishing touches on the grandstand, judges' stands, administration buildings, and field accommodations.[45]

Hotel lobbies filled with tourists, and some of them attended the Aviation Ball, a charity event held at Pasadena's Hotel Maryland. For San Diego Day around three thousand spectators traveled by train from that city. Delegations of San Franciscans occupied the stands on other days. As at Reims, some people rented boxes at the flying field for the entire meet. The grandstand held fifteen thousand viewers, and an equally large crowd watched from carriages and automobiles or simply stood. With lots of time between events they no doubt ambled around the grounds and patronized the concessionaires. The promoters took in more than $140,000 in entrance fees for the eleven days of the meet and earned an additional $4,000 from concessions sold to vendors.[46]

Glenn Curtiss—the only American to compete at Reims—brought two of his latest machines from his home in New York. On

Successful flight demonstrations in 1908 and 1909 launched tourist-luring competitions, like the 1910 Dominguez Field (Los Angeles) Air Meet, which gave thousands of Californians their first view of airplanes in action. *Courtesy of the San Diego Aerospace Museum.*

opening day Curtiss climbed into his biplane. Mechanics spun the propeller, and the plane rolled down a sawdust-covered, dirt runway. When the wheels lifted off the ground, many of the spectators saw an aviator in flight for the first time. Moreover, Curtiss lifted off from level ground, not from an embankment like a glider would, and without any kind of external launching aid. In the excitement band members forgot to play. A cheer rose from the astounded crowd, however, when people resumed breathing after an initial gasp.[47]

Curtiss's planes, flown by himself, Charles Willard, and Charles Hamilton, chalked up speed and endurance records. In all, the trio won more than $10,000 worth of prizes.

Together with Curtiss, Louis Paulhan, the only European aviator to compete at Los Angeles, gave the 200,000 awed spectators some of their most memorable moments. Paulhan had taught himself to fly in a Voisin and had finished fourth among the prize

winners at Reims. His style and daring made him the unques-
tioned favorite flier at Los Angeles.

On opening day Curtiss and Willard had already excited the
eager attendees with airplane flights up and down the course,
reaching heights of up to two hundred feet, and returning to the
starting point with well-executed landings. Lincoln Beachey and
Roy Knabenshue sailed their cigar-shaped dirigibles over the
grandstand, capturing every eye, and made a speedy return with a
stiff wind at their backs.

The crowds had not yet seen Paulhan. The Frenchman had
moved his Farman biplane out of its hangar and took off from a
position outside everyone's view. Suddenly the onlookers spotted
his plane as he circled the field. They scarcely had time to react
when he brought the plane down at high speed before the grandstand, waved his arms, shouted to the crowd, and took off for a second round. Halfway around the course he cut across and headed
for the grandstand, veered sharply and flew off, disappearing from
view behind the grandstand. He flew around the countryside for a
bit and then cleared the stands by a few feet when he approached
it from behind, shouting greetings to the dumbfounded people
diving for cover below.

The irrepressible Frenchman's aerial performance had already
lasted more than eight minutes, but he had not finished. When
Knabenshue took his dirigible up again, Paulhan started another
circuit. He positioned himself above the dirigible, matched its
speed, and then outdistanced the rigid airship. He darted one way
and then another over the countryside, ascended suddenly, and reversed direction just as quickly, until it appeared he might crash.
He dipped the plane to scatter groups of onlookers gathered
around the field, again headed for the grandstand, and pulled up
at the last moment. On this second trial he stayed in the air ten
chilling minutes and then performed as many antics in a third,
half-hour flight.

Richard Ferris, the air meet promoter, knew what this performance meant for the box office and would only say, "We cannot do
anything with that Frenchman. He pays no attention to rules and
regulations."[48]

On San Diego Day, when thousands of San Diegans in the grandstand shared the anticipation of more aerial drama, Paulhan went after the altitude record. His plane climbed slowly, while on-lookers in the stands and on the field craned their necks to follow his upward movement. After forty-five minutes he reached a record height of more than 3,600 feet, calculated from the ground by triangulation. The judges posted the achievement, and the spectators exploded in applause while Paulhan made a rapid, six-minute descent and landed.[49] On another day he surpassed his own achievement with a flight above 4,100 feet.

The confidant Paulhan continued to delight the crowds and to break rules and records. On the next-to-last day of the meet he put on a yellow cloak, helped his wife into the plane, saluted the multitude at the airfield, and headed toward the ocean. Flying at altitudes between 500 and 1,000 feet, he soared over Redondo and Venice beaches and ventured out over the waves for half a mile, with no life buoys in case they should land in the water. The twenty-two-mile trip took thirty-three minutes. Paulhan landed directly in front of the grandstand, where the closest viewers hoisted him to their shoulders and carried him around for others to greet.

Even though it was three o'clock in the afternoon on a winter's day, when the sun sets early, frenzied potential passengers besieged the French aviator for rides. Paulhan put Lieutenant Paul Beck of the U.S. Army Signal Corps in the seat just vacated by Mme. Paul-han and took off. Beck had carried several pretend "bombs" on the ride, dropped them overboard, but failed to place them within a premarked square on the ground. Paulhan flew with several other passengers in the waning afternoon light, including newspaper publisher, William Randolph Hearst. Not even Glenn Curtiss had turned his plane into an aerial busline.[50]

A parade on the final day of the air meet depicted the evolution of transportation, including horses, covered wagons, autos, and the airplane. If Paulhan intended for his passenger trips to demonstrate the utility of the airplane as a transportation mode, his pranks may have contributed to an opposite reaction. For one thing, a company agent informed aviator Frank Johnson that his

Daredevil stunt fliers astounded audiences on the ground and in movie theaters, competing for attention with airline interests that encouraged the development of regular air services. *Courtesy of the San Diego Aerospace Museum.*

life insurance policy would not be valid if he flew competitively at the meet and that future insurance policies would most likely carry an exclusionary clause related to aviation. Thrills had their place, but insurers did not have to underwrite them.

Nor did the *New York Times* express approval of the risk-takers:

> As a show the "aviation meet" out in Los Angeles promises to be as successful—that is to say as profitable—as its promoters hoped. . . . [H]owever, one gets the impression that flying of this particular sort is rather a futile business, interesting and amusing rather than important—not at all the thing that is really going to advance the art of aerial navigation. The contestants are constantly tempted to win unthinking applause by recklessly taking desperate chances, and the more that people are astonished by the performance of dangerous "stunts" the less of apprecia-

tion will they have for the sane and comparatively safe sort of flying that means something for the future of aviation.[51]

Although air shows turned aviation skeptics into believers that humans could fly, it would be several years before they gave serious consideration to the significance of the airplane as an economic factor or as a means of transportation. Rather, profitability had established the airplane as a form of sport and entertainment and air meets as tourist attractions. Even the Wright brothers, who had rejected participation at Reims and Los Angeles, would enter the lucrative exhibition business within the year.

Despite the admonitions of critics, financial rewards continued to motivate daredevil pilots. Paulhan took his $19,000 in Dominguez prize money, embarked on an exhibition tour of several cities in the western United States, and then headed for England to compete for the *London Daily Mail*'s still unclaimed (since 1906) 185-mile, London-to-Manchester prize. According to the *Daily Mail*'s rules, aspirants had to make the trip in less than twenty-four hours, with only two stops en route. Advances in aviation technology, Paulhan's accumulated experience, and his penchant for publicity and prizes convinced the risk-seeking aviator that he should give it a try.

Paulhan injected more than a little nationalistic fervor into the competition when he decided to challenge Claude Graham-White, the Englishman who had announced his intention to claim the prize. Auto dealer Graham-White had traveled to Reims as a spectator, inspired by Blériot's flight across the English Channel. Swept up in the excitement, he ordered a plane from Blériot and remained for some two months in Paris. He worked alongside the mechanics of the Blériot factory and became accustomed to the feel of the machine and the control mechanisms while he took the plane around the grounds. Then he actually flew it. The novice aviator demonstrated both confidence and boldness when he opened a flight school in the south of France, with the *Blériot XI* as his trainer plane.

Graham-White returned to England to transfer his flight-school operation to his homeland and took on the London-

Manchester flight to gain publicity. Instead of the Blériot, which Graham-White deemed not up to the grueling schedule and distance, the determined competitor shopped around for another plane. He decided on a Farman and, with less than two hours of flight time to master the controls, set off to enter the record books.

With a minimum of flying experience and a maximum of daring, Graham-White took off on April 23 and covered eighty-three miles in two hours before his first unscheduled stop. Headwinds and engine trouble forced him down, and a storm prevented his continuing that day. Before he could take off again, the ravaging wind overturned his plane, and the resulting damage forced him back to London. While he repaired his plane, Paulhan prepared for his own try at the prize.

With patriotism turning the event into a closely watched confrontation, Paulhan took off from London in a Farman biplane late in the afternoon of April 27. He followed a special train with Henry Farman and a group of reporters on board. The train flew a white signal cloth to show Paulhan the way, since he knew little or nothing about the geography of the English countryside. Reporters aboard the train filed their stories about the plane's progress, dropping them off at stations along the way, to satisfy an increasing contingent of flag-waving readers who bought their respective newspapers.

Paulhan literally caught Graham-White napping. The exhausted Briton had been trying to recoup the sleep lost during the day of flying and the two days of intense repair efforts. When he learned of Paulhan's flight, Graham-White hastily followed Paulhan into the air. He had lost about an hour. They had started out late in the afternoon, and when they landed for the night, Paulhan still enjoyed about an hour's lead.

The more-experienced Paulhan maintained his lead throughout the next day, and Graham-White concluded that he could gain the advantage only if he started the next leg in the dark of night. He knew the risks—no markings, no visible horizon, and no way to discern a flat area for landing if he needed one in a hurry. He managed, however, with the help of friends and supporters, defiant upholders of British pride, who drove motor cars and rode bicycles, with head lamps and lanterns to light the way. Graham-White gained time on his adversary before Paulhan started out at 4 A.M. The Frenchman, now with just a twenty-five-minute lead, continued to follow the train.

Graham-White battled a wind that rose with the dawn and grew stronger with daylight, tossing the plane around. With relatively little total flying experience, even less familiarity with the Farman, and worn down by the constant necessity to manipulate the aileron flaps and rudder, Graham-White reluctantly set the plane down and gave up the race. Though struggling against the same winds and the early morning chill, the veteran Paulhan, forty miles ahead when he started, managed to complete the flight at 5:25 A.M. and was greeted by spectators who had waited all night outside Manchester in the hope of observing a historic, cross-country flight.[52]

Even though Graham-White lost the contest, England made the good-looking, enthusiastic pilot its aviation idol and a symbol of the country's determination to participate in an international rivalry in which France had claimed the primary position and the United States struggled to regain the top rung.

Despite the Wright brothers' demonstrated superiority in aerial navigation just two years before, *Scientific American* conceded European supremacy in its coverage of the first U.S. aeronautics show, held in Boston in February, 1910. The display of airplanes, motors, gliders, and balloons created far less excitement than the previous month's air meet at Los Angeles but demonstrated the state of the art in U.S. aviation manufactures nonetheless. A dozen U.S. firms built planes, and nearly fifty produced aircraft parts and supplies.

Various combinations of airplane construction and motors inspired both those with an inclination to fly and those with mechanical ability who thought they could improve on what they saw. "The exhibition as a whole was a very creditable one," *Scientific American* concluded. "It leads one to believe that America will soon catch up to Europe in the aeronautic industry."[53]

Meanwhile, active aeronautical laboratories in France, Great

Britain, Italy, Germany, and Russia—some with governmental support—designed machines that revealed great potential.

Flying Circuses and Air Safety

It must have come as no surprise to the Wrights that patent suits and injunctions could not hold the competition at bay. To sell the planes coming out of the Dayton plant, they had to compete in an increasingly crowded and aggressive marketplace. The U.S. Army Signal Corps had bought one Wright Flyer but had not ordered any more. The Wright planes manufactured under license in France and Germany brought in little profit.

The success of the Dominguez Air Meet demonstrated that Americans, like Europeans, wanted to see airplanes in action. The Wright brothers could refuse to participate and try to keep others from doing so, but people who paid to share the excitement of human flight or to feel their skin tingle with the tension of daring competitions also constituted a market for planes. Hundreds of thousands of previously skeptical people saw their first flying machines amid the commotion and passion of a well-attended public performance or air meet. Newspapers publicized the events and provided the names of competing pilots and plane manufacturers. County fair organizers offered prize money to lure aviators, who attracted paying customers. Curtiss, who also built his own planes, began to follow the circuit and trained an exhibition team.

Even without increasing sales of Wright planes, entertainment opportunities returned a handsome profit. Two months after Dominguez, the Wright Company put together a team of fliers. Orville selected the team members and taught them to fly, and the brothers hired experienced flier Roy Knabenshue to arrange bookings, oversee the team, and deal with problems on the circuit. The team started off in the middle of 1910 with an exhibition at the Indianapolis Motor Speedway and went on to Montreal and Atlantic City. With event managers paying the company $1,000 per day, or $6,000 per pilot for the standard six-day meet, plus prize money (the pilots earned $320 per week: $20 salary and $50 for each day

Pilots trained in World War I continued to entertain the crowds with exhibitions and offered to give passengers a thrilling ride. *Courtesy of the San Diego Aerospace Museum.*

they flew), the Wright Company recorded nearly $100,000 in earnings for 1910, with the brothers retaining half.[54]

The Wright brothers' team flew straightforward exhibitions at first and only gradually succumbed to the showmanship that augmented the crowds but increased the dangers. Controlling the Wright planes demanded considerable manual dexterity on the part of the pilot, who moved levers forward or back to bank a turn and maneuvered the wrist of one hand to control the rudder and of the other to operate the elevator. Dives and stunts multiplied the stress on both pilot and plane; the team lost one member in a mishap at a Denver meet and then another. Wilbur Wright's 1908 prediction to *Scientific American* had been both insightful and mistaken. The exhilaration of flying did indeed appeal to many people, but the sport had not proved less dangerous than football.

Eight months after the Dominguez Air Meet, the newly inaugurated Harvard Aeronautical Society offered various cash prizes and trophies to bring the thrills of aviation to New England. The organizers apparently had significant financial backing, and the promise of $50,000 and paid expenses enticed England's hero, Claude Graham-White, to try his luck in America.

The Harvard-Boston meet attracted its share of the social register and political celebrities as well, including President William Howard Taft and Boston's mayor, John "Honey Fitz" Fitzgerald. A young New Yorker named Franklin Delano Roosevelt also attended. No doubt impressed by speed, duration, distance, and altitude events, President Taft most likely also took note of the contest in which each pilot dropped plaster-of-Paris "bombs" from a height of at least one hundred feet and attempted to hit the deck of a model man-of-war.

Graham-White flew both Blériot and Farman planes in Boston, took passengers on rides, and competed for prizes. He won first prize for speed and for landing accuracy and also ranked first in the bombing contest, demonstrating the excellent performance qualities of his French machines two years after the Europeans had their first look at the Wright Flyer. Ralph Johnstone ran the bombing run in a Wright plane, but Graham-White scored nine straight hits. With more than a touch of arrogance, Graham-White followed Boston with a trip to Washington, D.C., where he circled the Capitol dome and the Washington Monument and landed alongside the White House.[55]

Harvard had certainly attracted its share of the social elite, but the October meet at Belmont Park racetrack on New York's Long Island outclassed Boston in prize money and cachet. Belmont was billed as the social and sporting event of the year and lived up to its advance notice. Vanderbilts, Whitneys, Goulds, and Drexels took their place in the boxes, while thousands of ordinary folk paid one dollar for general admission.

Thanks to the Wright brothers, the Belmont meet also earned a reputation for contentiousness. In order to hold the meet at all, the promoters paid Wilbur and Orville $20,000 to back away from their demands for royalty payments on exhibition flights in America by Europeans who flew planes with the Wrights' patented equipment. Later the brothers tried to impound $198,000 in gate receipts in order to gain an additional $15,000.

In recognition of the importance of the Belmont Park meet, both the Wright and Curtiss companies unveiled new models. The Wrights' *Baby Grand* contained an engine twice as powerful as that in any of their previous machines and flew at seventy miles per hour on a trial run. Curtiss brought a new monoplane. Since the meet's promoters had scheduled the second Gordon Bennett speed contest—Curtiss had won the first at Reims—spectators expected to see the new Curtiss plane in action. Curtiss chose not to defend his title, however, after viewing the competition. Graham-White won the Bennett in a speedy Blériot with a fourteen-cylinder rotary, one-hundred-horsepower engine at a speed of 61.3 miles per hour, nearly fifteen miles per hour better than Curtiss's record at Reims just a year before.[56]

The Wrights' *Baby Grand* had crashed during a test flight, and, although Wright pilots set the altitude record and won $15,000 in prize money, the Belmont Park meet demonstrated once again that French plane builders were leading the pack.

Aeronautics had gone from science and engineering to business and entertainment, and the leadership in aviation development had moved to France. Except in the construction of sea planes, where Curtiss emerged as the design leader, American supremacy in aviation had ended. At the end of 1911 Frenchman Roland Garros set an altitude record of 12,828 feet in a Blériot. Moreover, French electrical engineer Edouard Nieuport captured speed and endurance records in a monoplane with a fully enclosed fuselage. French pilots flew French flying machines to new heights.[57]

The Wright brothers dissolved the exhibition team in November, 1911, but by 1912 three more Wright-trained pilots had died in Wright-built planes. Instead of positive publicity, the exhibition circuit threatened to damage the brothers' reputation as airplane builders. Most graduates of the Wrights' training schools still followed the county fair circuit and competed for various prizes, but they had to attract other sponsors for needed money for planes, spare parts, and other expenses. Moreover, the brothers' continued pursuit of legal actions injured their personal reputations. Even their long-time friend Octave Chanute questioned their motivation and judgment. Nevertheless, they continued to design and test new airplane models, and they trained both military and civilian pilots.[58]

Concerns about safety accelerated as aviators took more risks and flew more often from makeshift fields at fairs and carnivals. Flying teams evolved into flying circuses. A group of Belmont Park contestants formed John Moisant's International Aviators group, which included three French pilots, a Swiss, and various Americans. Traveling by special train with a built-in repair shop, the entourage included roustabouts, ticket sellers, press agents, a dozen airplanes, mechanics, and eight aviators. The troupe traveled across the southeast, Oklahoma, and Texas and then crossed into Mexico for shows in Monterrey, Mexico City, and Vera Cruz; from Vera Cruz they traveled on to Havana, Cuba. When John Moisant died in a crash at New Orleans in December, his older brother took charge. However, Alfred—obviously mindful of the dangers of aerial circuses—ended the tour early in 1911, disbanded the aviators, and opened an aviation school.[59]

At the same time that Alfred Moisant opted for a safer career, other pilots also began to give more thought to safety and showed less concern for spectators' acclaim. Exhibition flying began to move in other directions as well. For one thing, intercity races highlighted the possibility of air transportation as an alternative to sport and entertainment.

French planes and French pilots dominated the intercity, cross-border events, which no American-made airplanes entered. Several hundred thousand spectators turned out for the start of the Paris-to-Madrid race over the Pyrenees in 1911, and a crowd of about 100,000 assembled outside Madrid for the finish. Later, French citizens choked the roads around Versailles on their way to the starting point of the May, 1911, Paris-to-Rome race. Surging crowds greeted winner Jean Conneau after a flight of eighty-two hours and five minutes. Conneau also won the first Circuit of Europe in June, 1911, which went from Paris, through France and

Belgium, across the English Channel, and back to Paris. Although 52 planes entered the race, which required 9 flights over 13 days, only 9 planes finished.

A navy lieutenant, Conneau shared the spotlight and the public adoration with the two other French pilots who dominated the biggest flying events that year. Jules Vedrines, a former factory worker from Paris, had won the Paris-to-Madrid race, and veteran aviator Roland Garros lost to Conneau in the Paris-to-Rome race but steadfastly battled wind and rain to capture first prize in the ninety-seven-mile Circuit of Anjou.

A Military Game

International boundaries seemingly disappeared as country-to-country races flourished. Armies of people flocked to starting points and landing places, enjoying the circuslike atmosphere. The *Paris Journal* and *London Standard* announced a 1,600-kilometer Circuit of Europe, and hundreds of thousands of onlookers gathered at Vincennes for the start of the race. These spectators anticipated neither stunts nor fancy flying but simply wanted to be a part of aviation history and the industry's future, a future that increasingly focused on a military purpose—despite the transnational sentiment underlying the races.

The Circuit of Anjou, for example, was a triangular course between the towns of Angers, Saumur, and Cholet in the province of Anjou, "intended to test the mettle of planes and pilots by simulating the grueling conditions of wartime." [60] The two-day competition required seven turns around the course. France's best aviators and most advanced planes gathered at Angers, the starting point, along with military attachés from several European nations.

Just three years after the great Reims air meet had introduced the world to the sportsmanship of flying, Europe anticipated a deadlier game. Nevertheless, aviation attracted tourists to Angers, as it had to Reims. Spectators swarmed to the city from all over the continent, "and for a few days little Angers was a boom town, its cafes filled to overflowing, hotels jammed and landlords inflating their prices mercilessly." [61]

Although the U.S. government expressed minimal interest in testing pilots for wartime conditions, army officers at the January, 1911, air meet in San Francisco dropped explosive projectiles to demonstrate the utility of the airplane as a "war machine." The exhibition clearly carried the message that airplanes could revolutionize warfare between nations in the near future.[62]

At the same event an aviator landed his plane on the deck of the cruiser *Pennsylvania,* where ropes stretched between sandbags halted the plane's specially constructed skids. The pilot lunched with the ship's captain while the crew turned the plane around and cleared the sandbags. In less than an hour he took off from the deck, demonstrating that airplanes could serve the navy's needs for communication and reconnaissance.[63]

The absence of heart-stopping stunt flying disappointed some spectators at San Francisco who had come to be entertained and energized by high-risk aviation. However, the shocking death toll of stunt fliers had made aviators more cautious. Moreover, for an aircraft industry to develop, the frail pioneer airplane would have to cast off its image as an exhibition toy and leave behind the world of aerial circuses. These arguments gained urgency in influential periodicals, where debates about the future of aviation occupied journalists and editorial writers. *Scientific American,* for example, in its January 14, 1911, issue described the climbing fatality rate among pilots as a "thrill of horror" that threatened an unacceptable loss of faith in the usefulness of the new art of flying.

Unwilling to undermine a technology in which the science magazine saw great promise, its editors prescribed a path of recovery. First, determine the cause of serious accidents, "whether they lay in the faulty construction of the machine, or in the lack of skill or the overdaring of its manipulator" so that "every accident yields its quota of valuable lessons for guidance in future construction and future handling." Then, increase the margin of safety and strength in the various parts of the plane. In particular, improve materials to resist the abnormal stresses of stormy weather and the "spectacular dives and other attractive maneuvers which have become so popular with the race-going public."

Not unexpectedly, a journal that saw its purpose as recording "the world's progress in scientific knowledge and industrial achievement" turned to scientific method and engineering to mitigate the threat inaugurated by the transformation of an important invention into sport and entertainment. Let skilled engineers, it cautioned, not daredevil fliers, lead the exploitation of the flying machine.[64]

The warning did not go unheeded, but aviation proceeded on both tracks. Engineers improved airplane performance, while aerial acrobatics attracted crowds to live performances and to the movies. Thus, the flying machine magnified and expanded the desire of populations to transcend the ordinary, to participate in the cutting edge of society's experiments, to experience excitement and share it with others, and to be entertained.

In the first decade after the Wright brothers' Kitty Hawk flight, airplanes gained legitimacy as a tool of show business, as a way to move from place to place, and as a potential military advantage. Also within a ten-year span, from 1903 to 1913, a generation skeptical about human flight had experienced a profound transformation of consciousness. The world had accepted the reality of motorized flying machines, human pilots, aviation contests, and daredevil thrills, as well as the possibility of intercity air transport and aerial bombardment.

CHAPTER 3

Inventors and Entertainers: Movies

I N LESS THAN a decade airplanes turned the ancient dream of human flight into entertainment. Fliers thrilled crowds with races and daring stunts, and air meets transformed thousands of curious observers into tourists. At the same time, motion pictures projected dreams onto a screen and turned ordinary people into movie stars (sometimes only in their imagination).

Undoubtedly more people watched their first airplane in flight from a seat at the movies than in person. After decades of scientific experiments and engineering, inventors had created mechanical devices that made pictures appear to move. They used scientific principles of vision to create novelties and instruments of amusement, following a long history of diversions that trick the eye with mirrors and lights.

While flying machines engendered disbelief before rousing enthusiasm, the novelty of motion pictures startled and then quickly captivated viewers. Perhaps because the earliest motion pictures—the "actualities," with their everyday experiences—had acquired credibility with audiences, even skeptics accepted the reality of human flight when newsreels put the photographic evidence on movie screens.

Movies and airplanes both challenged people's perceptions of technological possibilities and personal capabilities and altered notions of distance and geographic barriers. More than passing fads, these mechanical inventions underpinned profitable industries, inspired spectator satisfaction, widened people's awareness of different societies, and transformed human aspirations, expectations, and behaviors. Profitability, in turn, engendered personal and national competition.

Inventors

Neither the pioneers of aerial navigation nor the inventors of photographic equipment viewed themselves as progenitors of international, mass-entertainment enterprises. Although the two life-altering inventions emerged in the public consciousness at about the same time as sources of entertainment, airplanes and motion pictures differed significantly in character and scope. Unlike movies, the airplane itself could not be separated from the entertainment it provided. Most airplane manufacturers only reluctantly entered the world of entertainment. If a mechanic or an engineer assembled various parts into an airplane and flew in it, people who witnessed the occasion recognized the unique phenomenon and applauded. However, how could the owner and builder recoup the cost, build another plane to improve performance, and promote sales? Circumstances often forced the entrepreneur to entertain or to compete for prizes.

An airplane builder demonstrated the machine, perhaps taught someone to fly, and sold an airplane to the novice aviator. Prohibitive cost and high risk limited the market, while uncertain reliability limited the plane's longevity in the entertainment business. By contrast, the Edison Company earned considerable revenue from the manufacture and sale of Kinetoscopes.

Unlike the spectators at an air meet who kept their eye on the airplanes, moviegoers watched the medium on which the photographs appeared—not the machine that produced the pictures or reproduced the images. The direct connection established between the spectator and the airplane and flier evaporated in the world of motion pictures. In fact, the movie viewer interacted with a product, not the mechanical invention itself.

Several people in the nineteenth century had devised machines that moved still photographs at a speed sufficient to produce the appearance of action. Others produced cameras that captured moving images on film. Still others constructed machines that projected the photographic images for the benefit of large audiences. Multiple photographic images were captured contiguously, stored on film, and then moved through machines to provide the entertainment. Unlike the thrill seeker who watched the airplane and pilot, the movie fan could totally engage the film and be completely unaware of camera, producer, development process, and projector.

Once innovators in the development of motion picture photography had created a way to reproduce filmed images, they entertained multitudes of people. Projectionists showed copies of many motion pictures to different viewers day after day. As people encountered and embraced motion pictures, profits grew exponentially relative to the investment in equipment and—unlike airplanes—with minimal risk to humans and property.

Moreover, as the producers of motion pictures learned to manipulate the viewer's perceptions of the material filmed, the variety of images imprinted encouraged a greater or lesser emotional bond between viewer and product. The considerable range of feelings engendered by cinema, from subtle well-being to consuming rage, outpaced the thrills and horrors of the typical air meet or flying circus.

A critical decade of experiment and innovation in motion picture entertainment began in the early 1890s. In the United States Thomas A. Edison's camera, the one-ton, massive Kinetograph, photographed objects in motion. George Eastman's celluloid roll film provided the medium. Edison and William Dickson built the Kinetoscope viewing box and connected the public to the experience of motion pictures.

Edison patented the camera and the viewing machine and displayed the Kinetoscope at the 1893 Chicago World's Fair. The

Kinetoscope, an upright, wooden box, approximately $3\frac{1}{2}$ feet high, $2\frac{1}{2}$ feet deep, and $1\frac{1}{2}$ feet wide, had a tapered top leading to the eyepiece and lens near the front. The viewer put a penny in the slot to activate the machine, bent over, and watched the presentation through the eyepiece. A battery operated a light and turned sprocketed spools to move perforated film past the light at a speed sufficient to create the illusion of movement.

That same year Thomas Lombard, Frank Gammon, and Norman C. Raff formed the Kinetoscope Company to purchase the coin-operated machines that Edison manufactured. The Kinetoscope Company intended to place the machines in convenient places where the public could enjoy the moving pictures, and Edison agreed to keep the new company supplied with film. Thus, production and exhibition—invention and entertainment—separated immediately. To fulfill his commitment Edison built an enclosure around a stage and used the Kinetograph to take pictures for the Kinetoscope. As straightforward as the agreement sounds, it represented a radical change in the world of entertainment.

Only one person at a time could view the Kinetoscope's wonders, of course, and ten machines located in a New York City amusement arcade in 1894 marked the first commercial use of Edison's invention. His first thirty-two-frame film, a few seconds long, had captured Fred Ott, Edison's handyman, sneezing. Now he made lengthier films of about a minute and used cats and dogs, as well as humans, to entertain.[1]

Edison produced films to supply his single-viewer Kinetoscopes, as contracted, but he still derived profits from manufacturing and selling the machines. However, the American Mutoscope and Biograph Company put out a rival machine based on flipped picture cards moved by hand crank and later demonstrated a projector, the Biograph, and also began to make movies.

To expand his repertoire of available films, Edison contracted with two American brothers, Otway and Gray Latham, to film a boxing match for display on the Kinetoscope. The popularity of the sports film at the penny arcade prompted the Lathams to seek bigger audiences per showing; they began to experiment with motion picture projection. William Dickson, who had worked with Edison, helped the brothers develop a projector. For their April, 1895, debut demonstration of film projection for simultaneous group viewing, they presented scenes of boys playing in a park and a man smoking a pipe. Audience appeal probably derived less from the subject matter than from the novelty of movement itself. Although poor visual quality doomed this particular projector, one technical innovation—sprockets that permitted looping the film for longer film length—became a standard projection device.

Six months later C. Francis Jenkins and Thomas Armat demonstrated a different machine, called the Phantoscope, at the Cotton States Exposition in Atlanta. The Edison Company manufactured the projector, changed the name to Vitascope, and introduced projected films to New York audiences in 1896 as part of a vaudeville show. Intended to be as entertaining as the live stage performances, the films covered more arresting material than Fred Ott's history-making sneeze. Although the "peep-show" viewers remained the dominant audience until about 1905, the motion picture business moved in the direction of film projection for simultaneous multiple viewing.

Known collectively as "actualities," the one-minute projected sequences recorded dances (the "Butterfly Dance," the "Skirt Dance," and the "Umbrella Dance"); travel ("Venice Showing Gondolas," "Cuba Libre"); slices of life ("The Barber Shop," "The Bar Room"); public interest ("Monroe Doctrine," "Kaiser Wilhelm, Reviewing His Troops,"); sports ("A Boxing Bout"); and nature ("Sea Waves"). The total time of a single program of films approximated the twelve-minute performance of one vaudeville act. Audiences accustomed to variety in a theatrical bill filled with live clowns, dancers, singers, and so on generally enjoyed the novelty of this last "act." If not, they left the theater.

John Harris and Harry Davis opened the first storefront facility devoted solely to projected motion pictures in Pittsburgh in 1905 and charged a five-cent admission for the patrons who filled its ninety-six seats. Unexpectedly, people willing to pay a nickel to watch the program of movies far outdistanced the store's seating capacity, and the partners soon operated the Nickelodeon (nickel theater) from 8 A.M. to midnight. Before very long, Harris and Davis took in $1,000 per week, the equivalent of 15,000 – 20,000 attendees, since they sometimes charged ten cents for special shows.

Two years later the United States counted some five thousand nickelodeons. (The name became a generic term for storefront movie houses.) The profits that accrued to their owners demonstrated the popularity of the movies. William Fox, for example, whose parents had brought their infant son to the United States from Hungary, invested in a Brooklyn nickelodeon and within several years owned fifteen of them. Not too many years later he produced his own films at his own studio, Fox Film Corporation.

Numerical and financial strength conferred market power on the nickelodeon owners, and they pushed the new and important form of mass entertainment in the direction of profitability rather than art. That is, producers churned out films to meet an escalating exhibitor demand: "I don't want it good; I want it Tuesday." If the primarily working-class audiences wanted filmed chases, producers obliged, linking a series of action sequences—cops and robbers, rescues of victimized women and children, and so on— in a skeletal narrative.

Americans could not lay exclusive claim to the development of motion pictures, of course. Across the Atlantic Ocean, four innovators, working separately, inaugurated the French film industry in the 1890s. At the Société Antoine Lumière et Fils, manufacturer of film plates and stock for still photography, Louis Lumière experimented with visual recording processes. Léon Gaumont also manufactured and marketed photographic and optical equipment.

Lumière and Gaumont both looked into the technical possibilities of motion pictures. First Louis Lumière learned how to register an image on a 35-mm film strip. Then he and his brother, Auguste, invented a portable combination movie camera and projector, which they patented as the Cinématographe. With this single device the brothers could take photographs and project them as moving images for a multiperson audience. They gave the first public demonstration of their invention the year after the Kinetoscope Company installed Edison's viewing box in the first Kinetoscope Parlor on lower Broadway in New York City. Then they exhibited projected motion pictures commercially for the first time in December, 1895.

Camera portability gave the Lumières an advantage over the Edison Kinetograph. That is, they weren't limited to studio filming. Their first effort followed workers as they exited the Lumière family's factory in Lyons, and the brothers' touring camera operators produced nearly one thousand short films over the next two years, a volume that confirmed the growing market for French commercial films. In 1900 projections of Lumière films on a large screen at the Paris Universal Exposition attracted more than a million spectators over a seven-month period.[2]

Meanwhile, Charles Pathé exhibited Kinetoscope films at fairgrounds, and Georges Méliès, the owner-manager of the Robert-Houdin Theater in Paris, began to film some of the magic acts and plays that filled his stage. He also built a studio and began producing short films for projection at the theater.

Typical nickelodeon programs included travelogues, films of current events or historical re-creations, and "industrials," along with narratives. The French company Pathé Frères, for example, the dominant supplier of nickelodeon films, distributed a Tours of the World series and industrial films that explained the unique properties of various economic endeavors. One film examined logging, while another demonstrated oil exploration and production. Pathé photographers also recorded farming practices in remote places and factory production techniques. Exhibitors, eager for products to fill the screens—and the seats—in their theaters, lined up to buy the French films.

The opportunity to be entertained at a reasonable price certainly changed people's daily or weekly routines. They made time for the movies. Moreover, the nickelodeon opened lives and minds. Moviegoers, seated in a dark room before flickering images, accessed a world beyond their social traditions, work, and communities without going far from home. Long before air travel, movies transported them to new locations and placed them among people of other classes and nationalities. In fictional films actors made decisions and took actions in situations that viewers had never encountered.

We might even conjecture that nickelodeons taught more people in the United States about their world than the secondary schools did. Early in the twentieth century, roughly thirty million Americans lived in cities of more than 2,500 residents and might have had access to a nickelodeon. If weekly attendance at the 5,000 nickelodeons in the United States (1907 estimate) averaged even 3,000 and we allow for repeat customers, perhaps ten million people saw movies each week. Fifteen million Americans fell between the ages of ten and nineteen, but a significant percentage of them worked. At the most, several million youngsters attended high school each year. While public school instruction implemented a curriculum designed by professional educators to promote the acquisition of knowledge, we might concede a personal and social benefit to the hours spent at the movies. We might well ask in what ways and to what degree did the direct appeal of persuasively told stories influence a relatively unschooled population of habitual moviegoers?

Observers quickly awakened to the breadth and depth of the rapidly unfolding phenomenon of motion pictures as a commodity, an entertainment form, an education tool, and a social force. Supporters of film censorship began to record what they perceived as negative relationships between movie content and behavior. For one thing—much as today—they connected portrayals of robbery and violent behavior in motion pictures with rising crime rates. For another, they decried the cultural values implicit in the settings, actions, and characters in foreign films as potential agents of denationalization or—in the case of immigrants—inhibitors of Americanization.

Motion pictures had entered—and altered—the world with amazing speed. Producers of motion pictures used new inventions to fill a rapidly accelerating demand for cheap entertainment; they formed companies and competed to show their products.

When tens of millions of ordinary people around the world came to know and love the movies and paid small admission fees to see them, audiences entered worlds they hadn't known before, or they saw familiar circumstances through others' eyes. Within a decade of the first commercial theatrical projections, people began to recognize the existence of an entertainment milestone with outstanding creative potential, as well as the social significance of large numbers of viewers going to see movies on a regular basis.

The evolution of the motion picture viewing experience from one-minute visual novelty to fully developed feature films covered approximately the same decade (1904–1914) that witnessed the evolution of the airplane from novelty to entertainment to the first suggestions of its utility in military operations and as transportation. Like the promoters of the Reims Air Meet, who saw profit in thrilling the public with daring aerial feats, investors discerned the value of motion pictures to the entertainment marketplace. They opened arcades, nickelodeons, and elaborate motion picture theaters to accommodate growing numbers of viewers, and the returns confirmed their foresight.

Unlike air meets, which required an expanse of empty land and viewers willing to travel to the entertainment venue, motion picture outlets flourished among concentrations of population. By the early twentieth century, urban, industrial, consumer societies in the United States counted millions of factory and transportation workers and office and retail clerks with a little time and money to spend. The effect of steadily rising wages and declining working hours had made itself felt in the variety of commercial entertainment for the popular classes, such as music halls, amusement parks, vaudeville theaters, burlesque, and movies. Even small factory towns like Lowell and Lynn, Massachusetts, supported vaudeville theaters that showed movies along with five or six acts of live entertainment. In summer the local amusement parks included films as an attraction.[3]

Entertainers

The millions of movie viewers rapidly underwrote a financially significant entertainment industry. In 1927, just two decades after the nickelodeon boom began, Harvard University saluted the motion picture business—producers, actors, directors, distributors, financiers, and exhibitors. Wallace B. Donham, dean of the business school, acknowledged entertainment's significance in the national economy, despite the peculiarities of its product.

Simultaneously self-congratulatory and apologetic, Dean Donham heralded a milestone for Harvard's prestigious, conservative Graduate School of Business Administration. Self-congratulatory because he welcomed the entire graduating class of 1927, over three hundred students, to a unique six-week series of lectures by prominent leaders of the fourth largest industry in the United States, motion pictures. Apologetic, as he admitted, because Harvard administrators had little contact with the motion picture business, an industry that counted its longevity in years, rather than decades, scores, or centuries.[4]

Few motion picture pioneers and leaders had earned college degrees, but by 1927 motion pictures represented an adventurous business, and America's filmed products dominated a worldwide market. Studio executives earned and paid enviable salaries; investors had made fortunes. The busy executives of this economically and socially significant industry had set aside other engagements to accommodate Harvard's rather hastily arranged course on business policy, Donham noted. Some of the industry's prime movers had agreed to travel across the country to share the experiences and problems of a unique enterprise with the select student body—the next generation of the nation's business leaders.

Harvard, in fact, had initiated the course on the motion picture industry more by chance than by academic design. For the privilege of listening to the industry's pioneers—its organizers, artists, and financiers—the students could thank alumnus Joseph P. Kennedy, Harvard College, class of 1912. Joseph Kennedy's career had taken an unusual turn for a Harvard graduate. He had left the socially acceptable world of banking and the stock market for the entertainment business. Once there, he recognized that mass entertainment created investment and job opportunities for graduates of Ivy League business schools.

Kennedy, who had recently become president of FBO Pictures Corporation, had suggested the lecture series to the business school faculty and quite emphatically urged that the students learn more about an industry whose life coincided chronologically with their own.[5]

The entertainment business had earned few previous academic honors. Reproved by moralists for exhibiting frivolous and suggestive stories to a vulnerable public, serious consideration in scholarly circles more often leaned toward accusations of social corruption. That is, social science researchers posited that bank robbers and bigamists acted under the mesmerizing influence of the movies.

Kennedy's fellow Hollywood entrepreneurs had made some money in manufacturing and retail businesses and then invested in a risky but exciting new opportunity. Now, in a curious pairing of Eastern elite and Eastern Europe, Harvard students listened attentively to course lectures offered by pioneer investors and innovators in the movie business, legendary figures like Adolph Zukor, Carl Laemmle, and William Fox, who never expected their personal experiences to become a business school case study. Zukor, Laemmle, and Fox headed powerful film companies in 1927—Paramount, Universal, and Fox—but they came from the ranks of recent immigrants. The movies, in fact, had found their first customers among the popular masses.

Harvard's acceptance of motion pictures as an industry and of the movies as a significant mass entertainment medium signaled a profound transformation in consciousness. In fact, the movie moguls stood on the shoulders of scientists, inventors, and early filmmakers who never imagined that their labors would inaugurate an international entertainment industry that was socially influential, politically powerful, and academically provocative.

Zukor could thank Kinetoscope pennies for substantial financial rewards even before he tried his hand at theater exhibition and film production. Despite the hardships of his early years in both Hungary and the United States, the successful furrier lived comfortably in New York at the turn of the century. Zukor had surplus capital, and his cousin Max Goldstein had an investment idea.

On a visit to the 1901 Pan-American Exposition in Buffalo, New York, Goldstein had met Thomas Edison's sales representative at the Fair's Edsonia Hall, which featured Edison's phonographs and his motion picture machine. Cousin Max wanted to follow the advice of the Edison salesman and open a Kinetoscope arcade on 125th Street in New York City. Zukor lent Max the money, and curiosity sent him to the arcade when it opened.[6]

Goldstein praised the entertainment innovation, but as fascinated as Zukor may have been with the Kinetoscope and its short pictures, he stayed with the business he knew, at least for a time. When Zukor finally gave in, he talked his partner in the fur business into a new venture. They opened their one-hundred-machine Kinetoscope arcade, Automatic Vaudeville, in a converted restaurant on New York's bustling Fourteenth Street, a thoroughfare filled with shops and frequented by working people who might have a penny or two in change to spend on the latest novelty. The traffic volume no doubt contributed to their good fortune, for they took in more than $100,000 in the first year of operation.[7]

If Benjamin Franklin likened saved pennies to earned pennies, the lesson in thrift lost considerable luster for thousands of wage earners when the peep-show arcades opened. On the other hand, spent pennies turned into earned dollars for arcade owners.

At a penny a peek, the exceptional total in dollars indicated that moving images fascinated a horde of curious people. They eagerly added motion pictures to an entertainment cornucopia that included circuses and world's fairs, amusement parks, and vaudeville shows. Kinetoscope and Mutoscope viewers spent their pennies to watch thirty-second or one-minute films about natural phenomena, ordinary human activities, or special events. Within a few years they exchanged nickels for the opportunity to enjoy ten-minute stories and song slides at nickelodeons. Later they willingly parted with ten cents, and then one dollar or more, for the hour-long entertainment of a scripted, costumed feature, sometimes in extravagantly decorated settings and starring their favorite actors.

In a provocative examination of the role of motion pictures at the St. Louis World's Fair, film historian Tom Gunning situates the future nickelodeon patron in a dynamic world of interactive visual culture. The great fairs intentionally engulfed the participants in a showplace, a visual culture, driven by novelty and spectacle—architecture, food, music, dance, and exhibits of unfamiliar people and cultural practices. In fact, they foreshadowed the movie experience.

A day of visual consumption at the fair might comprise a sampling of raw materials, manufactures, aspects of popular culture, practical arts, fine and folk arts, and machinery. The sometimes head-spinning "trip around the world" entertained as well as educated. Surprisingly, St. Louis fair promoters accorded no official recognition or high-profile reception to motion picture entertainment. Unlike the prominence given to wireless communication, automobiles, and the grand competition in aeronautic achievement, they overlooked the promise of the movies.

Nevertheless, Gunning suggests, the potentially confusing experience prepared future movie audiences to sequence separate scenes acted by diverse characters, to mentally integrate shifts in camera angles and distances, varying time periods and multiple plots, and to compile the variables into a single motion picture encounter.[8]

The technology that soon lured viewers to thousands of nickelodeons across the country played a secondary, mostly explanatory, role in St. Louis, far from the amusement-filled Pike. For example, the extensive City of Jerusalem display used motion pictures, accompanied by lectures, to convey the way of life in ancient Israel. Similarly, one U.S. Department of the Interior film series presented Native American ritual dances and handicraft production; another showed Yellowstone and Yosemite National Parks. The U.S. Post Office Department had filmed mail-handling techniques to demonstrate the government's work. Among private-sector displays, Westinghouse films described how its factories produced the goods on exhibit.

By contrast, commercial attractions on the Pike offered more mechanical than photographic amusements. Concessionaires manipulated elaborate technical effects and materials like scenic projections, electricity, steam, stained glass, celluloid, and silk to generate dramatic tension while they created illusions of devastating floods and terrifying fires.

Although French Pathé travel films, like *A Trip through Algiers* or *A Trip through Europe,* and Georges Méliès's fictional *A Trip to the Moon* had already crossed the ocean to play on the American vaudeville circuit, fair concessionaires relied on mechanical props. On the virtual trip "New York to the North Pole in Twenty Minutes," fairgoers paid their admission and mounted a mock-up of an Atlantic steamship that moved through still-picture panoramas of the city of New York, the Atlantic Ocean's northern waters, and then into arctic landscapes.

Another attraction offered travel to "The Hereafter" and sent customers on a mechanical voyage through imaginative representations of Hell to end at the impressive and fanciful gates of Heaven. Equally ambitious moving panoramas and voice accompaniment traced a trajectory back in time to the Creation, which was re-enacted through the use of props, lights, and projected images.[9]

Nevertheless, the fair's simulated trips and fantasy voyages undoubtedly encouraged George C. Hale to develop a novel form of filmed exhibition. Hale, a former fire chief of Kansas City, Missouri, operated a concession at the fair at which he demonstrated his city's fire-fighting techniques for amblers on the Pike. His location in the entertainment zone enabled him to observe the amusement choices of thousands of fairgoers, and he discerned their fondness for illusions of travel. The first "Hale's Tours," combining the experience of travel with motion pictures, opened in Kansas City some six months after the St. Louis fair closed.

Hale showed travel films in a small theater constructed to resemble a railway coach. A "conductor" took tickets as passengers entered the theater and found seats for the trip. As the lights went down, the coach "rumbled and swayed," and the filmed version of some travel route, taken from the platform of a moving train, appeared on the screen.[10]

The enthusiastic Kansas City reception of Hale's travel film idea motivated him to sell franchises that allowed other entrepreneurs to replicate the setting and use the same films. Among those who answered the all-aboard call, theatrical manager William A. Brady bought the rights for New York state and asked Adolph Zukor to join him in the business venture.

By 1906 Zukor had already opened a two-hundred-seat moving picture theater above the Automatic Vaudeville. The Crystal

Hall theater revealed Zukor's flair for selling. After all, the fur business doesn't sell dead animal skins; it sells style and glamour. To encourage his peep-show clientele to part with a nickel instead of a penny, Zukor created a theatrical adventure. He installed a glass staircase between the arcade and the theater, ran water through a trough under the staircase so that it resembled a waterfall, and played red, green, and blue lights on the water. New Yorkers understood the message: A nickel was a small price to pay to cross an exhilarating threshold of glass and lights and watery illusion.[11]

Zukor joined Brady, and the two entertainment entrepreneurs rented a store on Fourteenth Street, installed a Pullman car, turned the front of the store into a "train depot," and hired a lecturer to point out highlights to the "passengers." They opened with six different filmed tours and did so well that they quickly expanded to Coney Island, then Philadelphia, Pittsburgh, Boston, and Newark.

Unlike the Automatic Vaudeville and the Crystal Hall theater, Hale's Tours proved a costly mistake. Operators rented their travel films from the Selig film company. Selig's 1905 catalog listed twenty-five travel films, mostly tours of western U.S. locations. The limited range of choices forced frequent repetition and quickly exhausted the novelty of vicarious train travel. The size of the audiences dropped below profitability, and motion picture producers calculated that the market did not warrant the expense incurred in filming travelogues from a train platform.

Brady and Zukor kept the audiences coming for a while by showing *The Great Train Robbery,* which must have offered a unique sensation to patrons seated in a train car themselves. Though they eventually lost their investment in Hale's Tours franchises and found themselves heavily in debt, they did not give up on moving pictures. They ripped out the railway cars, put in seats, and kept the theaters open, showing short subjects and popular chase pictures. Then as now, audiences liked to see people running (or driving), careening one after the other to catch the "bad guys."[12]

Meanwhile, Selig shifted its output to service the expanding nickelodeon market with story films like *The Girl from Montana.* Although Vitagraph and Edison filmed their "Westerns" in New

Jersey, the Chicago-based Selig preferred location shooting. With both travelogues and western-location films seen by thousands of movie patrons, Selig films gained value as promotional come-ons for tourism to western states. Convinced that its films created a desire to visit the places where the pictures were made, Selig promoted the wild and beautiful scenery in its 1907 melodrama, *Western Justice,* as well as the story.[13] In 1933 RKO-Radio used planes and Rio de Janeiro, rather than trains and the American West, to send a travel message.

The rise and fall of Hale's Tours reveals a dilemma inherent in early motion picture theater profitability: A mass market spent small sums but had a great appetite for entertainment. To keep the revenue flowing, exhibitors depended upon a steady supply of new films.

The burgeoning motion picture industry necessarily adapted to supply the increased demand. For one thing, film-producing companies adopted technical standards for film stock so that films could be shown on a variety of projectors. Rather than travel with their own films and a projector, producers began to view exhibition as a separate entity. After the makers of equipment sold projectors to exhibitors, producers sold prints of the films they made to those exhibitors. Exhibitors purchased films from various producers, arranged them into programs, added music and/or narration, and traveled from place to place, leaving one location for another as audiences seemed to reach the saturation point.[14]

Although audiences responded with enthusiasm when a traveling exhibitor came to town, the limited supply of films determined the variety of the programs that could be offered and the length of the exhibitor's stay. The exhibitor made a circuit and earned enough to buy more films. Because profits depended on one's ability to purchase a sufficient number of films, the exhibitor considered them a commodity, an industrial product responsive to market preferences. Producers themselves referred to their film studios and print-processing facilities as factories. Their potential to increase production depended on sales, and the traveling exhibitor bought more films as the theater sold more tickets.

Two developments soon restructured the relationships within

the industry. For one thing, equipment manufacturers made projectors easier to operate, so theater owners were able to train their own personnel to run the films. They no longer relied on a traveling exhibitor who carried along the necessary equipment and films. Consequently, entrepreneurs—possibly former traveling exhibitors—bought films from several producers and opened film exchanges; that is, they rented films to vaudeville theater owners and storefront theater operators, who showed rented films on standardized projection equipment.

Market growth propelled the rapid expansion of film rental exchanges, the critical link between producer and exhibitor that facilitated frequent program changes. With unassailable business logic, these exchanges bought or leased films from producers and rented them to multiple exhibitors at half or one-fourth of the purchase (lease) price. The more films they had available, the more frequent the program changes; the more admissions the exhibitors collected, the more films they wanted to rent.

Railroad connections between cities facilitated film delivery to theaters and their subsequent return to the exchanges. When exchange services advertised their films in catalogs and trade papers to stimulate demand, producers began to appreciate the importance of name identification. That is, names like Vitagraph and Biograph assured the potential renter of quality films. Within five years, more than 125 exchanges were operating all over the country. Even as new exchange companies sprouted, older ones opened branch offices.[15]

In short, experiments in actualities and narrative films between 1899 and 1903 had accelerated a burst of entrepreneurial production and exhibitor activity. For the first few years camera operators recorded an action, activity, or place, relying on the novelty of movement itself to entertain the viewer. Gradually the early experimenters mastered the camera techniques—the ability to record movement, stop, and then resume filming—that imparted greater dynamic qualities to their films. By 1902, when audience appetites for actualities began to flag, producers developed longer, narrative films. Filmmakers selected a story—or wrote a new one—divided the material into scenes, filmed the actors against appropriate backdrops, and linked the scenes sequentially in an edited trajectory of events.

Innovative pioneers in the movie wilderness tapped a deep spring of psychological nourishment. Their stories catapulted a time-tested form of human communication into a global entertainment phenomenon. Narratives occupied an essential place in human history and society (and still do). Experiences that passed from mouth to ear to mouth became the essence of oral tradition. Without written language, the storyteller imparted advice, information, explanations, and instructions through the repetition of myth, legend, parable, fable, fairy tale, and anecdote. The teller, "the one who knew" (from the Greek *histor*), narrated the events and connected the listener to the group and to its history and values.[16]

The motion picture camera expanded the possibilities for storytelling and tapped into the profound human desire to share experiences. Viewing a well-crafted story became its own special kind of experience. Viewers' imaginations integrated separate shots — distance, medium, close, parallel actions, and so on — into a whole story. Audiences became accustomed to switched viewpoints, jumps, and time lapses and allowed themselves to sit in a dark room, watch a screen, and enjoy the diversion prepared for them.[17]

The early popularity of filmed fairy tales reflected the viewers' satisfaction in familiarity with the stories portrayed. The storytelling tradition reveals an unmistakable set of reactions to story repetition, regardless of whether the teller is a filmmaker. Listeners as well as viewers respond to the sensory stimulus each time. Anticipation — knowledge of what will take place — awakens a tension and heightens the pleasurable sensation when sharing the character's predicament. The storyteller may foreshadow events to enhance emotional involvement, so that we know what lurks in the shadows or how and when the rescue takes place. As we look forward expectantly, our involvement increases.

Silent films leaned heavily on melodrama for plot outlines and style. Like folk and fairy tales, the genre created menacing situations in which innocent heroes or heroines faced desperate situations due to natural disasters or human misdeeds. They remained steadfast until rescued, at which time the villains met their fates and virtue was rewarded.

The emergence of staged melodrama paralleled the nine-teenth-century migration of agricultural populations. As farmers and peasants moved from rural areas to industrial centers, the large-scale social upheaval disrupted local oral traditions. In Europe, for example, uprooted, preliterate urban dwellers turned to the theater, where live performances replaced the village story-telling traditions they had left behind.[18] As new types of stories—Westerns, for example—replaced familiar works of fiction in the films, genre conventions provided the tension.

The workers who filled the nickelodeons and movie theaters in the early twentieth century no doubt embraced the motion picture as previous generations had responded to the theater. Film pro-ducers elaborated the stories and improved the techniques of telling them, and more people paid to see them.

Most moviegoers willingly became emotionally involved and shared the hopes and fears of the characters on the screen. At times the narrative functioned as a safe arena in which to confront situations that people typically avoided in daily life. That is, the character faced a life-choice, a crisis, or a danger. The life of that character gained interest as the individual made choices that affected the lives of other people. The storyteller defined the circumstances and calculated the audience response as the plot unfolded and conflicts were resolved. When "The End" filled the screen, the moviegoer looked forward to the next opportunity to experience an emotional encounter.

The popularity of story films and the development of film exchanges fostered an extraordinary increase in the number of movie patrons and admissions. By the 1905–1906 season nearly every vaudeville house was showing moving pictures. Moreover, nickelodeons offered thirty-minute programs of films and illustrated songs from noon to late at night to a clientele of shoppers, off-work employees, and restless neighborhood residents. By the summer of 1907 the Chicago Film Exchange offered as many as seven film program changes per week—fulfilling the exhibitors' one-per-day demand. Thus, the popularity of cheap vaudeville and the nickelodeon created remarkable profits for owners and the film exchanges that supplied them.[19]

Unlike amusement parks and vaudeville houses, the nickelodeon could change its attractions frequently with little inconvenience. These low-budget mass entertainment outlets with the voracious appetites for new films introduced motion pictures to big-city neighborhoods in the United States. With a storefront, chairs, a screen, and a projector in place (at a cost of about $400), a steady supply of new films boosted profits through audience turnover. As a "drop-in" diversion, the short programs that repeated all day long encouraged people to sample whatever was playing. Most viewers saw each new program and clamored for more. In turn, increased film output swelled attendance figures and encouraged investors to open still more storefront shows.

The local cinema added a new attraction to centers of shopping and street life. Women and children patronized the bakeries, fruit and vegetable merchants, grocer, and butcher shops, and men enjoyed the sociability of the corner tavern. Now they also dropped in at the movie house for a break in the routine and talked about the latest program with friends and neighbors.

In this socially acceptable addition to urban activities, millions of people sought the excitement, release, and relief of watching movie stories. At the same time, their numbers unleashed an explosive energy, a new and different entertainment and business force, that affected their lives and their perception of the world. The scope of the shared experience—the laughter, wonder, and pleasurable tension—also shaped a community unconfined by geographic boundaries.

As the trickle of moviegoers grew into a torrent, the high demand for films strained the capacity of domestic film production and secured the domination of French films in both the American and worldwide markets. Unfortunately for U.S. film pioneers, production companies no longer controlled the industry when the nickelodeon boom began. Film exchanges and exhibitors exerted the power of the marketplace, and as they increased the pressure for more films to show, French companies had the capability to fill the demand.

French Cinema Supremacy and International Rivalries

Admittedly the imperial ambitions of the world's commercial powers at the turn of the twentieth century dwarfed the conflicts within the fledgling motion picture industry into insignificance. An international film market competition and the economic well-being of U.S. equipment manufacturers and motion picture producers seemed inconsequential, for example, beside the dramatic demonstration of power intended when the "Great White Fleet" left the United States in December 1907 on its fourteen-month-long, world-circling tour. One hundred million dollars worth of battleships—sixteen of them—stood for the country's sense of its own importance. The well-publicized muscle flexing focused attention on the ability of the United States to defend its commercial interests, even as those interests extended to Asian markets. Newspapers dutifully reported the fleet's visits to various ports, filled with the symbolic ceremonials that conveyed friendship and recognition. The completed mission accomplished its goal and established the nation as a force to be admired and respected.

On the other hand, the competition for colonies and trade— the subject of public debate and policy pronouncements at the highest levels of government—created a context for the astoundingly rapid, overlooked emergence of the new entertainment mode and its ultimate sweeping impact on people's behavior and consciousness and on international economic relations.

While the Great White Fleet traveled from sea to sea and port to port, the sales forces of filmed novelties visited the world's capital cities, moved into the hinterlands, and connected people through business arrangements, entrepreneurial opportunities, aesthetic satisfactions, curiosity, laughter, and the universal appreciation of the storyteller's art.

Millions of people in all parts of the world enthusiastically watched motion pictures and went to see another as soon as it reached the local exhibition venue. Two decades later, when representatives of the world's powerful nations worked to diminish dependence on armaments as instruments of international relations, movies and movie stars formed the basis for a global popular culture, and the United States dominated the worldwide motion picture industry.

In the end, one might argue, the international battle for commercial and political influence took place in movie houses as much as on the high seas.

The motion picture industry emerged without official backing, overshadowed by the worlds of finance, trade, and manufacturing. Within a decade of the first commercial public demonstrations of projected motion pictures, the elements of a major international creative and competitive industry took shape. Inventors of machines, experimenters in film, and entrepreneurs of exhibition turned a novelty into an entertainment milestone; that is, they made an inexpensive, engaging experience available to millions of people. Moreover, they built profit into the process. However, they could not have anticipated the social, cultural, and economic power that would result from their inventiveness.

Movie industry rivalries began earlier, developed more rapidly, and crossed more geographic boundaries than those that characterized the early years of aviation. Motion picture producers competed in the international marketplace before the Wright brothers flew their first plane. The expansion of an entertainment consciousness and the profit-and-loss potential of films went hand in hand. From the onset this business aspect of motion pictures fostered competition in the industry. French filmmakers confronted U.S. producers in the motion picture world, just as French planes and pilots rivaled American pioneers in the aviation arena. As in aviation, French production surpassed that of the United States and dominated the international market prior to World War I, including substantial inroads in America itself.

By 1905 the films of Georges Méliès and Pathé Frères had already proven their popularity. Méliès's *Cendrillon (Cinderella)* and *A Trip to the Moon* had inspired a taste for French story films and helped to accelerate the American market for that genre. Pathé had surged to world dominance by marketing reliable cameras and projectors and tripling its production. Then France's largest and most powerful film company had assembled a team of directors who headed production units that worked simultaneously at three studios—two with double stages—on the outskirts of Paris. Conforming to a factory model of production, Pathé's extensive laboratories processed and printed an average of forty thousand feet of positive film per day. Primarily story films, a good percentage of the output went to the U.S. market. Even before the nickelodeon, Pathé films entertained the customers who took advantage of the cheaper admission prices and shorter programs of the family vaudeville houses.

As Richard Abel demonstrates in *The Red Rooster Scare,* a study of early French film exhibition in the United States, the films of Georges Méliès and Pathé Frères supplied a thriving entertainment market in family vaudeville and summer amusement parks as well as nickelodeons.[20]

In 1904 demand for its films had encouraged Pathé to open a New York office. With sales offices in New York and then Chicago and connections to the rental exchanges, Pathé solidified its dominant position in the American market, as the company had done elsewhere. Between 1905 and 1909 the studio became America's leading supplier of films, pumping out six films per week by 1906, as the nickelodeons changed programs frequently to satisfy the market's constant demand for variety. By early 1907 some five thousand exhibition outlets in the United States scrambled to keep millions of daily attendees paying their nickels. The number of theaters swelled to 8,000 in 1908 and 13,000 in 1910, and moviegoers paid ten cents at some of them. Pathé's melodramas and comedies pleased the audiences, and Pathé probably sold twice as much footage in the American market as all the U.S. producers combined.

Even in the midst of an entertainment frenzy, most U.S. companies produced one film per week at most. They didn't have enough studios, directors, actors, or camera operators to manufacture the number of films the exhibitors requested. Meanwhile, Pathé's New York film office had advance orders for fifteen prints of each title shipped to the United States. Pathé films monopolized the Keith chain of vaudeville houses and enjoyed considerable strength in the rest of the U.S. market. In fact, by 1908 the French company may have provided 60 percent of the films in circulation in the United States.[21]

That year, Pathé Frères offered the largest number and greatest variety of film subjects in the international marketplace, a popularity that reflected a combination of vivid storytelling, camera techniques that unambiguously captured the emotions appropriate to the story, and elaborate settings (today's "production values").

Unlike many of the motion picture industry's earliest pioneers, Georges Méliès did not move from the photographic laboratory or workbench to a position behind a camera. Rather, the artist son of a well-to-do manufacturer had turned his interest in stage-performing illusionists from an avocation into a business. (A theater illusionist creates astounding effects that leave audience members at a loss to explain appearances and disappearances of objects and people.) Méliès left work in his father's factory and found his niche in the entertainment world.

Not surprisingly, Méliès, the proprietor of the Robert-Houdin Theater in Paris, sat entranced among the spectators at the first public showing of Lumière films. He immediately recognized the possibilities of cinema and used his theatrical and financial resources to further his fascination with the world of entertainment. He bought a projector and some films and in 1896 turned the Robert-Houdin Theater into the world's first cinema theater.

However, Méliès the businessman indulged his artistic bent as well. He carried a portable camera around Paris and took pictures; he filmed the acts on the bill at the theater. He also built a glass-sided, rectangular studio at his house, put the camera at one end and scenery at the other, arranged scenes, filmed them in a narrative sequence, and showed the resulting motion pictures in his theater. The technical ability to stop the camera and start it again opened any number of possibilities for the imaginative filmmaker to amaze the viewer with illusions. Méliès manipulated his subject matter to great effect and produced startling filmed trickery.[22]

In 1897 Méliès opened a shop and advertised his films for sale under the "Star Film" trademark. For one of his first story films, the familiar fairy tale *Cinderella,* Méliès incorporated the talents of thirty-five people in twenty scenes arranged in succession like a theatrical production. Each scene illustrated one aspect of the tale, and many included ballet and other diversions. In proper sequence the individual scenes, filmed by a stationary camera, illustrated the romantic poor-girl-to-princess progress of the story. By now an experienced entertainment entrepreneur, Méliès produced the imaginative *Cinderella* in 1899, when most film producers still concentrated on actualities. *Little Red Riding Hood, Robinson Crusoe, Joan of Arc,* and *Bluebeard* followed. He enlarged the studio to accommodate wider scenes and employed twenty people in the processing factory—each a specialist in one color—to tint the film prints.

Méliès's real triumph of this foundational period of narrative filmmaking came in 1902. In *A Trip to the Moon* Méliès told the story of the fantasy voyage in thirty sequentially arranged scenes filmed against elaborately decorated backdrops. Actors, singers, and acrobats provided the action—and some satirical humor—as they mimicked the meeting of scientists at the Astronomic Club, the planning sessions, construction of the space-traveling projectile, and astronomers boarding the vehicle and landing on the moon. Scenes of adventures on the lunar surface preceded departure, splashdown at sea, rescue, marches and processions, and honors by public officials. Méliès wrote a musical score for piano accompaniment to the highly theatrical story told with pictures. Success at the box office in Paris and then all over Europe pointed the direction for subsequent films.[23]

Méliès had not abandoned his understanding of profit when he stepped behind the camera to indulge his creative proclivities. After he sent three prints of his film to the United States, hundreds of unauthorized copies began to circulate. The enormous popularity of *A Trip to the Moon* and the absence of controls over film piracy prompted the French filmmaker to open a branch office in New York City. He put his brother, Gaston, in charge and built a printing lab to speed up the processing of his films so that he could place more films and more copies on the expanding international market.

No film comparable to *A Trip to the Moon* had been made up to that time. People who went to vaudeville shows and amusement parks enjoyed the ten or twelve minutes of boxing matches, nature studies, current events, comedies, and so on that constituted the movie experience—but the filmed adventure narrative inaugurated a new genre. Talented producers like Méliès and Edwin S. Porter enhanced the entertainment potential of motion pictures with good stories and secured an ever-wider market. Porter moved his camera as well as his actors and followed the action while making *The Great Train Robbery* in 1903. Where Méliès had arranged successive scenes to tell his stories, Porter edited the film footage to suggest the simultaneity of activity in a community, danger from bandits, pursuits, and gun battles. Porter's style, more cinematic than theatrical, created excitement, tension, and thrills.

Population size alone gave the United States filmmakers a larger market than the rival Europeans. The variety of exhibition outlets—vaudeville, peep show arcades, amusement parks, and then nickelodeons—generated sufficient revenue to allow motion picture producers in the United States to recoup their filming and distribution costs. By 1900 the northeast and midwestern sections of the United States counted dozens of major vaudeville houses that offered motion pictures as part of their entertainment lineups. To accommodate the geographically expanding network of venues, exhibition services packaged projectors, projectionists, and motion pictures and moved them by railroad around the various vaudeville circuits weekly.

Later, when the popularity of the nickelodeon increased the demand for movies in the United States, exhibitors had to rely on imports just to maintain the frequently changing programs. No other country's producers could depend on their domestic market alone and had little choice but to expand overseas. Conversely, U.S. producers could not meet the domestic demand, and exchange companies necessarily bought and sold foreign films.

By 1902 and 1903, Méliès and Pathé were perhaps the world's most prolific film producers, building the market even as they supplied it. French story films like Méliès's *Cinderella, Little Red Riding Hood,* and *Jack and the Beanstalk* appealed to audiences everywhere. So did Pathé's *Ali Baba and the Forty Thieves, Sleeping Beauty, Puss-in-Boots,* the biblical series *Prodigal Son,* and the fairy-land series, in which enchantments plunge a prince and princess into astounding situations. Though wildly popular in France, they quickly saturated the relatively small domestic market, and French movie producers moved to sell their products overseas.

The French competed successfully in the U.S. market at a time when the United states was making only small inroads abroad. Lumière alone had produced two thousand films by 1900, and the Lumière Cinématographe equipment vied with Edison's Vitascope and American's Biograph. The French seized the early lead in the worldwide film export market, with the Italians a close second. U.S. exhibition services advertised French films, and the French companies adopted identifiable trademarks (Méliès's star and Pathé's red rooster) as symbolic assurances of quality, much as Vitascope and Biograph relied on name identification.[24]

As silent-film buff Edward Wagenknecht recalls from the days of his youthful obsession, French films dominated the nickelodeon screens:

> All the films shown at [Chicago's Family Electric Theater] were French Pathé, and if I loved the posters I loved the titles and subtitles even more. They were always tinted red, with enormous lettering, and there were two of the famous Pathé roosters at the bottom of each title, one at the right and the other at the left. The rooster's feet were brought smartly together under his body and fastened to a bar on which the words "Trade Mark" were printed.[25]

Although the United States offered the largest potential market for film sales, Latin America also loomed large in the ambitions of early film producers. Argentina, Mexico, and Brazil had the most dynamic urban cultures in Latin America at the turn of the century, with most of the economic activity concentrated in the heavily populated capital cities.

In 1896 movies arrived in Argentina during a time of rapid population growth and urbanization. Strong historical and cultural ties may have inclined the Argentineans in Europe's direction, but the Lumière camera's portability bestowed an advantage in the equipment market as well. The first Argentine camera operators, for example, recorded scenes from the country's urban and rural activities and showed them in Buenos Aires's first movie theater in 1900. Domestic film production supplied only a tiny percentage of films seen in the country, however, with French and Italian imports supplying most exhibitors. The substantial population of Italian immigrants living in and around Buenos Aires figured in the evident preference for Italian films.

Lumière agents supplied the first moving pictures in Mexico, although Mexican entrepreneurs bought film stock, cameras, and projectors and evidenced a strong showing in Mexico City by 1903. An increasingly urbanized Brazil first enjoyed the excitement of the cinema in the 1890s, after the citizens established their republic in 1889. Infrastructure underdevelopment, particularly in the electricity generating sector, impeded expansion for a time, but Brazilians quickly began to produce their own films as well as to import foreign products.

The introduction of motion pictures in Argentina, Mexico, and Brazil gradually extended to neighboring countries, as itinerant show producers moved from place to place in Latin America. Once Cuba broke with Spain and recovered from the independence struggle, the island filled with movie houses—some two hundred by 1910, with local entrepreneurs involved in both film production and exhibition.[26]

Participants in the scramble for motion picture markets established offices in foreign cities and then worked to saturate the local entertainment venues with their equipment and films. Pathé's offices stretched from St. Petersburg, Russia, to Singapore and from New York to Calcutta by 1908. The company moved on to Australia in 1909 and South Africa in 1912 and had forty-one offices in major cities—with a virtual monopoly in China and the Middle East—before World War I.

French success overseas reflected a particularly astute business expansion strategy. Pathé Frères sent its sales force to underdeveloped regions, where they showed films and encouraged local entrepreneurs to buy equipment and to open their own theaters. After Pathé created a demand for films, the company would open a film exchange to maintain the supply and to keep out competitors.[27]

Thus, Pathé gained a firm hold in the small markets, as well as in the United States. For example, in India, which counted only six permanent theaters in 1910—four in Bombay, one in Calcutta, and one in Rangoon—and some seventy touring cinema outlets, only Pathé distributed films. The company sold its films to the local theater owners, who then sold the used films to the traveling shows at half price. Syria, which had an even smaller market, leased its French films from companies in Paris and its Italian films from companies in Rome—after they had been shown in Egypt.

Most U.S. companies employed a different strategy in the early years. Rather than dispatch company sales personnel, they contracted with established export firms, which acted as their overseas agents. Edison Company broke with this practice and used its phonograph subsidiary in London to handle direct sales in Europe. When both the market and the competition expanded, Edison set up an office in Paris to control European operations and to process its negatives into positive prints for sale in Great Britain and on the continent. Other producers soon established direct representation in Europe, began to make two negatives while filming, and sent one of them to Europe for processing and distribution. Between 1908 and 1910 U.S. production companies opened European distribution headquarters in London or Paris and then established branches and agencies in other locations.

With 2,000 theaters—300 in London alone—Britain became the primary target for U.S. producers. British investors, reluctant to put their money into film production, had left the motion picture field open to foreign firms. When the Americans arrived, French and German firms were firmly entrenched. By 1911, however, 60 percent of British imports came from the United States. Germany, with 1,500 theaters in 1912, provided the second best market, and the United States gained the largest foreign market share in that country before the war, with Italy second and then France. European competition elsewhere impeded U.S. gains, however, particularly in France. The French were loyal to French films, and Italy proved equally difficult. In turn, France and Italy dominated the small southern and eastern European market.[28]

Even in the earliest, awakening years of motion picture entertainment, the inventors and innovators kept a wary eye on rivals. Méliès's Star Film Agency and Pathé Frères both opened offices in the United States during the vaudeville market years both to prevent unauthorized duplication of their prints by film pirates and also to distribute their films.

Faced with this stiff foreign competition, U.S. film producers moved to control and then reduce the foreign share of the domestic market. For one thing, Thomas Edison brought patent infringement lawsuits against Méliès and Pathé in 1904, accusing them of using his designs in their equipment. (The Wright brothers used this legal maneuver a few years later.) Edison had patented his movie camera in 1897 and filed the first of many patent infringement suits within six months, charging that other companies, particularly Biograph, used equipment based on his design. Specifically, Edison complained that films made with cameras that used sprockets to move the film past the lens violated his proprietary interests.

The suits never came to court, however, and Pathé became the largest single supplier of films—and not only for the U.S. market. The French company established its hegemony in the international arena, while the United States struggled to catch up. Pathé's undeniable success produced a significant backlash in the United States, with attempts to control the industry in general and nationalist appeals to block Pathé specifically.

The Motion Picture Industry Trust

As in other industries that had experienced rapid, unfettered growth, one company set out to control the chaos that threatened its economic viability. By 1908 fragmentation and destructive competition characterized the motion picture industry in the United States. Rivalries among producers, distributors, and exhibitors had escalated the conflicts to near crisis proportions.

Confusion characterized the distribution system, and hostilities plagued the production companies.

The transition from the first nickelodeon (1905) to an attempt at monopoly control took an astoundingly brief three years. First, the Edison Company moved to dominate the unruly film industry, regulate its various elements, and gain leverage over the proliferating film exchanges. Then the company offered to license other producers, who then could make films but had to pay a royalty when they used Edison's patented items. The producers balked, but when the courts found in Edison's favor, producers agreed to pay the fee.

Edison issued the appropriate licenses. Under company direction the licensees then formed the Edison Film Combine and used its leverage as a single film source to bring the distribution system of film exchanges under control. To purchase films from the combine, a film exchange had to have a license and agree to certain rules, including minimum rental prices. Those exchanges that Edison licensed became known as the Film Service Association.

However, the bitter patent rivalry between the Edison Company and the Biograph Company continued. Because Biograph used a camera mechanism that Edison's patent did not cover, the company remained outside the combine. So Edison and Biograph each churned out films to satisfy exhibitors and hoped to deter them from defecting to the competing organization.[29]

The combine's licensing and product control mechanisms failed to significantly diminish either domestic or foreign competition or to exercise the desired power over the industry. Edison then reassessed the strategy and created the Motion Picture Patents Company (MPPC) as a holding company. MPPC pooled the disputed patents, dropped all litigation, and brought domestic producers Biograph, Vitagraph, Essanay, Selig, Lubin, and Kalem into the fold, along with the French Méliès and Pathé companies (in order to control film imports).

To restrain competitive practices, including talent raids, the trust also regulated wages. Members of the trust paid writers $25 per story, directors $50 a week, and limited performers to $60 a

162 / CHAPTER 3

week. Within two years the producers' trust had bought up exchanges all over the country and created the General Film Company to distribute their products. General Film Company collected a license fee of $2 per week from each member exhibitor, and the company's licensed exhibitors could not show films distributed through other exchanges.

The trust's authority in the film industry lasted nearly five years, until a lawsuit that filmmakers Carl Laemmle and William Fox had filed resulted in government restraints on the MPPC oligopoly. Laemmle's financial power rested on his ownership of film exchanges in major cities across the country. Although the MPPC had licensed his distribution organization, he decided to move away from the trust and operate as an independent. Laemmle and several other independent producers (that is, those who operated outside the Edison trust) formed the Motion Picture Distributing and Sales Company. The company bought films made by independent producers and sold them to independent exchanges. In turn, the exchanges rented to exhibitors who challenged the trust.

Laemmle also launched a production company, the Independent Motion Picture Company of America, playfully called the "Imp," and set out to challenge the MPPC's wage policies. While the trust regulated salaries and its members deliberately maintained the anonymity of performers, Laemmle just as deliberately publicized the names of actors who played the lead roles in his movies. In order to encourage paying customers to favor his films, he developed the "star" system, that is, higher salaries to certain actors and promotional efforts to publicize their names. Laemmle lured the talent he wanted with better pay, placed their photographs in theater lobbies, and garnered audience loyalty to individuals through personal appearances.

William Fox built his movie empire by integrating backward through the structure of the industry. That is, he profited first as an exhibitor, moved into film distribution, buying and leasing films through his Greater New York Rental Company, and ultimately started a production house with several associates, the Fox Film Corporation. He, too, challenged the hold of the trust, first by resisting attempts to buy out his distribution company and then with a lawsuit against MPPC for unlawful restraint of trade.[30] Like the plot of the melodramas they produced, the "victims" persevered against the machinations of a threatening power until some heroic judge rescued them. Then Laemmle and Fox became industry powerhouses.

The trust faced European defiance as well. Since three-fourths of the profits of the big European producers came from the American market, it surprised no one that most of them sided with independent U.S. producers like Laemmle and Fox in the effort to break the trust's power. Given MPPC's limitations on foreign film imports at a time of increased film demand, the significant English, French, Italian, and German producers met in Paris in March, 1908, set up a committee, and funded an operation to try to keep the U.S. market open to their products. In 1909 they formed the International Projecting and Producing Company (IPPC) to challenge the MPPC's limits and to export European films to the United States.

IPPC never produced films on its own but rather acted as agent for from eighteen to thirty-two companies at various times. The company managed to keep some market slots open for a small number of releases. Only after the U.S. government limited the MPPC's hold on the industry did the members of IPPC learn that the U.S. independent producers and exhibitors had little or no interest in promoting foreign films in their movie houses.[31]

Americanizing the American Market

U.S. producers had acknowledged Pathé as a formidable competitor as early as 1904, when the French company opened its New York sales office and a facility to make positive prints from its negatives (to counter uncompensated duplication of its films). Then Pathé Frères had joined the MPPC trust and enjoyed further financial success in the U.S. market. As a result, Pathé encountered another barrier, a campaign to restrict its market share through intimidation. In the struggle for domination, U.S. film interests began an antiforeign campaign, characterizing French films as "morally suspect" for their sexuality, violence, and distasteful sensationalism.[32]

Attacks on film quality barely disguised an Americanization agenda. The public debate over "foreign film" content played on dominant society concerns about the millions of immigrants who continued to arrive in the United States and who made up a significant proportion of the motion picture audience. In general, attackers claimed that films produced overseas unduly influenced the "raw material of future citizenship."[33] Could these as-yet unassimilated immigrants adapt as Americans, they asked, when European cultural influences dominated the nickelodeon screens? Newspaper articles and editorials charged that the subject matter and style of French films, the costumes, settings, and accessories became subversive elements, counterforces to the national interest.

Moreover, the arguments continued, the leading characters in Pathé films—some of them well-known French stage actors—did not have an "American look." To aid them in identifying with their new country, immigrants sitting in movie houses in the United States should see performers that resembled Anglo-Saxon types, like those portrayed in magazine ads.[34]

Under extreme social and political pressure, exchange companies bought fewer French films. The message to Pathé was clear: Inclusion in the MPPC did not confer free access to the U.S. market. Because the size of the U.S. market was sufficient incentive to address the criticism, the company responded with an announcement that it would henceforth produce and market "American" films. So Pathé filmed Westerns like *The Girl from Arizona,* shot on location, and films that dealt with Native Americans, like *Justice of a Redskin* and *Red Man's Revenge.*[35] The titles suggest a contrarian view of western settlement, that is, from the Native Americans' perspective.

Pathé films had flooded the American market between 1904 and 1908, but the company redirected its business strategy under pressure, joined the trust, and then produced American-themed pictures for U.S. audiences. The French filmmaker also moved to counter the nativist, anti-import campaign by playing its "high culture" card, that is, appealing to the image of French history and majesty that millions of Americans had seen at the St. Louis World's Fair.

Pathé invested in two new production companies to turn out high-quality, filmed adaptations of literary classics as well as popular French plays. The company declared new "standards of excellence" in advertisements in major, daily U.S. newspapers. First, its producers intended their new "art" films to educate the popular classes who regularly attended the movies. Second, they hoped to attract a more affluent and sophisticated clientele to the larger theaters, which had begun to compete with the nickelodeons.

From Nickelodeon to Theater

The transition from nickelodeon to movie theater reflected the American motion picture industry's struggles with (1) the MPPC monopoly, (2) maverick independent distributors and exhibitors, and (3) foreign competition. Despite the efforts of the trust to confine and regularize the industry—or perhaps because of them—the new entertainment sector stretched in new directions.

Adolph Zukor exemplified the trajectory in film exhibition, as he invested in a Kinetoscope arcade, then nickelodeons, and in 1909 a "combination" theater that presented live vaudeville and film. Zukor had signed leases on fourteen storefronts and had opened nickelodeons. He rented films, collected admissions, and operated profitably until he hit a downturn after the 1907 financial panic. The economic slump probably accounted for some of the slackening attendance, but Zukor also sensed a weariness with the chase pictures grinding through the domestic production houses. At his vaudeville theater he showed films along with live entertainment and tried unsuccessfully to persuade American producers to make longer, more substantive, movies.

The handful of producers who operated at the time kept their cameras rolling and their labs processing the one- and two-reel output that the nickelodeons demanded. The thousands of small venues counted on high audience turnover, based on short programs for a low admission price any time of the day. Hour-long

feature films threatened to curtail their profitability. Thus, producers with a dependable market for short films had no incentive
to make longer films and even argued, in their own self-interest,
that people would not sit long enough to see them.

When a new partnership with Marcus Loew and other vaudeville theater owners brought him both a dependable income and
free time, Zukor entrusted the day-to-day management of his theaters to Loew's Enterprises and went to Europe in search of quality
films. He admired the superior French and Italian productions of
the time. When he came across *The Passion Play,* Pathé's extremely
successful, hour-long, hand-colored film, he determined to take
the exceptional picture to America.[36]

The popular Pathé film, whose content could hardly be interpreted by proponents of Americanization as subversive in content
or cultural values, generated considerable controversy nevertheless. To some critics Pathé's filmed version of the life of Jesus
seemed unsuitable for exhibition in a venue meant for cheap
entertainment.

As Zukor later recounted the circumstances, he "did not dare
open [the film] in New York" and tested audience reaction in
Newark, New Jersey, first. He invested in elaborate musical accompaniment—an organ and singers—to set the proper tone and
opened on a Monday morning in the storefront theater next to a
big department store. Enthusiastic responses from the shoppers
who stopped to see the film encouraged Zukor's optimism about
his financial future.

However, as might be expected, the movie's title attracted a
priest along with the shoppers. The offended moviegoer complained that the subject matter belonged to the church, whose
social mission differed from that of the theater. When the priest
disclosed his intention to share his objections with the city authorities, Zukor pleaded financial hardship. Without this potential
source of income, he asserted, he faced bankruptcy. The compas-
sionate priest relented, and the picture stayed in Newark for
months. Subsequent long runs in Zukor's other theaters enhanced
his financial well-being.[37] Zukor judged the positive popular reac-

tion to the movie as indicative of audience maturation, that is, a readiness for more complex and involving stories.

While Zukor recounted his trials as a businessman, silent film devotee Edward Wagenknecht recalled seeing *The Passion Play* as a young boy. In response to public outcry, city authorities in Chicago, the first U.S. city to censor movies, had granted police the power to ban a movie even prior to its first showing. They didn't ban *The Passion Play,* but when Pathé's film opened, flyers "decorated with lurid pictures of Jesus on the Cross" appeared. The church and the media discussed the suitability of the nickelodeon as the place to show the life of Jesus. Wagenknecht's mother came down on the conservative side, and the family stayed away from the neighborhood theater. He loved going to the movies, however, and saw as many films as he could. Later the family "weakened," and Wagenknecht remembered the controversial movie as a sincerely told, "uplifting" story.[38]

Ironically, Zukor found his first opportunity to make the type of feature film he wanted—well-known stage celebrities in theatrical presentations—because the legendary Sarah Bernhardt failed in a play. Even though the "divine Sarah" played the title role in *Queen Elizabeth* on the Paris stage, the play folded in short order. In a bold, innovative attempt to recoup funds, the theater owner suggested she film the play. Bernhardt agreed. For one thing, she had invested in the stage production and stood to lose a considerable sum. Moreover, unlike other stage actors, Bernhardt had not scorned film performances in the past and consented to perform once again before the camera.[39]

Zukor bought the rights to *Queen Elizabeth* in November, 1911, without flinching at the exorbitant $35,000 price tag. The melodramatic film mixed love, politics, and betrayal in a story based on an affair between the British queen and the Earl of Essex. The compressed action, told mostly in pantomime with explanatory titles, necessarily eliminated some details of the play. In twenty-three scenes, acted against elaborate sets in period costumes, Bernhardt and her fellow actors played to the stationary camera set among the theater's front rows.

However, Zukor, the long-time exhibitor who had participated in the trust, ran afoul of it now. MPPC rules blocked his attempts to show the film. Movie theaters with Patents Company
projection machines could show only General Film Company
films. Not to be denied, Zukor turned to the legitimate theater for
bookings and advertised the film and its beloved star in the newspapers in New York and Chicago, the country's theater capitals.
Audience enthusiasm marked the July 12, 1912, New York opening
as a historic occasion.

Queen Elizabeth played in the country's two largest cities, and
Zukor monitored audience responses. Theater goers bought their
tickets and sat through a long production. Zukor may not have
fully recovered his investment on Queen Elizabeth, but he had satisfied himself that "pictures of the right type had a great future."[40]

For Zukor, this meant that he could fulfill his ambition to film
famous players in famous plays. He followed Queen Elizabeth
with James O'Neill in The Count of Monte Cristo (directed by
Edwin S. Porter, who had filmed The Great Train Robbery), and
then James K. Hackett in The Prisoner of Zenda. He had made his
point. Feature films attracted audiences who set out to be entertained, rather than the casual "drop ins" who paid their nickel each
time the program changed. As with live theater, they sat for an
hour or more and expected to pay appropriately for a filmed, dramatic theatrical experience.

Among film historians, the success of Queen Elizabeth stands as
a milestone in the "theatricalization" of the motion picture. Zukor,
like Pathé, targeted a middle-class audience and steered them toward the theater rather than the nickelodeon. However, like Pathé's
art films, Zukor's sophisticated dramas required some prior knowledge of the source material and depended on a substantial number
of intertitles—written explanations that interrupted the filmic narrative. Moreover, faithful adherence to the text of literary works often produced plodding films. Zukor undoubtedly moved the film
industry in his preferred direction, but he sacrificed box office rewards in the process. Both Pathé and Zukor chased a literary muse
to give movies legitimacy among the middle classes, but Zukor's
Famous-Players series did not last long.[41]

Meanwhile, other theatrical interests joined with motion picture distributors, imported European feature-length films, and showed them in large legitimate theaters at higher prices. The Italian-made *Quo Vadis?* played to capacity crowds at New York's Astor Theatre for twenty-two weeks in 1913, followed by other imports that helped to establish the appeal of feature films.[42]

The move to feature films over the next few years indeed brought on the decline of the nickelodeon. Like the arcade peep show with its minute-long "actualities," the nickelodeon's one- or two-reel narratives gave way to advances in production capabilities and techniques and to evolving relationships between moviemakers, their star performers, and loyal fans. Feature films, based on plays, literary classics, and original stories with more intricate plots and complex characters, became the mainstay of elaborate movie houses with one-dollar admissions and middle class audiences.

Whatever Zukor's filmed plays may have lacked in exciting visual storytelling, Biograph's David Wark Griffith unstintingly provided. Griffith lengthened the stories he filmed and developed a depth of character not required in chase films. His cinematic storytelling style and expressive camera work retained the loyalty of the mass audience built by the nickelodeon while extending their appeal to other social sectors.

Melodrama had already challenged comedy and chase films as the most widely produced genre when Griffith joined Biograph in 1908, at the height of its struggle against Edison's attempt to control the American film industry. With aspirations to a writing career, Griffith had offered to sell his stories to Edison and, when rejected, turned to the rival. Biograph remained outside the Edison Film Combine, competed to sell films to exhibitors, and needed stories to film. The company bought several of Griffith's narratives and even hired him to act in them. Then the producers asked him to direct *The Adventures of Dollie,* the story of a little girl kidnapped by gypsies and eventually returned to her parents. Griffith filmed *Adventures* in two days, and Biograph premiered it in July, 1908, in New York.

About the time when Zukor began to pursue films that required lengthy explanatory titles, Griffith typically subordinated words to images, developed character through action, and used camera and editing techniques to create a dynamic narrative. Cuts between scenes built drama and connected characters; lighting shaped the mood and atmosphere.

No titles interrupted the flow of Griffith's 1909 film, *The Lonely Villa*, for example. Griffith conveyed the isolation of the house in question with a long shot and then moved among scenes to reveal the family that lived there. Close-ups of appropriate details communicated that the father was leaving the house. Cross-cutting between scenes set the action: Robbers break in; mother and children barricade themselves in one room. The father learns their predicament by telephone and heads home. Cuts between the robbers, the family, and the husband let the audience know that the latter is in a race against time. Through scenes that were more cinematic than theatrical, the audience sensed the dramatic tension and felt suitably relieved when the plot resolved happily with the anticipated rescue.

By the time Zukor scored his success with *Queen Elizabeth*, Griffith had made more than four hundred films, almost all of them one-reelers for Biograph. Chafing under the restrictions the studio imposed, he stretched his cinematic reach in the direction of feature films, produced the four-reel biblical story *Judith of Bethulia*, and soon thereafter started work on the Civil War epic *Birth of a Nation*.

The transition to longer and more complex narratives had sealed the fate of the nickelodeon. The advent of the feature film ushered in a new era and gave the young industry a more glamorous personality, marked by the construction of elaborate theaters, an emphasis on movie personalities, dependence on publicity, and publication of fan magazines.

Imagine a Rip van Winkle-type character who had fallen asleep watching *The Great Train Robbery* zip by in twelve minutes and awakened ten years later, in 1913, with the eight-reel Italian spectacle *Quo Vadis?* on New York's Astor Theatre screen. The length of the film might have put Rip to sleep again but for the intense excitement of the enormous crowds filmed in the massive replica of the Roman Coliseum and the prowling lions eyeing the Christian martyrs.

Stumbling from the theater in confusion, Rip bought the *New York Times* and caught the prestigious paper's first film review— an anonymously written piece of a few lines that praised *Quo Vadis?* as a production with "many spectacular scenes" and strik-ing pictorial effects.[43] Despite its brevity, the *Times* review con-ferred legitimacy on the feature film as an entertainment medium worthy of notice.

As the movie industry evolved, production companies gener-ously compensated the actors, producers, and directors who brought in the audiences. The MPPC had recognized and tried to prevent the rivalries that drove up salaries. Nevertheless, inde-pendents like Carl Laemmle had challenged the trust's regulations and had stimulated audience preferences for certain actors. He promoted talent to sell his films and paid accordingly. Recogniz-able personalities became stars and connected to the growing ranks of movie fans. As producers competed to control talent, they offered inflated salaries for established box-office attractions and spent great sums of money on publicity and advertising. Zukor, who defied the trust to bring Sarah Bernhardt to the screen, paid star salaries along with the rest.

Film stardom challenged and at times surpassed the status, privilege, and wealth of twentieth-century monarchs. Fan loyalty conferred an aura on certain actors, a mystique that surrounded the person apart from the characters they played. While most people accepted the limits that common birth placed on access to royal circles, the humblest person might aspire to climb the ranks of the adored elite in the motion picture business. The popular mythology of the United States allowed any native-born boy to grow up with aspirations to be president of the country, but im-migrants and girls did not qualify. Moreover, the job had less glamour, and the salary did not compare to that of a film star. Ho-ratio Alger's hard-working fictional hero might rise from street urchin to middle management and marry the boss's daughter, but his was a pedestrian life at best and not the stuff of daydreams.

The nineteenth century had produced great captains of man-ufacturing and transportation, builders of cities, financiers, and stock market magnates. However, steel company presidents didn't publish popular, mass-circulation magazines that made stars of their managers and fans of consumers; neither did powerful bankers and railroad chiefs.

The leading characters of the Gilded Age contributed to the growth of the country and inspired both admiration and fear, but they remained remote figures to most people. The average person might not know the personal preferences and habits of Andrew Carnegie, J. P. Morgan, or Collis P. Huntington or write to news-papers asking about their marital status, where they lived, or what they ate for breakfast. Not so the movie stars that the fan magazines lionized.

Members of the Patents Group maintained stock companies and chose actors for parts from among the salaried players. They downplayed individual contributions in order to keep salaries low. Moreover, nickelodeons had emphasized the program itself, not the actors. Their film presentations contained no acting credits and needed none since many viewers adopted the habit of seeing whatever program was playing at the time. People went to see Pathé's *Passion Play* because of its content, not because they ad-mired the actor who played Jesus.

Nevertheless, the twentieth century brought fantasies of wealth wrapped in the magic of movie stardom. When the Patents Group started the *Motion Picture Story Magazine* in 1911, it in-tended the publication to impart information, not stir adoration. Nevertheless, the operational practices of the movie business, as much as product content, exerted a profound influence on people's perceptions of the world. An estimated half-million moviegoers read the early issues, in which producers promoted their pictures through story synopses and accompanying photos. They also paid for advertisements. *Motion Picture Story* and other movie maga-zines eventually awakened a widespread personal connection with stars and stardom.

Longer, more demanding film stories fostered a greater aware-ness of leading roles and the people who played them. Producers identified players by name on the film posters that they sent to exhibitors. *Motion Picture Story Magazine* and its popular rival, *Photoplay,* began to feature articles on film personalities and to tell the life stories of the emergent crop of stars. The mythicizing began as fan magazine readers transferred the fantasy from screen to actor and then wanted to know the story behind the story—marriage, romance, career. Eventually the fan magazine developed into an industry of its own and produced many publications from which fans could choose.

Real-life transformations further inspired thoughts of movie stardom. How many young women found inspiration in the career of Mary Pickford? Pickford worked for D. W. Griffith at Biograph for five dollars a day in 1909 and became Carl Laemmle's "Little Mary" the following year at $175 a week. Screen appeal and public popularity brought her financial power in the competitive film world, and in 1913 Zukor paid her $20,000 a year to join his Famous Players company. She became "America's sweetheart," and he raised her salary to $2,000 a week. By 1916 she was making $500,000 a year.

If the public thought of Pickford as everyone's favorite sister, that characterization hardly applied to the tailor's daughter that Fox Film Corporation catapulted to star status. Thanks to Fox's publicity operation, Theodosia Goodman of Cincinnati became the alluring, seductive Theda Bara of the Arabian desert. Because she captivated audiences in forty pictures, her salary climbed from $75 to $4,000 per week in four years.

The incomparable Charlie Chaplin generated profits for studios far in excess of whatever they paid him. He earned $250 per week in 1913 at the Keystone studio and $1,250 at Essanay in 1915. He made his classic film, *The Tramp,* for Essanay, and the company tried to retain its moneymaker with a $500,000-a-year deal. Chaplin defected, however, and earned more than $600,000 from a rival studio.

Both motion pictures and the motion picture industry had undergone profound changes in a decade. With the feature film becoming standard fare, new companies in the United States rushed to join the Europeans, who dominated both the production and the market. As audiences demonstrated a willingness to pay higher admission fees to see the features, investors opened larger and more elaborate theaters. The first nickelodeon had counted 96 seats. New York's Strand opened in 1914 with 3,300.

Just as the evolution in film quality and length altered the viewing experience, new movie palaces elevated the status and pleasure of attending movies. Edward Wagenknecht saw *A Trip to the Moon* in a converted Chicago storefront, with movie posters pasted over the plate glass windows; at another nickelodeon the low ceiling obscured the top of the screen and cut off the picture. His "rather dismal" neighborhood theater, a converted dance hall, showed three reels of film and an illustrated song, and he gave his nickel to the proprietor, who "stationed himself at the end of a long, dingy corridor." On the other hand, the later Victoria had a marble-faced exterior, with cupids on top of the building and carved figures holding up the interior ceiling.[44]

Feature films, theatrical settings, and mass media recognition marked the social acceptance of the young entertainment sector, much as the formation of the MPPC had signaled the passage of the motion picture industry into the world of big business. Its roots firmly planted in twentieth-century soil, the branches had worked their way into the global consciousness.

Daredevil Aviators, Feature Films, and Combat

Quo Vadis? and the Astor Theatre might have stirred the awakened Rip Van Winkle's curiosity sufficiently to send him to another movie for confirmation of what he had seen. However, nothing could have prepared him for the newsreel that showed human beings in flying machines. Like most people who first encountered proof of human flight surrounded by the darkness of a movie house, he probably shed his disbelief and acquired the optimism and enthusiasm of an increasingly air-minded era.

Still cameras had recorded numerous failed attempts by ingenious experimenters in a variety of imaginative equipment, and most people had dismissed flying machines as foolish flops. Now, by a fortunate coincidence of timing, motion picture newsreels carried the excitement of early flight demonstrations to millions of people.

Motion picture audiences had learned to love the action of chase films, but in time the predictability of the pursuit by horses, autos, and trains had eclipsed their appeal. At the same time, the thrills and excitement of airplane drama—and in 1910 every flight carried the potential for unscripted excitement—penetrated the consciousness of motion picture producers. Words and still pictures had not adequately conveyed the achievements of pioneering pilots, but aviators who astounded onlookers with their speed and death-defying maneuvers made perfect subjects for the new medium.

J. Stuart Blackton, a principal in Brooklyn's Vitagraph Studios, learned to fly so that he could appear in the company's one-reel aerial thrillers, along with daredevils who learned their craft in the flying circuses of the day. In 1911, Henry H. "Hap" Arnold, who learned to fly at Orville Wright's Huffman Prairie teaching center and later enjoyed a brilliant career in military aviation, piloted a Wright Flyer in two short films, *The Military Scout* and *The Elopement*.[45]

Mack Sennett directed his genius for action comedy toward airplane antics and put the formidable talent of Mabel Normand to work in the movie farce, *A Dash through the Clouds*. At the same time, film companies began to turn out that staple of the movie program, the multiweek, cliff-hanging serial. With actors already seen jumping from trains onto horses, suspended over chasms, dangling from ropes, surviving natural disasters, and escaping from villains, the next step—hanging from airplanes—proved a logical move for film producers. The legendary Pearl White did not actually fly in the classic *Perils of Pauline* serial, but studio editing skills put her on screen with a Curtiss pusher biplane (flown by flight instructor William Henry Bleakly) in several episodes.[46]

The start of World War I offered a different sort of opportunity for exhibition pilots to exercise their penchant for thrills. They competed against enemy aviators in a deadly game. The government also trained new cadres of flyers, some of whom tested their courage in battle and returned to demonstrate learned combat tactics in aerial shows and in the movies.

The war also proved a watershed for the worldwide movie industry and fostered a relationship of mutual interest between the motion picture industry and U.S. foreign policy. In fact, the U.S. government enlisted the producers of fictional films in the national cause as it mobilized support for participation in the military conflict. Two years after the war began in Europe, a significant segment of the population continued to express reluctance to become entangled in Old World fights. Even among those who saw a need to help the Allies, many thought in terms of material support rather than commitment of troops.

To rally the citizens behind the war effort and maintain morale, President Woodrow Wilson inaugurated the Committee of Public Information (CPI) shortly after the country declared war against Germany. Journalist George Creel, who headed the committee, accepted his mandate: to mold public opinion through information, inspiration, and persuasion and to convince people that they were engaged in a noble struggle to defeat antidemocratic enemies.

Feature films represented only a small part of the overall effort, but Creel acknowledged that their ability to influence viewers could be critical. Movie theaters counted attendance in the millions each day, a captive audience for the committee. While a committee-supported film, *The Kaiser—The Beast of Berlin,* acted as a virtual call to arms, any boy-meets-girl story played out in the context of personal sacrifice and loyalty conveyed a subtler, but moving, appeal.

When the United States entered the war in 1917, the film industry served as a partner in persuasion. Films and industry personnel mobilized support for wartime policies, raised money, and boosted military enlistments. Fans had forged links with movie personalities, and the stars carried messages directly to audiences at theaters that also served many communities as a hall for public debate and discussion. On the screen Mary Pickford, still America's sweetheart, might appeal to wartime sensibilities with a film like *Johanna Enlists,* aimed directly at the war effort, and follow it with *Rebecca of Sunnybrook Farm* as an escape from the tensions of the period.[47]

In an ironic twist of motion picture history, the most powerful U.S. film to express a political attitude toward World War I may have been *The Birth of a Nation.* The 1915 Griffith film portrayed the futility of war just as Wilson declared the country's neutrality in the European conflict. Griffith cut between corpse-strewn battle-fields and civilian populations suffering at home. Women and chil-dren shed copious tears at the destructiveness of the conflicts and became refugees fleeing the acts of unrestrained generals. Ex-planatory titles used words like "bitter" and "useless." Costly and destructive, war bred hatred rather than solved problems. For Griffith, no glory attached itself to battle, and only newer and more terrible conflicts resulted.

As an experienced director of melodrama, practiced at engag-ing audiences in the action, Griffith mixed anger and nostalgia, home and battlefield, North and South, and brutality and civility into a politically charged film. He incorporated romantic love into the plot and effectively played the personal lives of its beaus against the background of familial and civic duty.

The Birth of a Nation proved itself both as an artistic milestone and as a politically provocative motion picture, although the film itself had nothing to do with the contentiousness that had plagued Europe for decades. Griffith inadvertently aided a contemporary pacifist movement while dealing with the consequences of a previ-ous war. The film's antiwar sentiments echoed the pleadings of a growing voice that spread its message on both sides of the Atlantic Ocean the very spring that the controversial film appeared on the screen.

Opposition to the colonialism and militarism apparent in the emergence of the United States as a world power had spawned a significant, politically active, pacifist movement in the country. The American Peace Society organized against the 1898 Spanish-American War and lobbied against U.S. repression of the Philip-pine independence forces. The Carnegie Endowment for Interna-tional Peace had also been at work since the turn of the century.

Suffrage leaders like Carrie Chapman Catt, Alice Paul, and Jeannette Rankin added their voices to the peace chorus, as well as progressive social reformers Lillian Wald and Jane Addams. Two weeks after Europe embarked on the path of war, 1,500 women marched on New York's Fifth Avenue in protest.

The Women's Peace Party organized at a convention in Washington, D.C., on January 10, 1915, and elected Jane Addams as president. Addams and some fifty like-minded women traveled to Europe three months later for an international meeting of suffragists at the Hague. The thousand or so attendees placed the peace issue at the top of their agenda and formed the International Committee of Women for Permanent Peace. That organization also named Jane Addams its president.[48]

By coincidence, Griffith began shooting *The Birth of a Nation* in California within a month of the June, 1914, assassination of the Austrian Archduke Ferdinand at Sarajevo. The film opened in Los Angeles in February, 1915, and the following month in New York, just as hundreds of millions of dollars in Allied orders for merchandise placed with American manufacturers began to alleviate business conditions that had been depressed since 1913. While businesses supplying war equipment to the Allies raked in profits, pacifists questioned the strength of the president's commitment to neutrality.

President Wilson watched Griffith's sensational saga at a private White House showing that spring of 1915. Surrounded by the public commotion swirling around the film, the Virginia-born president who shared its Southern sympathies no doubt recognized its emotional impact and persuasive potential. Did he evaluate the possibilities of the motion picture industry as a political ally at the time? After all, women made up the majority of moviegoers, and the film industry had openly set out to attract more middle-class women, the pool from which many political movements drew their support, even though they could not vote.

Once Congress declared America's entry into the war, the Committee of Public Information had to overcome a reluctance to send young men to war on foreign soil, and the government acknowledged the movie industry's unique and tremendous power as a propaganda tool in the national interest. In bestowing his blessing on the industry, President Wilson spoke of the motion picture's importance in the development of national life and in the dissemination of public intelligence. When Creel enlisted the talents of screenplay writers and directors in the cause, he relied on proven abilities. Griffith, in fact, chaired the War Cooperation Committee, the liaison between the film industry and the Committee of Public Information.[49]

The U.S. motion picture industry gained much more than patriotic satisfaction during the war years. In fact, it gained the world. The studios took advantage of the war-caused disruption in Europe to replace France and Italy as major film suppliers. Film exports increased during 1915 and 1916 as Europe's industries declined and wartime disruptions interrupted transportation. The CPI's Division of Films worked closely with the commercial film industry and, by taking American films into markets around the world, probably helped to establish the industry's reputation in some new areas.

French audiences, who could be expected to favor French products if they were available, turned to American films and film stars. Performers like Pearl White, Charlie Chaplin, and Douglas Fairbanks captured wide popular acclaim.[50]

After 1916 U.S. producers adopted new marketing strategies. They opened more subsidiary offices outside Europe, for one thing, and established a level of control that other producing countries would later find difficult to erode. With non-European markets as the key to expansion, U.S. firms signed agents and opened offices in new locales. In May, 1916, U.S. producers supplied only 12 percent of the films used in South America. The two South American firms that controlled most of the nineteen film exchanges had typically obtained cheap films in Europe and pressured the theaters to book them. Pathé dominated the Mexican market, as it had in the United States before 1910. When the U.S. government encouraged trade with South America, the film industry followed the trend southward.

In the second half of 1916 the danger of Atlantic crossings motivated one of the biggest South American film buyers to shift operations from London to New York. In October, a new agency opened in Rio de Janeiro and handled quality U.S. films. Some of the newer U.S. companies, like Famous Players-Lasky, Universal, Goldwyn, and Fox, expanded sales operations abroad. Companies opened export departments, increased publicity, and made headway around the world. Fox opened its first foreign branch outside North America in Rio de Janeiro and expanded its distribution efforts from there.

U.S. films gained popularity, while France, formerly the world's single biggest film producer, lost ground. South America and Australia became the two key non-European areas in the wartime U.S. takeover of the global film market, with U.S. firms composing 95 percent of Australian film imports during the war.[51]

Thus, the critical 1904–1914 decade shaped film technique and witnessed the formation of a global film industry. By 1917, the motion picture industry had established its credentials at the highest levels of government in Washington, D.C., and in the worldwide feature film market. The hugely successful U.S. production-distribution-exhibition complex that the Harvard Business School recognized in 1927 in reality rested on scarcely ten years of worldwide dominance and had benefited from World War I to gain that exalted position.

CHAPTER 4

Surmountable Contradictions

THE WAR, the movies, flying circuses, barnstormers, and racers—all fed the romantic aura that surrounded airplanes and pilots in the 1920s. At the same time, a dedicated phalanx of businesspeople, aviation enthusiasts, and public officials struggled to overcome images of airplanes falling from the sky and of pilots who stared death in the face every time they flew. To transform the public consciousness, airline promoters fought to plant a new image in people's minds, one of transport instead of sport, of practicality and profit instead of thrills.

Not surprisingly, World War I temporarily shifted the perception of aviators away from entertainment and notions of aviation away from utopian fantasies. War weary and scarred by loss, former combatants rejected exultant projections of peace and harmony through flight. Airplanes that crossed national boundaries had carried destruction instead of benevolence. Engineers and inventors had mounted guns on planes and turned an instrument of sport and camaraderie into an agent of death.

On the other hand, the demands of aerial combat had improved the performance of flying machines and the skills of the pilots who mastered them. Thousands of mechanics had learned how to maintain an assortment of aircraft, and some no doubt suggested ways to improve the parts. In other words, the war bequeathed a significant body of expertise in airplane design, operation, and maintenance to civilian societies, some of them still uncertain how they might beneficially employ the equipment and personnel.

For others, like France and Germany, already convinced of aviation's future, the end of the war marked the beginning of commercial airline development in Europe, based on intensive wartime research that improved airplane reliability. Moreover, the oversupply of aeronautical resources—aircraft manufacturers, airplanes, and trained personnel—encouraged commercial air transport as a way to absorb the valuable asset.

Entrepreneurs of entertainment also inherited a windfall of cheap surplus airplanes and footloose pilots trained in the acrobatics of aerial combat. Veteran fliers, accustomed to risk, performed stunts in the movies and at exhibitions, air meets, and flying circuses. They perpetuated the aura of danger that had surrounded prewar aviation, now enhanced by the dramatic heroism and tragic deaths of wartime fighter pilots.

An air-minded, postwar decade battled an obvious contradiction; that is, daredevil thrills contributed to high mortality rates and deterred the serious consideration of mass air travel. It had been easy to lure masses of people into a grandstand to watch an air show. Convincing even a small segment of the population to take a seat as a passenger on an airplane, however, required considerable persuasion to overcome fear, cost, and the competition of trains, ships, and autos.

All through the 1920s builders of commercial airlines labored to put the genies back into their bottles. They needed pilots who could safely fly passengers to their destinations, not thrill seekers, and planes fast and comfortable enough to make the rather expensive trip attractive. Although government officials and businesspeople began to devote considerable effort to the pursuit of aviation as a viable mode of transportation, the issue of air safety dogged their heels, despite technological improvements in motors and aircraft design.

Most people who applauded human flight remained quite

content to forgo the pleasure themselves (not unlike our own experience with space travel). More people had the means to exploit commercial entertainment in their leisure time, but even as wages improved and workers enjoyed paid vacations, pleasure travel to distant places remained a privilege of the wealthy.

The prohibitive cost most likely precluded even the more adventurous members of the middle and working sectors from indulging their fantasies. For example, Pan American Airways charged fifty dollars one-way for the short, ninety-mile flight from Key West to the popular Havana, Cuba, tourist center in 1928. The round-trip fare alone represented a month's salary for most would-be vacationers. Only a thousand pioneering passengers traveled that year on Pan American's first commercial venture into Latin America, but they represented a link in the transformation of aviation from entertainment to transportation. Moreover, advances in aeronautical science and engineering made it possible to fly from Miami to Rio de Janeiro, Brazil, five years later. When Pan American Airways tried to persuade North American tourists to fly all the way to Rio, across hundreds of miles of open sea, a movie supplied the motivational images.

Entertainment and Aerial Combat

Between 1903 and 1914 the airplane evolved, through determined experimentation and competition, into a relatively dependable flying machine. Aerodynamic research focused on the most efficient shapes and materials for elements of airplane structure. For example, designers showed a preference for one of two types of wing arrangement and argued the relative efficiency of the monoplane for lifting large loads and the biplane for speed. Engineers redesigned wings to improve the lift- (ability of the plane to become airborne) to-drag (wind resistance) ratio and to enhance speed and stability. Manufacturers experimented with various kinds of woods for the beams of the fuselage and the wing spars and ribs, looking for lighter, more durable materials. They covered the wings and fuselage with a good grade of cotton and painted it with a weather-resistant compound that shrank the fabric and produced a taut surface. Some manufacturers preferred stick controls, others wheels, but they continued to experiment.

Glenn Curtiss built a seaplane in 1911, substituting a pontoon for wheeled landing gear on a biplane. An amphibious plane followed, with retractable wheels and flotation gear. Then he designed the Curtiss flying boat, with a watertight fuselage like a motorboat hull. By the end of 1913 Curtiss had sold more than forty flying boats, and other manufacturers—including the Wright Company—turned out aircraft that were capable of landing on water.

A decade after the Wrights flew for twelve wobbly seconds, airplanes could climb to twenty thousand feet, travel more than 100 miles per hour, and cover 600 miles without stopping. Pilots had set speed records; engineers had standardized plane construction. As airplanes grew in power, size, reliability, and distance, more people learned to fly, and pilots flew longer, riskier routes.

The first airplane manufacturers—Wrights, Curtiss, Blériot, Farman, Santos-Dumont, Voisin, and others—demonstrated their planes' capabilities at sensational air meets. They organized exhibition teams, trained pilots to display their planes to potential buyers, and formed flying circuses. Charles "Daredevil" Hamilton, star of Glenn Curtiss's exhibition team, survived sixty-three crashes. Each incident served as an enticement for hundreds of paying customers to see whether he would survive the next, but the excitement and tension built no confidence in air safety. On the other hand, the stunts and speed that drew crowds to aviation shows prepared the way for fighter planes and pilots.

In 1911, William Randolph Hearst had offered $50,000 to any airman who could fly across the United States in thirty days. Former motorcycle racer Calbraith P. Rodgers answered the challenge, and people cheered his audacity. Rodgers survived five major crashes, numerous mishaps and an almost total rebuilding of his plane at sixty-nine stops along the way, but the crossing took too long. Hearst kept his prize money, even though twenty thousand inspired spectators awaited Rodgers historic landing in Pasadena, California, on November 5, 1911.

Seven thousand more fans acclaimed Rodgers' courage when

he appeared at an exhibition in Long Beach four months later. The aviator acknowledged the crowd and headed out over the water, much as Louis Paulhan had done two years earlier at the Dominguez Air Meet. What must have gone through his thoughts as he dived to scatter a flock of seagulls riding the ocean's swells? He certainly did not consider that one bird might rise up in surprise and try to fly between the rudder and the tail, disabling the plane. What did the spectators think as Rodgers crashed into the waves? His death was not an unexpected occurrence in the world of contests and exhibitions, where fancy flying thrilled the crowds, but certainly did not encourage them to fly.

Daring stunt fliers increasingly maneuvered their planes to test the limits of acrobatic moves. Race and stunt pilots who flew planes for the entertainment of the spectators dived toward the ground and pulled up—undoubtedly what Rodgers had intended. They even flew upside down. Aircraft manufacturers improved their planes to reach the next level of speed and showmanship demanded by the pilots.

On September 21, 1913, Adolphe Pégoud performed some new tricks for journalists and spectators at a field near Buc, France. Pégoud worked as a test pilot for Louis Blériot, and he put the Blériot product through a heart-stopping performance of climbs and dives, falls and recoveries, to learn the plane's limits. At one point Pégoud flew straight, climbed steeply upward, slid backward tail first, recovered, dived head first, and leveled off again. He also flew forward, dived headlong downward, turned upside down, and rolled over into an upright position. But Pégoud's looping-the-loop maneuver, perhaps the most memorable of the day, sent him into a downward dive and a big circle, flying both upright and upside down.

Lincoln Beachey, who had learned to fly from Glenn Curtiss and had joined Curtiss's exhibition fliers, sent shivers through audiences with his vertical dives and upside-down flying. Like other daredevil pilots who pushed mechanics and designers to alter flying machines to accommodate ever-riskier aerobatics, Beachey ordered a specially built Curtiss biplane so that he could add loops to his performance.

Within six months of Pégoud's sensational aerial maneuver, some fifty other European and American aviators successfully performed the loop. Without anticipating their future application, stunt pilots developed the techniques to perform the climbs, turns, and dives necessary for evasive action in combat flying. They also encouraged the necessary advances in airplane design and performance that transformed airplanes from military reconnaissance instruments to full enemy engagement.[1]

In fact, European powers engaged in an arms build-up that included the development of new and more maneuverable airplanes. Better engines and stronger airframes supported pilots on longer, riskier flights. By 1912 the French Army counted some 250 planes, including the sleek, powerful Deperdussin and the Nieuport, a faster version of the Blériot. More than 350 French pilots had been certified to fly. They flew from Paris to Warsaw and from eastern France to Cairo. In the most daring feat of all, Roland Garros flew 512 miles nonstop from southern France across the Mediterranean Sea to the African shore.

The British established the Royal Flying Corps that same year with more than fifty pilots and held trials for suitable planes. Geoffrey de Havilland, who had designed double-decker buses before he turned to aviation, produced a speedy biplane, the precursor of a fleet of World War I fighters. T. O. M. Sopwith designed a highly maneuverable plane in 1913, the Tabloid Scout. Later the Sopwith Camel earned its reputation as one of the war's most effective fighters. The Germans borrowed from French designers like Henry Farman and others for its Albotros, but relied more on the planes of Dutchman Anthony Fokker, whose single-seat monoplane blazed through the skies on the western front.

Igor Sikorsky, a graduate of the Russian naval academy, designed and built a four-engine biplane in 1913, with an enclosed passenger compartment, pantry, toilet, and interior heating. The Russian Air Service ordered ten of Sikorsky's planes and then seventy more after the war started.

In contrast to the Europeans, the U.S. Army and Navy experimented a little with bomb dropping and shipboard takeoffs and landings but spent little money on military aviation. The U.S. Navy acquired its first airplanes in 1911. The Wright Company manufactured one, and Curtiss sold them one land plane and one amphibian. By contract, the Wright and Curtiss companies trained three navy men to be pilots. Six years later, with the country ready to enter the war, the navy had only twenty-one planes and barely enough pilots and mechanics to keep them in the air. The government quickly ordered planes and opened pilot schools but could not expect combat-readiness for many months.

Many observers and critics in aviation circles had chided the United States for falling behind Europe. Governments in France, Great Britain, Italy, Germany, and Russia provided some funding for science and engineering laboratories to advance aeronautical knowledge, while the U.S. government failed to act on the request of the National Academy of Sciences to develop an aeronautical laboratory. Congress legislated, and President Woodrow Wilson signed, a bill to create a National Advisory Committee for Aeronautics, but the committee remained advisory.[2] The country continued to depend on the dozen or so plane manufacturers in the private sector for aircraft design enhancement.

Despite the inadequacy of public expenditures, government action inadvertently accelerated airplane development with important repercussions for U.S. wartime aviation. In February, 1914, the U.S. Army banned pusher airplanes because engines mounted behind the pilot had been crushing fliers during crash landings. In response, Glenn Curtiss built a plane with a front-mounted engine and called it Model N. After a visit to England's Sopwith Aviation Company he designed Model J, an improved biplane, and then combined the best features of Models J and N into the JN-1. Continued upgrades evolved into the JN-4D, or "Jenny," the standard model that served as one of the backbones of World War I aviation—and as a postwar stunt flyer.

The warring countries of Europe had airplanes in 1914, but not all of the military leaders agreed on how—or even whether—they should use them. In a cavalry age many of the veteran leaders feared that the planes might frighten the horses.

In past military engagements balloonists had gathered information on enemy emplacements and movements. As early as

1911, however, the exhibition troupe of John and Alfred Moisant had demonstrated the feasibility of pilot reconnaissance as they watched the Mexican revolution unfolding. The Moisants flew their plane over the battlefield at Juárez, across the Rio Grande from El Paso, Texas, and viewed the action from the air. That same year Italy sent airborne scouting missions over the enemy's lines in Libya when they engaged Turkey in a colonial war in North Africa. In another glimpse at the future of aerial warfare, an Italian pilot carried grenades in a leather bag aboard his plane and tossed them at a Turkish encampment.

Planes designed for speed and stunts had less to offer for reconnaissance work than a slow, stable craft that permitted the observer sufficient time to look around and operate a camera. Daredevils need not apply. Although vulnerable to enemy action, the first World War I reconnaissance observers did not carry guns. While in flight, they sometimes threw stones and pieces of brick or chain at each other but usually returned safely to their bases.

The distribution of rifles to pilot-observer teams changed the airplane's mission. The observer served as a gunner, but the narrow confines of the cockpit impeded the gunner's capacity to load and take aim. Even with the development of more powerful planes that accommodated the mounting of a machine gun, shooting at moving targets through wires, struts, and whirring propeller blades endangered one's own plane as much as the enemy's.

Imagination and engineering augmented the death-dealing capacity of both the weaponry and the planes, at which point the acrobatic maneuvers of stunt flying proved their combat value.

First, French pilot Roland Garros, who had earned accolades with record-breaking flights before the war, devised a method of protecting the propeller while deflecting ricocheting bullets. The shield permitted the pilot to fly at opposing airplanes, while more than 90 percent of the bullets passed the propeller blades to destroy an enemy aircraft.

Garros's shields gave French pilots only a short-lived advantage, however. Forced by engine trouble to land behind German lines, Garros tried to burn his plane, as instructed, to keep it from the enemy. However, the wet plane would not burn, and the Germans took it to Berlin to examine the propeller shields. They took Garros to a prison camp.

Thus, the Germans learned the secret of the French pilots' air success. With the aid of Dutch airplane designer Anthony Fokker, who was working in Germany, they devised a mechanism that timed firing to the propeller movement. This interrupter device fostered a dangerous shooting war in the air as well as on the ground. Skillful, daring fighter pilots became the romantic heroes of the war, as fighter planes pursued observation planes and bombers and fought each other.[3]

The World War I "ace," characterized by the number of enemy planes the pilot had destroyed, watched the surroundings to spot enemy planes, maneuvered the plane, and handled the gun, all at great speed. High mortality rates (fighter pilots on the Western front averaged three weeks before being shot down) imparted a de served reputation for personal courage and sacrifice that carried into postwar life and into movie versions of the war.[4]

In August, 1914, Americans distanced themselves from Old World political conflicts and counted on the physical and psychological separation that the Atlantic Ocean provided to enforce their declaration of neutrality. In fact, the United States had little to contribute in terms of military aviation experience, particularly in the systematic training and deployment of forces. Actual combat operations consisted of naval action during the Mexican Revolution, when five Curtiss flying boats, hastily loaded onto U.S. ships, deployed in Vera Cruz harbor to look for mines and conduct sporadic reconnaissance flights. The army's limited experience in aerial scouting resulted from involvement in the same revolution, accompanying General John Pershing's forces into northern Mexico in pursuit of Pancho Villa.

Hardly prepared for aerial combat, the U.S. Army Signal Corps, whose aviation section carried the responsibility for U.S. military aviation, counted around 250 planes in April, 1917, mostly trainers, and scarcely more than a thousand enlisted personnel. U.S. manufacturers had built perhaps a thousand planes since the Wright brothers' 1903 flight. When the French government asked that 4,500 planes, 5,000 pilots, and 50,000 mechanics be sent to Europe before the end of 1918, Congress financed the necessary military expansion program.

The demands of war quickly accelerated the country's capacity for airplane construction. By November 11, 1918, the aviation section had more than 20,000 planes. Curtiss and various subcontractors had produced nearly 6,000 JN-4Ds for the U.S. government and 2,000 for export to other governments. Before the government stopped production, factories turned out another 2,000 after Armistice Day, and surplus Jennies flooded the market when the war ended.[5]

The wartime demand for pilots also developed the pool of trained personnel available for postwar commercial aviation. By 1918 most people associated pilots with the image of heroic fliers fighting war battles, but some military aviators returned to civilian life determined to prove the viability of commercial aircraft industries and air transport. Others became barnstormers or stunt fliers and put the Curtiss JN-4Ds or the Standard J-1s to peacetime use in the entertainment business. The Standard Aircraft Company's two-seater trainer had encountered engine problems during the war. Phased out of production, the company nevertheless had hundreds of the high-performing planes in storage when the war ended. When refitted with Hispano-Suiza engines, they proved more costly than the Jenny but gained popularity among the barnstormers.[6]

Surplus two-seater Jennies sold for as little as four hundred dollars, and most military fliers had trained on them. The plane's characteristic sixty-mile-per-hour speed and stability lent themselves to the plane changes and wing walking that stunt fliers performed above the heads of amazed crowds. The "flying gypsies" gave many people their first glimpse of an airplane at exhibitions and county fairs or even in some farmer's pasture. The itinerant fliers paid their way with one-dollar-a-minute airplane rides for the more adventurous spectators. They also flew their planes for movie producers who saw exciting prospects—and profits—in filmed, airplane-based adventures.

Entertainers crisscrossed the country and performed death-defying aerial acts for a public relieved to have the war over, appreciative of military aviators' bravery and their contributions to ending the war, happy to enjoy the live or filmed shows, but understandably unconvinced that they could rely on the airplane as an alternative means of commercial transportation. In fact, the high mortality rate among the picturesque and popular stunt fliers generated a fear of aviation that took powerful forces to overcome.

Press agent and promoter William H. Pickens moved into the center ring of the flying circus. Pickens had managed the career of Lincoln Beachey, America's first barnstorming hero, when Beachey flew for the Curtiss exhibition team before the war. He found three veteran army fliers, Ormer Locklear, Milton Elliott, and Shirley J. Short, signed them to contracts, purchased three planes, and sent the trio on a national tour. On May 16, 1919, in Uniontown, Pennsylvania, they opened a sensational routine of plane changes and aerobatics. The exuberant crowd at the Uniontown Speedway no doubt gasped as the stunt fliers hung from the landing gear, dangled from the wing bottoms, crawled along the fuselage, and waved at the spectators from the tail of the plane.

A penchant for reckless flying also opened up potentially lucrative, but unquestionably hazardous, careers in motion pictures for a handful of professional daredevil fliers. Universal Film Company made one of the first postwar aerial adventures. Company president Carl Laemmle, the independent movie exhibitor who had fought the Edison trust, marked its significance in the evolution of silent movies when he called it *The Great Air Robbery*. Instead of bandits who robbed a train, as in Porter's 1903 classic film, a band of air pirates tried to hijack a plane of the newly formed U.S. Airmail Service.

To replace stagecoach and train robbers with their airmail counterparts required production transitions, but few script writing challenges. Standard formula plots worked well in aerial adventure films, and a positive box office response encouraged their production. Movie studios paired stunt flying and crime stories; they pitted thieves, smugglers, hijackers, and secret agents against courageous, duty-bound pilots and substituted planes for horses or automobiles in the chase scenes.

Hollywood's Stunt Fliers

Universal's Laemmle signed William Pickens's barnstormer Ormer Locklear for his first aviation movie scarcely two months after Pickens had put the war veteran into a stunt plane. The Texas-born Locklear had trained as a military aviator but had never left the United States. Instead, November, 1918, found him in Texas, teaching others to fly—aviators who also never had experienced the tension of battle. Perhaps the stories told by war-tested veterans spurred Locklear to take exceptional risks in the air.

Laemmle, the film company boss, paid Pickens, the flying-circus promoter, for all of Locklear's fair dates for a month in order to obtain the services of the pilot-performer he wanted. It was worth the money. In a dazzling display of midair plane changes, an airplane-to-car transfer and a car-to-plane transfer (by way of a dropped ladder), Locklear thwarted the intentions of lawless gangsters who tried to steal gold shipments.

In a mutually beneficial conjunction of aviation and motion picture interests, Universal shot *The Great Air Robbery* at one of the three Hollywood-area airfields owned by famed movie director Cecil B. DeMille. Too old in 1917 to gain acceptance as a student pilot with the U.S. Army, DeMille had learned to fly anyway and obtained a pilot's license. His company, Mercury Aviation, sold rides and taught flying. In addition, DeMille provided planes, pilots, and movie locations for Hollywood productions.

Camera operators loaded their equipment aboard a second plane to catch the fast-paced action and inaugurated the highly specialized field of aerial cinematography. For close-up shots of Locklear in the plane, later edited into the action, Universal Film Company employees erected a platform and hoisted an airplane to the top. While grips rocked the plane, a camera operator stood alongside and shot the required footage.[7]

At the time Laemmle made *The Great Air Robbery,* about seven private airfields were located in the Los Angeles basin. Most depended either on exhibition flying to generate income or on several dozen motion picture studios that operated in the area. A number of film producers used Venice Airport, for example. The

B. H. DeLay Aircraft Company bought the field in 1919 and furnished both aircraft and a location for a number of silent films in the 1920s. Venice Airport also became the hangout for an informal group of exhibition and movie pilots who took passengers for rides above Venice Beach in the slow times between pictures.[8]

By 1921, several film companies had produced action films that centered on danger and risk-loving pilots. As might be expected, however, Hollywood also witnessed several deaths among the aviators, including that of Ormer Locklear.

Potential and actual destruction of life and property provided the peril and excitement that kept viewers returning to the theaters for aerial action dramas. In *The Skywayman,* made for Fox, Locklear played a World War I ace who had lost his memory as the result of combat wounds. His girlfriend devised a series of shocks to recapture his forgotten past—a simple story line designed to exploit Locklear's willingness to risk his life in daring film sequences. At one point his plane crashed into a church steeple. In another plot turn, Locklear climbed down from the plane by way of a rope ladder, fought with villains on top of a speeding train, climbed back up, and flew off. In the last scene, filmed at night, the plane spun toward earth. Crossed searchlight beams picked up the plane as it crashed. Locklear and Milton Elliott both died in the stunt, substantiating the widespread belief that the airplane remained a hazardous novelty. Undeterred by the appalling loss of life, the studio advertised the crash footage in its promotion of the film.[9]

Whether the script called for aerial battles, carrying the mail, or barnstorming, Hollywood's fictional pilot-heroes made sacrifices, established loyal friendships, attracted beautiful women, and demonstrated a capacity for leadership. On the screen or off, however, fearlessness often slid into the realm of recklessness. Breathtaking feats of flying—in aging flying machines—called attention to risk instead of to the increased reliability of newer planes and to mortality rather than utility. Barnstormers died in even greater numbers than movie stunt fliers. By 1923, when 85 people died and 126 suffered injuries in 179 accidents, pilots, aircraft builders, and editorial writers decried the escalating recklessness of daredevil aviators.[10]

Prompted by complaints, the federal government acknowledged the need for some authority to rein in the mavericks. Congress passed the Air Commerce Act of 1926, which set out air traffic regulations and guidelines for aircraft registration, inspection, and certification. With the goal of lowering the death rates, the legislation also required that pilots obtain licenses. By the middle of the 1920s, many of the military-trained stunt fliers took jobs testing planes for aircraft manufacturers or flying airmail routes.

Almost as if a struggle existed for the soul of aviation, former combat pilot John Monk Saunders approached movie producer Jesse L. Lasky with a war story focused on aerial combat, just as the aeronautics branch of the U.S. Commerce Department acted on behalf of safety in the civilian skies. Lasky liked Saunders's story idea, and Famous Players-Lasky Company (later Paramount Pictures) obtained the cooperation of the U.S. War Department—and $16 million worth of equipment—to make the movie *Wings*.

Lasky assigned William A. Wellman, World War I veteran combat flier, to direct the picture, which took more than a year to make. A romantic-triangle plot fulfilled audience expectations and provided context and continuity for battle scenes and wartime relationships: Three likable young people—two male and one female—live in a typical small town. Both young men like the girl, but she is smitten by the one who thinks of her only as a pal.

The war interrupts the potential romantic competition. The men take pilot training together, become good friends, go to the front, and risk their lives in spectacular aerial battles (actually filmed over Texas using multiple planes with photographers who operated cameras placed on gun mounts). Combat veteran Wellman knew the tension and confusion he wanted to portray, and he created a startling sense of battlefront participation for the audience. He also captured the camaraderie and intense loyalty that developed among the pilots, as well as the enmity that motivated the fiercest combat against Germany.

The most emotional plot turns and anxieties hinge on the two aviators' bond. When one is shot down behind enemy lines and presumed dead, the other's anger and grief propel him to destroy any representation of the enemy. However, his pal has been

The popularity of aviation action films fostered new careers for a small group of aerial cinematographers. *Courtesy of the San Diego Aerospace Museum.*

wounded, not killed, and has stolen an enemy plane to make his escape. Clearly, the most tension-filled aerial fight takes place between the friends. One kills the other, giving rise to an emotional farewell and aching despair. The survivor, who is the preferred partner of the girl next door, returns home a hero, asks forgiveness of his friend's parents, and recognizes his true love.

The $2 million film proved an enormous success, acclaimed for its awesome aerial photography and its tribute to military aviators. The film opened in New York in August, 1927, just months after the city feted Charles A. Lindbergh for his trans-Atlantic flight. In a year filled with aviation heroism, *Wings* won the first Academy of Motion Picture Arts and Sciences award for best picture. Ironically, Lindbergh, who had bought his first plane with $500 earned as a parachute jumper and wing walker and later became an airmail pilot, also served as a model of reliable flying when he flew alone from New York to Paris.[11]

Another ambitious young man of the air and motion picture

era, born too late to have been a film pioneer or a combat pilot—but an aviator and moviemaker nonetheless—set out to make a better aerial warfare movie. Howard Hughes Jr., born in Houston, Texas, to affluent parents who died before he was twenty years old, inherited the Hughes Tool Company. The business made equipment for a booming oil industry and provided him a comfortable income.

The now-legendary Hughes owned his own airplane factory and film studio when he was twenty-one years old. Although his first films caused little stir, he aspired to a loftier status in the industry. The competitive Hughes determined to achieve recognition and took advantage of the public's enchantment with aviation heroes.

The success of *Wings* inspired Hughes to film an even more compelling aerial drama. In *Hell's Angels* he submerged a weak romantic triangle in a powerful combat film. Two young brothers who fly for the British Royal Flying Corps become involved with the same girl. One loves her; the other merely has a fling. The girl herself prefers to keep her independence. The brothers, ordered to fly a mission against the Germans, are shot down and captured. The Germans promise to send them back, however, if they will reveal information about British plans. One battle-scarred brother cracks and almost blurts out the time of the British attack, forcing the other to shoot him. He dies in his brother's arms, and then the Germans execute the survivor. Few people went to see *Hell's Angels* for its potboiler love triangle, but audiences all over the world flocked to see scenes of Zeppelin warfare and aerial dogfights.

Hughes rounded up the necessary equipment and rebuilt planes as needed, laying out hundreds of thousands of dollars. Then he moved the Sopwiths, Fokkers, a Gotha bomber, and various other planes to open-space locations around Hollywood. He hired more than a hundred aviators and as many mechanics. Twenty-six aerial photographers took turns in ten camera planes. Hughes choreographed the air combat sequences and directed the filming and the actions of the pilots from his own open-cockpit plane, waving his arms to signal his intentions. At one point he flew so close to the ground to demonstrate to the "combat" pilots the effect he wanted that he crashed his plane. Fortunately, the film crew pulled him from the wreckage in time to save his life.

Hughes took three years to shoot the film, during which time other filmmakers had switched from silent film to sound. Understandably, he had to replace his Norwegian-speaking leading lady. He also wrote new material, hired a director for the dialogue sequences, and added a sound track for the aerial combat footage. Then he edited 2.5 million feet of film into a reasonable length for exhibition. *Hell's Angels* premiered in 1930 at Grauman's Chinese Theater and played for thirteen weeks. The single-minded novice filmmaker spent almost $4 million on *Hell's Angels,* twice the cost of *Wings,* and lost more than $1.5 million of his investment.

Howard Hughes made a great film. A convincingly suspenseful Zeppelin raid over London gripped the viewers with its powerful realism. Airplane pilots performed midair "collisions" and forced landings as well as aerial gunfights. Dozens of mechanics kept the planes in the air. Hughes's commitment to authenticity brought memorable action to the screen but danger to the actors. Sadly, Hughes's devotion to recreating the horror and heroism of a pilot's war mission cost four men their lives in the making of the film.[12]

Perhaps it was emblematic that Howard Hughes battled against himself, demonstrating on film the danger of flying, while trying to carve a niche for himself in commercial aviation. By the time Hughes's war film appeared on the screen in 1930, the focus of aviation had shifted to transportation.

Resolving the Contradictions

Barnstormers and stunt pilots introduced airplanes to millions of spectators as a thrilling form of entertainment. Public officials recognized a more serious responsibility: "to bear the brunt of the burden in the development of aeronautics in the United States until such time as the utility of aircraft for transportation has proven itself beyond doubt to the people of this country."[13]

The drive to possess the fastest planes, encouraged in the early teens by prizes and prewar air meets, continued into the twenties, with engineers and pilots pushing the limits of aircraft and engine design. The war had challenged utopian visions of a peaceful, progressive aerial age and a world without national boundaries, a world in which air transport fostered universal understanding. Instead, technological advances had encouraged national pride and competition. People whom the experience of modern warfare had touched acknowledged profound changes in their world, but they were changes that brought uncertainty. Airplanes could take off, fly, and land again, but to what purpose? Military needs had driven combatants to design and build sturdier, faster planes that depended on more powerful engines, and aerial exploits drew public attention to the airplanes' capabilities.

If aerobatics attracted its share of war-trained pilots, the desire to set new speed records lured others. As before the war, when speedsters competed for fame and prizes, aeronautical design and engines improved to satisfy the new demands. Aviators who had pushed planes above 100 miles per hour before the war began chasing a 200-mph threshold in the early twenties. Encouraged by new trophies and prizes—the Pulitzer Cup, the Schneider Trophy for seaplanes, the National Air Races, and the Bendix Trophy in the United States, for example—aviators traveled faster and farther.

General "Billy" Mitchell set a world speed record of almost 223 miles per hour in a Curtiss Racer in October, 1922. Lieutenant James Doolittle set a seaplane speed record of 245 miles an hour in a Curtiss machine in 1925.

> During the next several years, spectacular flights over the poles and across the oceans and the continents helped to stir national and international interest in airplanes. By 1929 the National Air Races at Cleveland were important events, for air racing was a big business.[14]

Because of the movies and the alarming accident rate—due as much to poorly maintained equipment as to risk-taking pilots—many Americans in the 1920s viewed aviators first in terms of military rashness and then as civilian speedsters and daredevils. Hollywood, as much as the military, focused public attention on aerial warfare. Military expenditures on aeronautics in fact had re-treated, since few top-ranking officers pressured the government to develop an air force.

Meanwhile, the aviation industry, composed of private-sector entrepreneurs interested in airplane manufacture and air trans-port, struggled to attract financial support. Air-minded in the extreme, they strained to alleviate the safety concerns of potential investors and passengers. They recognized the need to replace ro-mantic attitudes toward pilots with an acceptance of the practical uses of the plane and to replace an expressed enthusiasm for air-planes with the foundations for aviation development. Because convenience and time had to outweigh the high cost of airfares, several of the earliest airline efforts marketed tourism and leisure-connected air travel to affluent customers.

Postwar Civil Air Transport

Air transport developed more rapidly in Europe than in the United States. Blériot's flight across the English Channel and intercity races had directed attitudes toward the practical uses of airplanes before the war. From 1914 to 1918, combatants had equipped numerous airfields to accommodate observation planes, bombers, and fighters, which they quickly converted to commer-cial aviation and experimentation sites after the war. Within a year of the armistice Aircraft Transport and Travel started the world's first scheduled international air service—between London and Paris. Although numerous other airlines followed in the early 1920s, many of them failed after short periods of operation.

European governments had included aviation infrastructure in their wartime budgets. Later they granted subsidies to civilian airlines as a way to maintain both a cadre of trained pilots with ex-perience in flying load-carrying planes and a number of large planes that could be commissioned for military use. To encourage the development of air transport they also demonstrated a willing-ness to provide either aircraft and fuel or exemptions from various taxes. These subsidies allowed European airlines to offer fares at prices too low for sound business practices; they also recognized

Europe's reality. That is, excellent train and water transportation existed in a geographically limited area, where overnight ground trips could already take passengers to many desired destinations.

Even before the war ended, Germany and Italy had started regularly scheduled domestic air transportation and planned for postwar international services in Europe. With demobilization, they diverted planes to civilian use and put pilots and mechanics to work in a fledgling air transport industry. Although the Treaty of Versailles temporarily deprived Germany of military aviation and turned the country's airfields into scrap heaps of military airplanes sawed in half, the Allies had neither forbidden the Germans to establish commercial airlines nor ordered the destruction of civilian planes. By 1922, Germany returned to aircraft manufacture and developed civilian air transportation as a market for its aircraft industry. Aero Lloyd, A.G., a large transport combine, integrated two leading shipping companies, an important engineering company, and several aircraft builders.

With government subsidies in the form of free fuel, Aero Lloyd operated fifteen air routes in 1922, including one to Moscow. Junkers Airlines provided seasonal summer services as a way to promote the sale of the company's five-passenger planes. The government established Luft Hansa, a quasipublic airline, in 1925, expanded its domestic and European network of airlines, and exported the products of its aircraft factories.

By 1922, France was operating eight airlines; England, three; and Germany, two. Affluent travelers, willing to take risks to avoid border-crossing hassles, found an option in air travel. U.S. citizens composed a substantial percentage of cross-channel flights during the peak summer travel season. Because of its speed and relative independence of barrier-creating topography, air transportation also offered substantial advantages for business transactions and communications.

Europe's rapidly developing international air transport posed a challenge for international relations that countries met from a national-interest perspective. The 1919 International Convention for Air Navigation established the principle of national sovereignty in airspace. Moreover, aircraft—like ships—assumed a national-registry identity; that is, they "carried" the country's flag on the new routes between Paris and Brussels or London or between Vienna (Austria) and Padua (Italy).

France began with a network of international air services in Europe, established air routes to colonies in Indo-China and West Africa, and by 1927 moved on to South America (partly by sea). The French government heavily subsidized its air transport lines and encouraged the purchase and maintenance of as many aircraft as possible. The Netherlands extended its network in Europe in the 1920s and then opened an Amsterdam-Batavia route to its Indonesian possessions in 1930. Italy confined its routes to Europe until its political expansion into East Africa. By 1936, the Italians had inaugurated regular air service to that area.

Understandably, Great Britain's long-distance air transport efforts in the 1920s ran in two directions: southeast toward South Asia and Australia and south to Africa.[15] In addition to the advantages of timely transfer of documents and personnel, air service played an important role in developing resources—like minerals—in remote regions where terrain was a barrier.

To demonstrate route feasibility, two brothers, Ross and Keith Smith, took off from London in a converted World War I Vickers Company bomber in November, 1919. Their destination, Darwin, Australia, lay 11,000 miles away, and they needed to reach that city in their homeland in fewer than thirty days. The Australian government had offered $46,000 (10,000 pounds) to the first fliers who completed such a journey. Along the way they had stopped at Delhi, Rangoon (Yangon), Bangkok, and Batavia (Djakarta), all important centers of European colonial commerce. Just sixteen years after the Wright brothers flight, the Smith brothers landed triumphantly in Darwin with a little more than two days to spare.

Unlike Great Britain, France, Italy, and the Netherlands, Germany had no colonies to serve as bases for an international air transport service after World War I. Colonial possessions offered access to the considerable ground support required for transnational air travel—landing facilities, radio markers, beacons, weather reporting, and radio guidance. Nevertheless, Germany built its domestic and European routes. Chapter 5 covers the German move into South America.

On the other side of the world, in Asia, Japan confined its air transport to domestic and colonial routes until 1932, when airplanes followed the Japanese army into Manchuria and China.[16]

The United States took longer than the European countries to develop domestic and international air connections, more because of the absence of direct government financial support than because of a failure to recognize the potential importance of civilian air transport.

Like other economic sectors, domestic aviation had fallen on hard times after a brief period of war-generated prosperity. In 1923, five years after the war had ended, the country's leading commercial and financial center—New York City—still depended on Long Island's Mitchell Field, forty-five minutes away by train, for air service. Boston opened an airport in September of that year.

As secretary of commerce in President Warren G. Harding's administration, Herbert Hoover had defined the relationship between the government and a struggling commercial aviation sector as one of assistance rather than sponsorship. That is, industrial leaders should work through voluntary associations to overcome technical limitations and to improve market conditions, while the public sector provided and maintained an infrastructure for transportation (e.g., navigational aids, airports, and airport lighting) and disseminated publicity, technical data, and relevant economic information necessary for better management decisions and service.

In an industry marked by bitter patent battles between the Wrights and Glenn Curtiss, Hoover's model of a voluntary trade association had not developed. Manufacturers demonstrated little willingness to work with transport sector entrepreneurs. The Aero Club of America enjoyed wide membership but suffered from internal divisions. An Aeronautical Chamber of Commerce acted as the voice of the manufacturers, while the broader-based National Aeronautic Association promoted an appreciation of aviation without a financial stake in the industry.

While Hoover urged the industry to organize to promote its views, he strongly opposed direct subsidies. In his concept of an "associative state," the government played a secondary role to industry leadership. To encourage investment from a reluctant financial sector, the secretary willingly publicized air transportation as a way to boost business efficiency and enhance profits. To help aircraft manufacturers build a market for their planes, the Department of Commerce appropriately suggested practical uses such as crop dusting and aerial photography. If Americans associated aviation with daredevil entertainment, Hoover would use the power of the Department of Commerce to regulate civilian flying in an effort to mitigate the alarming accident rate. However, European-style subsidies did not fit the Republican model.[17]

Moreover, when Hoover took office, the aviation world still considered dirigibles as competition for airplanes in commercial transportation.

Before its service in World War I, the motorized, rigid Zeppelin airship had operated commercially as passenger transportation between Berlin and the resort city of Baden-Baden. Since the dirigible could be directed with certainty to a destination, promoters viewed the airship as competition for trains and steamships for carrying goods and passengers.

In fact, in 1923, German engineers investigated the feasibility of a commercial airship line between New York and Chicago for a group of investors that included Marshall Field, William Wrigley Jr., and Franklin D. Roosevelt. The plan called for a helium-filled airship to carry fifty passengers on an overnight journey between the two cities.

Thousands of onlookers craned their necks to watch the silver ZR-I dirigible cross over Newark, New Brunswick, and Camden in New Jersey, Philadelphia, and New York on a data-collection journey intended for commercial purposes. On an uneventful trip from its home port at Lakehurst, New Jersey, to the 1923 aviation meet at St. Louis (the site of airship thrills at the 1904 World's Fair) and back, the ZR-I reported fuel costs in a commercially favorable range for transporting goods.[18]

When the Zeppelin's inventor died in 1917, Hugo Eckener

took over the Friedrichshafen works. Eckener defended the airship's peaceful purpose as an inexpensive and reliable transportation mode over long distances. Although the Treaty of Versailles prohibited Germany's construction of airships, Eckener's arguments held sway. He persuaded the American government to accept a new ship, the LZ 126, and revived the Friedrichshafen Zeppelin plant. The Goodyear Tire and Rubber Company purchased the rights to manufacture Zeppelin dirigibles at its Akron, Ohio, plant in 1923, and in 1926 Eckener flew the LZ 126 on the first nonstop transatlantic crossing by dirigible. Its landing at Lakehurst generated tremendous excitement.

Eckener began work on the LZ 127 when the Allies lifted restrictions on German commercial aviation. At more than 700 feet long and 100 feet high, the largest airship ever built flew across the Atlantic Ocean to New York City and back in October, 1928, and around the world in August, 1929, establishing its reputation for safety and reliability.[19]

Thus, dirigible manufacturers laid claim to long-distance, transoceanic, commercial viability while airplane manufacturers struggled to find markets. Encouraged by activity in Europe, airline operators continued to promote the idea of airplane safety. The first nonstop, cross-continental flight landed at Rockwell Field, San Diego, twenty-six hours and fifty minutes after it had left the east coast. Thousands of people met the aviators as they landed, giving a boost to those who battled on behalf of commercial airplane service.

Transportation professionals compared the reluctant acceptance of airplane transport to the cool reception given the steam locomotive in the nineteenth century, when many individuals had questioned the superiority of the railroad over the stagecoach and canal boat. Similarly, twentieth-century investors recognized the importance of speed but doubted the airplane's economic feasibility. Could air transport produce sufficient revenue to cover the costs?

The federal government had initiated regular airmail service between New York City and Washington, D.C., in May, 1918, six months before the Armistice, with six U.S. Army Air Service Curtiss training planes and six military pilots to fly the planes back and forth. By the time the mail traveled by ground transportation to the airport on Long Island, then two and one-half hours by plane, and from the airport in Washington to the post office, it could almost have gone the entire way by train.

After several months of joint operation with the War Department, the U.S. Post Office Department assumed full responsibility for the highly experimental program. When the war ended, the post office increased its supply of planes from among the available surplus, hired pilots from among the newly trained fliers, and added new routes—Cleveland to Chicago and New York to Cleveland. By September, 1920, service had reached San Francisco, and the operation became an increasingly important element of business communication. For example, the banking industry moved checks and other financial instruments more quickly from city to city by air than by train. In 1924 the government pronounced transcontinental airmail service a success.

Coast-to-coast airmail had its limitations, however. Forced by the lack of navigational aids to land at dusk, pilots turned the mail over to railroad personnel, who carried it until dawn, when another pilot carried the cargo forward. This air-rail combination took seventy-eight hours but saved a full day over rail-only service.

The business community urged the post office to speed up the service with round-the-clock flights. A system of flashing beacons, flood-lighted main terminals, and intermediate emergency fields contributed to a reliable day and night operation that was completed by 1924. Many localities established airfields to accommodate the mail service, but the entire country had slightly more than a thousand such facilities in the 1920s.[20]

Not surprisingly, railroad interests took a dim view of government competition in mail transportation. Railroads carried mail under contract from the government, they argued, and airmail service should operate under the same conditions. Pennsylvania Congressman Clyde Kelly embraced their cause and, encouraged by prospective airline operators, pressed for the enabling legislation and the necessary appropriations for payment. The Kelly Air Mail Act received Congress's approval in February, 1925, and President Calvin Coolidge signed the act.

Implementation of the Kelly Air Mail Act advanced the infrastructure for commercial aviation. The United States had built no network of operational airfields and associated ground organizations comparable to Europe's during the war and had demonstrated no inclination to establish and fund airlines. Now public funds built airfields and paid for ground support, aircraft maintenance services, and a training school for pilots.

U.S. Post Office Department contracts settled the question of government assistance to the aviation industry, that is, contracts to private-sector competitors, but not European-style subsidies. The contracts proved a major boost to airline entrepreneurs, as the post office transferred airmail operations to private companies in 1926 and 1927.

Unintentionally, the government also supplied the movie industry with a new variation on a popular genre; air pirates tried to hijack airmail shipments, and the heroes chased the villains in the air as well as on land.

The Appeal of Airlines

As a factor in commercial competition, airplanes doubtless offered advantages to the business interests of one company—or one nation—over another, particularly in the rapid transmission of orders, shipping documents, credit advices, specifications, blueprints, estimates, samples, catalogs, and so on. Furthermore, salespersons, engineers, and executives could investigate the economic potential of isolated areas, develop closer contacts with traders, cultivate sales, solve problems, and even carry replacement parts for machinery.

Moreover, in international relations, prestige accrued to operators of well-run airlines. The perception of technical expertise followed the planes, pilots, mechanics, and radio operators to their destinations. Airlines that carried a nation's flag to a foreign country served a purpose not unlike the national navy; they represented a forward posture and a symbolic stature.

A number of prospective airline companies in fact opened offices in the country's larger cities after the war and hired young people to sell stock in anticipation of multimillion-dollar, commercial, air transport businesses. However, the promised high returns on investment failed to materialize. By 1921, enthusiasm was waning, the promoters had fled, and the public scorned commercial aviation as a profitable investment.[21]

In the wake of demonstrated private-sector skepticism, U.S. authorities tried a different approach. In 1922, the U.S. Army Air Service undertook the operation of a model airline to demonstrate the feasibility of such an enterprise and to rekindle investor interest.

The U.S. Army Air Service organized its demonstration airline on a route between Washington, D.C., and Dayton, Ohio, chosen in part because pilots had to cross the Allegheny Mountains. The six-month experiment, from June, 1922, to March, 1923, was intended to convince commercial organizations to enter the field of aviation by determining operational costs and developing planes and equipment for bad-weather flights. Out of 132 flights during the experiment, operational reports recorded nine forced landings because of adverse weather and six due to engine failure.[22]

If anything, the government's model airline preached to a choir of believers, aviators who wanted to fly but lacked financial backers. Passenger transport had taken its first tentative steps even before the war, when the St. Petersburg-Tampa Airboat Line demonstrated the safety of its twenty-minute flight. The war intervened, but a line between Seattle and Victoria, British Columbia, opened in March, 1919. Aero Limited used war-surplus flying boats for a series of flights between New York and Atlantic City, New Jersey, in August, 1919. American Trans Oceanic Company operated winter-season, round-trip services from Miami, Florida, to South Bimini in the Bahamas for two years, charging $25 for the relatively short flight.

By the 1920s, the Caribbean had become a playground where wealthy North Americans escaped the freezing temperatures, snow, and ice of winter. The islands had attracted foreign visitors for some time, with steamships the major mode of transport before the introduction of airlines and after. Advances in tropical medicine and sanitation in the early twentieth century had cleared the way for travelers to adopt a favorable view of the previously disease-plagued tropics. The therapeutic benefits of sunshine and warm weather accompanied winter voyages to the Caribbean, while restorative mineral springs refocused the image of the islands from pestilential to healthful.[23]

U.S. prosperity, wartime limitations on trans-Atlantic shipping, and promotional efforts fostered the acceptance of Caribbean destinations as convenient tourist resorts. Aeromarine Airways operated flying boats between Key West, Florida, and Havana, Cuba, beginning in 1920 — just after the start of Prohibition. During the winter season, from December 15 to April 15, thirsty passengers could take Aeromarine's daily 10:30 A.M. flight, with return flights from Havana at 3:30 P.M.

Aeromarine carried nearly 1,100 passengers on the ninety-minute trip in 1920, almost 7,000 in 1921, and more than 9,000 in 1922. The airline expanded its services to include Bimini and Nassau in the winter and moved its airplanes north for summer-season flights out of New York to Atlantic City and New England. Although Aeromarine flew more than 700,000 passenger miles in 1921 and 1922 without an accident, insurance costs constituted thirty percent of the company's operating expenses. Fuel, labor costs, overhead, maintenance, and inspection charges gobbled up the remainder of the revenue, and Aeromarine suspended operations in 1924.[24]

Compared to the air service established for golfers between New York and Newport, Rhode Island, Aeromarine enjoyed a remarkable longevity record. The *Graylark* made its first eighty-minute trip across Long Island Sound in early July, 1923, with convenient Friday and Saturday departure times and Sunday night and Monday morning returns. The *Graylark* and two sister ships each carried four passengers in the comfortable cabin of the world's fastest commercial flying boat for a one-way fare of thirty dollars. However, little more than a month after the inaugural flight, the air service announced the discontinuance of its passenger service. After a crash killed a prominent New Yorker, the company confined its loads to mail and newspapers.[25]

In 1922, the Security Trust and Savings Bank of Los Angeles analyzed the costs for round-trip air service between Los Angeles and San Francisco and estimated a ticket price of almost $100 in order to make a profit. The potential success for such an airline depended on the willingness of businesspeople, lawyers, doctors, entertainers, and travelers to value the shortened travel time—five hours compared to more than thirteen for the train—over the expense. The report's conclusion accepted confidence in safety as a major problem for potential airlines, along with price:

> While the patronage of tourists and sightseers could not be relied upon as the primary support of any such service, it is possible that a moderate number from this class would avail themselves of the opportunity to explore the country by air. If popular timidity of aerial flight is dispelled by ample demonstration that airplanes can fly over long distances, regularly without accident, an aerial service established at Los Angeles should have advantages for attracting tourists possessed by few other cities.[26]

Even with the safest of planes and a sufficient pool of financially secure passengers, profitability could not be guaranteed. For one thing, weather conditions added to concerns about both service and operating costs. The study estimated that fog might prevent planes from leaving Los Angeles or landing in San Francisco nearly 50 or 60 days of the year and strong headwinds or heavy rain clouds at either end of the line might detain flights on an additional 20 or 30 days. Without speed as a premium, why pay the additional cost?

Pleasure travelers took a chance on Claude Ryan's Los Angeles to San Diego airline. Tourists kept the young West Coast aircraft pioneer in business long enough to make aviation history as the designer of Charles Lindbergh's *Spirit of St. Louis*. Born in Parsons, Kansas, in 1898, Tuboe Claude Ryan moved with his family to southern California, which became a center of aviation activity during World War I. Glenn Curtiss also moved to San Diego and trained pilots at Rockwell Field, under the command of Major Henry H. (Hap) Arnold. The field on North Coronado Island became the primary flight school for the aviation branch of the U.S. Army Signal Corps, and Curtiss JN-4D trainers flew in and out of Rockwell. By 1920, the wartime Jenny had been replaced by the more powerful Hispano-Suiza Jenny, and the army maintained another flight-training school at March Field, near Riverside, California.

Ryan had learned to fly during the war and tried to earn his living as a pilot when it ended. He flew over towns in southern California and dropped leaflets advertising flights for $2.50 or $5.00, depending on the length of time aloft. The novelty produced a meager income, but when San Diego emerged as a tourist center in the 1920s, aerial sightseeing became popular, and Ryan offered visitors an opportunity to "See San Diego from the Air."

Prohibition contributed to the popularity of the San Diego-Tijuana area. Tour buses brought visitors from Los Angeles, and Ryan gave cooperative bus drivers a commission when they brought their passengers to his airfield. At five dollars per air passenger and two or three flights per bus, the Ryan Flying Company earned a steady income from tourist excursions.[27]

With an eye to expanding his business, Ryan adapted planes to carry more passengers, hired pilots, and offered forty-dollar, round-trip charter flights to and from Los Angeles. The charter business evolved into a scheduled airline. Planes left Los Angeles at 10 A.M. for the hour-and-one-half flight to San Diego and left San Diego at 4 P.M. Hollywood celebrities who liked to cross the border into Mexico helped launch the airline in March, 1925. However, at $14.50 each way, the novelty of flying attracted only a limited, affluent clientele and proved too expensive for regular transportation. Nevertheless, the airline lasted for a year and a half.[28]

Claude Ryan and his partner, B. F. Mahoney, also operated a Douglas Cloudster, the first airplane built by Douglas Aircraft Company in Santa Monica. On February 21, 1921, the Cloudster had become "the first aircraft to get off the ground carrying weight

San Diego's tourist attractions (and those of Tijuana, Mexico) could not produce enough fares or sufficient profits to keep the Ryan Airline in business in
the 1920s. *Courtesy of Greg Young Publishing.*

exceeding its own."[29] Ryan and Mahoney converted the large two-seat, wood and fabric, single-engine biplane into a cabin-type, twelve-passenger plane and used it to fly prospective customers from Los Angeles to San Clemente Island every Sunday. A real estate developer gave the passengers lunch and a sales talk and tried to sell a few lots.

Ryan's company made its reputation with the airplane that Lindbergh flew across the Atlantic, not with the Cloudster charters or its failed airline. But the airline's Los Angeles terminal lured a young man into the field whose name also left its mark on aviation lore. Seventeen-year-old Douglas Corrigan encountered his first airplane one day in 1925. A cloud of dust attracted his attention as a plane took off from a field—literally, a place where the brush had been cleared and a shed erected to protect a spare engine—near Exposition Boulevard.

On the following Sunday morning Corrigan went to take a closer look. The teenager stared at the biplane that stood in the northern terminus of the Los Angeles-San Diego airline. The converted wartime plane carried four passengers in a cabin up front, with space for the pilot in an open cockpit in the back.

A Curtiss JN-4D trainer parked behind the one-room office by the road attracted Corrigan's attention, as did the notice that the company offered fifteen-minute flying lessons for five dollars. Corrigan followed his destiny and flew his first solo flight in March, 1926. Not long after, Ryan and Mahoney discontinued the airline and closed the Los Angeles field. By the time Corrigan arrived in San Diego in February, 1927, Ryan had sold his share of the business to Mahoney, but Ryan Flying Company hired him to work as a mechanic at the San Diego field.

Mahoney planned to start another air service, and Corrigan and two other employees drove across the Mexican border to retrieve the Douglas Cloudster, which the company needed for the airline. The plane had been contracted out to a Mexican beer company after a rainstorm had washed out the road between Tijuana on the coast and the inland border town of Mexicali. Because of Prohibition, the beer company could not use U.S. roads to transport their product between the two towns and had hired a pilot and the heavy-load-bearing Cloudster to haul barrels of beer for two to three months until they could use the Mexican road again.

Corrigan worked as an airplane mechanic for several years before earning a transport pilot's license in 1929, and he piloted commercial aircraft for a number of years before his famous journey. On July 8, 1938, Corrigan set off from Long Beach for a nonstop flight to New York. On the return he left New York and became disoriented in the fog that blanketed the east coast. According to the experienced pilot's account, his compass did not function properly, and he mistakenly headed east rather than west, not realizing his error until it was too late to turn back. He landed safely in Ireland instead of California and returned to the United States a celebrity for his nonstop New York-Dublin flight. "Wrong-way Corrigan" stuck to his story despite considerable skepticism about his real intentions.[30]

Charles Lindbergh's Flight across the Atlantic Ocean

Douglas Corrigan had arrived in San Diego on February 2, 1927; on February 3, Ryan Airlines received a telegram inquiring about the company's ability to construct an airplane capable of flying nonstop between New York and Paris.

Ryan's aviation interests had included aircraft design and production as well as transportation. In 1926, he and Mahoney turned out the Ryan M-1, a monoplane aimed at the market created by the newly privatized U.S. airmail service. By 1924, planes carried the mail from coast to coast. They flew mostly during daylight hours and through arcs of light provided by airfields across level plains and prairies at night. The service had become a rigorous training ground for aspiring young pilots. Only the really good aviators survived the high mortality rates of the airmail service's early days.

Twenty-five-year-old Charles A. Lindbergh flew the mail on the St. Louis-Chicago route. He had learned to fly at the age of twenty, had flown for the U.S. Air Service, and in 1924 had earned the rank of lieutenant. He had tried his hand at barnstorming, had performed parachute jumps and wing walking, but had never flown more than five hundred miles at a stretch. As chief pilot on the St. Louis-Chicago route in 1926, Lindbergh had heard of Ryan's plane and about New York hotelman Raymond Orteig's $25,000 prize to the first aviator to fly nonstop between New York and France. By 1927, a number of fliers, including five groups of Frenchmen, had announced intentions to enter the competition. Lindbergh decided to attempt the trans-Atlantic crossing himself.

Although the trend in airplane design favored the efficient monoplane, many skittish pilots still questioned its safety. As had other aircraft designers before him, Ryan had sent his M-1 model around the country to perform at air meets to prove that the wings would stay on. In 1926, he built the *Bluebird,* a monoplane with an enclosed cabin, forerunner of Lindbergh's *Spirit of St. Louis.*

Among other Americans preparing for the competition, Clarence D. Chamberlain and Bert Acosta, a one-time auto racer, stayed aloft for more than fifty hours in an endurance test flight. They sipped soup, downed sandwiches, and took catnaps on a mattress in their monoplane equipped with a Wright engine. They covered more than 4,000 miles before they finally set the plane down—400 more miles than the distance between Manhattan and Paris.

Polar explorers Richard Byrd, Floyd Bennett, and George O. Noville also flew a test run in their new Fokker trimotor. They landed successfully, but the plane suddenly somersaulted as they taxied along the field. Noville injured his pelvis, Bennett suffered a cracked thigh, and Byrd, a broken wrist, eliminating the trio from contention.

French war aces Charles Eugene Jules Marie Nungesser and François Coli inspected their biplane, *White Bird,* at the Paris airport and headed for New York, expecting to reach their destination in thirty-five hours. They carried sufficient gasoline for forty hours of flight time. However, no ship sighted the plane once it passed the Irish coast, and the world waited in vain for its arrival in New York City. Nungesser and Coli apparently crashed unseen into the ocean.

With capable competitors who also longed to be the first aviators to fly across the Atlantic and collect the prize money, time loomed as a critical factor for Lindbergh and his financial backers in St. Louis. When Ryan Air Company responded favorably to Lindbergh's inquiries about the cost of the airplane and delivery time, he took a train to San Diego.

The self-assured young aviator arrived on February 23 and assessed the company into whose hands he would place his fate:

> The Ryan Airlines factory is an old, dilapidated building near the waterfront. I feel conspicuous driving up to it in a taxicab. A couple of loafers stare at me as I pay my fare. There's no flying field, no hangar, no sound of engines warming up, and the unmistakable smell of dead fish from a nearby cannery mixes with the odor of dope from drying wings.[31]

If the physical plant disappointed, the character of the workers he met put him at ease. Donald Hall, the engineer assigned to redesign the company's plane to suit Lindbergh's needs for the long-distance solo flight, especially inspired his confidence.

In mid-May, Lindbergh flew his new Ryan monoplane from San Diego to St. Louis and then on to Curtiss Field, Long Island. He put 451 gallons of gasoline into the plane's tanks but took very little "fuel" for himself—four sandwiches, two canteens of water, and emergency army rations. He took off about 8 A.M. on May 20, flew the great circle route to Paris, completed the trip in thirty-three hours and twenty-nine minutes, and landed on May 22, Paris time—just three months after that inauspicious introduction to the Ryan-Mahoney airplane factory.

Lindbergh's flight signaled a watershed in commercial aviation. The excitement that followed boosted the prospects of airline companies to attract financial backers. Only eight U.S. passenger airlines (as opposed to airmail service) operated in the mid-1920s: New York to Boston, Chicago to San Francisco, Chicago to Minneapolis, Los Angeles to Portland, Los Angeles to Salt Lake City, Los Angeles to San Diego, Detroit to Grand Rapids, Michigan, and Cheyenne, Wyoming, to Pueblo, Colorado. The planes traveled about three times as fast as equivalent train service, and the airlines charged three times the price.

Two decades after the *California Arrow* dirigible captivated spectators at the St. Louis Fair, aviation hero Charles A. Lindbergh returned to the same fairground and thrilled thousands of eyewitnesses as he flew the *Spirit of St. Louis* over Art Hill. *Courtesy of the Missouri Historical Society.*

Even for the potential airline passengers who could afford the fare, the concern for air safety still played a major role in the decision to fly. The Aeronautical Chamber of Commerce of America, which existed to promote commercial aviation, acknowledged the widespread skepticism that plagued the industry. In the chamber's 1924 *Aircraft Yearbook,* the editors had denounced barnstorming as a "romance-drenched activity of questionable value" that influenced public attitudes and hindered those who promoted safe aircraft operation.[32]

Despite the highly visible toll in planes and pilots on both sides of the Atlantic in preparation for the transoceanic challenge, Lindbergh's success became a symbol not just of courage but also of safety advances in airplane design. His personal transformation from barnstormer to airmail pilot to pioneer of oceanic air travel

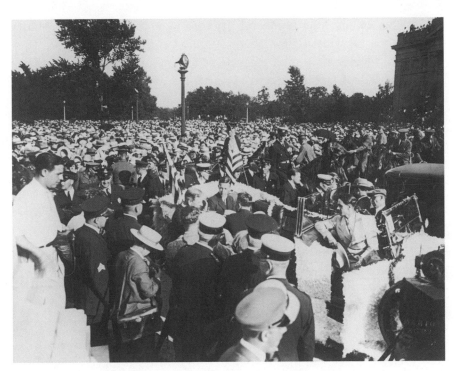

Lindbergh's solo transatlantic flight earned worldwide acclaim, nowhere more enthusiastic than in St. Louis, where the throngs in Forest Park made him their hometown hero. *Courtesy of the Missouri Historical Society.*

exemplified the goals of aviation's business sector. Within months of Lindbergh's triumphant return to the United States, a company announced a New York-Chicago route, connecting with the Chicago-San Francisco flight for a cross-country, thirty-two-hour flight costing four hundred dollars.

Safety—and the image of safety—critically affected the growth potential of commercial aviation. Between July 20 and October 23, 1927, Lindbergh joined a group of prominent aviators who participated in air tours to promote the building of airports and educational programs in the schools. Lindbergh's tour touched down in all forty-eight states. Of the millions who applauded his courage, at least some must have moved closer to a personal acceptance of air travel. Still, consistent reliability remained elusive for airplane engineers and designers. On October 24, just after Lindbergh's promotional tour ended, Ruth Elder took off with copilot George Haldeman to fly the Atlantic. They had to abandon their plane some 360 miles from the Azores. The crew of a Dutch tanker bound for Rotterdam rescued the pilots, but not the airplane.

Back to the Drawing Board

As much as anything else, the neglect of basic aeronautical research and technology impeded airline development. Prizes offered for airplane speed, distance, and endurance had commonly propelled advances in airplane design. But the 1927 Daniel Guggenheim International Safe Aircraft Competition focused manufacturers' attention on the vital necessity of ensuring safety as well as swiftness in air travel.

At the time, only ninety-six students in all of the United States studied for degrees in aeronautics. As an indication of the deplorable state of the industry, while twenty-seven companies entered machines in the competition, only two entries passed the preliminary tests and moved on to the stringent safety trials. The two-year-long contest finally named a Curtiss product—the Tanager—as the safest entry, but the real importance of the competition lay in the opportunity for engineers to develop design requirements to ensure safety.[33]

To advance aeronautical studies in the United States, few families—or individuals—had done as much as the Guggenheims, a name more often associated with mining than aviation. Daniel Guggenheim had developed an interest in airplanes during World War I, but his son, Harry, born into the aviation age in 1890, became the flier in the family.

Daniel's grandfather Simon had immigrated to the United States from Switzerland in 1848. Meyer Guggenheim, Simon's son and Daniel's father, had peddled household goods in eastern Pennsylvania alongside his enterprising father. They made a decent living, but Meyer turned from selling to manufacturing and then diversified into imports and mining. Colorado silver made Meyer a millionaire. With four sons in the mining business, M. Guggenheim's Sons expanded into smelting and mining explorations in other locations. The company became Guggenheim Brothers in 1916.

Harry Guggenheim enrolled in Yale's Sheffield Scientific School in 1907 to study mining but dropped out the next year and moved to Mexico, where the family had a smelting operation. Two years later the Mexican revolution threatened the Guggenheims' interests, and Harry enrolled at Pembroke College, in Cambridge, England. He studied economics and political science under John Maynard Keynes and minored in chemistry. When he earned his degree in 1913, he had already developed an interest in flying.

Harry began flying lessons in Florida early in 1917 and completed training with a naval reserve group in June, 1917. Commissioned a lieutenant, junior grade, he left for Europe and flew heavy bombers during the war. By the time of Harry's military discharge in 1921, his father had established the Daniel Guggenheim Fund for the Promotion of Aeronautics. In 1922, only five schools trained aeronautical engineers, and only the University of Michigan and the Massachusetts Institute of Technology granted degrees in the field. With Harry's encouragement, Daniel Guggenheim endowed an aeronautics school at New York University.

The Guggenheims created another fund in 1926, this one intended to awaken the American public to the advantages of air travel. The fund provided grants to promote aeronautical education, foster research, assist in the development of commercial aircraft, and encourage businesses to consider various uses for airplanes. After Lindbergh's flight, the fund also established a model airline between San Francisco and Los Angeles to promote commercial passenger-carrying air transportion.[34]

In the third decade after Kitty Hawk, a fledgling aviation industry found an ally in the Guggenheim family and a rallying point in Charles Lindbergh's spectacular solo flight. The late 1920s saw the construction of more than two thousand airports in the United States and a growing confidence in aviation that attracted capital to aircraft manufacture and airline operation. People called the investment influx the "Lindbergh boom."

Some observers characterized Lindbergh's achievement as an

end to the pioneering period in aviation. The Air Commerce Act of 1926 institutionalized the government's role in aviation with the new post of U.S. Assistant Secretary of Commerce for Aviation, responsible for regulating the industry and establishing airways. Airmail contracts served as an indirect financial subsidy to new airlines, and government authorities accepted responsibility for safety issues.

Despite the fact that no significant U.S. market for air transport existed besides the post office, several large holding companies emerged in the late 1920s. United Aircraft and Transport controlled several aircraft manufacturing companies and a few airmail carriers that composed United Air Lines. North American Aviation brought together several air transport companies, including Eastern and National. The Aviation Corporation combined eleven small companies into American Airlines, while the Aviation Corporation of the Americas operated Pan American Airways.[35] Airmail contracts nurtured the industry until a record of safety and time saving could be established.

The pivotal year that ushered in the new aviation era also marked an upheaval in the movie industry. Audience acceptance of the first talking motion picture, *The Jazz Singer,* changed the world of film production and exhibition and led directly to the incorporation of RKO-Radio Pictures. A closer examination of Pan American Airways, the first U.S. international airline, demonstrates the significance of *Flying Down to Rio* as a key to understanding critical alterations in attitudes toward air travel and the influence of movies on social behavior.

CHAPTER 5

Lines in the Sky

A S FASCINATION with flight passed from the mythical and fantastic to the mechanical, the more technically minded humans who had devised and mastered flying machines quickly turned to the domination of the air itself. To poets, the open and boundless blue sky still inspired thoughts of gods and the freedom of birds. Public officials and businesspeople, on the other hand, beheld a contested commodity subject to national sovereignty. This transformation of consciousness signaled a new reality in an aerial age. The air, essential to life itself and free to breathe, acquired a commercial character with a significance for flight. Governments plotted lines in the sky and awarded control of these "skyways" to airline companies.

Airline companies gained access to assigned routes between landing points and conquered the domain of the elements. The companies lifted passengers above the earth and extended the experience of flight to thousands—and then millions—of people. Their destinations might fulfill the dreams of a lifetime.

Of all the companies that flew those pathways through the sky in the 1920s and 1930s, Pan American Airways laid claim to the most geographically extensive continuous route network. Pan

American operated the largest seaplane-based network in the world, covering more than twenty thousand miles. By the end of 1931, the airline was carrying passengers from country to country on an aerial circuit of the Caribbean and South America—Miami to Cuba to Central America, down the west coast of South America to Chile, across the Andes to Uruguay and Argentina—or across hundreds of miles of open Caribbean waters to Colombia and along the east coast of South America to Rio de Janeiro.

Pan American's ambitions served as a testing ground to establish the feasibility of long-distance, overwater air transportation. The airline had flown its first passengers from Key West to Havana in 1928, a mere ninety miles. Its expansion to South America had thrust the company into the position of an "Atlantic laboratory," that is, improving the capabilities and performance of aircraft and refining the procedures necessary to inaugurate passenger travel across the Atlantic and Pacific Oceans.

The blueprint for an international air transport and tourist industry that connected the Americas to Europe and Asia still lay on Pan Am's drawing board in 1933, when the movie *Flying Down to Rio* consciously tempted audiences to fly Pan American Airways to one of the most exciting cities in South America. Even before Pan American's planes reached Rio and years before the airline crossed the Atlantic Ocean, Germany had lured affluent American steamship passengers with packaged air tours of Europe aboard the state-supported Lufthansa airline. For $399—affordable to only the most affluent travelers in the Depression year of 1931—tourists could leave their ships at the ports of Bremen or Hamburg and travel by air to Berlin, Dresden, Prague, Vienna, Munich, Zurich, Paris, and London in twelve days, with first-class accommodations and stopovers for sightseeing.[1]

Although millions of people had incorporated movies into their lives by 1933, the era of mass international tourism remained at least a generation away. Pan American Airways sold the romance as well as the convenience of flying to wary travelers of the 1930s. RKO's advertisements boasted of glittering dances set on the wings of giant airplanes. In the context of music and romance, the filmmakers demonstrated the speed and safety of flying, the dependability of Pan American's operation, and the rewards of contact with a foreign culture.

Airlines and Blood Lines

Nobody in the United States really knew how to run an airline in the early 1920s. The business ventures generally ended in financial ruin. To inaugurate an airline required a true believer, a missionary of aviation. How did one determine operating expenses in such a new endeavor? Who composed the market? Few investors had the courage to commit their money to such an obviously risky undertaking. Most start-ups lasted only a short time and failed because of high expenses and a lack of customers.

Despite the odds, a circle of wealthy friends pushed their airline ambitions along the uncharted path, bonded to each other by school ties and a love of flying. Pan American Airways benefited from the talents and passion of this group of first-generation aviators. More businessmen than barnstormers, these Ivy Leaguers from well-established patrician families tied their personal futures to the country's preeminence in air travel. Most of them had learned to fly before or during World War I. They came to maturity with the airplane and shared the camaraderie of wartime air service and the confidence gained from access to financial resources and the upper echelons of government. Willing to help make the rules for an aviation industry, they were not always careful to follow them.

Juan T. Trippe, the person most closely identified with Pan American Airways throughout its history, occupied the center of the airline's inner circle. Trippe could trace his family's history in Maryland back to the 1630s. He grew up in the privileged world of bankers and old money, went to prep schools, and entered Yale in 1917. As an impressionable schoolboy, Trippe had witnessed— along with thousands of other awed spectators— Wilbur Wright's 1909 flight around the Statue of Liberty. When the United States engaged in "a war to end war," service as a flier appealed to him more than his studies. He left school during his freshman year and volunteered for military service.

Trippe gained acceptance to Navy flight training, soloed for the first time in a Jenny biplane, and qualified as a fighter pilot. However, the war ended before he shipped out for France, and he returned to Yale in February, 1919. Not surprisingly, he joined the Yale Aero Club, a recreational flying organization, and, as secretary of the Intercollegiate Flying Association, which sponsored air races, Trippe copiloted Yale's 1920 winning entry. Upon graduation, he went to work as a Wall Street bond salesman but quit two years later and committed himself to a career in aviation. His entry into air transport taught him a powerful lesson about the risks in the field. He bought seven war-surplus navy seaplanes, started a flying service, and lost his investment in two years.

Trippe recovered quickly, as dedicated to flying as ever. His friends from Yale and various exclusive social clubs, all members of the eastern elite of transportation, financial, and industrial wealth, shared his commitment and his ambitions.

Juan Trippe's long friendship with C. V. (Sonny) Whitney began at Yale, although Sonny's wealth and social status far outclassed Trippe's. Grandson and namesake of Cornelius Vanderbilt II, considered the wealthiest man in the United States, Whitney also claimed forebears who had arrived in America early in the seventeenth century. Grandfather William Collins Whitney enjoyed more heritage than money until he married Flora Payne. With the help of his wealthy father-in-law, William gained the franchise for New York City's Metropolitan Railway in the 1880s. Appointed Secretary of the Navy, William and Flora moved to Washington, D.C., and joined the capital's social circles. C. V.'s father, Harry Payne Whitney, Yale 1894, loved polo and worked with his father in business, which included interests in the Guggenheim mining operations. Harry married Gertrude Vanderbilt in 1896, and C. V. was their offspring.

C. V. attended Groton and graduated—a less-than-stellar student—in 1917. He entered Yale in the fall and, like Trippe, left his studies to train as a military pilot. Whitney enlisted as an aviation cadet in the U.S. Army Signal Corps. He took flight training in Texas, but, also like Trippe, the war ended as he was about to leave for France to serve with a squadron of pursuit pilots. Discharged as a captain in the reserves, he returned to Yale. As might be expected of a flier prevented from fulfilling his military ambition, Whitney also joined Yale's Aero Club.

After graduation, Whitney's father put him to work in the family's silver-mining company in Comstock, Nevada, and then in New York's financial sector. Sonny Whitney served as an usher at Juan Trippe's wedding and joined him in several early airline ventures. Revenue from the profitable sale of his holdings in a construction company in Mexico's Yaqui Valley went into the foundation of Pan American Airways, and Sonny remained a major financial backer. When C. V. Whitney served as Pan American's board chairman in the 1930s, he brought cousin John Hay (Jock) Whitney, a patron of the arts, theater, and the movies, onto the board of directors.[2]

John Adams Hambleton, the third man who spearheaded Pan American's push into international aviation, traced his Maryland-based family back nine generations. His family and the Trippes had been in business together earlier in their shared history. Hambleton attended the elite St. Paul's School in Concord, New Hampshire, started Harvard in 1916, and left in February, 1917, to train as a pilot in the U.S. Army Signal Corps' aviation section. He left for France in October, served as a flight commander, was wounded in combat, and returned to the United States a decorated officer.

After the war Hambleton worked in the family banking business and kept his hand in aviation through a company that invested in aviation-related enterprises. In 1924, he married the daughter of the president of a railroad company. David K. E. Bruce, a boyhood friend from another wealthy old southern family, served as an usher. Bruce had married the daughter of Treasury Secretary Andrew Mellon. The connection proved particularly advantageous when Trippe and Hambleton pursued air routes for Pan American.[3]

Frederick Trubee Davison shared the indignation of his peers at the actions of German forces. September of 1914 found him at Yale. Davison's father was an executive with the Red Cross and a partner at J. P. Morgan and Company. During summer vacation in 1915, Trubee volunteered for duty with the American Ambulance

Field Service in France, where a family friend introduced him to several members of the Lafayette Escadrille—the squadron of American volunteers flying in the service of France.

The Yale campus must have seemed extraordinarily removed from Europe's travail that fall. After the summer's tumult, Davison's classes interested him less than discussions of the war and aerial combat. He and several classmates organized the Yale Aero Club in 1916, and their parents paid for a couple of seaplanes and flight instruction at the Trans-Oceanic Company base in Port Washington, Long Island. A few weeks later the Yale fliers joined U.S. Naval Reserve exercises held nearby. However, when the trainees tried to enlist in the navy's aviation service early in 1917, they were denied admission.

Trubee's father intervened. He cornered Jack Towers, commander of the Naval Reserve Flying Corps and told him about the group from Yale. Towers took the so-called Yale Aviation Unit to Washington, D.C., where Assistant Secretary of the Navy Franklin D. Roosevelt enlisted them in the U.S. Naval Reserve. David Ingalls, who was only seventeen—one year under the requirement age—could not join up with his roommate, Trubee Davison.[4]

Twenty-eight young fliers of the Yale Aero Club's First Unit paid for their own flying lessons at Palm Beach, Florida, for two months and then went to Huntington, Long Island, to continue training. By that time the United States had entered the war, and the former Yale students of the naval reserve were ordered to active duty.

Trubee Davison never flew in combat. Injuries from a seaplane crash off Long Island ended his dream of participation in the aerial war, but he later served as Assistant Secretary of War for Air Operations under Calvin Coolidge, and President Coolidge appointed him to the 1927 Interdepartmental Committee on Aviation, designed to assess the development of commercial aviation to Central and South America. Trippe, of course, would call on fellow Yale alumnus Davison to assist his Washington lobbying efforts on behalf of Pan American Airways.

Davison's First Yale Aviation Unit was followed by a second

and a third. David Ingalls continued to fly with the Aero Club until he reached enlistment age and then embarked for war duty with the third unit. He learned to fly the Sopwith Camel, one of the Allies' fastest and most maneuverable planes. Ingalls shot down five enemy planes, and his record as a World War I ace earned him the British Distinguished Flying Cross and the U.S. Navy's Distinguished Service Medal. The French made him a member of their Legion of Honor.[5]

David Ingalls, a nephew of former president William Howard Taft, became Assistant Secretary of War for the navy under President Coolidge.

Francis White, son of another old-line Maryland family, entered Yale a few years ahead of Trippe, Whitney, Davison, and Ingalls. He graduated in 1913, before hostilities broke out in Europe. As did many members of the eastern elite, White entered the Department of State to embark on a diplomatic career. He served as chief of the Latin American division from 1922 to 1926 and Assistant Secretary of State for Latin American affairs from 1927 to 1933. President Coolidge appointed him chair of the interdepartmental committee on aviation in 1927, on which Trubee Davison also served. Correspondence in White's papers at the Herbert Hoover Presidential Library documents his close association with Trippe, Hambleton, and other Pan American Airways officers. As a State Department officer, White opened doors around Latin America for the only U.S. overseas airline.

When Juan Trippe left Wall Street in 1922, he tapped into the passion for flying that he knew existed among his old classmates and other Yale alumni. With his experience as a bond salesman to guide him, he approached the potential backers and convinced them to invest in the airline that he intended to start with their capital. Seven navy surplus Aeromarine float planes cost $3,500. Adding more engine power and a second passenger seat to each plane increased the initial expense but added capacity.

Long Island Airways marketed its chartered services to a wealthy clientele: New Yorkers who owned summer homes on Long Island or vacationed in Atlantic City, the Caribbean, and

Canada. However, despite Trippe's commitment and hard work, expenses exceeded revenue. By 1924, he had sold off most of the company's tangible assets and closed the doors.

Trippe lost the company but not his friends or the desire to take another chance. Moreover, he had gained enough experience in commercial aviation to know that passenger traffic alone could not sustain an airline.

The collapse of Long Island Airways occurred just as the 1925 Kelly Air Mail Act authorized payment to private companies to carry mail for the U.S. Post Office Department. Although the U.S. government professed a no-subsidy policy toward its developing airline industry, this reliable source of revenue drew dozens of aviators and small airline operators into the bidding for various routes.

Yale buddies Trippe, John Hambleton, C. V. Whitney, and William Vanderbilt each put up $25,000 and formed Eastern Air Transport in New York to bid on Civil Air Mail Route One, New York to Boston. Colonial Airways, a rival group based in Boston, raised $200,000 in hopes of gaining the contract. Rather than risk a bidding war, Trippe approached Colonial and persuaded the investors to join forces. The two groups merged, combined the names, and, as Colonial Air Transport, won the contract. Trippe became general manager.[6]

The original Colonial Airways contingent had put up two-thirds of the investment in what both groups considered a potentially profitable endeavor. Therefore, those investors had the most to lose when Juan Trippe quickly proposed that Colonial carry passengers as well as mail and committed the company to two three-engine, Fokker F-7 transport aircraft and two Ford all-metal trimotor planes. The financially cautious participants from the original Colonial Airways balked. The company used the more economical, single-engine Fokker Universals on the Boston-New York mail route, and the majority of the company's board members saw no need to invest in new equipment.

In fact, differences of opinion over equipment masked the more fundamental rift in plans for the airline's future growth. The larger, more modern, reliable trimotors better accommodated a passenger airline, Trippe argued, but he failed to pass his vision on to the reluctant majority partners. They viewed the mail as certain income, while the passenger market remained precarious. The company was losing money, and the directors voted Trippe out of his management position. He and his friends sold their shares in Trippe's second failed attempt to run an airline.

Trippe apparently had not shared his more ambitious schemes with Colonial's partners at the time of the merger in early October, 1925, but his actions reveal that he had already considered the possibility of a future Key West-Havana mail route at that time.

While he organized Colonial Air Transport for operation as a domestic airmail carrier, he also spent considerable time in Washington, D.C., talking to government officials about overseas airmail opportunities. Trippe traded on his connections and arranged an introduction to Pittsburgh Congressman Melville Clyde Kelly, sponsor of the original airmail legislation. Kelly had also taken on the responsibility for a foreign airmail bill.

Trippe's college roommate, Alan Scaife, the son of a millionaire industrialist, came from Pittsburgh. Scaife had married the niece of Treasury Secretary Andrew Mellon, Congressman Kelly's richest Pittsburgh constituent. Scaife introduced Trippe to Mellon, and Mellon introduced him to Kelly. No doubt, at some point in the conversation, Trippe also mentioned his partner, John Hambleton, whose old friend, David Bruce, had married Mellon's daughter. Most certainly, Trippe came highly recommended to Kelly, and he used his passion for aviation to advantage when he spoke with Kelly about the proposed legislation.[7]

In addition to his visits to Washington, Trippe spent time in New Jersey, where Anthony Fokker, the Dutch citizen who had developed fighter planes for the Germans in World War I, had opened a factory to produce the F-7 trimotor plane. In December, 1925, Trippe convinced Fokker to fly him to Havana, purportedly to show off the new F-7, whose three motors provided sufficient reserve power and thus a margin of safety essential for overwater flying.

Clearly, Trippe's meetings with Kelly in Washington signified his interest in flying the mail to Cuba, and he had more on his mind than a round of golf with Fokker at the Havana Country Club. The fierce competitor had used the Yale network to meet Congressman Kelly, and Trippe turned to the network again, probably State Department official Francis White, to advance his ambitions in Cuba.[8]

Trippe and Fokker, in fact, followed a well-trodden path to Cuba. A significant contingent of U.S. businesspeople had invested, worked, and played on the island for some time, and U.S. officials of the business-minded Republican administration in Washington assisted when and where they were needed. Cuban officials responded to requests for favors and joined the business executives on the golf course or at the racetrack, both operated by North Americans. Cuban President Gerardo Machado had attended opening day at the racetrack earlier that December as the guest of John McEntee Bowman, who owned the Sevilla-Biltmore Hotel in downtown Havana and had just bought the Oriental Park racetrack in the Havana suburb of Marianao.

President Machado proved himself receptive to U.S. business interests in general, and Juan Trippe fared as well as others. The day after Fokker gave Machado an aerial demonstration of his plane, Trippe hired a Havana lawyer. At Trippe's request, the lawyer drew up an agreement granting Trippe landing rights at Camp Columbia, Havana's only airport. The document was presented to President Machado, and Cuba's head of state had an official sign what amounted to exclusive air rights to serve Havana.[9]

Thus, when Trippe and his friends ended their connection with Colonial Air Transport, they had already moved in the direction of carrying the U.S. mail to Havana. In fact, if Francis White aided Juan Trippe's aggressive advance into Cuba, his services aided U.S. government interests as well. That is, he fostered a preemptive strike to ward off a foreign airline's offer to carry mail between the U.S. and South America.

Pan Am's Push Southward

The United States had never disguised its political and economic interest in Latin America. The Monroe Doctrine, the Mexican War, the Spanish-American War, and the building of the Panama Canal represent just a sampling of the country's demonstrated will to identify the hemisphere's well-being with its own. Several of the U.S. world's fairs blatantly courted the nations that composed the Pan American Union. During the last decade of the nineteenth century, the United States made a concerted effort to develop closer commercial relations and to increase trade with Latin America through the negotiation of reciprocity agreements, that is, a mutual lowering of tariffs on imported goods.

Between Buffalo's Pan-American Exposition (1901) and the start of World War I (1914), the dollar amount of U.S. exports to Latin America increased by 240 percent. With European-Latin American trade thrown off track by the war, U.S-Latin American exports increased another 300 percent by 1925.[10] Unfortunately, the United States too often backed up the country's commercial ties with military actions, a circumstance noted and very much resented by Latin American governments.

In the matter of aviation, however, the United States had exhibited an uncharacteristic reluctance to take charge. The government's unwillingness to underwrite domestic airline operations after World War I carried over into foreign air operations. France and Germany had taken advantage of that void to expand their own interests in South America.

The end of the war left both Europe and the United States with bustling aircraft industries and a surplus of military airplanes and trained personnel. Wartime research had improved airplane performance sufficiently to stimulate efforts at commercial air transport, and in fact engineers, pilots, and mechanics sought to initiate various private enterprises based on their experience and expertise.

The war had not promoted aviation advances in Latin America, however, and the nations of the area remained without the technical or financial wherewithal to undertake airline development. Although European governments began to reach out to South America before the United States made a move, Latin America had neither trunk lines joining any two countries nor air connections to other continents until late in 1927.[11]

In fact, South American governments generally welcomed foreign capital and technical assistance to develop air transport and stood to gain by playing the United States against European powers. With little expenditure of capital on their part, governments gained air services needed to communicate with and to develop resources and trade in remote areas. In Peru, for example, the trip from the coastal capital at Lima to the interior Amazon River town of Iquitos took forty days by land, yet only six hours by plane.

European governments, meanwhile, were directly supporting airline development in their respective countries. French government-subsidized airlines not only provided a market for its aircraft manufacturers but also fostered renewed commercial contacts in Africa and South America that the war had disrupted. A few months after the hostilities ended, the French government granted a subsidy and a monopoly to a private company owned by Pierre Latecoere. Lignes Latecoere operated an airline between Paris and Casablanca via Toulouse, Barcelona, and Tangier. In 1924, a wealthy banker with holdings in South America acquired the airline. With a substantial subsidy from the French government, the renamed Compagnie Générale Aéropostale inaugurated an expansion program to build the airports and radio contact points necessary for mail service between Natal at the easternmost point of Brazil and Buenos Aires, Argentina.

The ambitious scheme to tie France to South America included an extension of the France-Africa airline operation to Dakar at the westernmost point of continental Africa (in present-day Senegal) and transportation by ship over the 1,900-mile gap between Dakar and Natal. Service between Natal and Buenos Aires opened in November, 1927, with the ocean-going portion added in March, 1928. That same year, when Aéropostale's Argentine subsidiary inaugurated mail and passenger service between Buenos Aires and Asunción, Paraguay, the link completed a chain that connected France with Brazil, Argentina, and Paraguay. Mail from Paris reached Buenos Aires in eight days, compared to twenty days by steamship from New York to the Argentine port city.[12]

Forbidden by the Versailles Treaty to pursue military aviation, Germany turned to commercial industries to support at least some of its factories, fliers, and support personnel. Germany's Junkers Airlines used Junkers-built, all-metal, five-passenger-cabin monoplanes. Consequently, the airline advertised the company's airplane as it transported travelers. By 1922, Germany operated fifteen air routes and had created Aero Lloyd, A.G., a large air transport company that comprised shipping companies, an engineering company, and aircraft manufacturers. In 1925, Aero Lloyd merged with Junkers into a single airline company, Luft Hansa (now Lufthansa), a state-supported aviation monopoly.[13]

German capital and government support also backed operations in South America. Local governments granted concessions to airlines incorporated as national companies. Germany generally contributed capital, and the airlines bought their planes from German manufacturers. Where permitted by local governments, Germany sent its pilots to fly the planes and brought South American residents of German descent to Berlin for aviation training.

Peter Paul von Bauer, an Austrian aviator who had flown with the German forces during the war, started the first successful South American commercial airline in 1920, the Sociedad Colombo-Alemana de Transportes Aereos (SCADTA), or Colombian-German Air Transport Association. Because of the critically needed transport service the airline offered, von Bauer's enterprise generated profits from its inception.

One can hardly exaggerate the transportation advantages that von Bauer's airline brought to Colombia. Using Junkers F-13 seaplanes and German pilots, SCADTA flew the 650 air miles from Barranquilla, Colombia's main port at the mouth of the Magdalena River on the Caribbean, to a spot on the river close to the country's mountain-ringed capital, Bogotá, in seven hours. The standard communication mode, a Magdalena River journey, took at least a week in the wet season and as much as a month in the dry season, when dwindling water levels impeded boat traffic.[14]

Topographical obstacles also spurred airline development in Bolivia, where high mountains obstructed surface travel. In 1925, German residents of La Paz, Bolivia, presented a plane as a gift to the Bolivian government. The government, in turn, provided operating subsidies to Lloyd Aereo Boliviano, the newly formed local company. German Bolivians operated the company with financial support from Junkers, the aircraft manufacturer, which at that time badly needed markets. The airline's first route shortened the time between Cochabamba and Santa Cruz, two hundred miles apart, from four days to three hours.

In 1924 Germans organized Kondor Syndikat with the intention of operating flying boats to connect various locations in South America with the Caribbean. Government-owned Deutsche Lufthansa retained financial control when the Brazilian-incorporated successor company, Sindicato Condor, opened the nine-hundred-mile Rio de Janeiro-Porto Alegre-Rio Grande do Sul line in 1927. German Brazilians also organized Viacao Aerea Rio-Grandense (VARIG) that year, which used equipment supplied on easy terms by Lufthansa and flown by German personnel. German-influenced enterprises generally exchanged free passes on the airlines for subsidies from local governments.[15]

Although Germany logically based its South American expansion in Brazil, with the goal of connections to Berlin to counter France's growing network, it was the SCADTA operation in Colombia that captured the attention of the United States. Word reached the U.S. military attaché in Bogotá that the highly successful von Bauer had plans to expand his operation to Central America and to the United States. The attaché forwarded reports to Washington-based, military intelligence officer Major Henry H. (Hap) Arnold (wartime head of air training operations in San Diego), indicating that a trans-Caribbean route would occasionally take SCADTA's planes over the Panama Canal.

Major Arnold took this information to Postmaster General Henry New. Meanwhile, SCADTA sent a delegation to Washington with the objective of linking North and South America through a trans-Caribbean mail service. SCADTA's application for landing rights in Florida and the Canal Zone to accommodate airmail planes further aroused government concerns. The possibility of an airline with German connections operating near the Panama Canal set off alarms in some quarters. Furthermore, the post office, state, and commerce departments had begun receiving complaints that Aéropostale's Latin America airmail service gave European business competitors a significant advantage over North Americans.

The SCADTA delegation went to Washington in 1925 to inquire about airmail contracts. As already mentioned, Juan Trippe used his Yale contacts to gain access to Cuba's President Machado and acquired landing rights in Havana in December of that year.[16]

When the postmaster general informed Major Arnold that only the existence of a competing U.S. airline justified his refusal of the SCADTA request for landing rights essential to his mail service plan, he kindled the pent-up aspirations of several contenders for foreign airmail contracts, including Hap Arnold, who then determinedly jockeyed for position.

In the summer of 1926, Arnold and several friends came to Postmaster General New's rescue and completed the paperwork for an airline that they named Pan American Airways. All four of the participants in the Pan Am proposal had military aviation backgrounds. Three of them, including Arnold, still held the rank of army major when they put together the documents for the airline. They intended to resign and pursue civilian careers in commercial aviation. The fourth partner, John Montgomery, had flown with the navy. The group had not yet acquired the planes necessary to give the airline viability when it convinced President Machado to award Pan Am the right to carry mail from Havana to Florida.

The Pan American project seemed ready to fly. However, an unanticipated complication—the court martial of General William (Billy) Mitchell, the commander of America's expeditionary air force in World War I—detoured Arnold and his military associates.

An outspoken defender of military air power and sharp-tongued critic of military leaders who opposed the idea of an air force, General Mitchell lost rank, command, pay, and credibility as a result of the court's judgment against him. When Mitchell resigned from the army, Arnold and his fellow military aviators felt compelled to forgo their civilian ambitions in order to continue the struggle to develop an air force. John Montgomery carried on alone, looking for money to buy equipment for an airline with just a name and a contract to carry Cuban mail to the United States. He found his backers in Richard D. Bevier and Grant Mason, men with connections in New York banking circles who signaled an interest in financial participation.

Montgomery, Bevier, and Mason incorporated Pan American Airways in New York in March, 1927, just as the U.S. Post Office Department invited bids on the first foreign airmail contract from Key West to Havana.

Although Pan American existed only on paper at the time and had neither planes nor operations personnel, the post office awarded the Key West-Havana route to Montgomery's group in July. To keep the contract, they had to be ready to fly by October 19. Pan American Airways faced several potentially disastrous problems. It needed planes, equipment, and a departure location. More importantly, the company's potential investors lost confidence that the airline could be operational in the short time required by the post office department and declined to put up the funds that they had pledged. Without capital, the airline could not buy planes and equipment. Furthermore, it had no landing rights in Havana.[17]

Two rival aviation groups, both experienced, domestic airmail contractors, kept a close watch on the turbulence surrounding Pan American.

Captain Edward V. Rickenbacker, former race-car driver, learned to fly during World War I. Eddie Rickenbacker became the leading U.S. ace and returned home a decorated and esteemed aviator. He had organized Florida Airways in 1926 with Reed Chambers, another combat ace, and Virgil (Vic) Chenea, as partners. Chenea had sold various properties to take advantage of airline prospects. Florida Airways, backed by an impressive group of investors, including Percy Rockefeller and Richard F. Hoyt, chairman of the Curtiss-Wright aircraft manufacturing company, acquired the contract for the airmail route from Atlanta to Miami, via Tampa, and looked like a winner.

Unfortunately, Florida Airways went bankrupt in the spring of 1927. Chenea later called it the "worst investment he ever made." The airline bug had bitten him, however. He, Chambers, and Hoyt formed a new company called Atlantic, Gulf, and Caribbean and approached Pan American Airways with an offer to bring their experience and money as a reinforcement to the airmail contract bid. However, they made no headway with John Montgomery.[18]

Juan Trippe, with his Washington contacts and an agreement for landing rights in Havana, obviously intended to be a player in the international airmail game. In a highly dramatic air-minded year, personal disappointments, lost investments, and failed enterprises set the stage for the almost operatic birth of a new airline connection to Latin America, acted out by irrepressible advocates of the aviation age.

Here is the scenario. In the spring, Montgomery formed Pan American Airways; Chambers, Chenea, and Hoyt folded Florida Airways; and Trippe, Hambleton, and Whitney left Colonial Air Transport. Atlantic, Gulf, and Caribbean incorporated. Lindbergh flew the Atlantic in May. The United States prepared tumultuous welcomes. In June, President Calvin Coolidge decorated the latest aviation hero with the Distinguished Flying Cross. A ticker tape and confetti parade on New York's Broadway followed. End of Act One.

July brought the first foreign airmail contract, awarded to Montgomery with the challenge of an October deadline. Pan American lost financial backing but turned down overtures from Atlantic, Gulf, and Caribbean. Trippe and college friends John Hambleton, Sonny Whitney, and William Vanderbilt started the Aviation Corporation of America (AVCO) and invited other friends and relatives to invest.

The ten members of AVCO's board of directors composed an extremely impressive roster. Besides the four friends, four members had banking connections: W. Averell Harriman, a 1913 Yale graduate; Edward O. McDonnell, graduate of the U.S. Naval Academy; John Hay Whitney, a Yale graduate five years younger than his cousin Sonny; and Seymour Knox, 1920 Yale graduate. Two more came from the aviation world. Grover Loening, 1908 Columbia graduate, had served as general manager for the Wright Company and then founded Loening Aeronautical Engineering. Sherman Fairchild was president of Fairchild Aviation Corporation.

Hoyt approached AVCO, which controlled Cuban landing rights, had planes on order (originally for Colonial Air Transport), could muster flight personnel, and had access to copious financial resources. Trippe laid his cards on the table. If AVCO could take over Pan American Airways, with its Key West-Havana airmail contract, and, if the Trippe group controlled the company with Trippe as president and general manager, he would join forces. End of Act Two.

The October deadline hung over the squeamish Pan American investors when Trippe boldly proposed merging the groups. The post office would not extend the time limit, and Trippe refused to budge from his insistence on control. He also rejected a three-way split. With scarcely two weeks to go, the other groups agreed to give AVCO the major interest, with Juan Trippe as president. The Hoyt group and Pan American Airways accepted lesser shares in the new company.

With a week to go before the deadline, Trippe sent representatives to New Jersey to accept delivery of a Fokker trimotor plane that he had ordered for Colonial Air Transport. He assigned other personnel to an island just off Key West to smooth out a landing strip. With the tension mounting to a breathtaking finish, the first airmail delivery to Havana took place as scheduled on October 19. Pan American Airways fulfilled its first foreign airmail contract — but not in the untested Fokker, as it happened. In fact, when the airline failed to complete all of the necessary preparations in time, the determined Trippe borrowed an available Fairchild FC-2 floatplane and loaded the cargo. The pilot took off and carried the mail to Havana's harbor, not Havana's airport, where Trippe had the landing rights. Nonetheless, Pan American fulfilled the contract requirement.[19] Curtain calls.

The airmail drama had come to a satisfactory conclusion. However, Trippe had not given up on a passenger-carrying airline. Pan American had its Fokker trimotor airplane, and Havana attracted a wealthy tourist trade. Trippe understood the market potential. With a dependable aircraft operating from a newly functioning airport, in less than three months Pan American Airways carried its first seven passengers, along with the mail, from Key West to Havana.

Trippe and John Hay Whitney's sister Joan joined the inaugural January, 1928, flight. A total of seventy-one passengers traveled between the two points that month, and around one thousand made the trip during the first year of operation. Pan American had taken the first step toward carrying fun-loving tourists all the way to Rio de Janeiro.

Pan American's well-timed, first passenger flight took place at the height of Cuba's winter tourist season, when the English-language *Havana Post* would publicize the flight to thousands of wealthy, vacationing North Americans. The particular date, however—January 16, 1928—capitalized on the hemispheric-wide media attention accorded the sixth Pan American Conference, then under way in Havana. U.S. President Calvin Coolidge and Cuban President Gerardo Machado greeted Trippe and his entourage at the airport, and tourism secretary Carlos Miguel de Céspedes gave the principal welcoming address.

With mail service to provide the cash and passengers to supply prestige and glamour, Pan American Airways opened the air link to Latin America. In February, Charles Lindbergh, Pan Am's new technical adviser, flew into Havana for a five-day visit to promote the new air connection. The press followed Lindbergh, of course, as they had since the previous May. This time, Lindbergh had flown the *Spirit of St. Louis* from Washington, D.C., to Mexico City and had made a circuit around the Caribbean before his well-publicized stop in the Cuban capital.[20]

Even with all the business demands, inaugural tensions, and Havana hoopla, Trippe kept his eye on Washington's policymakers. The U.S. Post Office Department had granted the original Key West-Havana airmail contract for a period of only nine months. With termination scheduled for April, 1928, the company they had formed in October, 1927, had just six months to retain their hold on the airmail route. As Bender and Altschul assert in their history of the airline, "Pan American Airways . . . was built in Washington, D.C. . . . . Mail routes were created in the office of the Postmaster General, in the cloakrooms of Congress and in other corners of the Administration."[21] Lobbying tirelessly for renewal of the contract, Trippe worked the cloakrooms and the corners, often accompanied by John Hambleton, and they succeeded.

Pan American Airways (PAA) promoted Cuba as a destination and airplanes as the preferable travel mode for tourists. *Courtesy of Greg Young Publishing.*

In November, a month after Pan American completed the first foreign airmail delivery, President Coolidge set up the Interdepartmental Committee on Aviation. Francis White chaired the committee, and Trubee Davison served as a member. Trippe and Hambleton called on their friends and strenuously argued that competitive bidding on airmail contracts could result in chaos, with awards given to inexperienced low bidders with high failure rates.

The administration proved receptive. Secretary of Commerce Herbert Hoover promoted the country's business interests in Latin America and understood the competitive advantages of airmail. Moreover, the war department had misgivings about foreign aircraft flying over the Panama Canal Zone but could not prevent foreign companies from submitting bids.

When the committee completed its work, its recommendations reflected these concerns and Trippe's warnings. It advised flexibility in mail contract awards, with contracts going to the company that best served U.S. interests, not necessarily to the lowest bidder. Furthermore, the committee recommended better compensation to contract holders and the opening of two new Latin American routes. President Coolidge quickly approved the recommendations and directed the post office department to send authorizing legislation to Congress.

Congressman Kelly, whom Trippe had wooed earlier, introduced the foreign airmail bill in January, 1928—the same month that Coolidge and Machado greeted Trippe in Havana. The bill authorized the postmaster general to enter into contracts with private carriers for up to ten years. The legislation enacted on March 8 also called for $1.75 million to pay for mail carried on contracted routes. Coolidge signed the measure into law.

The post office department then awarded the Key West-Havana contract to Pan American Airways for five years and awarded additional contracts to carry the mail between Miami and the Panama Canal Zone and on a Miami-to-Trinidad route, via Cuba, Puerto Rico, Haiti, and the Dominican Republic.

In July, 1928, Trippe called a meeting of the Pan American Airways staff in the office that had been opened in the Sevilla-Biltmore

Hotel in Havana and announced that the airline would soon fly mail and passengers all around the Caribbean.[22]

After the celebration Trippe sent Lindbergh to survey the new routes and identify appropriate landing locations. He cranked up the publicity machine when Amelia Earhart opened the company's new terminal at Havana's airport. With an unerring sense of celebrity, Trippe captured the aviation icon of the moment to enhance the airline's stature. Earhart had completed a transatlantic flight from Newfoundland to Burry Port, Wales, in June, 1928. Even though she was a passenger on the flight, and not the pilot, and a fuel shortage forced the plane to land in Wales instead of the target destination at Southampton, England, London crowds exploded in applause when Earhart arrived by car. Thousands of Americans turned out for her parade up Broadway when she returned to New York, and the mayor greeted her at City Hall.[23]

Pan American had scarcely organized the Key West-Havana operation and surveyed the new Caribbean routes when Trippe called a meeting to inform the company's officers that he would bid on the extension of airmail service to Paramaribo in Dutch Guiana (now Suriname) on the South American mainland. They would have to be ready to go in six months. Met with an understandable outcry against additional obligations, Trippe cited European competition in South America and the necessity for the United States to catch up.[24]

Pan American Airways as the "Chosen Instrument"

Competition with European interests in South America had acquired a dimension beyond trade and investment. The southern half of the hemisphere constituted a battleground for air supremacy. Not just Trippe's statement to his colleagues, but also official correspondence of his friend Francis White (at the State Department) connected the airline's interests to those of the U.S. government. Because of German and French competition, White explained in his memorandum on aviation in Latin America, the State Department wished "to have American aviation predominate." While representatives of the U.S. government moved diplomatically to counter SCADTA's favorable position with the Colombian government, "the Pan American Airways vigorously pushed forward their program. . . . If the United States were not to be excluded from South America, it appeared necessary to act at once and President Coolidge supported legislation permitting the Post Office Department to grant airmail contracts to South America."[25]

Two months later White defended a policy of diplomatic support for those U.S. aviation companies that had been awarded post office department airmail contracts. White acknowledged that the administration would incur criticism and complaints from rival airlines but cited considerations of "vital national interests" over the "particular interests of individual companies"[26] as justification for his recommendations.

White laid out an argument for a policy of monopoly over competition and based it on the nation's well-being: (1) American mails should be carried by air to Latin America and should be carried by American companies in American planes; (2) because of European competition in Latin America, the U.S. government should not let American companies fight one another for concessions in Latin America, lest all Americans lose out to French or German airlines; and (3) for strategic regions the United States should control aviation in the Caribbean region in order to protect the Panama Canal.[27]

White made an additional appeal for monopoly and State Department support based on the contracted company's economic interests. That is, given the effort and expenditures required to establish an airmail route abroad, "No company wanted to go in and make the financial outlay and run the risk and, after that work had been done, have other companies get the contracts and the cream of the business after they had done the unprofitable pioneering work."[28]

In fact, while public monies supported domestic airways with construction and maintenance of airports, radio communications, weather bureaus, beacons, and so on, the international carrier faced a more daunting task. First of all, the airline negotiated with the governments of various nations for permission to operate on their soil. Each nation had complex and often shifting political

institutions and leadership, and each government established its
own customs, immigration, and shipping regulations.

Moreover, foreign governments undertook no obligation to
finance the agreed-upon operations. Although the countries benefited, Pan American paid to construct its own landing, radio, customs clearance, and weather service facilities. Much of the territory covered by the contracted routes had never been flown over
before, and the company undertook its own surveys to fill in uncharted map areas with descriptions of topography.[29]

A company brochure marking Pan American Airways' fiftieth
anniversary made the process of building Latin American airfields
seem much more adventurous than bureaucratic and costly. The
text plays on the romantic aura that in retrospect often surrounds
the pioneer:

> Often, in Central and South America, [bases] were hacked
> out of dense unexplored jungles. Pan Am survey planes
> would fly low over the crocodile-infested swamps, locate a
> suitable site, then drop sacks of flour to make white
> splotches in the matted green of the jungle. Construction
> crews hired by Pan Am would come in from the nearest
> town by canoe, on burro or on foot, and clear the ground.
> Food and supplies were dropped from planes. Indians, of-
> ten hostile until won over with dime store trinkets, were
> put to work, trekking from the nearest seaport to the in-
> land base with five-gallon cans of aviation gasoline on
> their heads—then fleeing in terror when the "thunder
> birds" arrived. Eventually Pan Am would establish 160
> land and marine bases and 93 ground radio and weather
> stations in Latin America.[30]

Sometimes the company built its own roads and filled in
swamps. For locations that proved totally unsuited to land routes,
the airline purchased Sikorsky S-38 amphibious planes and established their facilities on water contiguous to the shoreline. For
the essential landing point on Mexico's Yucatán peninsula, for
example, en route from Cuba to Central America, Pan Am used a

Juan T. Trippe, the force behind Pan American Airways, hired Charles A. Lindbergh to promote the airline and to survey air routes to South America. *Courtesy of the San Diego Aerospace Museum.*

lagoon on the offshore island of Cozumel. Amphibians also solved the landing problems posed by the hard volcanic terrain of the eastern Caribbean islands from Puerto Rico to Trinidad.

Just two years after Pan American's first ninety-mile airmail flight between Key West and Havana in October, 1927, the international company operated a 12,000-mile system that linked twenty-three hemispheric countries.

In forging that chain, the airline company often called on the good offices of the State Department to use its influence with various Latin American governments that impeded its onward march. Francis White not only defended Pan Am's contract monopoly but also opened doors around Latin America. In return, company officials fed information they deemed useful to their friends in positions of authority in the U.S. government. For example, Pan American extended its reach around the Caribbean in July, 1928, and began to negotiate landing rights with various governments. While visiting Guatemala City, Juan Trippe sent White a translation of what he termed a "very interesting editorial" from the July 16, 1928, edition of *Nuestro Diario*. He wanted to give White "a first hand view on the present local situation," he said. The newspaper, which Trippe characterized as "usually very anti-American," had urged the government to "make the best arrangement it can" with Pan American in order to secure certain "privileges." [31]

The editorial reflects a resentment of the power of the United States, not enthusiasm or excitement at the opportunity to send its mail by airplane. "Our suspicions are confirmed, in that the company . . . counts on the official favor of the U. S. A. . . . Fatally, the Central Amrican [sic] Governments are in the position of being obligated to accept the services of the Pan American Airways. We should prepare ourselves [in order] that the terms of the contract may not be too one-sided or disastrous." [32]

Because Pan American depended on airmail contracts for revenue and on landing rights in foreign countries to fulfill those contracts, the airline's expansion into Latin America necessarily involved the company in controversy. Latin American suspicions of U.S. intentions stemmed from a long history of political, economic, and military aggression in the hemisphere that included the occupation of territory, interference with domestic politics, control of markets, and protection of companies that extracted natural resources and exploited native labor.

To the south of Guatemala, the occupying U.S. Marines engaged in a prolonged battle against the rebel Nicaraguan nationalist Augusto César Sandino, while Pan American officials arranged to build their facilities. Pan Am forwarded translations of company correspondence to Francis White, who thought they would be of interest in view of references to the Nicaraguan political situation. The airline's Nicaraguan attorney in Managua lobbied on Pan Am's behalf in the Nicaraguan congress. In explaining the difficulties of gaining favorable consideration of the airline's requests, he referred to the administrative anarchy, combined with a strong spirit of misdirected patriotism, that reached the point of considering any North American company an enemy of the republic. After the lawyer-lobbyist succeeded in guiding the Pan American contract through the Nicaraguan congress and a presidential signature, White congratulated Trippe: "It is gratifying to know that Pan American Airways has been able to accomplish so much towards bringing about closer relations between this country and Nicaragua."[33]

Pan American gained the access it needed in country after country, strengthened commercial ties, and promoted Latin America as a desirable tourist destination. The State Department supported the only U.S. international airline, and the bargain helped them both.

Skyroad to Rio

After two years of operation (1927–1929) Pan American controlled airmail routes through Mexico and Central America to Panama and through the Caribbean to Dutch Guiana. With airmail contracts in hand and favored by a prosperity-driven speculative investment climate, Pan Am sold stocks, bought planes, marketed routes, and encouraged passengers to try the new mode of speedy transportation. The next two years (1930–1931) closed the gaps in the circuit and took the airline to Rio, but not without the flexing of economic and political muscles. That is, the company used the resources of financial backers to gain control over companies that stood in its way and availed itself of the political connections necessary to influence the U.S. Post Office Department.

More than 17,000 passengers flew at least some part of the Pan Am route in 1929, and the February 24, 1930, issue of *Pan American Air Ways,* the company's magazine, boasted of its commercial and tourist passenger service. The magazine also announced that a career State Department official (not Francis White) had resigned his post to join the airline.

With Brazil still under survey in anticipation of additional routes, Pan American had moved from Panama down the west coast of South America as far as Santiago, Chile, and then across the Andes to Buenos Aires, Argentina, and Montevideo, Uruguay.

Pan Am's southern march had taken a significant step with the formation of Pan American-Grace Airways (Panagra), in partnership with W. R. Grace Company, the powerful shipping corporation that operated along the coast of Peru. An agreement with Colombian officials allowed Panagra free passage along the country's Pacific coast to reach Peru, but no landing rights.

SCADTA, the Colombian airline whose northern expansionist ambitions had triggered the formation of the first U.S. international carrier, blocked Pan Am's access to the entire region immediately to the south of its terminal in Colón. In September, 1928, John Hambleton had written to Francis White about his suspicions that Lufthansa intended to take over SCADTA and then to expand as rapidly as possible throughout South America.

Hambleton also alluded to an expected lack of cooperation with SCADTA. By the end of 1929, SCADTA offered air services as far north as Barranquilla and Cartagena in Colombia and Cristóbal in Panama and as far south as Guayaquil in Ecuador. The airline clearly intended to command the northwestern corner of South America, with a foothold in Panama, a situation of concern to both Pan American Airways and the U.S. government.

In the ensuing months State Department correspondence referred to German propaganda against Pan Am in Colombia and Ecuador and competition with the Germans over airmail contracts in Peru.[34] By February, 1930, Pan American had disposed of its formidable rival on its western South America route. Trippe approached Peter Paul von Bauer, SCADTA's founder and managing director, and arranged to purchase eighty-five percent of the company's stock. SCADTA discontinued its lines along the north and west coasts of South America and into Panama in favor of route development in the interior. In turn, the Colombian government signed an agreement with the U.S. Post Office for an exchange of airmail at Barranquilla to be carried to and from Bogotá and other interior cities on the SCADTA lines. The agreement no doubt pleased the U.S. State and War Departments as much as it did Pan American Airways.

At the same time, Pan American launched an assault on another airline to establish a direct Rio connection and close the South American circle. A look at the map shows west coast service as the shortest route from Miami to Pan Am's southernmost terminals at Santiago, Buenos Aires, and Montevideo. Extension northward to Rio from Buenos Aires and return accommodated that service. However, the rival New York, Rio, and Buenos Aires Air Line (NYRBA) had tied up the potentially lucrative direct route to South America's east coast cities.

The Fight for Rio

Brazil's four-thousand-mile coastline had almost no facilities for air travel in 1927. The German-backed Sindicato Condor began operations in 1928, and the French also carried some mail along the coast. Ralph O'Neill, a former World War I ace and marketing representative for Boeing Aircraft, had been in the area and recognized its transportation shortcomings. O'Neill seized the opportunity to put together an airline company for the South American market. He convinced James Rand of Remington Rand, F. C. Munson of Munson Steamship Line, Lewis Pierson of the Irving Trust Company, and Reuben H. Fleet of Consolidated Aircraft Company that Brazil offered a profit-making opportunity. They put up several million dollars and incorporated NYRBA in February, 1929.

While Pan American Airways moved south on the strength of its U.S. mail contracts, NYRBA acquired mail contracts from the governments of Argentina, Chile, and Uruguay. Between August and November, 1929, the airline extended its reach from Buenos Aires to Santiago in one direction and to Montevideo and Asunción in another. It also gained authorization to operate within and along the coast of Brazil, for which routes O'Neill created the NYRBA do Brasil ("NYRBA of Brazil") subsidiary.[35]

NYRBA operated Ford Trimotors on the Buenos Aires-Santiago Route, and eight-passenger Sikorsky S-38 amphibians between Buenos Aires and Montevideo and between Brazilian coastal cities. The airline also bought, as promised, six twenty-two-passenger Commodore flying boats from Reuben Fleet's Consolidated Aircraft Corporation.

Reuben Fleet knew airplanes. He had served in the military during World War I and stayed with the air service until 1922. When the federal government inaugurated its airmail service in 1918, Major Reuben H. Fleet piloted the first flight. Eagerly pursued when he left the military, Fleet turned down jobs with aircraft manufacturers Glenn Curtiss and William Boeing and opened his own company. The money that he invested in NYRBA represented profits on contracts for military planes. In fact, Consolidated had originally designed the Commodore for naval patrol work and then adapted it for commercial use. The Commodore's comfortable interior—upholstered chairs and carpet—had been designed to make the trip enjoyable for pleasure travelers. Its thousand-mile range accommodated long, overwater routes, giving NYRBA an apparent advantage over Pan American.

In February, 1930, NYRBA made its inaugural, week-long flight from Buenos Aires to Miami, stopping along the east coast of South America and hopping between the chain of islands in the Caribbean. The airline had positioned itself to challenge Pan American for South America's east-coast airmail route to Rio. The United States generated most of the mail between North and South America, and NYRBA needed the revenue as much as Pan Am did. NYRBA held contracts in South America, owned a fleet of planes, and had both knowledge of the routes and impressive financial backers, but Pan American controlled the route from Miami south to Paramaribo in Dutch Guiana.

Clearly, NYRBA made an attractive contender for the Miami-Rio contract, and Juan Trippe knew it. Pan Am and its backers launched a takeover effort after a series of competitive price cuts had weakened NYRBA's financial position. They formalized a merger on September 15, 1930, and nine days later the postmaster general awarded the east-coast South American mail contract to the enlarged Pan American Airways.[36]

The takeover of NYRBA, with its South American contracts, facilities, and fleet of long-range Commodores, paved the way for Pan American to shorten the air time between Miami and Rio. The airline started mail service between the United States and Brazil on November 10, 1930, and carried its first passengers over water to Panama by way of Cuba and Jamaica—in hours rather than days—on January 1, 1931.

Pan American had no doubt lobbied aggressively in Washington on this contract. In the division of the sky, Pan Am used its political contacts to win air routes and its financial strength to buy the planes and equipment—and airlines—necessary to maintain its monopoly.

Enticing the International Air Traveler

The 1920s opened a new frontier, that is, the previously unexplored commercial territory of international air travel. The 1930s added the challenge of long-distance, overwater passenger service. Between 1927 and 1931, Pan American Airways had directed its pioneering efforts toward route development, and, after a few "shoot-outs," the one remaining U.S. international airline dominated air travel between North and South America. The company marked its first profitable year in 1931. With multiyear airmail contracts in hand, Pan Am increasingly turned its attention to passenger development.

The twin-engine Commodore flying boats acquired along with NYRBA's other assets enabled Pan American to take the first step in long-range, overwater air travel. The acquisition of the comfortable planes helped to attract passengers, of course, but, faced with a market made wary by widely publicized crashes of daredevil pilots and their Hollywood counterparts, the airline company had to build a record of passenger safety as well.

Flights covering more than six hundred miles of open water increased and complicated safety concerns. For one thing, pilots flying over the Caribbean between Jamaica and Panama could not rely on the visual orientation of landmarks, topography, lights, and so on to find their way. Compared to ocean-going ships facing the same empty expanses, fuel limitations permitted far less navigational leeway. Airplanes had to reach their destinations within the time frame imposed by weight constraints. Furthermore, the advantage of air transport was speed, which meant that planes strayed farther faster, once they lost their way. Neither could they slow down or stop to calculate their position.

Pan American's communications engineer solved the problem with radio direction finders installed in the Commodores to facilitate communication with the company's bases. The licensed radio operator who traveled with each flight reported the plane's position, determined by sextant, every fifteen minutes to the land-based radio operator, who then radioed back any necessary course correction in less than two minutes. Furthermore, the airline's fifty-six ground stations reported weather conditions to the planes every half hour—important at any time, but critical in the Caribbean's hurricane season.

Both the navigation and weather-reporting systems contributed to Pan Am's record of safety and dependability and, in turn, to the airline's 175-percent increase in passenger miles between 1931 and 1934. However, given the small passenger base in 1931, even a tripling of air travelers represented only a small percentage of the potential market. Nevertheless, the newer aircraft carried more people. The Sikorsky S-38 amphibian had accommodated seven passengers; the Commodore, twenty-two.

Flying had advanced considerably since the Wright brothers lay on their stomachs and worked the controls with their hips and hands. The graceful Sikorsky S-40 landed on outrigger pontoons. Its four powerful engines hung beneath a high-braced wing just

PAA's "Clippers," like this one flying over Miami, connected the United States to Latin America for fun and profit. The ample, flat wing served as a model for the fantasy dance floor in RKO-Radio Pictures' 1933 musical comedy, *Flying Down to Rio. Courtesy of Greg Young Publishing.*

above the passenger cabin. Two first-class cabin suites located behind the cockpit and three standard compartments with eight chairs each accommodated some thirty travelers. Polished walnut covered the interior walls, with floors carpeted in blue. Stewards prepared hot meals in the galley. To enter the plane, passengers crossed floating platforms to an air bridge that reached the door.

Pan American put the first of the S-40s, christened the American Clipper, into service in November, 1931. The airline used the word "clipper"—after the sailing ships—in the name of all of its four-engine planes and featured the term in much of the company's publicity. Thus, the choice of "Yankee Clipper" as the name for the orchestra in *Flying Down to Rio* was no coincidence.

Pan American clearly intended to tap an identified luxury tourist market with faster, more comfortable flights and tried to impart the familiar sense of crew efficiency and the formalism of an ocean liner to its passengers. Uniformed attendants called "All aboard!" to round them up, and bells sounded to mark the time. In an October, 1931, *Scientific American* article, timed to introduce the S-40's inaugural flight, the company's public relations director pointed out that a six-week air trip would take tourists to more countries than they could visit in a year by other modes of transportation.

Only the most affluent travelers had six weeks of free time and the luxury to experience "the lure of gay old Havana," the "marvel" of Santo Domingo's cathedral, "quaint Jamaica," the "incomparable hills and valleys of Panama," and Buenos Aires, "the Paris of the Americas," all in one trip.[37]

Pan Am pitched its services to the business community, as well as to the high-end tourist market. Fares of $25 to Havana, $200 to Panama, and $600 to Rio de Janeiro became wise business expenses, according to company publicity. Increased trade followed improved communications, and the businessperson who reached the customer first gained a competitive advantage. South America imported $3.5 billion worth of goods a year—two-thirds from Europe and one-third from the United States. That commerce fueled the race for aerial supremacy and assumed even greater importance with the economic collapse of the 1930s.

To facilitate the passenger loads it anticipated and encouraged, Pan Am set up a nationwide reservation system, using more than six thousand Western Union and postal telegraph offices, and inaugurated a campaign to educate travel agents about the importance of international travel. Letters to travel bureaus suggested Latin America as a winter destination for their clients when travel to Europe declined and also called attention to the prospects for their own profit in booking this travel option. With Pan Am profits up sevenfold in 1932 ($700,000 compared to $100,000 in 1931), the company ordered ten S-42s, the latest Sikorsky thirty-two-passenger, luxury plane, with delivery scheduled for mid-1934.

Despite the Depression, passenger service between the United

States and Latin America increased in 1933, and so did Pan Am's profits. Pan American's expansion plans looked to more passengers on current routes and eventually to transoceanic flights, which only the Zeppelin dirigible flew in 1933.

Airships versus Airplanes

When interviewed in Berlin in 1909, Orville Wright had dismissed the dirigible as a rival for the airplane. Professing admiration for Count Zeppelin personally, Wright concluded that "the airship occupies the same relative position as the steam engine does toward the gas engine. The possibilities of the former are, as engineers agree, pretty well exhausted, while wholly undreamed of things are to be expected from the gas engine."[38]

Wright's bias notwithstanding, the airship had accomplished wholly undreamed of voyages. Even when most people's attention focused on airplanes in the late 1920s, the dirigible gained acceptance as a practical and stable mode of air transport.

Count Zeppelin's successor, Hugo Eckener, oversaw the construction of a 776-foot-long, luxury airship and sent the *Graf Zeppelin* on a round-the-world voyage in 1929. Those who saw it talked about a new era of air travel in the comfort and quiet of the dirigible's lounges and staterooms. After paying $2,500 each, twenty passengers left Lakehurst, New Jersey, on August 8, 1929, and headed east. Large windows facilitated observation of the scenery from a height of 3,000 feet as they reached the *Zeppelin*'s base at Friedrichshafen in the afternoon of August 10.

After a four-day layover the airship headed over the Balkan countries and Russia toward Asia. They crossed the great stretch of Siberia and reached Tokyo on August 19. In six more days they circled San Francisco and landed in Los Angeles on August 26. They flew over Chicago on August 28, reached New York the following day, circled the Statue of Liberty, and landed at Lakehurst, having covered nineteen thousand miles in 21 days, 7 hours, and 34 minutes.

The *Graf Zeppelin* went on to make more than 600 flights, 181 of them intercontinental. The big airship crossed the Atlantic on scheduled trips between Germany and Brazil for five years.[39] Its sleek outline and quiet mobility fascinated crowds of people wherever it went. The U.S. Post Office featured the *Zeppelin* on a postage stamp in 1930, and millions of Americans sat entranced as Howard Hughes's replica menaced London in the 1930 movie *Hell's Angels.*

Between May 18 and June 6, 1930, the *Graf* made its first flight from Germany to Brazil and then made three scheduled passenger flights in the fall of 1931. The operational and financial success of the passenger flights encouraged the Zeppelin company to schedule twelve round trips at two-week intervals between May and December. Nine passenger crossings in 1932 were followed by nine more in 1933. They settled into a routine for cross-Atlantic passenger traffic. On the third trip of the 1933 season, the *Graf* stayed in Rio only an hour and twenty minutes before it started its homeward journey. By the end of October, 1933, when the *Graf* visited Miami, Akron, and Chicago on its return to Friedrichshafen from Rio, the public had become so accustomed to its travels that people hardly took notice of the visits.[40]

Creating an Air Travel Market

Neither Zeppelin nor Clipper flights qualified as mass travel, but air transport companies engaged in salesmanship to create mass awareness and desire. They portrayed the excitement of travel and appealed to the same emotional responses that other advertisers used to sell consumer items. Like newspapers, magazines, and other media, movies could carry that same appeal.

By the late 1920s, when movie moguls Kennedy, Zukor, Laemmle, and Fox talked to the graduate students at Harvard, the United States owned half of the world's movie theaters and made 80 percent of the films seen in South America. Many, if not most, people suspected that movies stimulated a demand for goods, and American movies fostered consumption of American-made products. Moreover, admiration for the lifestyle portrayed in films, enhanced by identification with film stars and encouraged by fan magazines, gave the United States undue cultural influence.

The attraction of young people and women to the movies—the same group that advertisers targeted—became an object of concern to community leaders and parents. In an effort to stave off yet another censorship movement, William H. Short, president of the Motion Picture Research Council, encouraged a series of investigations into media influence on children. The study, conducted by social scientists at Yale University, University of Chicago, University of Iowa, New York University, and Ohio State University, focused on the impact of film viewing on health, attitudes, behaviors, and values.

The studies revealed the complexity of the issue. Movies do not incite viewers to deviant behavior or exert negative moral influences, but children and adolescents emulate motion picture heroes and heroines, pretend to be movie characters while at play, and decorate school lockers with pictures of film stars. Both youngsters and adults form personal judgments about body types, mannerisms, and habits based on what they see.[41]

The findings of the 1929–1932 study may have laid out arguments against censorship, but they certainly encouraged filmmakers to employ movies to influence audience attitudes and behavior. When RKO-Radio Pictures released *Flying Down to Rio* at the end of 1933, the studio had many reasons to portray a romantic, entertaining trip to Brazil and to encourage people to fly on a Pan American Clipper along an airway in the sky.

CHAPTER 6

PAA and RKO: The Rio Connection

Y EARS BEFORE Pan American Airways lobbied on behalf of
foreign airmail contracts or sent its first airmail plane to
Havana in 1927, the motion picture industry had forged
links to Latin America. In Cuba, Mexico, Argentina, Brazil, and
other Spanish-speaking markets, "Hollywood" had come to sig-
nify North American movie stars, material culture, and lifestyle, as
well as the major U.S. film production location. American movies
became the mainstay of a growing world market for filmed entertainment, and by 1925, the motion picture industry earned some
$15 million in overseas trade, or 30 percent of its gross revenues.
When investors still regarded air transport with a wary eye, motion
picture production merited a Harvard Business School graduate
seminar.

By the end of the 1920s Hollywood led the world in the export
of entertainment, with the foreign trade in films vital to the industry's expansion. Longer lengths and more sophisticated plot exposition, better film, variety in lighting and camera angle, and editing that moved the viewer's perspective from one actor or location
to another all enhanced the appeal of movies. Two-thirds of the
world's almost fifty-seven thousand cinemas operated outside of
the United States, a significant business consideration. Argentina,

Brazil, and Australia contracted for the largest numbers of imported American films during the 1920s, while Hollywood production comprised 80 percent of films shown in South America.[1] Brazil, for example, emerged as one of the best customers for American films. Some 1,250 films from the United States passed through the São Paulo censor's office in 1926 alone, compared to 10 from Germany and 24 from France.[2]

Aside from financial returns to the studios, the abundance of films exported (silent and then dubbed or subtitled) brought aspects of U.S. life and culture to the societies where they played. Settings, costumes, dialog, and music, as well as plot and action conveyed interpretations of history as well as issues of contemporary concern. For example, viewers perhaps thought they understood the experiences that characterized the settling of the "wild" West of the United States because they saw a motion picture (or many of the western genre films). Similarly, some people developed attitudes toward aviation and airplane safety through movie portrayals even before they ever actually observed a plane.

Both industries—motion pictures and aviation—necessarily concerned themselves with international relations. The airline needed landing rights in Cuba and in other Latin American countries as their routes spread out. Hollywood also had to maintain the good will of local interests. The same year that Pan American organized to bid on the Key West to Havana airmail contract, the Warner Brothers studio made film history with the production and release of a feature-length movie with sound, *The Jazz Singer*. With its tremendous financial stake in foreign distribution, Hollywood took a big risk introducing sound to their profitable silent films. Talking pictures carried a potential threat to industry profits if language barriers limited the foreign market and exports declined. Could the popularity of U.S. movies and film stars overcome the hesitation of moviegoers baffled by the English-language dialogue? Moreover, the thousands of existing foreign movie houses lacked the equipment necessary to project talking films. Would theater owners incur the expense of new equipment?

Moreover, a potential loss in foreign film distribution menaced large segments of the U.S. manufacturing sector, whose members remained convinced that the presentation of American lifestyles and material possessions in the movies stimulated foreign consumption of U.S. goods. So prevalent was this view among manufacturers and merchants that the U.S. Congress had authorized a motion picture section attached to the Bureau of Foreign and Domestic Commerce in the Department of Commerce under Secretary Herbert Hoover. The motion picture section promoted U.S. movies overseas, reported on available equipment and theaters capable of exhibiting them, and published surveys of overseas film markets.

In fact, the same year that the Warner brothers introduced *The Jazz Singer* to movie audiences, Commerce Secretary Herbert Hoover personally welcomed ambassadors from Central and South American nations to a banquet in their honor, sponsored by motion picture advertisers. Since Hoover supported the expansion of the film industry into Latin America, not surprisingly, he used the opportunity of the dinner to extol the virtues of the international trade in motion pictures. Among the benefits of that commerce, Hoover took particular pains to point out that filmmakers felt a special obligation to present the peoples of the western hemisphere in ways that would promote mutual respect.

Hoover unwittingly touched a sensitive nerve. Putting aside diplomatic niceties, the Chilean ambassador responded candidly to Hoover's show of bonhomie. Leaders in Latin American capitals warily eyed U.S. economic and political goals in their countries. Rather than fostering closer ties, the ambassador objected, Hollywood's stereotypical presentations of both romantic and villainous Latinos insulted the history and culture of some hemispheric nations.[3]

If American movies signaled cultural insensitivity and exacerbated Latin American resentments of U.S. intentions, Secretary Hoover had a problem on his hands. As the architect of U.S. commercial expansion in the 1920s, Hoover understandably concerned himself with Latin American attitudes. The country's growing financial stake and trade interests in the area derived from U.S. efforts to improve its postwar economic outlook. Significantly increased agricultural and manufacturing output had met wartime

demands for goods at home and abroad, but postwar retrench-
ment took an inevitable toll on those sectors. Latin America's capacity to absorb imports from the United States depended on the
area's selling its own goods abroad.

Although England, France, and Germany had dominated
Latin American trade and financial relations before the war, armed
hostilities had diminished Europe's ability to provide investment
capital or to transport goods to European markets. With Latin
America perceived as a potential battleground for economic advantage, Hoover encouraged U.S. financial interests to lend funds
to Latin American nations in order to expand their capacity to
import U.S. goods. By the time war-torn Europe recovered, the
United States had gained a foothold in Latin American commerce—including the export of its movies.

Faced with a powerful trade rival, Europeans played up the
idea of a "Yankee menace," a shorthand communication that recalled to Latin Americans a history of U.S. military adventurism
and political aggression. The European-U.S. contention for influence and trade in Latin America underlay the tricontinental relationship from the 1823 Monroe Doctrine through various U.S. in-
vasions, occupations, and protectorates to the rivalry for air
transport supremacy in the 1920s and 1930s.

Even as Secretary Hoover tried to placate Latin American officials, the introduction of movies with sound contributed an additional source of friction to expressed discontent over stereotypical
characterizations and historical misinterpretation. An editorial in
Mexico's *El Universal* charged that talking pictures, because they
were "the most popular of entertainments," forced the English
language on the population. Victimized by a change they could not
control, Mexicans needed to protect their native Spanish language.
Joining economic complaints to cultural nationalism, the editorial
also expressed sympathy for the technologically unemployed musicians who had formerly accompanied silent films. Imported talking pictures constituted an "invasion" by Mexico's northern neighbor, an imposition that called for an official response. Moreover,
costly new equipment impinged on the profits of exhibitors who
were required to pay higher film-rental fees for talkies. Money

would leave Mexico, the editorial concluded, to the benefit of the United States film industry.[4]

Some Cubans demanded import duties on sound films, with the derived revenue to compensate displaced theater musicians. Echoing the alarm sounded by Mexico and Cuba, Argentineans claimed that as many as a thousand musicians had lost work. Brazilians complained that few patrons understood English and those who had some familiarity with the language found the use of colloquialisms confusing. Others considered the English dialogue unpleasantly guttural. Charging cultural imperialism, one Argentine newspaper cited the harmful effects of talkies on the national language. A call went out to ban sound pictures in Buenos Aires. Another proposal suggested increasing import taxes to curtail the abuse. Nevertheless, the continued shipment of silent films to some markets helped push film exports to record levels in 1929.[5]

Although understandably nettlesome to nationalist sentiment, the introduction of movies with sound posed no significant threat to established U.S.-Latin American relationships. Despite protests to U.S. embassies and consulates, American films continued to dominate the markets of Cuba, Brazil, and Argentina as well as Mexico. Moviegoers liked talking pictures. Despite the commotion created at official levels, talkies gained in popularity among the thousands of patrons who had grown attached to that form of entertainment.

One response to the problem of language differences elevated music from an accompaniment to the screen action to the focus of film content. Hollywood released numerous musical revues between 1929 and 1931, films that required little dialogue and consequently minimized language problems. Songs with orchestral accompaniments became highly popular. Some studios distributed dubbed versions of popular musical films, but, to the horror of language-protecting nationalists, audiences preferred the English-language versions.[6]

Clearly, the introduction of the "talkies" steered film production and the movie industry in new directions. For example, the technology that added sound to film and gave birth to the movie musical also underlay the formation of RKO-Radio Pictures. Pictures with sound brought movies and radio together. Joseph P. Kennedy, Harvard graduate, film studio investor, and father of future president John F. Kennedy, paired with David Sarnoff, head of Radio Corporation of America (RCA) and National Broadcasting Company (NBC), and created RKO.

RKO-Radio Pictures

The nickelodeon era had spawned most film studio moguls of the 1920s, but not Joseph Kennedy. For Kennedy, studio ownership represented a timely financial investment, not a life-defining experience. In 1926, the New York investment firm of Hayden, Stone, and Company bought one of Hollywood's smaller studios, the Film Booking Office (FBO) of America, from British interests. FBO turned out low-budget Westerns, melodramas, and comedies for the expanding ranks of small neighborhood movie houses. Kennedy purchased a controlling interest in FBO and, like the pioneer movie men he rounded up for Harvard, moved to build an entertainment enterprise that controlled the production, distribution, and exhibition of moving pictures. With money borrowed from the Rockefeller-dominated Chase National Bank (not from friends and in-laws like the previous immigrant generation), Kennedy purchased a majority interest in the Keith-Albee-Orpheum (KAO) theater chain and then consolidated film production, distribution, and exhibition under FBO's management.

Kennedy moved from the financial world into films; David Sarnoff came from radio. Sarnoff had parlayed his knowledge of electronics into a position as head of RCA. His life story outstripped any Horatio Alger tale as he rose to the presidency of RCA. The child of an impoverished Russian Jewish immigrant family, Sarnoff had spoken no English when he arrived in New York. He dropped out of grade school in order to work and contribute to the family income. Self-taught in the basics of electronics, he climbed to the top ranks of RCA in three decades and to the leadership of the communications industry in four.

Radio came of age in the 1920s, but during World War I the United States had lacked an American-owned, international com-

munications apparatus. Arguing on behalf of national security requirements, the navy pressured for a consolidation of patents for
wireless communications. RCA dominated the resulting patent
pool that included General Electric, Westinghouse, and American
Telephone and Telegraph (AT&T).

Sarnoff envisioned RCA as an entertainment conglomerate
and inaugurated its radio-broadcasting component, NBC, in 1926.
RCA owned NBC at a time when nationwide radio networks
brought ever larger audiences together in shared experiences. Radio broadcasts brought news, information, sports, music, comedy,
drama, commercials, and political announcements to isolated
households in rural communities as well as to those in crowded
urban centers.[7]

Thus, in the same decades in which airline companies inaugurated and organized passenger air travel, the communications
and entertainment industries experienced tremendous expansion
based on technological advances. People flocked to see silent motion pictures first; then they listened to the sound of radio, and finally they embraced the talkies—sound wedded to pictures. With
the success of *The Jazz Singer,* Sarnoff moved to enter the movie
world with a rival sound-on-film process called Photophone.

In an age ever more enthralled by entertainment, tycoons with
vision, like David Sarnoff, employed capital and technology to ensure access to audiences numbering in the millions. In this case
Sarnoff had a sound process and needed film production capability. He found Joseph Kennedy. RCA Photophone, with Sarnoff at
the helm, bought into Kennedy's enterprise. Consequently, Sarnoff
became chairman of the board of a new RCA subsidiary, Radio-
Keith-Orpheum (RKO) Corporation. None of the Kennedy-
purchased KAO theaters had the capacity for sound films, a shortcoming that RCA electronics expertise could readily rectify.

In a synergy of name identification, the RKO Corporation
spawned RKO-Radio Pictures, whose logo displayed a radio tower
balanced on a globe, flashing its signal to a media-connected
world. Financially well rewarded for his efforts, Kennedy left the
company, and Sarnoff named a more experienced corporate executive as president of RKO Corporation.[8]

Sarnoff's fledgling entertainment empire expanded with the purchase of additional theaters and production facilities. Capacity for sound production gave RKO-Radio Pictures its first box-office hit, *Rio Rita,* the filmed version of a long-playing Broadway musical, and the studio earned respectable profits in its first years of operation.

Sound technology revolutionized picture making but didn't doom the industry, as some pessimists—concerned about the reception of "talkies" in the export market—had speculated. Audiences everywhere wanted more product, not less. The change affected not only motion picture content and style, but also the structure of the industry itself. Pictures with sound elevated production costs and raised the level of revenue required to make a profit. Studio heads borrowed funds or issued stock to raise capital in order to purchase theaters where they could exhibit their own films and thus enhance their profits. As they increasingly depended on loans or equity capital to fund operations, the studios tightened the relations between Hollywood and the east coast's corporate world. For RKO-Radio Pictures, the parent company, RKO Corporation, controlled the purse strings.

By the late 1920s, Sarnoff's involvement in the communications industry encompassed radio, telegraph, phonograph, and motion picture theaters and production. He also kept his hand in electronics research and technological development, radio and phonograph manufacture, finance, marketing, trade, and the economics and politics that both promoted and impeded the connections that profited RCA.

On the other hand, the hard-driven businessman maintained his appreciation of and commitment to the idea of communication as a service to humanity. Sarnoff, who had been the young telegraph operator on duty in New York when the *S.S. Titanic* transmitted its distress calls from the North Atlantic, no doubt internalized both the extraordinary potential of communication and the frustration of its technological shortcomings.

Thus, when RCA launched NBC, its announcement self-consciously proclaimed, "The day has gone by when the radio receiving set is a plaything. It must now be an instrument of service."

Moreover, RCA ambitiously declared that NBC would broadcast every event of national importance, not for political advantage or selfish power, but because the company wished to act in the public interest.[9]

With their ability to reach millions of homes, radio executives wielded significant power to direct public cultural preferences, and RCA seized the opportunity to enhance public access to music and drama through radio. After RCA added the movie studio to its properties, the RKO Theater of the Air, which was broadcast over NBC's forty-four-station Red Network, brought stories to listeners' homes every Friday night.

Never a person of narrow vision, Sarnoff embraced his own version of the earlier technological utopianism, that is, he fostered a crusade for human enlightenment through media. RCA's radios, Victrolas, radio broadcasting, and motion pictures occupied a potentially powerful position in a world increasingly tied together through mass communication. During RCA's late-1920s business expansion, which included the inauguration of NBC and RKO, Sarnoff also linked the company to entrepreneur, philanthropist, and arts benefactor John D. Rockefeller Jr. In the twists and turns of this history of aviation, movies, and tourism, even this strategic move affected the making of *Flying Down to Rio*.

The RCA-Rockefeller connection evolved from the late 1920s proposal to find a more suitable location and build a new home for that icon of upper-class culture, New York's Metropolitan Opera Company. Prosperous New Yorkers had moved farther north on Manhattan Island to large residences closer to Central Park. These opera patrons thought it was time for the Metropolitan to move also.

John D. Rockefeller Jr. spearheaded the relocation effort and settled on several midtown Manhattan blocks then owned by Columbia University. For more than a century, the university had derived considerable financial support from these real estate holdings. By the mid-1920s, however, the brownstone houses and commercial properties that occupied the space had experienced considerable physical deterioration, with a commensurate decline in the nature of the tenants.

Rockefeller formed the Metropolitan Square Corporation, leased the land from the university, and leveled the offending structures. According to the development scheme, Metropolitan Square would spearhead a general renaissance of the entire area. In the agreement designed to satisfy all participants, revenue from the lease would continue to support the university, and commercial development around the new opera house would contribute to the opera company, as well as to the Rockefeller interests.

However, before workers could begin to turn the earth for the opera house, the stock market crashed. Regrettably, the Metropolitan Opera Company withdrew from the development. Rockefeller found himself without his major tenant and committed to a long-term lease for the land. He changed the architectural plans to suit the circumstances and refocused the cultural and commercial development on a tall office building instead of an opera house.

Rockefeller Center architects expressed the expansive, exuberant, speculative optimism of the precollapse 1920s in the decorative motif for the project, "New Frontiers and the March of Civilization." By the time construction began in 1931, however, the country had marched into economic depression.

Sarnoff saw an opportunity in adversity. He no doubt considered his various communications efforts as the vanguard of Rockefeller's march across frontiers. Mass culture, the *raison d'être* of RCA and its subsidiaries, would take the place of the elite-oriented Metropolitan Opera as the focal point of Rockefeller Center. RCA negotiated space in two office buildings (named for RCA and RKO) and two theaters, with the right to name the entertainment section of the development as well. Only NBC could broadcast from the RCA complex, which Rockefeller agreed to call Radio City.

Convinced that modern mass communications would liberate and inspire humanity, Sarnoff enshrined his universalist convictions in a mural commissioned for the space above the recessed western entrance to the RCA Building at Rockefeller Center (now the General Electric building, but still home to NBC). In Barry Faulkner's stunning, intricate 1933 mosaic, *Intelligence Awakening Mankind,* sound waves carry information and ideas that vanquish the world's afflictions.

Also under contract to RCA, prominent sculptor Gaston Lachaise cast his vision of the spirit of progress and the conquest of space in limestone on the building's façade above the mosaic. Observers who direct their gaze up from the Avenue of the Americas can see Lachaise's figures with their motion picture cameras ready to record a scene to share with unseen audiences.

With negotiations for leases and naming rights completed in June, 1930, RCA and RKO embarked on the design and construction of a magnificent showplace for entertaining the masses. In January, RKO had contracted with well-known New York theatrical entrepreneur Samuel L. Rothafel to oversee the development of its Radio City theaters. Known to everyone as "Roxy," Rothafel had earned a reputation as the builder of a theatrical monument to cinema. His $10-million, Spanish Renaissance "cathedral of motion pictures" opened on the Manhattan corner of Seventh Avenue and Fiftieth Street in 1927. The Roxy Theater incorporated a Kimball organ into its golden-brown Moorish interior, and three organists accompanied vocal and orchestral music, as well as ballet, before the movie began. At the time of its opening, the Roxy was the world's largest theater.[10]

Roxy conceptualized the Art-Deco masterpiece Radio City Music Hall as a palace for entertainment, built to accommodate more than six thousand spectators in its cavernous auditorium. Designed in the first year of the Great Depression, before people realized the extent and depth of its toll, Radio City Music Hall occupied the ground floor of the RKO Building, a tall office structure next to the taller RCA building in John D. Rockefeller Jr.'s exuberant but debt-ridden project. They stood as expressions of faith in the March of Civilization and in the value of midtown Manhattan commercial real estate.

The magnificent theater enthralled viewers even before their imagination transported them to the fantasy world of entertainment. Rothafel intended to fill the music hall stage with theatrical extravaganzas, and three large panels on the external wall facing Fiftieth Street symbolized dance, drama, and song. Perhaps as a metaphor for show business itself, Ezra Winter's mural titled "The Quest for the Fountain of Eternal Youth" dominated the lobby.

The size of the theater and the nature of the presentations embodied Sarnoff's populist ideal of disseminating culture and entertainment to the masses. However, visions of a fabulous world did not pay the mounting bills. RKO broke ground on the project in 1931, when RKO-Radio Pictures already faced severe financial strain. Radio City Music Hall, RKO's premier theater, offered seventeen carefully chosen acts to a public in need of uplift in December, 1932. The earlier theatrical expression of Rothafel's interpretation of entertainment grandeur, the movie house, now renamed the RKO Roxy, opened two days after the music hall and shortly before an overextended RKO-Radio Pictures went into receivership.

As an illustration of Hollywood unreality, what could be more poignant? Depression-weary audiences enjoyed expensively produced entertainment in colossal palaces while the studios bled red ink.

When the glorious, massive monument to entertainment modernity opened, the RCA and RKO Buildings stood almost ready for occupancy. Unfortunately, few businesses wanted to commit to Rockefeller Center office space in the depths of the Depression. Even the newly completed rival, the Empire State Building, earned the derisive description "Empty State Building." Sarnoff canceled some of RCA's leased space in Radio City and issued 100,000 shares of preferred RCA stock to the Rockefeller-controlled Metropolitan Square Corporation as compensation.

A Movie Brought to You By . . .

David Sarnoff had linked RKO-Radio Pictures to an East Coast establishment of business and cultural interests that frightened most of Hollywood's pioneer movie producers, according to *Time* magazine. "Their consternation seemed to have a reasonable basis," *Time* acknowledged. RKO Corporation, launched in 1929 and capitalized at $20 million, included prominent, wealthy manufacturers, bankers, communications executives, and even a retired major general on its board of directors, a group "sufficiently powerful to rock any industry." Moreover, behind RKO stood the resources and power of RCA.[11]

On the West Coast, *Time* suggested, revealing more than a touch of ethnic bias, "crafty" studio heads, "one-time fur peddlers, garment dealers, second-hand jewelers—mostly Jews" who "settled their biggest deals over all-night poker games" discussed RKO's power and business acumen in awe-stricken whispers and "comic strip dialect." Keeping a watchful eye on the new player, industry moguls warned each other, "Vait till ve see vat Radio vill do." [12]

In fact, "Radio" maintained a presence on each coast—corporate headquarters in New York and its creative operations in Hollywood. RCA's David Sarnoff, whose family history closely resembled the experiences of Hollywood's poker-playing studio heads, persuaded the film-making son of movie pioneer Lewis Selznick to join RKO-Radio Pictures in 1931 as chief of production. In turn, David O. Selznick hired Merian C. Cooper as his assistant. Selznick and Cooper came from completely opposite ends of the social hierarchy, brought together by motion pictures, and their personal relationship and creative energies gave rise to a string of RKO aviation-related movies.

Merian Cooper serves as one more outstanding example of the social, economic, and cultural contributions made by World War I aviators. He built a career on three youthful passions: aviation, adventure travel, and movie making. Marguerite Harrison, who shared with Cooper the adventure of filming the documentary *Grass* in the mid-1920s, describes a man who wanted to become a great explorer, who possessed an "essentially dramatic" creative sensibility, whose vivid imagination favored "startling climaxes," and who demonstrated "a flair for the bizarre and unusual." [13] Once in Hollywood, Cooper precariously balanced his creative sensibilities against box-office demands.

One might characterize Cooper's wartime service as his first great travel adventure. A letter written to his father from France in 1918 expresses both the thrill the young man derives from flying and the flash of dramatic exposition:

I am the happiest I have been since I have been in France. I am at the front at last and expect in the next few days to be actively operating across the [enemy] lines. . . . I am in a day bombing squadron which means we put out quite a bit of fighting too, I hope. It surely is great to have a machine all your own. . . . When you open her up she jumps like a stricken deer, and you can take her nose up to the sky and go up like an elevator. I haven't looped or stunted her yet but expect to give it a thorough try out shortly. . . . I don't know whether I will make good at the front here or not. . . . But I'm just as happy as a man can be to be up here at the front, and if I happen to get mine don't worry or grieve a bit. . . . I am where your son should be.[14]

Merian Cooper descended from a family that had owned plantations along the Georgia-Florida border before the War for Independence. One of his forebears, John Cobb Cooper, commanded a cavalry unit in the revolutionary struggle and later served as governor of Georgia. By the twentieth century the family benefited from an extensive network of long-standing business and political connections. Merian's father, a lawyer and banker, served as head of the Federal Reserve Bank in Florida. Florida's Senator Duncan U. Fletcher had recommended Merian for appointment to the U.S. Naval Academy at Annapolis.

Cooper left the academy during his senior year, most likely due to some academic or behavioral shortcoming. He later expressed regret at not graduating, along with feelings of failure, and recalled having been a high-spirited youth who loved excitement and took chances—attributes more appreciated at the front, perhaps, than in the classroom. After he left Annapolis, he worked aboard a merchant ship and as a newspaper reporter and then served with the Georgia National Guard in General John Pershing's 1916 expedition into Mexico in search of Francisco "Pancho" Villa.[15]

When the United States entered World War I in April, 1917, Cooper weighed the possibilities of a commission as first lieutenant in the Georgia National Guard or a commission in the army. He wrote to a West Point graduate friend of his father's in the War Department for advice and to his father for solace. He confessed a "bitterness" at past events and a willingness to die for the country's honor and asked his father to "Pray that I may go to France and there win such success as I may merit, that our name may still stand proud and true. . . . I failed the service of my country in time of peace. Now I only ask humbly that I may prove worthy in the test of steel and blood." [16]

When Cooper graduated first in his class from the School of Military Aeronautics at Georgia School of Technology in Atlanta, he wrote gleefully about his pride in completing the course with honors "because I was an Annapolis failure, and a failure too at every other school I had been at." Once in France, he confided both his joy and his sense of inadequacy: "Thousands of better Americans than I have died gladly over here," and he hoped to measure up to their sacrifice. [17]

In fact, Cooper's war experiences proved even more dramatic than his words and more worthy than he could have imagined. The eager patriot turned a passion for flying into a love of battle, which he confided to his father in his letters from the front. Each success raised his self-confidence as he redeemed his reputation and the family's honor.

Cooper contentedly piloted his bomber until shot down behind enemy lines and taken prisoner in September, 1918. The Germans treated his wounded hands, which had been severely burned when bullets set his plane on fire. The Germans kept him in a prison camp until after the war ended. Offered a medal for staying with his flaming plane rather than abandon his wounded fellow aviator, Cooper declined, citing equivalent actions by others in his squadron. [18]

Repatriated to France in January, 1919, Cooper left for Poland the following month to establish a food mission, set up to relieve the suffering of Poles who had been battling the invading Bolsheviks. Returning to Paris once more, he helped to recruit a dozen American aviators into the Kosciuszko Squadron, and they all joined the Polish Army—much as the Lafayette Escadrille had formed to help the French.

Again the family honor combined with Cooper's love of adventure to influence his commitment to the Polish cause. General Casimir Pulaski, the Polish nobleman who had joined the colonists against the British, had fought alongside Cooper's great-grandfather at Savannah and had lost his life in the battle. "Would it not be a fine and honorable thing," he wrote to his father, "if I could pay with my life for the debt our name owes to Pulaski for the great service he did with our ancestor at Savannah?" [19]

Anyone but a truly adventurous spirit would have gone home after several months as a prisoner of war, but Cooper longed for another battlefield. He arrived in Warsaw with the Kosciuszko Squadron on the anniversary of being shot down and taken prisoner and could not wait to begin strafing the enemy. He expected to have a "splendid" winter at the front, he declared on October 24, his twenty-sixth birthday, and when the cold and snow immobilized the troops, he expressed the hope that the two sides would not make peace before the spring and deny him the opportunity to fight again. [20]

Cooper flew again in the spring on the Ukraine front, spent a few weeks resting, and then returned to the front. On July 13, he failed to return from an observation flight over the battle lines. After months during which the Polish authorities listed him as missing and looked for him, Cooper escaped from the Russian prison camp near Moscow, where he had been held, along with two Polish soldiers. They reached the Latvian border after a twenty-six-day trek and paid a smuggler to help them cross. [21]

With the family honor more than adequately upheld and having encountered significantly more adventure that most people experience in a lifetime, Cooper returned to the United States in 1921 and went to work as a reporter for the *New York Times*.

Movies had not yet become crucial to Cooper's life, but they soon would. With his desire to explore the world still unsatisfied, he arranged to join a round-the-world cruise as a ship's officer and a writer. When the expedition's cameraman quit after a storm at sea, Cooper contacted a wartime acquaintance, Ernest B. Schoedsack. Schoedsack had worked in Hollywood and then as a combat photographer. He and Cooper had met in Europe after the war and before both of them had linked their fates to the Polish cause.

Schoedsack accepted a position as photographer on the cruise.

He introduced Cooper to the possibilities of adventure-film making when the ship stopped in the culturally distinctive African country of Ethiopia. So, at the age of thirty, Cooper once more appeared to be embarking on a career, this time as an explorer and filmmaker. He and Schoedsack borrowed money—not unlike most novice movie producers—and took off for Persia (now Iran). Newspaper correspondent Marguerite Harrison, whom Cooper had met in Poland, put up $5,000 and became the third partner.

The subject of their documentary film, the seasonal migration of Bakhtiari herders in search of grazing lands, took them from the high mountain valleys of central Persia to the shores of the Persian Gulf. The trio lived with the tribe and photographed its daily activities until their money ran out. Cooper and Schoedsack developed the film themselves, edited the footage into a coherent narrative called *Grass,* and took the completed work around the lecture circuit in 1925. In a fortuitous circumstance that Hollywood itself might adopt for a screenplay with a happy ending, Paramount-Famous Players' Jesse Lasky saw the film and arranged for theatrical distribution. And the rest, as they say, is history.

The veteran photographer and his recruit took the money they made on *Grass* and went off to the jungles of northern Thailand to film *Chang,* the story of an elephant. Paramount distributed this second documentary adventure also, and Lasky hired Cooper and Schoedsack to produce and direct their first dramatic film, *The Four Feathers,* a tale of soldiering and comradeship that certainly appealed to the two combat veterans. Perhaps even more attractive, the studio sent the two adventurers off to Africa to photograph natives, wild animals, and location footage for the film, which Paramount released in 1929.[22]

By then Cooper had experienced the motion picture business from story development to distribution. He and Schoedsack had bridged the passage from silent to talking pictures, from documentary to feature film, and from location to studio work. Nevertheless, the multitalented Cooper soon left Hollywood for New York to pursue yet another career path, one that indulged his passion for aviation.

Back on the East Coast and in contact with old friends John Hambleton and Sonny and Jock Whitney, Cooper joined their effort to advance the cause of U.S. air transport. On Hambleton's advice, he invested part of his earnings from *Grass, Chang,* and *The Four Feathers* in aviation stocks. As a result of his substantial financial participation, Pan American Airways and other air transport companies named Cooper to their boards of directors. He worked in New York on behalf of the new industry and at the age of thirty-five seemed to have settled on a career in aviation.

Before very long, however, the desire to make another animal-adventure film, combined with his passion for airplanes, sent Cooper back to Hollywood. No doubt his experiences in African, Asian, and Manhattan jungles influenced the evolving film concept that became *King Kong.* One version of the inspiration for the film suggests that the idea of a battling gorilla came to him when he was in Africa, filming animals for *The Four Feathers.* Another reconstruction places Cooper in his Manhattan office, actively at work in the airline industry. Interrupted by the sound of an airplane motor, he looked up to see a plane flying past the New York Life Insurance building, then New York's tallest structure. According to this version, the idea of a giant gorilla shot down from the top of a skyscraper by men in airplanes represented to him an epic battle between nature and technology.[23]

In *King Kong* a film crew captures and transports a gigantic gorilla to Manhattan for exhibition purposes. When the frightened animal breaks loose, police trackers use radios to communicate the rampaging Kong's whereabouts in the city. Once Kong climbs to the top of the Empire State Building, beyond the reach of ordinary people, heroic pilots risk their lives (one plane whirls to its doom during the standoff) to protect the metropolis. Airplanes save Manhattan from a destructive, untamed force and facilitate the rescue of the beautiful blond maiden that the beast carries to the man-made pinnacle where it had unwittingly sought escape from the multitudes.

Merian Cooper's life took yet another turn. He enjoyed all of the advantages of inherited status in eastern elite social and financial circles, but his connection to the West Coast immigrant movie pioneers enabled him to develop his concept for an action-adventure film about a gorilla in civilized society. The association came not through family ties but as a result of his work on *The Four Feathers*. He had met the young David O. Selznick (probably best remembered as producer of the Civil War epic film, *Gone with the Wind*) at Paramount Pictures.

David's father, Lewis J. Selznick, had immigrated to the United States from eastern Europe, settled in Pittsburgh, and opened a jewelry store. On the advice of a friend, Lewis moved into the film industry as a business venture, not because he had creative ambitions. When he imposed himself on the fragmented, squabbling owners of Universal Pictures in 1912 as a self-appointed general manager, he moved his family to New York. Once he learned the fundamentals of the operation, he launched his own company, Select Picture Corporation. Selznick and Select became well known, but not necessarily well liked, through the years of fierce competition and industry growth. Nevertheless, Lewis's family lived comfortably in Manhattan on income derived from the movies' popularity.[24]

Some of Lewis Selznick's status in the industry derived from his position as a founding member of the Motion Picture Producers and Directors Association (MPPDA), launched in 1922 to combat widespread criticism of film content and suggestive promotional materials and to deflect the censorship pressures placed on local exhibitors by civic and religious leaders. With studio heads sensitive to political and trade issues that might affect profits, they formed the trade association, developed guidelines responsive to public opinion, lobbied against government regulation, and protected the industry's interests in the international marketplace.

Like Merian Cooper, David Selznick benefited from his father's business and political connections. When Lewis's business fell on hard times in the 1920s, he moved to Hollywood to start again. David and his brother, Myron, followed. The Selznick name still opened doors in the interconnected world of film studio pioneers. Myron became a talent agent, and David worked in production at Paramount when the studio made the aerial war classic *Wings* in 1927. The following year he put together an action drama, *Dirigible*, as a follow-up. However, the navy's dirigible development unit refused to assist the studio unless the story demonstrated the airship's safeness. Since the script called for the dirigible to encounter various dramatic, tension-building episodes, the studio had to abandon the project.

A decade younger than Merian Cooper, David Selznick had missed the defining experience of service in World War I. Although nurtured in the early-twentieth-century American culture of striving immigrant entrepreneurs, Selznick had entered his adult life in the commercial, political, artistic, combative, tribal world of the movie business.

In the serpentine, real-life scenarios that often surpass fiction in their dependence on coincidence, Selznick, son of one movie mogul and son-in-law of another, facilitated Cooper's return to Hollywood just when the aviation executive wanted to make another picture.

Selznick's assignment as associate producer on *The Four Feathers* had put him in close contact with Cooper and Schoedsack. Cooper returned to New York. Selznick continued to work at Paramount and married Irene Mayer, daughter of legendary Metro-Goldwyn-Mayer chief, Louis B. Mayer. Like the movies they made, film producers' lives encouraged a belief in wish fulfillment. Mayer, the Russian-born Hollywood powerhouse, active in the California Republican Party and an outspoken supporter of President Herbert Hoover, arranged for the newlyweds to dine at the White House on their way to a European honeymoon.

David Selznick returned to work at Paramount after the honeymoon. Later that year, RCA chief David Sarnoff offered Paramount $50,000 for Selznick's services, in the hope that the talented young producer could strengthen RKO-Radio Pictures. Although the company had made money, the studio had produced a string of mediocre pictures after several early successes.[25] Paramount declined Sarnoff's offer, but Selznick found himself increasingly discontented in the position of assistant production manager and left Paramount the following June after a salary dispute with the studio.

Constrained by studio politics and determined to produce films on his own, Selznick put together a production company—on paper—with his friend, director Lewis Milestone. He took the train east to find financial backing for the project and met with banker Otto Kahn, one of the money men behind Paramount, and with representatives of Chase National Bank. He also wrote a proposal for RKO Corporation, offering to supervise the production of six pictures to be released through RKO-Radio.

After he made the rounds of financiers, Selznick called on his former Paramount colleague Merian Cooper. They shared burning ambitions: Selznick needed money for his independent film company; Cooper needed a studio to make his gorilla film. Cooper had already told his friend David Bruce, son-in-law of Treasury Secretary Andrew Mellon, about his film idea, and Bruce had met with Sarnoff on Cooper's behalf. Now Cooper introduced Selznick to Bruce, Trubee Davison, and Sonny Whitney (all of them old friends of Juan Trippe and associated with Pan American Airways), and they strategized about funding sources.

Perhaps when Cooper approached Bruce to make the pitch to Sarnoff, he also reasoned that with Selznick at RKO-Radio, the studio would surely make his film. At any rate, Sarnoff once again offered Selznick a position at RKO. Convinced he would find backing for his own company, Selznick refused. However, he was still in New York when Lewis Milestone bowed out of the prospective partnership and accepted a job offer in Hollywood. When Sarnoff repeated his offer, Selznick accepted and returned to California in November, 1931, as RKO-Radio Pictures executive vice president and production chief.[26]

Selznick immediately put Cooper on the payroll, and the aviator/filmmaker moved to Hollywood to make his travel-adventure-thriller movie. Selznick worked hard to sell studio executives on Cooper's technically creative, but highly experimental, film. However, at the time, both RCA and RKO worried about company expenses. Given the overcommitment at Radio City and a studio on the verge of bankruptcy, the cautious RKO officials authorized production of only one reel, to be evaluated by the sales force before embarking on full production. Several months passed before Selznick obtained approval.

While most films took several weeks or at most a couple of months to produce, *King Kong* took a year—from early 1932 until its release in March, 1933. After Cooper arrived with a story idea, writers took months to come up with scenarios and dialog. Model-animation techniques and other special effects had to be developed and tested. The studio had to hire actors, and the actors had to perform certain scenes before the cameras, while technical people performed magic with a mechanical gorilla, rear projections, miniature sets, process shots, and so on. Then they edited thousands of feet of film into a coherent, exciting story.

Airline executive Merian Cooper connected the two worlds of commercial aviation and motion pictures when he joined RKO late in 1931 and used his influence in movie production to advance the acceptance of air transportation. As assistant to Selznick during the year that *Kong* took shape, Merian Cooper worked on various other studio projects as well as his own film. His influence is obvious in several RKO-Radio, aviation-related pictures. Five studio releases, beginning with *The Lost Squadron* in March, 1932, and ending with *Flying Down to Rio* in December, 1933, after Cooper replaced Selznick as RKO-Radio production chief, reflect an aviation enthusiast's optimistic attitude toward air transport. That is, airplanes are not inherently dangerous and in fact benefit society.

In several RKO films made under Cooper's aegis, not only did airplanes offer entertainment and excitement, but they also represented safe, convenient, and speedy transportation. If accidents occurred, the fault lay with the way in which people used and abused the planes' flight capability, not in the machines themselves. The story lines of the five films, taken as a whole, encouraged a transition in the viewers' image of airplanes from an instrument of war, entertainment, and sport to an expression of civilized life, a transportation mode, and access to the pleasures of tourism.

Merian Cooper signed on at RKO-Radio Pictures the same month that pilot Charles Lindbergh and aircraft designer Igor Sikorsky launched the inaugural S-40 *American Clipper* flight for Pan American Airways. Lindbergh and Sikorsky attended a dinner at the first stop—Kingston, Jamaica—on the triumphal circuit to mark the occasion. The world's first four-motor seaplane performed perfectly under Lindbergh's expert hand. The next day Lindbergh and Sikorsky flew on to Barranquilla, Colombia, and then to Cristóbal in the Panama Canal Zone.

With the arrival of the air service, Jamaican authorities anticipated a revitalization of their country's steamship-dependent tourist trade. Regularly scheduled air travel would appeal to the businessperson or middle-sector worker whose time constraints restricted ocean travel. Indeed, Kingston's *Daily Gleaner* later recalled that before Pan Am linked Jamaica to the United States, the island had catered almost exclusively to a wealthy clientele. *Clipper* service opened the island to a broader vacation market and facilitated its mass tourism industry.[27]

Although the speed with which travelers could reach a destination was critical to tourism's growth as a mass industry, the expansion of industrial tourism also depended on safety and promotion. Latin American tourism gained from Pan American's advertisements in various media as a comfortable, reliable passenger carrier and from the company's image as fostered by its public relations team.

On the other hand, millions of moviegoers internalized other—possibly inhibiting—messages about flying. Understandably, Merian Cooper had both personal and financial reasons to use his position at RKO-Radio Pictures to alter the communication. He loved to fly, held firm convictions about the value of air transport, and had funds invested in aviation stocks.

Although film historians consider *The Lost Squadron* David Selznick's first RKO production, Merian Cooper clearly took a hand in the film's evolution from script to screen. Selznick knew virtually nothing about aviation, whereas Cooper lived and breathed airplanes. RKO had already acquired the story, written by stunt pilot Dick Grace, when Selznick and Cooper joined the studio. Grace had flown stunts for *Wings* in 1927 and looped, dived, and crashed for *The Lost Squadron,* too, despite his story's criticism of death by entertainment. The self-reflective film depicts Hollywood's exploitation of stunt pilots in order to make exciting movies. The caustic tale of a callous film director who risks lives for cinematic thrills reflects Grace's extensive Hollywood experience as a movie plane crasher. Altogether, he had wrecked thirty-eight planes on cue.

Dick Grace's behind-the-scenes look at aerial movie making set a squadron of stunt fliers against an egotistical, overbearing, jealous director, played by director Eric von Stroheim in an easily recognizable self-caricature. He struts and poses, wears spats and gloves, and carries a cane; he berates the film crew and belittles the actors.

The film-within-a-film plot—the studio under scrutiny is making a war movie—condemns the industry's misuse of stunt pilots but provides ample opportunity for daring combat flights. The fliers, merely cogs in the machinery of filmed thrills and crashes, are expendable and interchangeable to the director. To emphasize that point, Grace's original story gives them no backgrounds, no lives before they assemble at the airfield the studio uses. Their lives are emblematic, and he condenses their reality to a day and a half of action—flying, rolling, crack-ups, and blood and guts after the inevitable crash—and personal interactions— love, jealousy, and revenge—involved in the gory glory of aerial film production.

The film script adaptation expands Grace's serialized short story to acknowledge the stunt pilots' military service. It opens with a rousing, joyful homecoming from the war. Added vignettes of personal history explain why these men have assembled on a California airfield to risk their lives in the stunt game. They had met personal disappointment on their return to civilian life, and the public soon forgot them. When the Depression took their jobs, they went to California to change their luck. After all, says one, the studios paid $50 a day for flying, and there would be no enemy planes to shoot at them.

RKO-Radio Pictures began filming *The Lost Squadron* in November, 1931, just as Selznick took over as production chief and Cooper dug in as his assistant. RKO-Radio script files indicate that added scenes dated January, 1932, moved the film's opening to the last days of World War I. The first scene recorded an aerial dogfight between American and German forces on the Western front.

When the shooting ends, three pilots return to base and then gather in a café in a French village. The last remaining pilots of their squadron, they celebrate the war's end and their return home. They have forged the bonds of wartime buddies and will renew that sense of loyalty when they fly together years later in Hollywood.[28]

That new opening directly parallels Merian Cooper's war combat experiences, that is, the action, the return to base, and the camaraderie. His letters home had described his friendships and his anguish at the deaths of so many fellow pilots. Cooper stamped an unmistakable mark on the film. Moreover, he undoubtedly agreed with author and stunt pilot Dick Grace that the movies had taken too great a toll on the war's heroic aviators. At the end of the film, as in the story, the diabolical director dies at the hands of two stunt pilots. One of them puts the director's body in his plane, takes off, and crashes to hide the murder.

The lone surviving pilot marries the kid sister of another of the director's victims. Their marriage will end his foolhardy movie flying, she warns. He can go to work flying the mail. This film sent an airmail message to the audience: Airplanes will carry you safely to your destination; the crashes you see in the movies are ordered for your entertainment.

The Lost Squadron's success at the box office no doubt encouraged the financially strapped studio to make *Flying Devils* the following year. The low-budget story of barnstorming, flying-circus performers used lots of stock aerial footage and claimed little originality of plot. An older, jealous husband manages a troupe of fliers. His young, attractive, wing-walking wife falls for a young man who has left college to join his brother as a performer with their circus. The wife and the young man perform a stunt that calls for close physical contact, and the sexual tension mounts. They spend the night together. The lover asks the husband to divorce the wife. In a jealous rage, the husband devises a scheme to cause an aerial accident during the show to get rid of his rival. The protective older brother sacrifices his own life in the stunt, and the husband dies also.

The film presented no fictional challenge to the film industry but rather reinforced Grace's point—Hollywood put pilots at risk to provide entertainment thrills. Nevertheless, the last sequence

probably reflected the weight of Cooper's experience and authority, as it left no doubt where aviation was headed: A Ford trimotor
passenger plane taxis to an air terminal. Workers bring a canopy
and roll a carpet to the stairs. A uniformed attendant opens the
door and assists the passengers as they leave the plane. Then the
pilot appears—the young man from the flying circus, of course. A
woman, the widow of the flying-circus's owner, now the pilot's
wife, waits for him. They go off together.

The sentimental ending of the action thriller linked flying with
mundane satisfactions, the ordinariness of coming home from
work, not with daredevil thrills. Not only is the passenger plane
mechanically sound, it says, but the pilot wants to return safely to
the wife he loves and therefore will take no risks. He and the former wing walker will live happily together for years to come.

RKO did not want to lose the potential ticket buyers who
made *The Lost Squadron* a success, but the studio chose a story line
that reinforced the transition to commercial aviation. Studio executives made no secret of the fact that they closely followed the market when selecting the films they would make and the actors to star
in them. Given the studio's precarious financial condition, RKO's
corporate heads in New York understandably weighed every expenditure and every decision against potential profits.

In *Tracking King Kong,* Cynthia Erb's book about Cooper's
classic film, the cinema studies professor affirms that the cold logic
of the marketplace guided the content of the movie. While working on one expensive film, *The Lost Squadron,* Merian Cooper
completed his dream film, which cost even more money to produce. Since women constituted a significant segment of the movie
audiences, the studio promoted the picture either as a jungle-
action film or as a love story, depending on test market responses.
As one film distributor admonished the studio, promotional materials must play up the romantic aspects of the adventure film lest
they lose the lucrative women's market.[29]

Hardly in a financial position to disregard the advice of the
people who booked their films, RKO included both adventure
and romance in both the film and the advertisements. In fact,
Cooper's alter ego in the movie—the producer of adventure

films—wistfully articulates the inherent dilemma of the industry: that creative people answer to a sales force tied to box-office receipts and to corporate executives.

In the movie the producer is ready to start a new, wild-animal action film but awaits the hiring of his female lead. He has made adventure films before without women, he tells a theatrical agent, but the public demands a pretty face. Everyone wants romance, he complains. The exhibitors argue that a picture with a love interest grosses twice as much as one without. This time he's going to give them what they want, says the fictional producer.

The scene appears early in the movie, a bit of dialog swallowed up in the excitement that follows, but it conveys a real discontent. Nevertheless, Cooper's real-life production and promotion decisions, coerced or not, paid off. *King Kong*'s audiences responded as prompted to both the adventure and the romance and returned the studio's investment plus substantial profits.

The Feminine Approach to Flight Safety

True, the movie-going public liked pretty faces, but critics had difficulty placing Katherine Hepburn in that category when she made her first film for RKO. Hepburn had trained as a stage actress and brought a strong presence and personality, as well as a distinguished Broadway reputation with her to Hollywood. Her 1932 stage appearance in a comedy loosely based on Aristophanes' *Lysistrata* prompted a well-known New York society matron to share her enthusiasm for both the performance and the actress in a telegram to Merian Cooper.

Hepburn's screen test impressed David Selznick as well, and he offered her the role of John Barrymore's daughter in *A Bill of Divorcement* at a salary considerably higher than Broadway standards. Critics and audiences liked the film and newcomer Hepburn, so RKO signed Hepburn to a five-year contract and looked for a starring role suitable to her potential for forceful on-screen characterizations.

The studio selected a novel, *Christopher Strong,* with a plot about doomed love, suitable to 1930s' melodrama. A vigorous, independent female—Lady Cynthia Darrington—a race-car driver whose passion is speed, belongs to the British social elite. The title character, Sir Christopher Strong, a man of civic and personal virtue with a loving family, has arrived at "the dangerous age" and succumbs to her looks and vibrant personality, thus setting up the romantic conflict that drives the action.

RKO's film adaptation recast Lady Cynthia's persona from dedicated race-car driver to accomplished and ardent aviator. When the audience first meets Lady Cynthia, she is headed for the airfield to check on the preparations for her participation in an air show in Paris. She exudes confidence, strides rather than walks, dresses in form-fitting flying garb and trench coat, and is as comfortable with airplane mechanics as with English country-weekend hostesses.

Lady Cynthia lives to fly and does not want to compromise her independence or ambition, obviously the reason she has neither married nor even had an affair. She prefers to set aviation records, and when she enters a round-the-world competition, she wins. The audience watches as she departs from New York and heads east toward Europe. As the tension mounts, the moviegoers follow her course and share the excitement as the triumphant pilot lands her plane—in a rousing finish—in New York once again.

Now this tale of a self-motivated, freedom-loving woman takes a detour. Famous for her acknowledged accomplishments in aviation, Lady Cynthia nonetheless longs to fulfill a need for sexual passion. She and Sir Christopher become lovers, with disastrous consequences, of course. As in most other filmed melodramas of the period, female transgressors meet a difficult end. In this case, however, the woman who has exercised control over her life also controls her death. Pregnant, but unwilling to force Sir Christopher to break up his family, she nobly commits suicide by crashing her plane while setting an altitude record—another act of aviator self-sacrifice, like those scripted into *The Lost Squadron* and *Flying Devils*.

Did Merian Cooper's ties to the aviation industry influence the decision to make Lady Cynthia a flier for Hepburn's first starring role after her successful film debut? Film devotees not surprisingly identified the plucky, independent character of Lady Cynthia with aviator Amelia Earhart, who completed her trans-Atlantic voyage just months before RKO chose *Christopher Strong* for Hepburn and fashioned a bold female flier with an intense longing for excitement.

The choice of film genre suggests more than coincidence. Although Lindbergh's solo trans-Atlantic flight boosted the prospects for air transport, the overwhelming majority of people who had the opportunity to make the choice still refused to fly. With more women flying competitively in the late 1920s and early 1930s, the airline industry launched a campaign to tame the image of flight safety and made the female pilot its symbol of safety and ease of operation.[30]

Perhaps women pilots graciously indulged the overt condescension in the message: If women can fly a plane, the skill must be easy to learn; if they wanted to fly, it certainly could not involve too much risk. That publicity campaign might sell seats on an airplane, but it denied reality. Women pilots willingly took risks, and many of them died while participating in competitions.

As early as 1910, Bessica Raiche flew a Wright-type plane that she and her husband had built at their Long Island, New York, home. Harriett Quimby learned to fly in 1911, received the first international pilot's license issued to an American woman, and flew across the English Channel before she died at a Boston air meet in 1912. Laura Bromwell, an accomplished aviator by 1920—the year that Amelia Earhart learned to fly—fell to her death while looping her plane. Laura Ingalls performed aerial acrobatics.

Ruth Elder and Frances Greyson attempted trans-Atlantic flights in 1927. When engine trouble ended Elder's flight, a passing freighter plucked her from the sea. No one rescued Greyson when she went down, however, nor did searchers ever find her or her plane.

Amelia Earhart earned her pilot's license, but Wilmer (Bill) Stultz piloted her first voyage across the Atlantic in 1928, with Louis (Slim) Gordon as copilot. Earhart had a contract to write the story, and she did. She continued to fly and write, and four years later she flew solo from the United States to Ireland, the first person to cross the Atlantic twice in an airplane. That year she became president of the women pilots' association, the Ninety-Nines, named for the number of charter members in the organization. Before Earhart's acclaimed feat, Ruth Nichols had crashed her plane and broken five vertebrae while attempting the transoceanic voyage.[31]

Meanwhile, a pair of daring English women could easily have served as models for Lady Cynthia Darrington. Lady Sophie Heath flew solo from Capetown, South Africa, to Croydon, England, in 1928. When the Sudanese government insisted that she have an escort plane flown by a male pilot while flying over their national territory, she took off without warning and left her escort behind at Khartoum. The flamboyant, adventurous party-goer had married a wealthy aristocrat whose money supported her aerial exploits. An air crash in 1929 left her with some disabilities, and she did not fly solo in an airplane again for almost two years, by which time she had divorced Lord Heath.

Lady Mary Bailey married South African millionaire Abe Bailey in 1911 and had given birth to five children when she took up flying in 1926. She flew solo across the Irish Sea the following year and in 1928 flew from Croydon to Cape Town and back. Adventurous but more subdued than Lady Sophie, this Dame of the British Empire participated in numerous international aviation competitions and ferried British military planes during World War II.[32]

Phyllis Fleet earned her pilot's license in 1929, the same year that her father, Reuben H. Fleet, invested in New York, Rio, and Buenos Aires Air Line, Pan American's rival for the Miami-Rio airmail contract. Phyllis Fleet studied mechanical engineering at Cornell University and served as secretary of the school's flying club before she went to work for her father's company, Consolidated Aircraft. By the time RKO made *Christopher Strong,* Fleet had traded aviation for marriage and family, but she retained her membership in the Ninety-Nines.[33]

Orville Wright himself signed Evelyn Trout's international pilot's license the same year that the record-setting aviator participated in the first National Women's Air Derby. Will Rogers called the 1929 race from California to Ohio the "Powder Puff Derby," and the name stuck. A 1922 flight in a Curtiss Jenny determined the course of Trout's life. She set her first record—for endurance—in January, 1929, competed with Elinor Smith to keep it, and then set a women's altitude record in June of that year. While Katherine Hepburn accomplished Lady Darrington's fictional aviation feats through movie magic, Evelyn Trout set real records and taught other airplane enthusiasts how to fly.[34]

RKO script writer Zoe Akins certainly had superb material from which to create the persona of a head-strong, dedicated aviator. The heroine of *Christopher Strong* demonstrated once again that well-intentioned, self-sacrificial pilots might cause crashes, but the people who built airplanes designed them for safety.

Nevertheless, the studio's attempt to mix romance, speed, and excitement failed to work as a starring vehicle for Hepburn. The film opened with considerable fanfare at Radio City Music Hall. The *New York Times'* reviewer found her convincing as a flying enthusiast and sympathetic as a woman who loves another woman's husband, but audiences did not like the movie. Perhaps they preferred Mae West's unapologetic sexuality to Hepburn's self-recriminations and suicide in the cause of family sanctity.

Depression Woes Relieved by Movie Musicals

By the time RKO-Radio released *Christopher Strong* in March, 1933, David Selznick had left the studio, Merian Cooper had become production chief, and the studio had piled up huge operating losses. In January, the RKO house organ, *Radio Flash,* had laid out a grim scenario of financial curtailment. Even as RCA president Sarnoff sent employees an optimistic message in the company newsletter and exalted the socially significant role of the studio's product, he tightened his fist around its money supply.

The nation's economic woes had precipitated a general crisis in the movie industry. Unemployment deprived the working-class audience of disposable income. Box-office receipts declined by one-third between 1929 and 1933, and diminished revenues failed to cover the escalating costs of longer, more technically elaborate movies. All of Hollywood's dream factories struggled against a tide of red ink.

RKO-Radio Pictures needed a box-office success or two, given the economic crisis that plagued the entire movie industry. The studio had released twenty-nine films and earned more than three million dollars in profits in 1930, but a fifty-film schedule resulted in a $5.6-million deficit in 1931. The studio lost more than $10 million dollars in 1932, and two years of disastrous box-office receipts forced RKO-Radio into receivership in 1933.[35]

RKO's losses drained financial resources from the parent company, RCA, which the media conglomerate found difficult to justify to stockholders. David Sarnoff, president of RCA and board chairman of its subsidiary, RKO Corporation, openly and understandably expressed an eagerness to see RKO-Radio work its way back to profitability. RCA had invested substantially in RKO-Radio Pictures and, in 1933, owned more than half of RKO Corporation's stock.[36]

RKO's story department may have added to the decline in revenue, as it routinely combed the press for topical events on which to base screenplays. Increasingly, audiences across the country voiced a preference for lighter fare, and reality-based scripts lost favor. Who wanted to pay money to see the grimness of daily life reflected on the screen?[37]

Financial problems notwithstanding, the studio dedicated the opening receipts for the May, 1932, debut of *State's Attorney*, John Barrymore's first picture for RKO, to the Women's Division of the Emergency Unemployment Relief Committee. When President Hoover wired his good wishes to the RKO executives and employees gathered for that year's company sales convention, his warm greeting acknowledged RKO's generosity, as well as the movie industry's potential to entertain an otherwise dispirited nation.[38]

Sarnoff also expressed a vision about movies that transcended their market value. In his statement to RKO-Radio's 1932 sales convention, he lamented the Depression's toll on the nation but optimistically regarded the movie industry's potential contribution to the good of society. Machines had contributed to overproduction and led to the high levels of unemployment, he explained, following an economic analysis popular in business and government circles. On the other hand, machines that cut work hours afforded more leisure time. Both during and after a "transition period" to correct the imbalance between overproduction and labor requirements, Sarnoff suggested, the motion picture industry would provide films to enrich people's lives through wholesome entertainment and education.[39]

In January, 1933, officials of RKO Corporation traveled from New York to confer with Benjamin Kahane, president of RKO-Radio Pictures, and David O. Selznick. The studio would have to cut expenses, they insisted, including reductions in payroll costs.[40] Selznick left the next month and went to work for his father-in-law at Metro-Goldwyn-Mayer.

By 1933, the steady, dependable weekly moviegoer, having grown tired of Hollywood's gangsters, gritty urban settings, corrupt officials, and scheming businessmen, contentedly greeted a resurgence of musical comedies that gave a happy ending to people's misfortunes. They countered human conflicts with escapism and ended in reassurance, a formula sure to assuage the insecurities of the time. Hollywood had released sixty musicals in prosperous 1928 and seventy in 1930, but only fifteen in 1932. It was time for a change.

In addition to revues and adaptations of popular Broadway shows, the studios introduced stories about theatrical productions—the so-called backstage musical. In a discernible formula, the narrative involved characters in recognizable conflicts: stagestruck singers and dancers with unfulfilled ambitions; financial pressures and theatrical conflicts; and romantic rivalries that coupled and then frustrated the stars, chorus girls, producers, directors, secretaries, and wealthy patrons of the arts. By the final scene, clashing notions about show business priorities or class and family loyalties melted in the heat of passion. A compelling romance eclipsed differences in social status and culture. Loving couples, kept apart by scripted obstructions, ultimately reunited and married.

Musical numbers—humorous songs, romantic ballads, extravagant dance fantasies—interrupted the misunderstandings and complications that kept romantically inclined couples apart until the curtain-descending reconciliation. Exuberant dance sequences filled the screen with energy, sumptuous settings, chorus girls, and melodies. Freedom of movement in the musical numbers contrasted with the social or fiscal restraints depicted in the story. By the end of each film, characters had overcome obstacles and put on a spectacular show.

Responsive to the market, RKO moved deliberately from portrayals of a dark reality to the world of extravagant musical fantasy. Early in 1933, a three-reel RKO musical comedy short subject titled *So This Is Harris* proved surprisingly popular with audiences. Phil Harris, the real-life orchestra leader at the Cocoanut Grove nightclub at Los Angeles's Ambassador Hotel, inspired the film. Although few people around the country had ever visited the Hollywood nightclub where he performed, millions of radio listeners had heard Harris and liked his show. In the film, Harris plays a band leader and singer adored by women and resented by their husbands, a dilemma that instigates various comic sequences.

Positive audience and exhibitor response to the short film encouraged RKO studio executives to put Harris in a feature-length musical comedy. *Melody Cruise* cast Harris as a bachelor millionaire pursued by a dozen or so single young women on a winter cruise that travels between New York and California. The film's vacation-outfitted characters romp through fun-filled stops in Havana and Panama.

Harris devoted his weekly NBC radio broadcast to the film's music as part of an elaborate public relations and advertising campaign. A six-column, full-page *New York Times* advertisement featured scantily clad young women under a banner that invites "All Aboard for the Melody Cruise." Cunard Steamship Line assured readers that its cruises to Trinidad, Venezuela, Curaçao, Panama, and Havana matched the movie's gaiety and romance.[41]

Melody Cruise opened at Radio City Musical Hall, the elaborate showplace of New York's Rockefeller Center, on June 15, 1933, to excellent box-office returns and good reviews, and a film formula took shape around the combination of romance, music, and travel.

With *Melody Cruise* ready for distribution, RKO announced a second musical feature, with the songs, dancing, and romance located in Rio de Janeiro and aboard a Pan American Airways *Clipper* instead of on a pleasure cruise headed for California. Lou Brock, producer of *So This Is Harris* and *Melody Cruise,* wrote the story.

Pan American Airways board member Merian Cooper became production chief just in time to release *King Kong,* which brought RKO almost $700,000 in profits, and to launch the big-budget musical production *Flying Down to Rio.*

When RKO-Radio Pictures went into receivership that January, Metropolitan Square Corporation lost more than $1,250,000 in theater and office rental revenue at Rockefeller Center. RKO Corporation issued 100,000 new shares of common stock, worth $350,000, to Metropolitan Square. The large block of stock that RKO turned over to the Rockefellers to satisfy its obligations ultimately gave them controlling interest in the studio and put Nelson Rockefeller, John D. Jr.'s son, in the movie business.[42]

According to Allen Woll in *The Latin Image in American Film,* the newly acquired Rockefeller interest in RKO-Radio Pictures revealed itself quickly. The Rockefellers possessed extensive business interests in Latin America, and Woll claims that *Flying Down to Rio,* more than any other Hollywood movie released in the 1930s, treats Latin characters with dignity and places them in a sophisticated city, rather than in some backwater location. Woll also states that Nelson Rockefeller instructed the studio to triple the amount budgeted for the film.

Merian Cooper had actively participated in the expansion of Pan American Airways and of course knew that the company had set up a nationwide reservation system for passenger traffic in 1932. With Western Union and postal telegraph companies under contract, a total of 6,500 offices could book reservations for air travel to Latin America. By the end of the year, Pan Am had advised a thousand travel agencies in the United States about the com-

pany's service and the desirability of winter trips to tropical destinations. Moreover, the new forty-passenger Sikorsky *Clipper* flying boats were already on order.

In March, as Cooper and RKO-Radio president B. B. Kahane
went to New York to confer on film proposals and studio problems, *Pan American Air Ways,* the airline's monthly magazine,
carried photos of RKO executives, the head of its export division,
and the general manager in Panama meeting in Mexico City before
they embarked on a 20,000-mile tour on PAA airliners. The
March, 1933, issue also carried a photograph of Raoul Roulien,
Brazilian movie star, composer, and producer, who flew on Pan
American from Miami to Rio.[43]

In April, the studio hired veteran Broadway playwright Ann
Caldwell to take Brock's story idea for an aerial musical and turn it
into a screenplay. Vincent Youmans began writing the music in
May, the same month that RKO signed Raoul Roulien for the film.
During the summer, the studio dispatched its photographers to
take pictures of Rio de Janeiro.

Flying Down to Rio began filming in August, 1933, with Mexican film star Dolores Del Rio playing opposite well-known leading
man Gene Raymond and screen idol Roulien as the boyfriend who
eventually loses Del Rio to Raymond.

Del Rio had already endeared herself to RKO with high box-
office returns for her role as a pulchritudinous Polynesian princess
in the 1932 South Seas' adventure film *Bird of Paradise.* In that film
the brunette beauty captivates another wealthy playboy, played by
Joel McCrea. Conflicting traditions doom their cross-cultural romance, but the sight of a scantily clad Del Rio leaping into a flaming volcano to save her people—while McCrea anguishes at his
loss—swept audiences into an emotional frenzy. RKO no doubt
counted on Del Rio's seductive appeal to attract audiences to *Flying Down to Rio,* another love match with a wealthy playboy that is
threatened by cultural differences. Unlike *Bird of Paradise,* the conventions of musical comedy required happy endings, not flaming
tragedies, and the script writers complied.

Del Rio's assignment, in fact, proved an unexpected public relations coup for the studio and demonstrated the powerful role

that movies had achieved in international relations. The secretary general of the Asociación Nacionalista de México (Nationalist Association of Mexico) lauded RKO for featuring Mexico's much-admired actress in its film about Latin America. This politically well-connected Mexican gentleman, Alberto L. Godoy, a respected lawyer and the son of a former Mexican ambassador to the United States, enjoyed an occasional invitation to the White House. His opinions carried considerable weight in Mexico. To what degree the studio calculated the Mexican response I could not determine, but all of the studios depended on the foreign film market to cover costs and produce profits—just as they do now.

Thus, as a *Film Daily* columnist points out, the casting was not inconsequential. RKO had earned itself a place "on the inside," by which the Hollywood reporter no doubt meant that RKO could count on increased sales of its films south of the border.[44]

Although Del Rio and Raymond played the romantic leads, most critics and film historians attribute *Flying Down to Rio's* memorable contribution to film art to the almost accidental pairing of Fred Astaire and Ginger Rogers as the glamorous dance duo that performs the carioca in a Brazilian nightclub.

The studio hired Broadway musical comedy favorite, Fred Astaire, after his back-to-back stage successes in *The Band Wagon* and *The Gay Divorcee.* Prominent arts enthusiast John Hay "Jock" Whitney, an investor in *The Band Wagon,* recommended the dancer to RKO production chief Merian Cooper. Whitney also served with Cooper on the board of directors of Pan American Airways. A film novice, Astaire's screen test elicited negative comments (not good looking and lacks romantic appeal). Nevertheless, Cooper cast the Broadway star as second lead, Fred Ayres, and Astaire's dancing ability and distinctive way with song lyrics ultimately paid off handsomely for RKO.[45]

In fact, Hollywood gained a movie legend because Cooper and Whitney connected RKO-Radio Pictures and Pan American Airways. Dorothy Jordan, originally scheduled for the dance role opposite Astaire, eloped with production chief Cooper in May, 1933. RKO contract player Ginger Rogers, who had performed in two of the year's outstanding movie musical extravaganzas, Warner

Brothers' *42nd Street* and *Gold Diggers of 1933*, replaced Jordan when the newlyweds took a honeymoon just as production started.

Film historians generally credit Warner Brothers' trio of 1933 triumphs with initiating the musical comedy revival. The studio's financial free fall, from profits of $17 million to losses totaling almost $8 million in two years, gave investors nightmares. Nevertheless, Warners mounted increasingly lavish and costly musicals. The songs, dances, and new personalities of *42nd Street, Gold Diggers of 1933*, and *Footlight Parade* seduced customers back to the theaters.

Warner's story editors transformed characters who had inhabited its gritty films of social concern into villains of show business, while downtrodden, abused social outcasts gave way to confident problem solvers. Screenplays pit scoundrels and spoilers, vengeful competitors (in business and in love) against hardworking theatrical strivers. People with questionable ethics or dishonest and deceitful financiers plagued the handsome actor and warmhearted chorus girl just as they had bedeviled other honest citizens in more sinister films. In the lighthearted, optimistic musicals, the underdogs won.

In *42nd Street*, a hard-times, backstage story, a seasoned Broadway showman turns a chorus girl into a star. His show is a great success, and matrimony waits in the wings for Hollywood's newest movie sweethearts, Dick Powell and Ruby Keeler. *Gold Diggers of 1933* followed, with more theatrical angst. Keeler and unemployed fellow showgirls despair when a producer who offers them jobs turns up broke. Powell, a wealthy Bostonian working incognito as a songwriter, provides the money, joins the show, and falls for Keeler. Another hit show. *Footlight Parade* adhered to the formula of romance and hard knocks. Dedicated show people, including James Cagney as a theatrical producer, engaged in an uphill battle to mount a stage production and won the day.

Warner Brothers' scripts used auditions, rehearsals, and finished performances as devices to interrupt the narrative with musical segments like love ballads or comedy songs and dances. They also effectively employed the choreographic genius of Busby

Berkeley to woo audiences. Berkeley extracted musical fantasies from a seemingly endless imaginative storehouse of dance routines, camera angles, and kaleidoscopic movements, and his fully realized production numbers, photographed as the cameras shifted position and distance, plunged audiences into new movie experiences. Hundreds of beautiful chorus girls pranced and danced, moved in timed perfection to create geometric patterns, posed on giant turntables, or swam in pools of water. From tap dance to water ballet, overhead shots to underwater cameras, Berkeley defined movie musical innovation.

While *Flying Down to Rio* certainly fit the musical comedy formula of narrative and musical fantasy, obstacles to romance, and happy endings, it moved beyond Warner Brothers' backstage plots to a new setting. Financially strapped studio heads at RKO authorized sets and costumes, hired actors, rolled the cameras, and offered their own flamboyant extravaganza to downcast moviegoers.

Flying Down to Rio thrilled audiences, stirred imaginations, and temporarily released people from the tension and restraints of the Depression. The investment paid off: The film opened spectacularly as the Music Hall's 1933 Christmas show. An almost half-million-dollar profit indicated that the combination of music, romance, and faraway places attracted its share of moviegoers. While economic hardship precluded a heavy demand for pleasure travel in the 1930s, movie theaters offered a convenient, inexpensive substitute. Not to be ignored, ticket purchases at thousands of box offices also helped bring RKO back from insolvency.[46]

The overwhelming majority of North American viewers could not afford to travel to Brazil, but the bewitching carioca dance sequence sent thousands of financially strained moviegoers to dance studios, where they paid to learn the steps they saw in the movie.[47] Incidentally, Rio's citizens, the real-life Cariocas, also learned the dance—a choreographed movie invention unfamiliar to Brazilians.

RKO connected romance to airplanes and distant destinations. Travel—as much as show business—emerged as a reason to sing and dance. Rio's carioca and chorus girls on airplane wings generated as much excitement as Busby Berkeley's patterned perfection. Depression-stricken audiences, familiarized to the formula, anticipated the film's romantic outcome. They enjoyed the experience and shared—at least for a moment—an optimistic confidence in a well-ordered world, even though travel plans had to wait.

RKO had perhaps more creditors than revenue prospects in 1933 when it spent almost $675,000 on the extensive animation and special effects for the adventure thriller *King Kong* and then more than $400,000 on *Flying Down to Rio,* with its lavish nightclub sets, dozens of costumed dancers, and chorus girls on airplane wings.

In fact, RKO-Radio counted two musicals among its four big hits in the 1933 lineup. *Melody Cruise* and *Flying Down to Rio* joined *King Kong* and the sentimental Civil War family drama *Little Women.*[48] Three came from original stories and one adapted a popular novel. For a change, the studio had good news to report. Like the rest of the movie industry, RKO turned the corner on its climb back to profitability.

The resurgence of movie musicals may have anticipated a new mood engendered by Franklin D. Roosevelt's 1932 election. The hope, energy, and persistence of the fictional theater people who vanquished their opponents in the movies perhaps mirrored for viewers FDR's forceful early days in office. Audiences demonstrated a renewed appetite for a genre that had once delighted them but, like too much candy, had satiated the craving. Now musicals attracted crowds in the mood for romance and song. Ticket buyers delighted by flights of fancy, they lined up at the box office. When they asked for more, the studios obliged. Hollywood brought new stars, creative camera work, and clever choreography to the screen and released thirty musicals in 1933 and fifty in 1936.

Flying Down to Rio entertained those audiences, but it also carried Pan American Airways' message to millions of moviegoers: We can fly you to the Caribbean and South America safely and in timely fashion. Belinha, the beautiful Brazilian played by Dolores Del Rio, needs to reach her father quickly, but she misses the daily Pan Am flight. Pouncing on the opportunity for romance, Roger

Bond comes to her rescue. He flies her to catch the missed plane at its first overnight stop. Counting on the persuasive power of imagination, RKO placed the actors in a seductive situation but salvaged Belinha's honor, maintaining audience expectations for the romantic genre. Once in Brazil, a virtual tour of Rio and lush and lively musical numbers encouraged potential Pan American customers to envision themselves aboard a plane, winging their ways to new experiences and the excitement of exotic travel.

The aggressive airline, intent on increasing its passenger traffic, chose a medium with proven appeal. Few people doubted the influential power of motion pictures. Repeated attempts by civic and religious institutions to exercise control over the narrative and visual content of movies attested to their persuasive capacity. "Throughout the world the moving picture has . . . become a major influence, molding the mentality of mankind," proclaimed *The Literary Digest* the very week that *Flying Down to Rio* opened across the nation, seconding Pan American's judgment. In laudatory—somewhat overblown—prose, the magazine also referred to movies as "the real ambassadors of the United States to other nations," "the equivalent of a thousand Broadways," and the "Arabian Nights of the machine age."[49]

By 1934, the motion picture industry had acknowledged the public's concern over its influence and, in a prudent move to avoid legislated restraints, adopted its own codes for "moral standards and good taste." Pan American Airways hoped to influence attitudes and behaviors with regard to flying, however, not sexual relations. The seductive tension of *Flying Down to Rio* fell well within acceptable boundaries, and the film ended in marriage.

Flying Down to Rio served more interests that those of RKO-Radio Pictures and Pan American Airways. The new administration pledged hemispheric friendship, and the film's well-meaning Yankees seconded FDR's signals to Latin America. Roosevelt had told Latin America's leaders that the United States had no territorial ambitions in the hemisphere and wished to cooperate with its good neighbors. In the movie, aggressive, single-minded, rule-bending, risk-taking Roger Bond visits Rio, learns to appreciate

President Franklin D. Roosevelt supported tourism as a way to enhance relationships in the hemisphere. *Flying Down to Rio* reinforced his Good Neighbor message. *Courtesy of the Franklin D. Roosevelt Library and Archives.*

Brazil's culture and tradition, and changes his behavior. Members of the Yankee Clippers band learn to esteem Brazilian music and musicians, and they rescue the fortunes of Brazilian friends.

The film's ending—marriage between North and South Americans—paralleled Roosevelt's foreign policy goals. The next chapter suggests that the timing and content of the RKO musical comedy were not coincidental.

CHAPTER 7

Musical Fantasies, Political Realities

T HE TITLE OF RKO-Radio Pictures' 1933 box office hit, as an exhibitor might have displayed it on the theater marquee, produced the immediately recognizable presidential initials FDR. More by coincidence than contrivance, the acrostic expresses the intersection of popular culture and public policy that turned *Flying Down to Rio* into an intriguing device for historical investigation.

Flying Down to Rio

In that turbulent, poverty-stricken, pivotal first year of Franklin Delano Roosevelt's presidency, RKO's studio heads authorized this romantic musical comedy centered on a visit by North Americans to Brazil via Pan American Airways (PAA). While a new administration in Washington struggled to devise a workable Latin American policy, motion picture chorus girls sang and performed an airborne dance routine above Rio de Janeiro. In the film, American tourists and Brazilians watched and applauded. In the real world, unemployed, hungry, and homeless populations in North and South America kept an eye on Washington and waited for "happy days" to appear again.

RKO-Radio Pictures developed its story about friendly Latin Americans just as FDR committed his administration to good neighborliness, renounced any acts of territorial aggression, and promised improved hemispheric relationships based on respect, cooperation, and increased personal contact. In the convergence of movie fantasy and international politics, Pan American Airways and RKO-Radio Pictures communicated the essence of Franklin D. Roosevelt's Latin American policy. That is, the midair marriage of Roger and Belinha cements a partnership between North and South Americans at a time when Latin Americans questioned the good will of their powerful northern neighbor, when the economic viability of vulnerable hemispheric nations depended on U.S. markets, and when the growing threat of fascism required a show of hemispheric solidarity. In movie conventions, marriage at the end of a film signals to viewers that the couple will live happily ever after.

A mutuality of acknowledged interests in Washington, New York, and Hollywood suggests more than happenstance in the timing and plot of this film. For one thing, the new administration had hoisted two warning flags; one waved in the direction of executives at Pan American Airways and the other at all of the Hollywood studios. Consider first the outspokenly political, experienced lobbyist-executives at Pan Am. The company depended on government airmail contracts for its very existence, and Republican friends in the Coolidge and Hoover administrations had aided its ambitions. In turn, the good relations that Pan American Airways built with Latin American governments helped the Republicans dispel long-held negative images of a hegemonic and interventionist United States. Both Pan American Airways and President Calvin Coolidge greeted hemispheric leaders at the Pan American Conference in Havana in 1928 in anticipation of improved commercial relations.

After the 1932 election, Pan Am would depend on the Roosevelt Democrats for its survival but had few friends in that camp. The newly elected administration announced its intentions to investigate a suspected favoritism in the U.S. Post Office Department's previous contract award practices. Across the continent, Hollywood faced the prospect of government-imposed regulations over movie industry distribution practices, labor relations, and salaries. With no little trepidation, the predominantly Republican studio heads determined to make friends with the new people in Washington.

Thus, the film represented (1) a political as well as a financial investment for RKO-Radio Pictures, (2) a well-timed demonstration of Pan Am's support for the administration, and (3) an advantageous means of mass communication for President Roosevelt. Pan American Airways and RKO-Radio served the government as instruments of foreign policy, promoting tourism as a way to improve hemispheric relations. In fact, Hollywood studios filmed a dozen or so stories that depicted North-South American romances and marriages during Roosevelt's four terms in office.

FDR's Latin American Strategy: Good Neighbors and Intranationalist Economics

By 1933, U.S. citizens had accumulated a huge financial stake in Latin America—a third of all U.S. private foreign investment—much of it in bonds made worthless by the Depression. Moreover, trade with Latin America had become a critical element in the U.S. economy. One-third of the country's exports went to hemispheric neighbors in 1929, almost a billion dollars worth, and the nation imported slightly more than it sold. Increased tariff rates legislated under the Hoover administration had forced dramatic cuts in that exchange and contributed to the economic crisis throughout the hemisphere. By 1932, the United States imported only one-third as much in Latin American goods and exported only one-fifth the 1929 total value.[1]

The substantial amounts of private capital invested in Latin America in the 1920s had generated considerable uncertainty regarding U.S. intentions in the hemisphere. The checkered history of both friendship and aggression afforded little assurance to Latin American leaders, and Pan Americanism, defiled by U.S. military interventions, did little to allay suspicions of "Yankee imperialism." Even Hollywood movies with English-language dialog aroused cries of cultural domination, and ambassadors from Latin American nations challenged then-Secretary of Commerce Herbert Hoover over filmed portrayals of their countrymen and women.

As governor of New York State prior to the presidential election, Franklin Roosevelt had had little influence over foreign policy. In 1933, the most up-to-date Latin Americanists at the State Department belonged to the Republic Party, now out of power. Roosevelt, in fact, intended to control the reins of international policy. Cordell Hull, Roosevelt's choice for Secretary of State, displayed a single-minded commitment to free trade but had little familiarity with Latin America or diplomatic affairs. A courteous "Southern gentleman," Hull had served more than twenty years in the House of Representatives and two more in the Senate, where he expounded on economic internationalism and the peace and stability emanating from the multilateral exchange of goods.

The 1932 presidential campaigns had scarcely touched on issues of foreign relations. Most of Roosevelt's speeches dealt with farm relief and worker protection, as well as the restoration of a balance between the nation's increased productive capacity and the people's limited ability to consume. By the time of Roosevelt's inauguration in March, 1933, his priority list of legislative measures reflected the strong domestic slant of the campaign: temporary relief for the jobless and needy, agricultural adjustment, farm-debt and home-debt refunding, banking reform, rural electrification, and regulation of corporations.[2]

The understandable emphasis on critical domestic concerns did not preclude preparation of foreign policy initiatives, however. While his advisers in the "brain trust" focused on domestic issues during the campaign, Roosevelt asked his good friend, career foreign service officer Sumner Welles, to prepare briefs and drafts of speeches on Latin America.

In one policy statement draft, Welles suggested conciliatory gestures that acknowledged U.S. respect for national sovereignty as well as a desire for a healthy flow of commerce among the hemisphere's nations. His draft for the inaugural address included a commitment to reciprocal tariff cuts as essential to inter-American trade. However, the speech, when delivered, emphasized the emergency at home over efforts to restore world trade. Roosevelt used the opportunity to announce a nonspecific "policy of the good neighbor" and promised to dedicate the United States to respect for the rights of others and fulfillment of obligations and agreements. A similar vagueness marked Roosevelt's first Pan American Day speech in April, 1933, when he spoke rather perfunctorily of friendship and respect and barely touched on actions to abolish artificial barriers to trade.[3]

Statistically and experientially the Great Depression hit bottom in 1932 and 1933, as Franklin D. Roosevelt succeeded Herbert Hoover. Corporate profits, the gross national product, personal savings, and motion picture attendance all plummeted to their lowest levels in that winter of discontent. While the new president urged optimism and offered hope, most people struggled to find or retain employment, to keep the family farm or home, and to put food on the table. For them, travel to Latin America was not an option or even a dream.

Given this reality, tourist visits to Latin America as an element of foreign policy should have seemed the height of folly. Disposable personal income, the sine qua non of pleasure travel, stood at scarcely more than half the 1929 levels, and money spent by North Americans on foreign travel had dropped by almost two-thirds. Even those travelers who sailed to foreign destinations watched their expenses carefully. Despite the cheerful assessment of the *New York Times* that an eager interest in travel existed, filmed travelogues garnered more customers for the movie houses, while vigorously promoted voyages found fewer clients.[4]

Improbable as it may have seemed, however, foreign travel played a role in New Deal plans for domestic economic recovery as well as in international relations. Roosevelt's incorporation of tourism in foreign policy formulation, in fact, recognized that sector's growing importance in the international economy.

The rationale for tourism promotion followed this logic: If the decline in foreign commerce contributed to the economic crisis, then travelers who put dollars at the disposal of the nation's trade partners provided funds they could use to buy U.S. goods. As a Commerce Department study pointed out, travelers from the

United States spent some $570 million dollars in foreign lands in 1932, down from the peak year of 1929 but still a substantial sum. Even if travelers cut expenses—if they traveled tourist or third class and stayed at cheaper hotels—their journeys abroad enhanced their personal experience and aided their host countries, while augmented trade improved the economic well-being of those who stayed at home.[5]

In 1933, Latin America's ability to buy U.S. products depended on dollars earned by selling their wares to the United States or else brought to their shores by tourists. Although analysts argued that increased trade with Latin America could put people in the United States to work and ease the nation's way out of the Depression, domestic political circumstances mitigated against tariff reductions. To open U.S. markets to foreign goods required both presidential action and congressional support. Neither appeared forthcoming.

For one thing, presidential advisers, elected officials, and government agencies at all levels had yet to reach a consensus on the underlying causes of the Depression, a necessary antecedent to determining remedies. Theorists who proposed lessening trade barriers so that surplus agricultural products and excess manufactured goods could find markets abroad clashed with analysts who wanted government controls and regulation to constrain overproduction. Among the population at large, some producers (who were also voters) relied on internal markets for their goods and feared competition from imports. Other producers (also voters) depended on foreign trade and argued for imports in order to increase the demand for exports. Roosevelt, who strained to build a Congressional majority favorable to his proposals for relief of the nation's ills, hesitated to alienate the elected representatives of those voters.

While the factions debated their respective positions, the desperate need of Latin American nations for access to U.S. markets succumbed to the political demands of the domestic legislative agenda. Roosevelt had finessed the issue of Latin American trade in his inaugural address, as he consigned hemispheric relations to the optimistic, but ill-defined, fellowship of good neighbors. April's annual Pan American Day speech alienated no potential supporters as it promulgated ideals of mutual helpfulness, respect, and solidarity and disavowed U.S. territorial ambitions.[6]

On the one hand, relief and recovery policies evolved into specific legislation and programs in the frenzied period after inauguration; on the other, tariff and trade issues languished in uncertainty and ambiguity. Secretary of State Hull (*Business Week* called him the most out-and-out free trader in American public life) argued in vain that unrestricted markets would increase trade and in turn put people to work.[7] Sumner Welles, Hull's assistant for Latin America at the State Department, agreed with the secretary and recommended an opening of U.S. markets to alleviate the economic distress of hemispheric neighbors and enable them to purchase U.S. goods. The president, however, couched any commitment to increased trade in the obfuscating language of "intra-nationalism." As government spokespersons explained the doctrine, a United States restored to prosperity at home could then afford to pay higher prices (that is, with the tariff burden included) for the exports of other countries.

Developed for the June, 1933, World Economic Conference held in London, intra-nationalism justified Roosevelt's focus on domestic recovery over international trade cooperation. The conference foundered on FDR's poorly disguised economic nationalism and his refusal to approve an international agreement to stabilize currency on the basis of its relationship to gold.

Six months later, at the seventh Pan American Conference at Montevideo, Uruguay, the White House still refused to discuss tariff matters despite the continued desperate state of Latin American economies. In a statement formulated as a practical expression of the Good Neighbor policy, the administration avoided an anticipated discussion of renewed trade and instead gave its official benediction to the development of transportation and tourism.

The president's personal secretary, Louis M. Howe, delineated the White House stance in a letter of instructions to Secretary Hull for material to be covered in his speech to the conference delegates. Howe reiterated FDR's reluctance to deal substantively with trade issues, which he knew ran counter to Hull's inclination. First, Howe admonished, offer "the usual kind words about good neighbors." Second, suggest that better understanding depends on enhanced communication. "We cannot know each other better until we can meet each other oftener," so the United States would like to improve transportation (steamship, railway, auto, and airplane). Also, he advised Hull to remind the conferees of the plan for "a great highway between the two continents." Talk about the development of air communications and improved radio facilities. Then "touch with regret on the present international economic situation . . . which makes it impractical at this time to reach definite conclusions on several of the suggestions [regarding currency stabilization and trade openings]." Avoid "like the plague" any discussion of customs duties (tariffs), Howe concluded, but the promotion of tourist travel seemed "perfectly safe." [8]

Coupling tourism and transportation, Secretary Hull's speech to the conference promoted air travel to Latin America. Specifically, on Roosevelt's instructions, he offered funds to place beacon lights at Latin American airports to facilitate nighttime flying. It takes little insight to detect the efforts of Pan American Airways behind this offer. Pan Am flights between Miami and Rio de Janeiro or Buenos Aires took seven days because the lack of beacon lights restricted planes to daytime travel. To the American businessperson, decreased travel time meant increased sales and profitability. By 1933, regularly scheduled dirigible flights carried passengers and freight from Germany to South America in two and a half days.

Thus, the airline leadership, so accustomed to the ways of Washington, had good reason to work with FDR on U.S.–Latin American policies, and the president—like Herbert Hoover before him—could take advantage of PAA's cordial relations with the countries in which its planes landed. Airport lighting aided the only United States carrier serving the Latin American routes, while improved flight times pleased export-oriented, private-sector U.S. interests concerned with aggressive European competition for prospective Latin American trade. [9]

However, policy formulations that benefited U.S. businesses did not necessarily satisfy Latin Americans. While the U.S. delegates urged travel as a step toward good relations and transportation improvements to facilitate face-to-face communication, representatives of Latin American nations with prostrate economies waited in vain to hear about expanded markets for their products and a moratorium on their debt.

Franklin Roosevelt, Cordell Hull, Sumner Welles, and others responsible for Latin American policy knew that restoration of large-scale trade depended on access to U.S. markets, not just tourism abroad. Nevertheless, they couldn't make it happen in that whirlwind hundred days of legislative activity or even in the months that followed. The administration had to expend its political capital on domestic issues.

Tourism suited Roosevelt's publicly proclaimed good-neighbor goals and kept political opponents at bay. Weighing his options, Roosevelt promoted an understanding and appreciation of other cultures and peoples through personal contact. Familiarity fostered friendship and diminished suspicion of U.S. power, while tourism's hard currency transfers enabled the purchase of U.S. goods without alienating domestic interests opposed to free trade and unwilling to open U.S. markets. Besides improving the potential to sell U.S. goods and put people to work, the administration argued, increased overseas travel aided Latin American governments that owed an aggregate $374 million to private lenders in the United States.

The nagging issue of debt repayment extended beyond the hemisphere to Europe, where the amounts owed to the United States dwarfed the Latin American obligations. By 1932, the complications of debt payment had become a major contention in U.S.-European relations. The United States had lent its allies more than $10 billion during World War I and some $3.2 billion after the war. These were Liberty loans that were paid for by selling Liberty bonds. Most of the money had been spent in the United States for food, munitions, commodities, and so on. Bond holders expected the government to redeem the bonds when they came due, of course, with the debtor governments providing the resources through their loan repayments.

In 1922, Congress had agreed to cut the original obligation almost by half. As of June, 1931, the United States had received

$750 million in payments on the principal and $1.9 billion in interest. The Allies had received more than that amount in reparations payments from Germany, but Germany borrowed from private U.S. financial sources (not the government) to make those payments. When the U.S. economy deteriorated after 1929, the dominos started to fall. U.S. capitalists no longer had money to lend; Germany stopped making reparations, and the Allied governments could not make payments on their debts to the United States.

In June, 1932, President Hoover asked for a moratorium on debt collection. Congress approved but insisted that the debt should be neither reduced nor forgiven. Opponents of the stipulation argued that debt reduction would free up the gold used for payments, which could then be used to secure dollars to buy farm products and industrial goods.

Roosevelt inherited both the crisis and the controversy. In November, 1932, just after the election, Britain asked to defer its December 15 debt payment and requested that the whole situation be reviewed. Congress still favored neither cancellation nor reduction, and Roosevelt needed congressional support for his own relief and recovery programs. Therefore, he argued for private negotiations by the executive branch through diplomatic channels—not through congressional action. In other words, he advocated resolution through inaction: The debtors did not pay—because they could not—but their obligation to pay remained on the books.[10]

Philadelphia businessman Louis H. Lehman championed a scheme to facilitate debt payment through tourism that may have influenced policy makers in Washington. Lehman, inspired by the Commerce Department's 1932 balance-of-payments report, which showed a significant aggregate sum of money left in Europe by U.S. visitors, wrote *Traveling to Prosperity*. U.S. tourists abroad had spent some $5 billion more than had visitors to the United States between 1921 and 1931, Lehman pointed out. On the other hand, he argued, the United States had received less than $3 billion in principal and interest payments from European debtors during that decade. So, he suggested, the United States should issue vouchers to travelers who paid, for example, one thousand dollars for these coupons, the same amount to be deducted from the public debt when honored by a debtor nation. Lehman concluded that patriotic, voucher-carrying travelers could enjoy themselves and still contribute to debt reduction.[11]

While Lehman's innovative proposal never translated into policy, U.S. support for tourism at the Montevideo conference indicates a knowledgeable awareness of its value in international economic relations. RKO-Radio Pictures sent its photographers to film background shots of Rio de Janeiro not long after Roosevelt's Pan American Day speech urged hemispheric neighborliness. Moreover, the studio released *Flying Down to Rio* the same month that the president offered transportation and tourism, instead of free trade, to Latin American delegates at Montevideo. During the course of Roosevelt's first year in office—concurrent with the planning, production, and release of *Flying Down to Rio*—the administration accepted travel as both a viable element of hemispheric relations and a factor in economic recovery.

Neither incidentally nor accidentally, good neighborliness infused the film's plot, characterizations, music, and choreography. RKO maintained a careful watch on the entertainment market and on politics. When musical comedies attracted audiences, the studio filled the screen with evocative and appealing songs and dances. Brazil was a lively, friendly place to visit and airplanes a safe way to get there. One should not allow fears or inhibitions to limit opportunity, the film suggested, because risk takers both get the girl and solve problems.

Merian Cooper, the RKO-Radio Pictures production chief who approved casting, budgets, promotions, and so forth for *Flying Down to Rio,* also sat on the board of directors at Pan American Airways. His dual role was not inconsequential; both companies had experience in placating politically powerful officeholders. Thus, it should have come as no surprise that *Flying Down to Rio* carried the messages of Pan American Airways and the Roosevelt administration.

In fact, travel statistics indicated growth in 1934 and 1935, and the travelers no doubt contributed in some measure to local economies. Most people traveled by ship to Central and South America and by auto to Mexico, but Pan American Airways reported a forty-four-percent increase in passenger miles in 1934 over 1933.[12]

The administration's tourism policy most likely helped the airline more than it aided the farmers, workers, and manufacturers of either continent. Meanwhile, behind the scenes, Roosevelt began to work on reciprocal trade treaties with Latin American countries, even before Congress took up the measure in 1934.

Pan American Airways Meets FDR

When Roosevelt assumed the country's highest office, Pan American Airways had completed its southern extension. The officers at the helm of this twentieth-century Clipper fleet had labored and lobbied their way to preeminence in a Republican administration that promoted international business interests through both the Commerce and State Departments. One hand washed the other. Well-placed friends had extended government assistance when called upon, and Pan American had turned financial losses for 1929 and 1930 into profits in 1931 and 1932. In return, airline personnel afforded an information source and a communications conduit between Washington and the various Latin American cities where the company operated.

Franklin Roosevelt's hands-on experience with both aviation and Latin America stemmed from his service as Assistant Secretary of the Navy. He had supported naval aviation as early as 1913 and expanded his commitment to meet wartime demands. Concerns about German penetration in the hemisphere during World War I prompted Roosevelt's support for U.S. interventions in the Caribbean and Mexico.

Pan American Airways' years of extended service into Latin America occurred while Roosevelt served as governor of New York State, an office with little or no involvement in diplomacy or international aviation. Thus, the 1932 Democratic victory brought uncertainty for Pan American: Influential government officials, friends from Yale like Trubee Davison, David Ingalls, and Francis White had left Washington, and Juan Trippe trod fresh ground among the Democrats and Roosevelt's circle of advisers from Harvard and Columbia Universities.

Moreover, the new leadership had its eye on the process by which the Hoover administration had awarded airmail contracts. No doubt some of Roosevelt's political supporters had a financial interest in reopening the bids. When Postmaster General James A. Farley, who had managed Roosevelt's successful presidential campaign, suggested a need for hearings on the issue, Pan American's executives and board members understandably fretted over the fate of the airline's lifeblood contracts.

Veteran lobbyist Trippe had dealt primarily with Republicans. He knew how to work the congressional and administrative networks in Washington; now he had to establish his connections among the new players in town. As Trippe built his fortifications against an investigation that might return the airmail contracts to competitive bidding, he lined up the weapons in his arsenal, that is, people and performance.

One link to the new administration came through marriage. Trippe had married Elizabeth (Betty) Stettinius, whose father, Edward R. Stettinius Sr., had served as Assistant Secretary of War during World War I, when FDR was Assistant Secretary of the Navy. However, the most useful—but unexpected—association turned up in the person of Pan American Airways stockholder and board member Cornelius Vanderbilt (Sonny) Whitney, whom Trippe had known since their days at Yale. Sonny Whitney ran for Congress in 1932, as the sacrificial Democrat in a Republican district in Queens, New York, an act of service that earned Roosevelt's gratitude. Whitney capitalized on this political favor to Roosevelt and used his access to apprise the president of Pan American Airways' value to the nation.

With Whitney's insider status as his wedge, Trippe called on FDR and worked his way into the ranks of supporters. Whitney's and Trippe's service as fliers during the war afforded them a common interest with the president, and their familiarity with Latin America provided a bargaining chip when dealing with an administration whose expertise in that area lacked both breadth and depth. Trippe also gained a position on the committee that planned the January, 1934, presidential birthday gala, a fund-raiser for the polio treatment center at Warm Springs, Georgia.[13]

The airline's long-standing relationship with Charles Lindbergh worked in Trippe's favor, of course. Lucky Lindy, with his wife, Ann Morrow Lindbergh, as radio operator flew a thirty-thousand-mile journey to twenty-one countries in 1933, a reminder of Lindbergh's survey work for Pan American that had helped to establish its routes and predominance in Latin America.

Pan American identified another popular aviator who had recently established White House connections. Amelia Earhart had officially opened the airline's Havana terminal in 1929 and then continued to fly and write about flying. Spurred on by other ambitious women fliers, she picked the fifth anniversary of Lindbergh's 1927 flight to start her own journey from New York to Paris. Although bad weather forced her to land in Ireland instead of France, enthusiastic crowds in Europe and the United States acclaimed her as the first person to cross the Atlantic twice in an airplane.[14]

Earhart met Eleanor Roosevelt later that year, just after the 1932 election. The celebrated aviator gave a talk titled "Flying for Fun" at a high school in Poughkeepsie, New York, a half-hour's drive from the Roosevelt home at Hyde Park. Earhart had written a book on flying, *The Fun of It,* the previous spring but had left the last chapter unfinished until after her trans-Atlantic flight in May. The publisher capitalized on the publicity and put the book in the stores within weeks after her return to the United States. The Poughkeepsie lecture kept the public relations machine going. Earhart described her solo flight and showed films of her receptions in Europe.[15]

Eleanor Roosevelt introduced Earhart at the talk, and the Roosevelts invited her for dinner. The two women became friends, and the friendship gave Earhart clout in Washington. The new first lady put Earhart on the White House guest list.[16]

Earhart had access to a president and first lady who recognized the real and symbolic importance of air transport. Franklin Roosevelt had often flown when he was Assistant Secretary of the Navy and had worked with Naval Secretary Josephus Daniels to build the navy's air service. Roosevelt had traveled by air several times during his unsuccessful campaign for the vice presidency in 1920 but then had not flown for several years while he dealt with the crippling effects of polio and served as governor of New York.

When the 1932 Democratic convention announced Roosevelt's nomination for the presidency, he and Eleanor, along with family members, close friends, and advisers, flew from Albany, New York, to Chicago for the acceptance. Roosevelt wrote his acceptance speech aboard the plane. He told reporters, "The whole idea of flying here was to bring forward the idea of getting the campaign started."

However, flying to the convention represented more than the start of his presidential campaign. The airplane trip communicated speed and vigor to the ten thousand people who greeted the candidate at the Chicago airport and to everyone who read about the trip in the newspapers or heard about it on the radio. The image of the presidential flight inspired voters who were—or had been—uncertain of the candidate's physical condition and suggested a forward-looking individual who was unafraid to move in new directions.[17]

In fact, when passenger air travel increased in the months after Roosevelt's inauguration, some analysts attributed improved public acceptance of air transport to the president's own example. Others gave more credit to Eleanor Roosevelt, who took frequent air trips and matter-of-factly explained them as the only way she could maintain her crowded schedule of events. When the first lady routinely used the country's airlines, the accompanying publicity helped to dispel fears about safety.[18]

President and Mrs. Roosevelt's air travel notwithstanding, behind the scenes of the new administration, Depression-influenced cost cutters took aim at several key government aviation offices. Aviation promoters reacted with alarm as government officials eliminated the positions of assistant secretary for aeronautics in the War, Navy, and Commerce Departments. The new budget director ordered the Aeronautics Branch at Commerce to return more than two million dollars of its allotment and subsumed the

First lady Eleanor Roosevelt (fifth from the left) flew to many of her official public functions and boosted confidence in the safety of air transport. *Courtesy of the Franklin D. Roosevelt Library and Archives.*

branch's work under an assistant secretary for transportation. Since the political supporter who was awarded that office knew nothing about aviation, people devoted to airlines and private flying launched a vigorous lobbying crusade and managed to restore the Aeronautics Branch.[19]

Once they had reinstated the office's budget, the battle-scarred victors then intended to fill the post with their choice of qualified individuals. Amelia Earhart worked her White House connections on behalf of veteran flier and airline executive Eugene L. Vidal. The son-in-law of Tennessee Senator Thomas Gore, Vidal had powerful political backers as well, and Roosevelt announced his appointment in September, 1933. With civil aviation reestablished as a public priority, the federal government's jobs program hired more than fifty thousand workers to build some six hundred new airports.

Juan Trippe had left his footprints on the White House doorstep, but the issue of airmail contracts remained unresolved.

Pan American Airways could help Roosevelt publicize his Latin American travel policy. Trippe also had connections in Hollywood, that is, members of PAA's board of directors who were significantly placed at RKO.

RKO embarked on preliminary arrangements for *Flying Down to Rio* in the spring of 1933, right after the presidential inauguration. Studio president B. B. Kahane and new production chief Merian Cooper conferred with New York corporate officers late in March. (Cooper flew; Kahane took the train.) Cooper returned to Hollywood in time to participate in the "New Deal Expedition," the meeting of studio officials in which Motion Picture Producers and Directors Association (MPPDA) chief, Will Hays, outlined the administration's proposed new economic order for the film industry: Reorganize and cut costs.

Blue Eagle over Hollywood

Hollywood's studio heads, mostly Republicans, worried about New Deal policies. The Republicans' governing philosophy—the business of government is business—had suited Hollywood's pioneers. They had organized to protect their interests through the MPPDA and collectively called on the Commerce and State Departments for assistance as necessary. In turn, the federal government viewed the movie industry's international stature as a financial asset and its product as a political boon.

Although Hollywood's film industry ranked far below the people's suffering and the nation's recovery among Roosevelt's concerns, presidential criticism of high executive salaries, eploitative labor practices, and monopolistic tendencies in film distribution had put studio heads on notice and raised the specter of government regulation. Hollywood preferred an administration in Washington that would not restrain the movie industry's business practices.

High-salaried Hollywood moguls understandably identified with Republican attitudes toward taxes and recoiled at the brain trust's analysis of the Depression, which called for a redistribution of wealth. An industry responsive to a ruthlessly competitive marketplace also listened apprehensively to talk of government-business partnerships. On the other hand, filmmakers understood from their MPPDA experience that they could placate their adversaries, make some concessions, and retain control over their product and its distribution.

The 1932 election had created a fissure in Hollywood's solid Republican bloc. Like the overwhelming majority of his colleagues, Louis B. Mayer, the highly visible political activist, continued his long-term, loyal support of Herbert Hoover. However, Mayer's arch-rivals, the Warner brothers (Harry, Jack, Sam, and Albert) switched their allegiance and backed Roosevelt. Joseph Kennedy—David Sarnoff's original partner in RKO-Radio—in his capacity as fundraiser for FDR's 1932 presidential campaign, had recruited Harry Warner to the Democratic camp. Harry convinced Jack and the other Warner brothers to join him in supporting Roosevelt. Jack Warner headed the campaign effort in Hollywood, complete with some of the country's first rousing political rallies anchored around the appearance of movie stars.[20]

Roosevelt won California by a half-million votes, and Jack Warner led a delegation of movie stars to the inauguration. During the early months of the New Deal, when Warner spent considerable time at the White House, the smiling portrait of FDR and the Blue Eagle of the National Recovery Administration (NRA) appeared prominently in the finale of Warners' 1933 *Footlight Parade*.

Hollywood demonstrated an adaptability to political winds. Studio executives used the pages of a special inaugural edition of *Film Daily* to assure Roosevelt of the industry's support for his administration. Personal messages and studio advertisements pledged Hollywood's loyalty. The financially prostrate industry expressed its hopes for "speedy enactment of measures to restore the country and the motion picture business with it, to prosperity." RKO plugged *King Kong*, its latest release: "King Kong inaugurates a New Deal for the forgotten showman." MGM timed its release of *Gabriel over the White House* with the inauguration. The studio's *Film Daily* ad quoted the *Hollywood Reporter* reviewer's reference to *Gabriel*'s "message to the American people . . . showing them how a President of the United States handled the situation and the marvelous results he attained."[21]

The less-than-lighthearted, staunchly Republican Louis Mayer, welcomed at the Hoover White House because of his active support, never doubted Hollywood's potential for political influence. In fact, *Gabriel over the White House* enraged Mayer because of the duality of its presidential personality. *Gabriel* starts with an irresponsible, corrupt president who is redeemed after the Archangel Gabriel brings a message from the Almighty. Armed with a new morality, the militant, although autocratic, leader moves vigorously on both domestic and foreign fronts, ousting crooked politicians and chastising foreign heads of state on their failure to disarm.

The "benevolently dictatorial" chief solves all of the country's problems, *The Literary Digest*'s reviewer wrote. Then, at the climax, "he terrifies the foreign diplomats by a display of Uncle Sam's potential air prowess, forces Europe to disarm and pay her debts, and then dies gracefully, a new national hero."[22]

Mayer resented the presidential characterization and an obvious bias toward an activist president-hero who rallied the support of the people with radio addresses, solved the country's problems, and then died, a martyr to good government. He condemned the film as an insult to all Republicans, a slap at the Harding administration, and a testimonial to FDR. He agreed to allow MGM to release *Gabriel* only after considerable cutting. The film's widespread box-office appeal and commensurate earnings most likely did not offer Mayer any solace.

Across town, the Warner Brothers' studio acted as political cheerleader with three classic musical comedies, *42nd Street, Gold Diggers of 1933,* and *Footlight Parade,* all back-stage musicals in which money problems and unemployment plague the characters. Optimism and cooperation overcomes all obstacles, however, a message wrapped in elaborate settings, romantic ballads, lavish costumes, and intricately choreographed dance numbers. The Roosevelt administration, notable for its expansive use of public relations and the media to mobilize support for its policies, no doubt recognized and rewarded the Warners' efforts.

If the public and the administration responded positively to Hollywood's version of New Deal optimism, Harry Warner's public appeal for wage-scale readjustments surprised and dismayed his industry colleagues. In the unlikely setting of the Rye, New York, Country Club, Warner warned the *Film Daily* golf tournament dinner guests that exorbitant salaries required reappraisal. "We must take from those above and give it to those below," Warner admonished. "The higher-ups cannot be selfish."[23]

This spirit of cooperation had its limits, however, and the industry's elite showed few signs of conversion to Harry Warner's new religion. Fictional heroes made sacrifices, but their creators protected their paychecks. "By the mid-thirties nineteen of the twenty-five highest salaries in America and forty of the highest sixty-three went to film executives. Louis Mayer earned more money than any other individual in the country—well over $1 million, even in the depths of the Depression." The Warners returned to the Republican camp in 1936.[24]

Warner Brothers paraded FDR's likeness across the screen; MGM portrayed a presidential hero in *Gabriel over the White House*; RKO-Radio Pictures produced a Rio-based musical comedy that supported Roosevelt's Latin American policy. Perhaps they all had one eye on profits and the other on Washington.

Less than a week after FDR's April 14 Pan American Day address reiterated the president's commitment to hemispheric cooperation, RKO made the first announcement related to the production of *Flying Down to Rio*. The studio had hired New York playwright Ann Caldwell to develop the screenplay for a musical comedy from a story idea by Lou Brock, producer of the studio's shipboard musical, *Melody Cruise*. The new film would center around an airliner bound for Rio de Janeiro. Merian Cooper, an experienced pilot and Pan American Airways board member, authorized the air-musical and assigned Brock to produce it. At the same time, the Pan American Union devoted its entire April, 1933, *Bulletin* to travel in the Americas, which the organization presented as a major effort to promote better understanding among nations.

RKO-Radio Pictures purposefully publicized Pan American

Airways' Clippers to benefit the airline. The movie also deliberately enticed moviegoers to visit South America at a time when such a message suited the goals of the nation's industries and the needs of the federal government. Meanwhile, RKO emblazoned the NRA logo and the accompanying slogan "We Do Our Part" on the front page of the August 12, 1933, *Radio Flash* (the RKO house organ), along with a reminder to readers, "Are You Proudly Displaying These?"

Flying Down to Rio went before the cameras at the end of August, and two weeks later RKO's president headed a unit that marched behind an NRA/RKO banner in an NRA parade in New York City.[25] Advertisements for the film's well-publicized New York opening also carried the NRA's Blue Eagle.

Clearly, the studio embraced the Roosevelt administration's domestic revival effort, and studio executives had good reason to support its Latin American policies as well. The same month that RKO started filming *Flying*—August, 1933—Hollywood's studio heads met in New York at the request of NRA's director Hugh S. Johnson to discuss a code of operation for the movie industry. The president had asked for a full report on unfair practices, including excessive salaries to artists and to executives and their families. For four months, representatives of the industry's producers, distributors, and exhibitors engaged in a free-for-all fight on distribution practices, censorship, and salaries with NRA deputy administrator Sol A. Rosenblatt before they devised a code agreeable to both Hollywood and the government.[26]

The code became law in December, 1933, the same month that *Flying Down to Rio* opened at Radio City Music Hall and Cordell Hull preached tourism at Montevideo, on instructions from the White House. RKO's double-page *Film Daily* advertisement on January 3, 1934, as the film opened nationwide, featured the "Flying Armada of Beauty" chorus girls and carioca dancers. The company also linked the familiar RKO-Radio logo to the ubiquitous NRA Blue Eagle "We Do Our Part" symbol.[27]

With Roosevelt moving to regulate the film industry through the NRA and the postmaster general questioning Pan American Airways' airmail contract awards, RKO Corporation and its parent, RCA, as well as the Pan American Airways board member who worked at RKO-Radio devised a story idea and a movie that entertained and enticed its audience and served the companies' immediate political concerns. Everyone shared the rewards. The film earned money for a studio in dire need. Audiences learned a little about Rio de Janeiro. The Roosevelt administration demonstrated its respect for and friendship with Latin America. Viewers saw Ginger Rogers dance with Fred Astaire for the first of many times, and some of them even took lessons and learned to dance the carioca.

While renouncing intervention in 1933, the United States nevertheless maintained its preeminent position in the hemisphere. Three twentieth-century industries came together that year in *Flying Down to Rio* and contributed to the country's stated and unspoken goals. Hollywood dominated the movie screens of Latin America, Pan American Airways controlled its skies, and U.S. tourists began to earn a critical place in the Latin American economy.

In the end, Postmaster General James Farley reconsidered the lack of competition in Pan American Airways airmail contract awards and concluded that withdrawal of contracts and resubmission to open bidding would prove too disruptive to U.S.-Latin American trade and commerce. Pan American won this battle, but another one loomed.

The German Threat in Latin America

In 1925, the active German presence in Latin American aviation had generated an energetic lobbying effort in Washington in support of airmail contracts to U.S. carriers that could service the region. By 1931, Pan American Airways, born of the resulting competition, had come to dominate air transport among the nations of the hemisphere. A newly elected U.S. president, bent on convincing Latin American neighbors of his benign intentions, recognized the contributions of the only U.S. international airline and fostered its best interests.

In 1933, the United States faced a new German leadership eager to compete for the Latin American market, just as the Depression-plagued administration tried to reinvigorate hemispheric commerce and generate peaceful relations through improved understanding and shared cultural appreciation. For the United States, the Depression-relieving struggle for trade and influence in Latin America rested on its ability to dispel the negative image of Yankee aggression, as well as its willingness to open markets. Faced with trade competition, threats of German expansionism, and Latin America's historically based cultural affinity with Europe, the Roosevelt administration moved to forge a supranational hemispheric bond.

Flying Down to Rio promoted this heightened sense of Pan Americanism. The film affirmed that well-meaning Yankees brought friendship, tourists, and solutions to economic dilemmas to Latin America and even gained acceptance there. The movie communicated a set of circumstances, a conflict and a resolution that presented North Americans in a favorable light to significant numbers of people. Moreover, it portrayed Europeans as suspicious characters with unethical motives.

Competition with Europe for Latin America's trade began long before 1933, and every trading company and country viewed international commerce through the prism of its own best advantage. No doubt Roosevelt recognized the public relations value of a widely heralded film in which North American musicians fended off the shadowy European enemies of an honest Brazilian businessman. Clearly, silver screen images conveyed messages of friendship to millions of people that Pan American Day speeches never reached.

Does the trio of stealthy Europeans who cast a dark shadow on the Brazilian coast suggest the rival interests of the commercially expansive National Socialists who gained power in Germany early in 1933? Germany's early claim on South America's air transport development had generated an aggressive United States response, but the National Socialists could still count on connections built by the industry with various national governments—just as the United States looked to the good will that Pan American Airways generated.

In 1931 Germany experienced severe foreign exchange problems. When its own protectionist trade policies closed western Europe's doors to the country's exports, Germany saw a market for its manufactures and a source of raw materials in Latin America. In turn, the Latin Americans had surplus mineral and agricultural products, a need for manufactured goods, and a shortage of foreign exchange. Germany initiated an intensive drive for barter arrangements, and the extremely successful trade strategy increased German exports to the area, in direct competition with the United States.

As the United States looked southward, the size of the potential market—assuming its economic recovery—compensated for an expressed anti-Americanism that might impede U.S. efforts. The administration embarked on bilateral negotiations to mutually lower tariffs with significant trading partners. The prospects for increased U.S.-Latin American trade appeared brighter in 1934 than in 1933 and in fact prompted some improvements in living standards for trade partners.

The U.S. relationship with Brazil improved through reciprocal agreements that made the United States Brazil's best customer for its coffee. Nevertheless, Brazil became Germany's leading trade partner after 1934. Brazilian leader Getulio Vargas eagerly expanded commercial ties, maintained cordial relations with the Third Reich, and played the trade rivalry to his country's advantage. Moreover, as Adolph Hitler consolidated power in Germany and expanded commercial relations, the National Socialists also accelerated competition with Pan American Airways in Latin America's air transport sector. Lufthansa began to increase its market share at Pan Am's expense. Only the hostilities that erupted in Europe curtailed Germany's advances. Then, when cuts in service weakened its rivals, the U.S. government secretly backed Pan American's purchases of its competitors.[28]

To his consternation, when looking at Latin America, Roosevelt saw a resident population of German descent whose potential influence—economically, culturally, and politically—dwarfed that of any North American presence. By 1933, an estimated one million Brazilians claimed German origins or German antecedents. Almost a quarter of a million German citizens had arrived in Latin America as settlers between 1870 and 1930. Almost half of the emigrants went to Brazil, where their descendants grew up. They farmed or opened shops, just as German immigrants had done in the United States. As a result, the local hardware or music store might be German owned. A German paint or chemical factory owner hired local employees; the banker of German ancestry lent money in the community. No similar exodus from North America to South America had taken place, and consequently no comparable U.S. émigré community existed.

The National Socialist regime intentionally drew the German émigré communities closer to Germany and cultivated a German national identity abroad. The predecessor Weimar Republic had disbursed financial subsidies to maintain German schools, theaters, and newspapers overseas, and in 1933 the National Socialists took over the organization that administered the subsidies. Moreover, the Nazi authorities maintained contact with National Socialist groups in foreign countries and paid particular attention to ethnic German populations living in Latin America. The Nazi swastika appeared on the Brazil-bound Zeppelin dirigible for the first time in August, 1933.[29]

Even as RKO-Radio wrote the screenplay, cast the parts, and filmed the story, the menacing shadows of a real European threat lengthened. By the summer of 1933, Adolph Hitler had consolidated power in Germany, and Nazi excesses were fueling a growing distrust. Brown-shirted German thugs began to intimidate citizens, primarily Jews, while local policemen turned their backs. The Nazis ordered a boycott of Jewish-owned shops on April 1. On May 1, the German government proclaimed a holiday, "The Day of National Labor," invited labor leaders to Berlin, and claimed solidarity with the country's workers. The very next day, the National Socialists occupied trade union offices, arrested labor leaders, confiscated union funds, and dissolved the independent unions.[30]

Reports of physical and political repression in Germany circulated in the world press. By the time RKO released the film in December, the American Federation of Labor had called on American workers to boycott German goods and services to protest the destruction of the unions and the open abuse of Jewish people and property.[31] The film's fictional European threat against Brazilian (and, by implication, hemispheric) interests had gained credibility through reported real-world events.

Roosevelt's cooperative policy for the Western Hemisphere, a sharpened New Deal focus on an inherited retreat from interventionism and economic domination, acquired an unexpected urgency. Collective security against the threat of European fascism supplanted a pledge of friendship and acquired a consciousness of shared destiny. In the event that European contentiousness spilled into the hemisphere and the United States had to join Latin America in military defense, the government built a rationale for unity.

A Commitment to Solidarity

In an unintended consequence of dynamic expansion, the web of relationships woven by the airline, movie, and tourist industries meshed with the determination on the part of hemispheric governments to advance from amity toward solidarity. Pan American Airways, which stood to gain from hemispheric tourism and had used a musical comedy feature film to impress its name in the mind of travelers, solidified its position as an instrument of U.S. policy. Although the occasional aerial action drama or thriller might still appear on the silver screen, air transport had achieved a status beyond sport, daredevils, and barnstormers.

The Pan American Airways logo—a globe carried on wings, displaying the North and South American continents—reinforced the hemispheric connection everywhere it appeared. Advertisements, stationery, brochures, and the planes themselves carried the symbol of an air transport service that brought people together. At the same time, limited disposable income curtailed air tourism's potential to cement Latin American friendships through much of the thirties. Many travelers who ventured outside the country in search of a "foreign" experience still headed for Europe, although tourism to the Caribbean and Mexico increased when steamship companies introduced bargain summer rates and when the mass production of automobiles lowered the cost of land transportation.

Pan Am recognized its value to the government and publicly articulated the strength of its position as the country's standard bearer and symbol of technological superiority:

> The development of the Pan American Airways system had been the answer of the U.S. government and of American aviation to the threatened domination of international air transport services by European companies heavily subsidized by their respective national governments. The first area in which the activities of European air lines commenced to have an adverse effect upon American trade was Latin America, one of the most important world markets for both Europe and the United States.[32]

In 1934, the U.S. Post Office Department acknowledged the political benefits reaped from Pan Am's efforts in the hemisphere, as well as the competitive edge offered to U.S. businesses, and renewed the company's noncompetitive airmail contracts. Capitalizing on its accumulated experience, the airline expanded its operations—and the U.S. aviation presence—across the Pacific Ocean all the way to Hong Kong in 1936 and opened the first trans-Atlantic passenger service from New York to Marseilles, France, in June, 1939.

Just six months before that inaugural Atlantic flight, the United States and twenty other American republics extended the pledge of cooperation and mutual respect at the Eighth Pan American Conference in Lima, Peru. Confronted with a growing fascist threat, the participants committed themselves to American solidarity, agreed not to permit any armed power to invade the hemisphere, and pledged to maintain the peace, security, and territorial integrity of any one country in case of a threat by an overseas power.

Roosevelt's 1939 message to Congress on the state of the union warned of a fascist menace to the country. Americans had to confront aggression against democracy, defend its institutions against attack, and maintain respect for the rights and freedoms of others. In light of the December, 1938, Lima declaration, that defense might require action to protect Latin America as well as the United States.

Friendship with Latin America was one thing; commitment of human and material resources to maintain the region's freedom was another. With the U.S. electorate suspicious of involvement in a European war, to what degree could the administration muster enthusiasm to defend Latin America? On the other hand, would the Axis powers' demonstrated military strength erode pledges of hemispheric solidarity? Since the announcement of the Good Neighbor policy, Roosevelt had insisted that the neighbors needed to meet and become acquainted in order to improve relations. Cordell Hull had carried the president's message to Montevideo in 1933 and had promised assistance to improve transportation and communications as facilitators of contact.

Over the years, the issue of hemispheric relations had evolved from friendship to mutual security. Could tourism and movies help to define allies and differentiate enemies? Of the three—air transport, tourism, and motion pictures—movies undoubtedly afforded the greatest degree of contact and opportunities for people to become acquainted with the world and to cultivate impressions about their hemispheric neighbors.

Increased Tensions and Hemispheric Solidarity

By the time *Flying Down to Rio* opened nationwide in January, 1934, Hollywood and Washington had institutionalized the government-movie studio relationship. Hollywood had agreed to a code of self-regulation under the NRA, and Roosevelt had signed the lengthy and elaborate document. Among other provisions, the president declined to impose federal censorship, and the industry pledged to maintain moral standards and good taste, both in the pictures it produced and in promotional materials. The code afforded some protections to exhibitors against the monopolistic business practices of motion picture producers and distributors and to the poorly paid movie "extras." In keeping with the administration's redistributive economic philosophy, the studios agreed to cut the excessively high salaries of some movie stars and studio executives.[33]

To some observers, the Washington-Hollywood pact signaled the entry of a maverick business into the industrial establishment and the official recognition of its economic and social importance. They reasoned that since U.S. citizens alone spent an estimated one billion dollars a year at the movies, filmed entertainment had earned a place among the country's major enterprises. Moreover, because of its global reach, Hollywood merited consideration as an unofficial ambassador for the nation.[34]

As with airplanes, attitudes toward movies had changed. A generation had grown up with motion pictures. People watched movies, formed opinions about them, and discussed them with friends, family, and coworkers. They incorporated selected screen behaviors into their own lifestyles, chose favorites among actors, and even modeled their appearance after movie stars. In the 1930s some eighty million Americans attended approximately sixteen thousand theaters each week. The scorn of the middle classes toward this entertainment of the masses had dissipated, although concerns about negative influences remained. With the possibility that up to eleven million people in the United States might be watching films at any given time, plus millions of others around the globe, the movies spread ideas and encouraged common perceptions among film fans.

However, the communication of character, action, dialog, and meaning could not be held to a certainty. Filmmakers made no pretense of expertise in the peculiarities of any region; few would claim knowledge of Latin America beyond some familiarity with Mexico and perhaps Cuba. Undeniably, some portrayals of local practices, along with confusion about cultural and linguistic distinctions, misinformed viewers. They also engendered anger and mistrust, rather than appreciation, among Latin American audiences. While *Flying Down to Rio* may have promoted good relations, other examples of Hollywood musical comedy entertainment proved less-than-reliable instruments to promote neighborliness.

Paramount's 1935 film *Rumba,* for example, illustrates the

332 / CHAPTER 7

potential for a studio to ensnare itself in an international wrangle over insensitive or uninformed stories, settings, and character portrayals. As one might expect, Paramount turned out a product in response to the market. When audiences responded favorably to one movie, similar films followed. In this typical Hollywood pattern, *Rumba* both followed and imitated a melodramatic musical romance called *Bolero* that had packed the movie houses and brought welcomed profits to the studio in 1934. In *Bolero* George Raft plays the owner of a Paris café whose love interest and dance partner, Carole Lombard, leaves him for a rich suitor. Raft goes off to fight in World War I, returns with a weak heart but opens another night club. On opening night, his new partner—Lombard's replacement—is too drunk to perform the featured dance with Raft, choreographed to Maurice Ravel's haunting "Bolero." Lombard is in the audience and substitutes for the incapacitated partner. She and Raft dance to great applause amid a hint of rekindled romance, but Raft has overtaxed his weak heart and dies in his dressing room. The film's huge success encouraged the studio to revive Raft through the magic of the movies.

Paramount counted on the Raft-Lombard chemistry to recapture the excitement of *Bolero* in a similarly scripted romantic film located in another foreign setting. If France worked for *Bolero,* why not Cuba and *Rumba?* In general, motion pictures that appealed to audiences in the United States proved popular south of the border, and the better-known Hollywood stars had loyal fans among the moviegoers there.[35] If Paramount read the market correctly, the Latins should produce sizable box-office receipts.

Cubans, in particular, loved U.S. movies. As historian Louis A. Pérez Jr., relates:

> The popularity [in Cuba] of U.S. films was unrivaled. . . .
> It is difficult to imagine any other country where North
> American films formed a more prominent part of popular
> culture. Hollywood captured the public imagination, and
> all the evidence suggests that moviegoers in Cuba were as
> hopelessly if happily immersed in movie star culture as au-
> diences in the United States.[36]

Affinity for Hollywood films and film stars notwithstanding, the steamy *Rumba* turned up an unexpectedly intense heat in Havana. The filmed story took place in both New York City and Cuba, where the sensual, folk-based rumba had moved from the sugar mills, docks, and streets into the ballroom. While *Flying Down to Rio*'s time-consuming carioca song-and-dance segment took eighteen minutes to complete, the colorful rumba, repeated in various outdoor locations and night club scenes, occupied substantially more of this movie's running time.

Raft plays a New York dancer whose personality mimics some of the actor's other roles—tough, suspicious, and sometimes disapproving. The edgy New Yorker dances his way to fame, to Havana, and into a romantic triangle that pits his regular dance partner against an interloping blond heiress, played by Lombard. Once again Lombard takes over the dance role in a pinch. This time Raft's female partner refuses to go on stage because the mob has threatened to shoot Raft—and they might miss him and kill her. Clearly, the story simply provided an excuse for the stars to display their dancing ability and romantic attraction.

However, one dance sequence takes place in the Cuban "interior," where "natives" perform a sensual, exaggerated rumba that potentially plants an image of erotic primitivism in the minds of some viewers. The segment so offended urban, middle-class Cuban officials that they banned the picture, threatened to bar presentation of any Paramount pictures if *Rumba* was not suppressed in the United States, and moved to set up a Cuban-controlled censorship board in New York to view films destined for Cuba. They insisted on the right to examine all movies—not just those produced by Paramount studios—and to forbid shipment to Cuba of any that could not pass their standards of good taste and appropriate portrayals of Latin Americans.

Cuban-American relations had only recently surmounted another of the intermittent periods of tension between the two governments. Cuba had turned to political violence in 1933 to remove dictator Gerardo Machado from office, but Washington had moved to shape the new government to its own interests. Then abrogation of the Platt Amendment had convinced some Cubans that Roosevelt would respect Cuban sovereignty, and a new trade treaty with the United States promised to restore the island's prostrate sugar economy. Tourists, frightened by the 1933 revolution, slowly renewed their vacation or weekend trips to Havana.

State Department officials acknowledged the movie's cultural insensitivity but, adding insult to injury, expressed the view that the designated "misrepresentation or exaggeration" of the Cuban rumba promised to substantially enhance tourist traffic from the United States. Cubans vociferously disagreed and hurled charges of assaults on Cuban dignity. The false impression of Cuban customs and culture, they objected, would diminish Cuba's tourism prospects, not help them.

Obviously, administrators in the State Department held a less lofty opinion of U.S. tourists' motivations than did the Cuban officials. Whereas the Cubans protested that the portrayal of exaggerated sensuality among the "natives" would discourage tourists, the U.S. officials regarded the movie as promotional. In fact, Cuba had built a thriving tourist industry in the 1920s, based in large measure on the attractions of rumba, rum, and romance, only to see it crumble under the weight of economic crisis and the violent upheaval of revolution in 1933. The change in government had brought reformers into the official tourist agency who wanted to restructure Cuba's appeal. These idealists dedicated their efforts to improving the island's image and to attracting family-oriented travelers. Hollywood certainly overlooked the shift under way in Cuba when Paramount used the island as an exotic backdrop for a rather sordid story.

The tropical storm over the film never grew to hurricane proportions. The U.S. ambassador to Cuba sat down with the indignant mayor of Havana and representatives of Paramount studios, and they watched the film together. When Paramount agreed to delete the most egregiously offensive fifteen feet of film, the Cubans withdrew their censorship demands.[37]

The confrontation, engaged with angry threats of boycotts, censorship, and economic damage inflicted on a callous film industry, reached a mutually agreed-upon resolution and quickly exited the arena of diplomatic crossfire. However, the conflict illustrates an awareness of Hollywood's power to influence perceptions and to direct the flow of tourists. Cubans acted on their considerable experience with movies, which they viewed as a "means of transport to distant places" and a way to "inform the imagination and alter consciousness."[38] They argued against the appropriation and distortion of cultural elements offered to the world as Cuban and concluded that unsophisticated viewers would attribute the characteristics portrayed on the screen to actual Cubans—not to fictional Hollywood creations. While they worried needlessly about the loss of potential revenue—tourists favored a bawdy Cuba—their concerns for the type of tourist attracted by promises of erotic native dances warranted consideration. Moreover, notions of sovereignty elevated national self-representation over movie-made portrayals.

Although they may have disagreed on whether suggestively sensual stories served the goals of tourist bureau officials, all three parties to the flare-up over *Rumba*—that is, the Cuban government, the U.S. State Department, and film industry representatives—viewed feature film portrayals as tourist motivators. As either incentives or disincentives, movies influenced the choice of destinations, as well as the decision to travel at all. The consciousness of that connection wove itself into efforts to bring the hemisphere together through the distribution of Hollywood's products and to encourage inter-American travel.

In 1937, the federal government officially acknowledged the tourist industry's economic potential and inaugurated the U.S. Tourist Bureau to assist private-sector expansion of the $5-billion-a-year industry. Summertime travel—domestic and foreign—exceeded all previous vacation travel records that year, and the tourist bureau set out to lure more Europeans and Latin Americans to the United States in order to balance citizens' expenditures abroad. The government had no plans to establish a publicly financed tourist industry, of course, but could print and distribute brochures, encourage the development of attractions, influence motion picture content (both feature films and travelogues), and ease the process of gaining entry into the country.[39]

The following year, the Pan American Union, which had published a number of articles on travel in the Americas in its *Bulletin,* initiated a campaign to promote tourism in the hemisphere and organized an Inter-American Travel Congress to be held in San Francisco in 1939. The delegates at the 1938 Lima Conference, motivated by both politics and economics, supported the travel congress and extolled the virtues of travel to stimulate understanding, good will, friendship, and trade.[40] Unlike Franklin D. Roosevelt's abstract pairing of tourism and communication presented five years earlier, the representatives of twenty-one nations produced an agenda for the travel congress that covered several dozen specific topics critical to tourist operations, from necessary governmental actions on passport and immigration matters, improvements in infrastructure, and customs exemptions to transportation, marketing, and promotion. All of the issues the delegates put forth required some level of international cooperation.

When Laurence Duggan, chief of the State Department's Division of the American Republics, addressed the Inter-American Travel Congress on Pan American Day, April 14, 1939, Europe stood on the brink of war. Duggan used the opportunity to reiterate the U.S. commitment to hemispheric solidarity and to distinguish the American peace from Europe's turmoil. The nature of the occasion required a tourism theme for the speech, of course, and as he enumerated the actions already taken to facilitate transportation among the American nations, Duggan emphasized the potential of cars, planes, ships, and trains to bring people together peacefully. He contrasted travel between nations by car with the movement of tanks. The hemisphere's merchant vessels carried passengers and products to mutual advantage, he reminded his listeners, while other nations sent battleships and submarines. The hemisphere's airplanes brought people close together rather than rain death and destruction from the air. Duggan concluded with an appeal to the delegates to move their nations along the road to a "richer and happier life for all of our peoples."[41]

Clearly, Duggan's road to happiness carried tourists, and President Roosevelt buttressed the commitment to tourism when he proclaimed 1940 "Travel America Year." With war closing popular

European destinations, the declaration reflected political realities as well as a show of friendship.

War in Europe also undercut Hollywood's foreign receipts, revenue that was needed to cover production costs. Between boycotts, the closing of theaters, blackouts, and unreliable distribution and transportation in the belligerent nations, studios could not depend on the European market. Gloomy prospects in Europe enhanced Hollywood's appreciation for Latin America's enthusiastic movie fans.

The controversy over *Rumba* had put the State Department on notice to keep an eye open for signs of irritation over Hollywood's films and attempts at censorship. By the end of the 1930s, when both the movie and tourist industries played an even larger role in hemispheric relations, misrepresentations of both the United States and Latin America gained greater importance in the struggle to build and maintain solidarity.

As an aggressive fascist movement increasingly threatened the international movie market, Hollywood and the U.S. government listened more carefully to the complaints and discontents of its neighbors. Furthermore, Germany actively pressed its interests in the critical Brazilian, Argentine, and Mexican markets, calling on governments to censor some films and to ban others. Some studios responded with self-censorship and withheld controversial anti-Nazi films from Latin American distribution rather than provoke a quarrel with foreign authorities.[42]

In fact, one could entice more viewers into the theaters with musical fantasies set in Latin America *and* encourage tourism at the same time. If people couldn't afford to "travel America" in person, they could experience Argentina, Brazil, and Cuba vicariously through Hollywood's versions of Latin life in movies like *Down Argentine Way, That Night in Rio,* or *Week-End in Havana.* Carmen Miranda starred in all three of these films and a dozen more, as the lovable representation of a fantasy Latina.

Christened María do Carmo Miranda da Cunha when she was born in Portugal, Carmen Miranda grew up in Brazil and became a popular singer. Opportunely for the U.S. tourism policy, Brazil had produced an entertainment idol. Impresario Lee Schubert brought Miranda to the United States in 1939. After she dazzled Broadway audiences with her sparkling eyes and personality, colorful costumes, flamboyant style, samba rhythms, and Brazilian songs, Twentieth Century-Fox put her in the movies. For better or worse, the highly talented performer came to symbolize Latin America for millions of North American moviegoers.

To suit the format of the musical comedy genre, Miranda generally played a nightclub or stage performer whose romantic entanglements developed alongside and in between the musical numbers. Story lines unfolded in the interludes between song-and-dance extravaganzas and involved sufficient complication to create an obstacle to romance, but little else. It was enough that the plots brought North and South Americans together in beautiful locations and ended with the appropriate romantic pairings.

By 1940, Cuba's indignation over *Rumba*'s distortion of the island's culture had faded to a dim memory. However, Brazil's lament that Hollywood had "Americanized" Carmen Miranda, a symbol of national pride, as well as complaints from Brazil's southern neighbor that Miranda sang in Portuguese when she played an Argentinean in the movies, reawakened a consciousness of Latin sensibilities in both the movie and political capitals of the United States. Profit-conscious movie producers took the criticism seriously. For the U.S. government, unity of antifascist purpose in the hemisphere superseded market considerations.

In June of 1940, President Roosevelt's administrative assistant sent a memorandum to the chief executive. "You may be interested in this letter from John Steinbeck who has just come to Washington from Mexico where he has been making a movie," he wrote. A penciled notation identified Steinbeck as the author of *Grapes of Wrath*. Steinbeck's own letter to the president made reference to an imminent crisis in the western hemisphere, "to be met only by an immediate, controlled, considered, and directed method and policy." Roosevelt responded, "I want to see John Steinbeck the author of Grapes of Wrath tomorrow for 20 minutes."

We can assume that Steinbeck conveyed to Roosevelt the concerns he expressed in a letter he had written to a friend, a copy of which he attached to his letter requesting time with the president:

> The Germans have absolutely outclassed the Allies in propaganda. If it continues, they will completely win Central and South America away from the United States. They have the finest argument of all, and one that the peoples of this lower hemisphere can understand. They will trade goods for goods, and there is no bonded indebtedness to add to the price. . . . I propose that a propaganda office be set up which, through radio and motion pictures, attempts to get this side of the world together. Its method would be to make for understanding rather than friction. . . . I have a smoothly functioning movie crew here and could gather several more very quickly. I could also work with some Hollywood people. . . . I do think a decent and honorable job could be done down here [Mexico] and in South America, but I doubt if it can be done by the people who are directing it now.[43]

In Steinbeck's opinion, both policymakers and U.S. citizens whom he had encountered in Mexico, where he was making a film, had "botched" the good neighbor policy. At least one State Department official agreed. The U.S. Embassy in Buenos Aires reported in July, 1940 — just as Steinbeck lamented the country's failures in the hemisphere — that a Hollywood product shown in the Argentine capital had fallen far short of its goal. The movie engendered "exactly the opposite effect to that intended and illustrates the danger of reproducing a synthetic Latin American background with serious faults in language and technical details, all of which go to make a bad vehicle for propaganda."[44]

The film so described was an RKO-Radio release, *Escape to Paradise*. According to the report, the Argentine media hardly knew how to interpret the picture, not sure whether to laugh or take offense. Argentines — and most likely other South Americans — argued that North Americans obviously knew nothing about Latin

America's history and culture since they dressed twentieth-century women in Spanish mantillas and presented gauchos with Mexican accents.

The *Cine Argentino* reviewer cited in the report regarded the film as a mockery. The audience "limited itself to loud laughter in those moments which were made even more ridiculous by the attempts to depict Argentine customs":

> In any case, it is a joke on the brotherhood of all America. . . . . [T]he intention is to flatter us gauchos. A young Yankee finds his paradise, with love and a guardian angel, in a corner of Argentina. The gauchos are picked from a New York district where Italians are intermixed with natives of Guatemala, Costa Rica, Porto Rico, Cuba, Mexico, Colombia, and Venezuela. . . . All this is done for the mutual knowledge of the brother countries.[45]

RKO-Radio hit the right ideological buttons but failed in its cultural research. In the unintentionally offensive film, the popular singer Bobby Breen plays a young North American tourist who takes a trip through South America, leaves the ship at a port called Rosarito, and finds his paradise. Called on to say a few words at a party, he advises North Americans and South Americans to get to know each other. He obviously takes his own advice and falls in love with a young lady in the city.

As with the movie *Rumba,* misrepresentation of Latin America may not have deterred potential tourists, but the ignorance the filmmakers displayed alienated the people that Hollywood wanted to attract to the theater and that the government needed as allies.

Roosevelt had already begun an effort to coordinate and exercise control over hemispheric relationships before John Steinbeck presented his brief in the Oval Office. By July, 1940, Roosevelt had proposed the development of a media-based, cultural-relations program in the fields of art, music, education, and science. At the time, the proposal lacked both focus and funding and had fallen victim to interdepartmental politics. Then he selected Nelson Rockefeller, a man knowledgeable about Latin America, as his coordinator of Inter-American Affairs. Rockefeller also had a financial stake in RKO-Radio Pictures, which established his credentials in the movie world. By the end of the year, Rockefeller had formatted an organizational structure and appointed John Hay Whitney—long-time friend and colleague of Juan Trippe, Merian Cooper, and David Selznick—to head the motion picture division.

The division had a policy-related office in Washington, production offices in New York, and a Hollywood office that "maintained contact with the industry and advised producers on their problems which related to the other American republics." Its objectives included (1) increased production of feature films about the United States and other hemispheric nations for distribution throughout the Americas; (2) the elimination of Axis-sponsored pictures from exhibition in the hemisphere; (3) voluntary, motion picture industry restraint in the matter of material that might be objectionable in other hemispheric countries; and (4) an effort to persuade producers not to distribute pictures in Latin America that might negatively portray the United States and its way of life.[46]

Hollywood had formulated and then accepted the NRA's regulations to fight the Depression in 1934 and signed on in 1940 to implement FDR's Latin American policy and to fight fascism under the direction of Coordinator of Inter-American Affairs (CIAA). In March, 1941, the CIAA begat the Motion Picture Society for the Americas, an organization devoted to familiarizing moviemakers with the "peoples, the problems and the countries" in the hemisphere in order to use their craft to achieve closer cultural relations.[47]

Whatever their utility and shortcomings as shapers of people's consciousness, movies and tourism had gained powerful champions in a short span of time. Along with air transport, they had grown into international industries within one generation and showed great potential to influence the way in which people made choices and thought about the world and other people in it. Leaders of nations had developed a faith in the ability of motion pictures and tourism to motivate people, and they put that belief into practice. War-era movies, for example, vilified enemies and justified their destruction.

Tourism afforded a more ambiguous political instrument. Like the promoters of world's fairs, some advocates of cultural contact borrowed the optimism of the technological utopians and posited a better, more peaceful world that could be achieved through familiarity. For the transformed generation that lived between 1903 and 1933, however, increased contact did not mean acceptance of people who had formerly been strangers. Nor does it now.

Movies, Airplanes, and Touristic Urges

And they shall beat their swords into bar stools
And their spears into golfing sticks.
                    —Prophet for an entertainment century
                              (with apologies to Isaiah)

A VIATION, MASS tourism, and the movies, three economically, socially, and culturally significant industries, evolved
independently, each surrounded by its own romantic
aura tinged with glamour, excitement, and risk. By 1930, each
had achieved importance in international commerce. As three elements of an increasingly complex and interdependent world, they
influenced the way in which people used their leisure time and affected their thoughts about themselves and the global society in
which they lived.

While North Americans had spent more than $800 million
dollars on foreign travel in 1929, they paid out scarcely $300 mil-
lion in 1933. Anticipating a near-term improvement in economic
conditions, hard-pressed Cunard Lines arranged for installment
purchases of vacation cruises in 1932, with payments stretched
over twelve or even twenty months. Analysts attributed a slight

increase in transatlantic passenger travel in mid-1933 to an encouraging stock market rise that prompted some stockholders to
liquidate holdings and spend the cash.[1]

Whether prearranged as a promotional tie-in to the movie or
simply coincidental, *The Literary Digest* published "Big Gain in Air
Travel" the same month that RKO released *Flying Down to Rio*.
Readers learned that they could visit thirty-three foreign lands and
colonies in the Caribbean and Central and South America on a
two-week vacation via Pan American Airways. Travel statistics in
the hemisphere in fact showed growth in 1934 and 1935. Although
most people still traveled by ship to Central and South America
and by auto to Mexico, Pan American reported a forty-four percent increase in passenger miles in 1934 over 1933.[2]

RKO-Radio Pictures captured a confluence of forces in
1933—air travel and tourism—that, separately and in combination, occupy an even more critical position in international relations today. Industrial tourism evolved from the effort to accommodate the needs of travelers into a planned, carefully marketed,
government-promoted business. Now airplanes connect even the
remotest locations to a tourist network. Tourists contribute to the
economic well-being of their chosen destination, where the money
they spend turns over in the local economy. Tourism revenues also
pay for imported goods, an exchange whose criticality does not escape policymakers and economic planners on either the sending
or receiving end of the transaction.

An affluent society follows its fantasies more freely in the
twenty-first century than in the economically depressed 1930s and
sometimes into unexpected territory. For example, two tour companies in still-fascinating but less glamorous Rio de Janeiro now offer daily excursions to the city's sprawling, hillside squatter slums.
Tourists from various countries ply its narrow passageways, past
stray dogs, garbage, and graffiti slogans to take photos of themselves
and the local residents.[3] Such "reality tours" would have held little
appeal for the deprived movie audiences of the thirties but now
compose their own segment of a huge array of travel possibilities.

Both the air transport and tourist industries take advantage of
movie-awakened sensibilities, as do government officials. Millions

of people receive impressions based on a filmmaker's interpretation of people and events. In an international audience that spans divisions of age, class, gender, and ethnicity, as well as regional boundaries, viewers respond to the manipulation inherent in filmmaking, as the movie industry intends they should. Audience members adapt, adopt, or reject attitudes and behaviors, but the experience of viewing itself contributes to transformations in consciousness. Some viewers may decide to visit the place they have just experienced vicariously.

Tourism's Connections

The lowly T-shirt has joined the ranks of popular art and culture as a ubiquitous, location-identifying tourist souvenir. Few airport or hotel gift shops fail to display creatively designed, colorful T-shirts that let travelers—and everyone else—know what city they have visited. Every tourist attraction also sells its version of the simple garment. How many people bother to connect the growers, transporters, and processors of cotton; the cutters, sewers, packers, and shippers; the graphic artists, producers of inks and other art materials; wholesalers and retailers; and buyers of souvenirs and receivers of gifts?

The worn and faded shirt enters the worldwide used-clothing market. One day a tourist aboard a small boat on an isolated waterway in a seemingly remote part of the world spies a man on the shore; he is fishing. As they pass, the fisherman lifts his arm in greeting. His shirt says, "San Diego Zoo." The tourist takes his picture, and the humor connects a global reality.

Air transport has facilitated a global tourism culture that connects millions of people with disposable income or borrowing power—mostly from many countries' numerically expanding, middle social sectors. Every year a larger portion of the world's population participates in tourist activities, and for many locations tourism represents one of their most dynamic economic sectors.

Global citizens have developed a shared set of tourist expectations and behaviors. Every tourist has stories, and some of the links are extraordinary. The following experience is mine. A genial, accommodating social director on a cruise ship trades his usual dark suit or sport jacket and slacks for an open-necked shirt as he leads a group of lively German, British, and American passengers through an animated rendition of the macarena. (The group dance circled the world and found a favored place in the cruise ship repertoire.) Combed-back, shiny black hair highlights an angular, smiling face. The leader extends his arms, turns his hands, places them appropriately on head and hips, swivels his derrière, and jumps a quarter turn to the driving beat of the familiar music. The passengers mimic his movements. Applause and laughter express the delight of participants and onlookers as the dance ends.

Talent night festivities continue as the vivacious, assistant tour director leads eight enthusiastic Nebraskans, men and women, through a game of musical chairs. The players dodge and collide, try to circle and then to occupy the diminishing supply of chairs while the music starts and stops. The amicable guide appropriately encourages and gently mocks the antics of the players, while fellow passengers enjoy the good-natured competition of this children's game. Then the Nebraskans don red T-shirts and sing the state university's song.

The German tourists, who had traveled together before, perform a choral number. A karaoke singer, well-practiced in his rendition of a familiar Elvis Presley tune, soon has most people joining in. Members of the ship's staff—bartenders, dining room servers—sing and dance. The evening's entertainment generates an atmosphere of well-being and international camaraderie that carries over into daily contact.

The evening's entertainment could have taken place aboard a cruise ship in the Caribbean or Mediterranean Seas or the Atlantic, Pacific, or Indian Oceans. This time the macarena and other talent night festivities surfaced in the salon of a ship plying the waters of China's Yangtze River. The German, British, and American tourists all knew the cruise ship routines, and the Chinese staff had adopted them.

Tourism, as much as any international policy or endeavor, has contributed to the opening of China. Market driven, today's Chinese pleasure tourism industry woos travelers with modern hotel accommodations, a variety of food preparations designed to appeal to foreign tastes, and the opportunity to view eternal landscapes, admire the relics of ancient peoples, and shop endlessly in fully stocked souvenir stores and street market stalls.

China's tourist industry engages the world and operates alongside the country's tangled intergovernmental relations. Closed for years to outside influences, China has emerged as a tourist powerhouse, ranking fifth in international tourist arrivals (behind France, the United States, Spain, and Italy). After the Red Army defeated the Nationalist forces in 1949, tourism—either domestic or international—ceased to exist as an economic activity in China. Then, after Mao Zedong died in 1976, China's new leadership embraced tourism as a potential contributor to the country's modernization. Paradoxically, Mao's successor, Deng Xiaoping, resurrected elements of traditional Chinese culture and important heritage sites—denigrated under Mao's rule and laid waste by loyal supporters during the years of the Cultural Revolution—as tourist attractions.[4]

Some thirty million pleasure seekers invaded the people's republic in 2000. In the summer of 2001, China's national tourist administration sent a four-bus caravan with a troupe of performers and replicas of Chinese landscapes to six U.S. cities, along with travel professionals to answer questions. Curiosity about an ancient culture modified by a recent half-century of communism no doubt stirred tourists' interest, heightened by newspaper stories, current events, and movies.

Perhaps well-placed advertisements by tour agencies and feature stories by paid travel writers caught their attention. In a United Airlines advertisement, a young, westernized Chinese man stands in the front of a sampan being poled along a crowded waterway. A blurred waterfront adds a touch of the exotic. The ad copy reads, "There are nearly 1.2 billion amazing people in this land of incredible beauty. . . . And now we've made it easier than ever for you to connect with them. . . . Just imagine the possibilities."[5]

Destination, transportation, imagination, and motivation—

readers, targeted by marketing experts, project themselves into the front of that small boat and become potential tourists. They may even begin to think about the Beijing Olympics in 2008.

A latecomer to the global tourist market, China rapidly learned to manipulate its national attributes to attract foreign travelers. The huge dam under construction for years on the Yangtze River is complete, and water is beginning to accumulate behind it. The dam will consign a huge part of the river valley to an underwater existence. During the few years available to see the beauty of the acclaimed Three Gorges region before it disappears beneath the flood waters, China marketed Yangtze River cruises.[6]

Tibetan women may struggle under heavy loads of wood along the unpaved streets of Xianggelila, but to the Chinese government the mountain city is paradise. At least the English language sign on the brand new airport identifies the location as "Shangri-La," the mythical fountain of youth described by James Hilton in *Lost Horizon*. In keeping with their tourism ambitions, China's enterprising leaders approved a name change for the town. Now James Hilton's remote enchanted sanctuary might attract another Hilton to accommodate tourists who have read the book or seen the movie.[7]

China exemplifies but does not define the remarkable economic and social phenomenon of invention and reinvention. Industry planners constantly prepare to beguile a growing market with ever more tempting, hard-currency-earning possibilities. They have every reason to do so: By the year 2000, tourism emerged as the primary source of international trade receipts.

Just a sampling of tourism-related conferences held in 2000 suggests the magnitude and ingenuity of the worldwide tourism network. Delegates met in Vienna, Austria, to explore innovations in city tourism; in Warsaw, Poland, they discussed local and regional tourism development. Conferees in Santo Domingo, Dominican Republic, put their heads together on behalf of ecotourism. They considered spa and health tourism in Rotorua, New Zealand, and traded ideas on ethnic festivals in Beijing, China. Tourism promoters debated the benefits of agrotourism in Perugia, Italy, and sport-generated tourism in Canberra, Australia, cultural tourism in Budapest, Hungary, and possibilities for peace through tourism in Amman, Jordan. Wine tourism attracted delegates to a conference in Marlborough, New Zealand, and connections between local cuisine and tourism took others to Nicosia, Cyprus. Participants addressed the sociology of tourism in Suva, Fiji, and the interconnected world of tourism in Singapore. Interconnected we certainly have become.

The Air Transport-Tourism Connection

The world's airlines carried the overwhelming majority of the international delegates just now mentioned to their tourism conferences. Later, airplanes will transport the tourists who respond to the attractions under consideration. Mass tourism has introduced billions of people to the rewards and sometimes the inconveniences of foreign travel. Without international airlines, tourism could not have achieved its acknowledged global importance in both trade and economic development.

The international tourist industry showed its greatest expansion between 1970 and 2000, when two hundred million annual tourist arrivals more than tripled to seven hundred million. Asia increased its share substantially, and Africa and the Middle East showed significant gains. China even outpaced Great Britain in rate of growth between 1999 and 2000. International tourists generated revenues of almost half a trillion dollars, and U.S. travelers dominated the spending spree. They contributed sixty-five billion dollars to various destinations around the world.[8]

Unfortunately, the world became suddenly and painfully aware of the criticality of air transport to a valuable industry after the destruction of New York's World Trade Towers in September, 2001. The psychological reaction was swift and drastic. The sense that a fundamental, inexplicable change had engulfed the world compounded the profound sadness. People battered by loss and uncertainty hesitated to be away from home, much less to fly. The seemingly irrevocable freedom to travel fell before the threat of violence.

Photographic witnesses to mass destruction and terror, millions of people experienced a heightened awareness of the world around them and of their own vulnerability. With security and safety in the air and on the ground under siege, they confronted an altered reality. When asked for reactions, many a stunned person expressed a need to reassess goals and values. As individuals, they made personal choices, but the cumulative effect of decisions not to fly to a family reunion, to a conference, or to a vacation destination critically impacted the livelihoods of citizens and the economic prospects of cities and nations around the world.

New York City probably felt the blow first and most thoroughly. The city anticipated multibillion-dollar revenue losses and thousands of unemployed workers in the travel and tourism sector. To avoid a financial catastrophe in the tourist sector that would ripple through the entire economy, the leadership quickly mobilized hundreds of Broadway show people. New York called on entertainers to turn back a crisis, and cast members of then-current productions filled Times Square with an emotional public performance designed to lure visitors back to the stricken city. Thus, entertainment functioned as tourism's salvation, as well as its attraction.

The economic damage quickly spread nationwide and then worldwide in the air-traffic-dependent tourism sector. Within three weeks 40 percent of Los Angeles County's hotel workers had lost jobs or suffered reduced hours when a majority of overseas travelers canceled reservations. Even tourists from neighboring Mexico and Canada declined to visit the famed site of movie studio tours and Hollywood glamour.[9]

In Anaheim, California, home to Disneyland and the West Coast's most popular convention site, conference managers canceled, leaving hotel rooms empty and setting workers adrift. Skittish tourists stayed away from Florida's Disney World and Universal Studios, too, and President George W. Bush traveled to Orlando to try to shore up the state's depressed vacation industry. Las Vegas lost millions of dollars in convention and overseas business. Japanese tourists deserted Hawaii, as did travelers from the mainland, leaving the island's tourism-dependent economy desperate. The disaster shook Caribbean island tourism, as dependent on airlines as Hawaii. Nervous U.S. vacationers canceled flights to Mexico's popular resort areas, and Mexico saw its hotels and beaches empty.

Since the country that suffered the greatest loss on September 11 also leads the world in international tourist expenditures, the refusal to fly unleashed waves that broke upon numerous foreign shores and threatened to swamp economic development plans in the most vulnerable of them.

Egypt suffered a 50 percent decline in visitors from England and Germany, who usually show up after the summer heat but decided to avoid the Middle East in the fall of 2001. Tourism is the Egyptian government's largest source of revenue and accounts for 10 percent of the country's gross domestic product. So, with thousands of group tours canceling reservations, the land of the pyramids tried to lure Russian replacements with promises of inexpensive charter flights and sunshine.

With tourist inflows accounting for one-fifth of Turkey's exports of goods and services, the loss of tourism revenue threatened its commerce, too. Brazil anticipated a 30 percent decline in U.S. visitors, and many Brazilians canceled trips to the United States. The small Mediterranean island of Malta, whose 380,000 people welcome almost three times as many tourists every year—most of whom arrive by air—faced a precipitous decline in advance bookings for the winter season.

By contrast, China anticipated a boost to its industry from Japanese tourists hesitant to fly to Hawaii and the mainland United States and who perceived China as a safe alternative.[10] The situation reversed in 2003, however, when China's tourism fell victim to Severe Acute Respiratory Syndrome (SARS) as the communicable virus caused cancellation of 80 percent of the country's foreign group tours. Other southeast Asian destinations also suffered drastic tourism losses.

If the World Tourism Organization awarded a prize for the most optimistic tourism-promoting government, Afghanistan certainly deserved the accolade in 2002. The country that bore the brunt of retaliation for the September 11 terrorist attacks epitomizes the desperation of impoverished peoples to find their deliverance in tourism. Many of the world's poorest developing nations consider tourism the most promising among limited opportunities to open avenues of economic growth and provide jobs for their people. The situation is particularly precarious, however, when potential tourists perceive the destination as politically unstable and dangerous.

Nevertheless, hardly a month after assuming power, with U.S. forces still bombing caves and raiding camps, the interim Afghan government of Prime Minister Hamid Karzai reinstated the pre-Taliban minister for civil aviation and tourism, who proclaimed the cash-strapped country ready to invite tourists once again.

Relying on media-fed curiosity about Afghanistan to build a market, the overconfident tourism minister declared his readiness to organize various history and culture tours, one to Kabul and Kandahar and another to the Bamiyan Valley, site of the giant stone Buddhas that the Taliban destroyed. He planned a tour of the route Marco Polo followed and trekking excursions into the Hindu Kush mountains, once land mines were removed, of course.[11]

Tourists are consumers of experiences as well as relaxation and romance, and the anticipation of adventure or of contact with other cultures and environments will eventually coax them to overcome their trepidation and buy their plane tickets to some enticing destination. Whether they choose Afghanistan might depend on the price.

On the other hand, no country can claim to control the circumstances that determine its tourist fortunes. In the year of the Wright brothers centennial anniversary, the uncertainties of war, violence against civilian populations, and the spread of a deadly virus have damaged the air transport and tourism industries.

Another Movie, Another Time

The lure that overcomes travel inhibitions might be a movie. The darkly humorous film *Fargo* may not have inspired people to pack their snow boots and seek out the expanses of frigid North Dakota, but thousands of people traveled to Iowa to stand in the cornfield that had been converted into a baseball field in *A Field of Dreams*. *Gandhi* turned travel thoughts to India, and the Scots heard cash register bells when Hollywood released the history-based films *Rob Roy* and *Braveheart*. To increase any pro-Scottish inclinations, they invited travel writers to tour the movies' settings and then sent them home to praise the beauty of it all in newspapers and magazines.

The English Patient offered an apparently rousing, travel-inducing combination: the mystique of foreign places, the beauty of the Tunisian desert, adventure, romance, passion, and betrayal. Even before *The English Patient* won the Motion Picture Academy's award for best picture of 1996, requests for travel information from the Tunisian Embassy in Washington, D.C., increased by 50 percent. On Oscar night hundreds of millions of people around the world viewed the handing over of nine of the familiar statuettes to various people associated with the film. Glamorous Hollywood and filmed fantasy acted as travel promoters.

The film opens slowly and ambiguously—the tip of a paint-brush moves across a sand-colored background. Brush strokes sketch a figure; an arm appears, a leg perhaps, only abstractly defining a human. The scene fades to sand dunes casting shadows similar to the brush strokes. The camera widens its focus to encompass the desert and catches a small airplane that the audience hears before it becomes visible. The open-cockpit, two-seater biplane swoops low over the dunes. A beautiful woman reclines in the front seat, perhaps asleep.

Suddenly the plane drops from the sky, brought down by guns fired from below. Subsequent scenes reveal wounded soldiers and a badly burned and bandaged individual who cannot speak. We learn the circumstances leading up to the opening scenes in patches of unconnected disclosures, bit by bit, pieced together from information in a diary, the revelations of a witness, and memories. Not unlike a historian, the filmmaker assembles the evidence and weaves the story. Breathtaking expanses of sand viewed in the clarity of the desert light interrupt the narrative from time to time, backed by soaring music that carries one along with a lush romanticism that contrasts with the stark desert. You really want to be there.

Tourist agents provided the balm to soothe the travel itch. In the brief time that it took to make air and lodging arrangements, an enterprising New York-area travel agent packaged a "Golden Tunisia" trip, including hotel accommodations, meals, guides, and visits to film locations. A notation understood by moviegoers read, "No biplanes will be used." [12]

Moving pictures, now a commonplace time-filler on long plane rides, captivated international audiences early last century, even as aeronautical inventors and engineers struggled to keep their planes in the air. Travelogues filled some of the earliest movie screens and introduced viewers to foreign, sometimes exotic, locations. Travel fantasies connected people even before airline companies and a tourist industry took them where they wanted to go.

The possibility that human ingenuity could develop a mechanical device to carry people through the air had fired imaginations and tested the skills of scientists and engineers long before the Wright brothers managed to remain aloft in their motorized flying machine. However, neither dreamers nor designers could have imagined chorus girls cavorting on airplane wings in front of movie cameras. What observer at Kitty Hawk, watching Wilbur or Orville lying on his stomach in the winged biplane and manipulating machinery amid the unpredictable air currents, ever conjured up a vision of eating lunch high above the seas one day on the way to Rio de Janeiro?

Georges Méliès filmed an imaginary rocket trip to the moon in 1902, but he never thought of the motion picture as a sales tool for air transport. The competitors at the Reims Air Meet exhibited their fragile craft and hoped to win fame and prize money. They could not have guessed, however, that in their lifetime airline companies would compete to carry passengers and cargo among continents. The combat pilots who battled to dominate the skies over France and Germany gave no thought to a competition among wartime adversaries for control of commercial airways over South America.

At the 1893 World's Columbian Exposition, which of the sober scientists discussing aeronautics conceived of an air transport industry? How could the social scientists divine the curiosity about preindustrial peoples that would itself shape an industry? How many of the visitors to that great tourist attraction foresaw that pleasure travel to foreign lands might one day function as a bargaining chip in international relations? As they bent over that unadorned brown box with the moving pictures inside, which fascinated watchers of Kinetoscope peep shows predicted the power of a motion picture industry?

Tourism has taken its place on the worldwide political chess board. As countries expand their tourist industries and increasingly rely on the revenue for their economic viability and on the foreign exchange for purchases in the global marketplace, they become vulnerable to political gamesmanship. That is, the more affluent, tourist-sending countries can hold tourist-receivers hostage by playing up negative conditions—crime, political unrest, and health risks—in the media. Moreover, political dissidents can render destinations uninviting when they target tourists for violent, well-publicized actions. In 1933, the notion of tourist blackmail would have seemed absurd, but tourism fantasies have turned into political realities.

At the turn of the twentieth century, a world in transition from the farm to the factory and from rural to urban existence witnessed the wobbly beginnings of three new industries—air transport, motion pictures, and mass tourism. No one recognized their future power as multibillion-dollar, global enterprises or guessed the excitement that would accompany their growth. They were beyond imagining.

Notes

Introduction

1. *Los Angeles Times,* May 14, 2002.
2. See Robert W. Rydell, *All the World's a Fair: Visions of Empire at American International Expositions, 1876–1916,* for the fairs' contributions to U.S. imperial ambitions.

Chapter 1

1. Cindy S. Aron, *Working at Play: A History of Vacations in the United States,* 138.
2. Ibid., 140, 143.
3. Earl S. Pomeroy, *In Search of the Golden West: The Tourist in Western America,* xii, 112.
4. Andrea Boardman, *Destination Mexico: "A Foreign Land a Step Away," U.S. Tourism to Mexico, 1880s–1950s,* 10, 17, 22, 24, 32.
5. Alfred R. Conkling, *Appleton's Guide to Mexico,* 1–4.
6. Rydell, *All the World,* 155.
7. Mary Beth Norton, David M. Katzman, Paul D. Escott, Howard Chudacoff, Thomas G. Paterson, William M. Tuttle Jr., and William J. Brophy, *A People and a Nation* (Boston: Houghton Mifflin, 1996), vol. II, 355; Rydell, *All the World,* 40–41; John F. Kasson, *Amusing the Million: Coney Island at the Turn of the Century,* 19–22; Robert Mucigrosso, *Celebrating the New World: Chicago's Columbian Exposition of 1893,* 82–83.
8. Rydell, *All the World,* 69.
9. Ibid., 87, 102, 147.
10. Ibid., 114.
11. Ibid., 115–16, 179.
12. Mucigrosso, *Celebrating,* 164–65.
13. Rydell, *All the World,* 138–39, 143, 148.
14. Alexander L. Holley, "The Inadequate Union of Engineering Science and Art," *Transactions of the American Institute of Mining Engineers, 1876,* 191, in *Science and the Emergence of Modern America, 1865–1916,* ed. A. Hunter Dupree, 9–10 (Chicago: Rand McNally, 1963).
15. Alfred North Whitehead, *Science and the Modern World* (Cambridge: Cambridge University Press, 1946), 120, quoted in *Science and the Emergence of Modern America 1865–1916,* ed. A. Hunter Dupree, 3.
16. Vernon L. Parrington, "The American Scene," introduction to *The Beginnings of Critical Realism in America,* vol. 3 of *Main Currents in American*

Thought (Harcourt, Brace, 1927), reproduced in *Democracy and the Gospel of Wealth,* ed. Gail Kennedy, 27–28 (Boston: D. C. Heath, 1949).

17. Kasson, *Amusing the Million,* 26–27.
18. Tom D. Crouch, *A Dream of Wings: Americans and the Airplane, 1875–1905,* 80.
19. Ibid., 30–32.
20. Crouch, "Engineers and the Airplane," 15; Crouch, *Dream of Wings,* 20, 24.
21. Crouch, *Dream of Wings,* 37–38.
22. Ibid., 43, 50–54.
23. Ibid., 87–95. A number of schools and a small airport in San Diego memorialize Montgomery's work. A monument marks the place where he flew his glider in 1884.
24. Ibid., 80–82, 97–100.
25. Crouch, "Engineers and the Airplane," 16–17.
26. Walter Lord, *The Good Years: From 1900 to the First World War,* 93–94.
27. Words by Andrew B. Sterling and music by Kerry Mills, in Theodore Raph, *The Songs We Sang* (New York: A. S. Barnes, 1964).
28. Dorothy Daniels Birk, *The World Came to St. Louis: A Visit to the 1904 World's Fair,* 51, 56, 91, 92; John Allwood, *The Great Exhibitions,* 113–14.
29. Rydell, *All the World,* 62, 179.
30. Kristin Hoganson, "Cosmopolitan Domesticity: Importing the American Dream, 1865–1920," 62–63.
31. Birk, *1904 World's Fair,* 63–64.
32. Ibid., 92.
33. Ibid., 92, 64.
34. Ibid., 92–93.
35. "The Cliff Dwellers of the St. Louis Exposition," *Scientific American* (Nov. 12, 1904): 339.
36. Nick Haslam, "Life with a Volcano in the Backyard," *Financial Times,* Dec. 22–23, 2001.
37. Grand Circle Tours company brochure, *Asia 2003.*
38. San Diego Natural History Museum, *Educational Programs* (Summer, 2002).
39. *New York Times,* May 20, 2001.
40. Jean-Luc Maurer and Arlette Ziegler, "Tourism and Indonesian Cultural Minorities," in *Tourism: Manufacturing the Exotic,* ed. Pierre Rosse, 82–84.
41. Ibid., 75–78.
42. Gerard Roville, "Ethnic Minorities and the Development of Tourism in the Valleys of North Pakistan," 158–59, 170.

Chapter 2

1. Rydell, *All the World,* 62.
2. Susan J. Douglas, "Amateur Operators and American Broadcasting: Shaping the Future of Radio," 39, 41.
3. Wilbur Wright, "Flying as a Sport," *Scientific American* (Feb. 29, 1908): 139.
4. Octave Chanute, *Progress in Flying Machines,* 268; Joseph J. Corn, *The Winged*

Gospel: America's Romance with Aviation, 1900–1950, 31, 37; Michael Paris, *From the Wright Brothers to "Top Gun": Aviation, Nationalism, and Popular Cinema,* 4.

5. Birk, *1904 World's Fair,* 63.
6. *New York Times,* Sept. 4, 1904.
7. *Scientific American* (Oct. 29, 1904): 302.
8. Tom D. Crouch, *The Bishop's Boys: A Life of Wilbur and Orville Wright,* 270–71.
9. Ibid., 274, 249.
10. Percy Rowe, *The Great Atlantic Air Race,* 22; Curtis Prendergast, *The First Aviators,* 24–25; Crouch, *Bishop's Boys,* 250.
11. Birk, *1904 World's Fair,* 63.
12. Marvin W. McFarland, ed., *The Papers of Wilbur and Orville Wright,* 416, 421.
13. Ibid., 421.
14. Crouch, *Bishop's Boys,* 279–81.
15. McFarland, *Wright Papers,* 421, 445; Crouch, *Bishop's Boys,* 282.
16. Lord, *The Good Years,* 268–69; Frank F. Taylor, *To Hell with Paradise: A History of the Jamaican Tourist Industry,* 6.
17. Prendergast, *First Aviators,* 26–27.
18. Ibid., 22, 24, 29.
19. *Scientific American* (Apr. 4, 1908): 238–39.
20. Prendergast, *First Aviators,* 34–35.
21. Ibid., 57–58.
22. Crouch, *Bishop's Boys,* 380–81.
23. Ibid., 385, 388.
24. Prendergast, *First Aviators,* 50–51.
25. Ibid., 52–53.
26. Ibid., 37–41.
27. Rowe, *Great Atlantic Air Race,* 212. A despairing Santos Dumont hanged himself on July 23, 1932, however.
28. *New York Times,* Aug. 8, 1909. I have used the Rand McNally *World Atlas*'s spelling of the German city, rather than the *Times*'s "Frankfort-on-Main" and also use the *Atlas*'s spelling of "Reims" rather than the variation "Rheims" for the French city.
29. *New York Times,* Sept. 5, 1909.
30. Robert Wohl, *A Passion for Wings: Aviation and the Western Imagination, 1908–1918,* 100.
31. *New York Times,* Aug. 8, 1909.
32. *New York Times,* Aug. 19, 1909; Prendergast, *First Aviators,* 61.
33. Henry Serrano Villard, *Contact! The Story of the Early Birds,* 73–77.
34. Prendergast, *First Aviators,* 63–65.
35. Ibid., 68–71.
36. Villard, *Early Birds,* 99.
37. Peter Demetz, *The Air Show at Brescia, 1909,* 25, 29, 43, 216.
38. Prendergast, *First Aviators,* 78; Wohl, *Passion for Wings,* 111–12; Demetz, *Air Show,* 11, 14, 64.

39. Prendergast, *First Aviators*, 80.

40. Rowe, *Great Atlantic Air Race*, 27–32.

41. Prendergast, *First Aviators*, 72, 76–77.

42. Ibid., 87.

43. Crouch, *Bishop's Boys*, 406–10.

44. David Daniel Hatfield, *Dominguez Air Meet*, 3–5.

45. *New York Times*, Jan. 9, 1910.

46. *Dominguez Air Meet, Dominguez Ranch, Los Angeles 1910*, vertical file, San Diego Aerospace Museum Archive (hereafter, vertical file, SDAM).

47. Dorothy K. Hassler, "Aeroplanes, Then," *Flying* (Dec., 1953): 15; Hamilton Wright, "With the Bird-Men at Los Angeles," *The World To-Day*, photostatic copy, n.d., vertical file, SDAM.

48. *New York Times*, Jan. 11, 1910.

49. *The Outing Magazine*, 753–55, vertical file, SDAM.

50. *New York Times*, Jan. 20, 1910.

51. Ibid., Jan. 13. 1910.

52. Prendergast, *First Aviators*, 92–94.

53. "The Aeronautic Show at Boston," *Scientific American* (Feb. 26, 1910): 183.

54. Crouch, *Bishop's Boys*, 426–29.

55. Prendergast, *First Aviators*, 96–97; "The Harvard Aviation Meet," *Scientific American* (Sept. 17, 1910): 216–17.

56. Villard, *Early Birds*, 106–107; Prendergast, *First Aviators*, 100–101.

57. Crouch, *Bishop's Boys*, 432–33; Prendergast, *First Aviators*, 117.

58. Crouch, *Bishop's Boys*, 434–37.

59. Villard, *Early Birds*, 114–16.

60. Prendergast, *First Aviators*, 147.

61. Ibid.

62. C. A. Bosworth, "Army Men Find Planes Useful at Frisco," *Aero* (Jan. 28, 1911): 67.

63. Bosworth, "Great Flying at the Golden Gate," *Aero* (Feb. 4, 1911): 90–92.

64. "The Death Roll of the Aeroplane," *Scientific American* (Jan. 14, 1911): 28.

Chapter 3

1. Robert H. Stanley, *The Celluloid Empire: A History of the American Movie Industry*, 2–3.

2. Richard Abel, *The Cine Goes to Town: French Cinema, 1896–1914*, 15.

3. Abel, *The Red Rooster Scare: Making Cinema American, 1900–1910*, 12–14.

4. Joseph Kennedy, ed., *The Story of the Films*, 5.

5. Ibid., 4–5.

6. Neal Gabler, *An Empire of Their Own: How the Jews Invented Hollywood*, 17.

7. Ibid., 21, 17.

8. Tom Gunning, "The World as Object Lesson: Cinema Audiences, Visual Culture, and the St. Louis World's Fair, 1904," 422–25.

9. Ibid., 436–38.

10. Edward Wagenknecht, *The Movies in the Age of Innocence*, 13–14.

11. Undated, untitled clipping in Zukor file, New York Public Library of the Performing Arts at Lincoln Center, quoted in Gabler, *Empire,* 22.
12. Ibid., 23.
13. Abel, *The Red Rooster Scare,* 153–54.
14. Gunning, *D. W. Griffith and the Origins of American Narrative Film,* 58–59.
15. Stanley, *Celluloid Empire,* 9.
16. Walter Benjamin, *Illuminations,* ed. Hannah Arendt, trans. Harry Zohn (New York: Schocken Books, 1976), 83–87; Michael Roemer, *Telling Stories: Post-Modernism and the Invalidation of Traditional Narrative,* 3, 11.
17. I. C. Jarvie, *Movies and Society,* 127–28.
18. Roemer, *Telling Stories,* 13, 24–25.
19. Abel, *The Red Rooster Scare,* 9–10.
20. Ibid., 1.
21. Ibid., 34, 50–52.
22. Albert R. Fulton, *Motion Pictures: The Development of an Art,* 14–16.
23. Ibid., 23–27.
24. Abel, *The Red Rooster Scare,* 11–12; Kristin Thompson, *Exporting Entertainment: America in the World Film Market, 1907–1934,* 1–2.
25. Wagenknecht, *Age of Innocence,* 16–17.
26. John King, *Magical Reels: A History of Cinema in Latin America,* 9, 15, 20, 25.
27. Thompson, *Exporting Entertainment,* 4–5.
28. Ibid., 33–38.
29. Gunning, *D. W. Griffith,* 60–65.
30. Stanley, *Celluloid Empire,* 14–16.
31. Thompson, *Exporting Entertainment,* 11, 19–20.
32. Abel, *The Red Rooster Scare,* 87, 94, 97.
33. Ibid., 119.
34. Ibid., 118–19, 138–39.
35. Ibid., 150–51. Abel points out that half of the Westerns made at that time had Native Americans or Mexicans as central characters. Some plots depicted the native heroes as working out problems created by contact with white society and featured Native American rituals, dress, and physical surroundings.
36. Kennedy, *Story of Films,* 60–61.
37. Ibid., 58–60.
38. Wagenknecht, *Movies,* 20.
39. Fulton, *Motion Pictures,* 45.
40. Ibid.; Kennedy, *Story of Films,* 62–63.
41. Paula Marantz Cohen, *Silent Film and the Triumph of the American Myth,* 36–37.
42. Stanley, *Celluloid Empire,* 18–19, 21–22.
43. Anthony Slide, *Early American Cinema,* 224.
44. Wagenknecht, *Movies,* 14–15.
45. James H. Farmer, *Celluloid Wings,* 8.
46. Ibid., 10.
47. Leslie Midkoff DeBauche, *Reel Patriotism: The Movies and World War I,* xvi, 50.

48. Rhodri Jeffreys-Junes, *Changing Differences: Women and the Shaping of American Foreign Policy, 1917–1994,* 1, 11, 15. 17.
49. Thompson, *Exporting Entertainment,* 94.
50. Ibid., 86.
51. Ibid., 70–71, 40–42.

Chapter 4

1. Prendergast, *First Aviators,* 145.
2. Roger E. Bilstein, *Flight in America, 1900–1983: From the Wrights to the Astronauts,* 30.
3. Gene Gurney, *Flying Aces of World War I,* 13–15, 19–21.
4. Stephen Pendo, *Aviation in the Cinema,* 70.
5. Paul O'Neill, *Barnstormers and Speed Kings,* 25; Gurney, *Flying Aces,* 148.
6. O'Neill, *Barnstormers,* 28.
7. Jim Greenwood and Maxine Greenwood, *Stunt Flying in the Movies,* 20–31.
8. Farmer, *Celluloid Wings,* 13–14, 20.
9. Pando, *Aviation in the Cinema,* 142, 150.
10. O'Neill, *Barnstormers,* 39.
11. Bilstein, *Flight in America,* 60–61.
12. Greenwood, *Stunt Flying,* 52–63; Pando, *Aviation in the Cinema,* 85–87, 93.
13. Thomas Hart Kennedy, *An Introduction to the Economics of Air Transportation,* 55.
14. Mark Friedlander Jr. and Gene Gurney, *Higher, Faster, and Farther,* 39.
15. Ibid., 145–47, 154–55; Oliver James Lissitzyn, *International Air Transport and National Policy,* 5.
16. Lissitzyn, *International Air Transport,* 5–8.
17. David D. Lee, "Herbert Hoover and the Golden Age of Aviation," 127–31.
18. *Time Capsule/1923: A History of the Year Condensed from the Pages of* Time (New York: Time, 1967), 134–35, 140.
19. Peter Fritzsche, *A Nation of Fliers: German Aviation and the Popular Imagination,* 138, 143.
20. Bilstein, *Flight in America,* 41, 50–51.
21. Kennedy, *Economics of Air Transportation,* 68.
22. Ibid., 55.
23. See Rosalie Schwartz, *Pleasure Island: Tourism and Temptation in Cuba;* Taylor, *To Hell with Paradise.*
24. Bilstein, *Flight in America,* 55.
25. *Time Capsule/1923,* 136–37.
26. Kennedy, *Economics of Air Transportation,* 68.
27. William Wagner, *Ryan, the Aviator,* 3, 11, 25, 28, 37, 45, 47, 52.
28. Ibid., 58, 72.
29. *Los Angeles Times,* Aug. 4, 2002.
30. Douglas Corrigan, *That's My Story,* 59–60, 63, 72, 83–85, 115, 181.
31. Charles A. Lindbergh, *The Spirit of St. Louis,* 79.
32. Richard P. Hallion, "Daniel and Harry Guggenheim and the Philanthropy of Flight," 21.

33. Ibid., 25, 31–32.
34. Ibid., 19–23, 28.
35. Lee, "Herbert Hoover," 136–37.

Chapter 5

1. *The Havana Post,* Apr. 26, 1931.
2. See Cornelius Vanderbilt Whitney, *High Peaks.*
3. Horace Brock, *More about Pan Am,* 3–4.
4. Theodore Roscoe, *On the Seas and in the Skies: A History of the U.S. Navy's Air Power,* 68–69.
5. Gurney, *Flying Aces,* 134, 147.
6. Roy Allen, *The Pan American Clipper: The History of Pan American's Flying-Boats, 1931 to 1946,* 14–15.
7. Brock, *Pan Am,* 6; Robert Daley, *An American Saga: Juan Trippe and His Pan Am Empire,* 16–17.
8. Marilyn Bender and Selig Altschul, *The Chosen Instrument: Pan Am, Juan Trippe, the Rise and Fall of an American Entrepreneur,* 71. Bender and Altschul state that Trippe contacted Cuban President Gerardo Machado through a Yale connection, without mentioning a name, but White is the Yale colleague most likely to have had connections in Cuba.
9. Schwartz, *Pleasure Island,* 51; Brock, *Pan Am,* 6. Brock points out that Trippe sought to exclude other U.S. carriers, not other foreign operators.
10. *Bulletin of the Pan American Union,* 1933, 761.
11. William A. M. Burden, *The Struggle for Airways in Latin America,* 10, 15.
12. "Roaring Down to Rio," *World's Work* (July 1932): 49; Burden, *Airways in Latin America,* 17.
13. Fritzsche, *A Nation of Fliers,* 177.
14. Burden, *Airways in Latin America,* 17.
15. Fritzsche, *A Nation of Fliers,* 339.
16. Burden, *Airways in Latin America,* 22.
17. Brock, *Pan Am,* 7–8.
18. Ibid., 8–9.
19. Ibid., 9–10; Allen, *Pan Am Clipper,* 15–16.
20. Schwartz, *Pleasure Island,* 65–66.
21. Bender and Altschul, *Chosen Instrument,* 91.
22. Ibid., 91–95, 153.
23. Ibid., 98; Susan Butler, *East to the Dawn: The Life of Amelia Earhart,* 151–53.
24. Brock, *Pan Am,* 14–15.
25. Mr. [Francis] White to the Secretary, Apr. 25, 1929, Aviation File, Francis White papers, Herbert Hoover Presidential Library (hereafter cited as White papers, HH).
26. Mr. White to the Undersecretary and the Secretary, "Policy of the Department regarding Aviation Companies," July 6, 1929, Aviation File, White papers, HH.
27. Ibid.
28. Ibid.

29. Virgil E. Chenea, "Skyways That Link the Americas," 343.

30. Pan American Airways, *The First Fifty Years of Pan Am,* 1977, 2.

31. Bender and Altschul, *Chosen Instrument,* 125; J. T. Trippe to the Honorable Francis White, Aug. 3, 1928, Pan American Airways File, White papers, HH.

32. Translation of editorial from *Nuestro Diario,* July 16, 1928, enclosure with Trippe to White, Aug. 3, 1928, Pan Am Airways File, White papers, HH.

33. J. D. MacGregor to Francis White, Apr. 12 and 15, 1929, and enclosures, Pan American Airways File, White Papers, HH; Francis White to J. T. Trippe, June 1, 1929, Pan American Airways File, White papers, HH.

34. John A. Hambleton to Francis White, Sept. 12, 1928; Francis White to John A. Hambleton, Mar. 16, 1929; Francis White to Secretary of State, Apr. 29, 1929, Pan American Airways File, White papers, HH.

35. Allen, *Pan Am Clipper,* 23.

36. Ibid., 24–27.

37. W. I. Van Dusen, "Wings over Three Americas," *Scientific American* (Oct. 1931): 234–36.

38. *New York Times,* Sept. 5, 1909.

39. Friedlander and Gurney, *Higher, Faster, and Farther,* 128–44.

40. Harold G. Dick, *Graf Zeppelin and Hindenburg,* 39–40; "Big Sister for the 'Graf'," *Literary Digest* (July 29, 1933): 30; "The *Graf* at Chicago," *Literary Digest* (Nov. 4, 1933): 10.

41. Kathryn H. Fuller, *At the Picture Show: Small-Town Audiences and the Creation of Movie Fan Culture,* 172, 175, 178, 185, 187, 197.

Chapter 6

1. Robert Sklar, *Movie-Made America: A Cultural History of the American Movies,* 216–18; Emily S. Rosenberg, *Spreading the American Dream: American Economic and Cultural Expansion, 1890–1945,* 99–102; Garth Jowett, *Film, the Democratic Art,* 203.

2. Donald Crafton, *The Talkies: American Cinema's Transition to Sound, 1926–1931,* 418; C. R. Cameron, U.S. Consul, São Paulo, to the U.S. State Department, Report No. 220, Mar. 16, 1929, 832.4061/26, General Records of the U.S. Department of State, Record Group 59, National Archives, Washington, D.C. (hereafter cited as RG 59, SD/NA).

3. Allen L. Woll, *The Latin Image in American Film,* 21, 29.

4. Hershel V. Johnson to U.S. Secretary of State, dispatch no. 1269, enclosure no. 1, "Negative Response to Talkies," 812.4061/113, RG 59, SD/NA.

5. U.S. Consul, Havana, to U.S. Secretary of State, dispatch no. 351, Sept. 5, 1930, 837.4061/19; J. C. White, Chargé d'Affaires, Buenos Aires, to U.S. Secretary of State, May 15, 1930, 835.4061/2; C. R. Cameron, U.S. Consul, São Paulo, to U.S. Secretary of State, Aug. 12, 1929, 832.4061/24; all RG 59, SD/NA.

6. Crafton, *The Talkies,* 418, 422, 425, 443.

7. See Alice G. Marquis, *Hopes and Ashes: The Birth of Modern Times, 1929–1939,* 17, 20, 25–26, 30.

8. Richard B. Jewell, *The RKO Story,* 8–10.

9. "Announcement of the NBC Network," www.flash.net/~billhar/nbcanoun .htm (copy in author's possession).

10. Friton Hadden and Henry R. Luce, eds., *Time Capsule/1927* (New York: Time-Life Books, 1968), 207.

11. *Time* (Nov. 16, 1931): 23.

12. Ibid.

13. Marguerite Harrison, *There's Always Tomorrow,* quoted in Rudy Behlmer, "The Adventures of Merian C. Cooper," in Merian C. Cooper Papers, MSS 2008, L. Tom Perry Special Collections Library, Harold B. Lee Library, Brigham Young University, Provo, Utah (hereafter cited as Cooper Papers, BYU), 4.

14. Merian C. Cooper to father, no date, Box 2, Folder 5, Cooper Papers, BYU.

15. Behlmer, "Cooper," 2.

16. Cooper to father, no date, Box 2, Folder 5, Cooper Papers, BYU.

17. Cooper to father, no date, Box 5, Folder 6, and Box 2, Folder 5, Cooper Papers, BYU.

18. Comptroller of the Currency to John C. Cooper, Apr. 5, 1919, Box 2, Folder 6, Cooper Papers, BYU.

19. Cooper to father, July, 1919, Box 3, Folder 1, Cooper Papers, BYU.

20. Cooper to father, Sept. 26, Oct. 24, and Dec. 24, 1919, Cooper Papers, BYU.

21. Behlmer, "Cooper," 3.

22. Ibid., 7–9.

23. Ronald Haver, *David O. Selznick's Hollywood,* 77.

24. Gabler, *Empire,* 93.

25. *Time,* Nov. 16, 1931, 23.

26. Haver, *Selznick,* 69–70, 76; David O. Selznick, *Memos from David O. Selznick,* 111, 115.

27. Taylor, *To Hell with Paradise,* 194–96.

28. RKOS 173, "The Lost Squadron," RKO Script Materials, Special Collections, University of California, Los Angeles.

29. Cynthia Erb, *Tracking King Kong,* 61.

30. Corn, *The Winged Gospel,* 73–75.

31. Butler, *East to the Dawn,* 151–53, 159, 233, 259, 266; Corn, *Winged Gospel,* 72.

32. Elizabeth S. Bell, *Sisters of the Wind: Voices of Early Women Aviators,* 39, 40, 48, 189, 193–94.

33. *San Diego Union-Tribune,* Mar. 6, 2003.

34. *New York Times,* Feb. 2, 2003.

35. *Radio Flash,* May 4 and 16, 1932. This publication was an RKO company newsletter.

36. As the name suggests, RKO-Radio Pictures produced motion pictures. RKO Corporation controlled the distribution and exhibition of the films as well as studio operations. Thus, RCA's dominant position in RKO Corporation gave the company control over RKO-Radio Pictures, too.

37. *Radio Flash,* May 28, 1932, and Feb. 4, 1933.

38. Ibid., May 4 and 16, 1932.

39. Ibid., May 28, 1932. The house organ carried production information, as well as columns written by various department heads.
40. Ibid., Jan. 14, 1933.
41. Ibid., Dec. 17, 1932; Feb.18, Mar. 25, Apr. 15, and June 8 and 24, 1933.
42. Robert Sobel, *RCA*, 102.
43. *Pan American Air Ways*, March, 1933.
44. *Radio Flash*, Aug. 12, 1933; *Film Daily*, Aug. 14, 1933, 2.
45. Haver, *Selznick*, 76.
46. Woll, *The Latin Image*, 39; Sobel, *RCA*, 102–105; David Reich, *The Life of Nelson A. Rockefeller: Worlds to Conquer, 1908–1958*, 94–100.
47. "Flying Down to Rio," *The Motion Picture Guide*, vol. 3, 882.
48. *Radio Flash*, Jan. 14 and Mar. 18, 1933; Jewell, *The RKO Story*, 56.
49. P. W. Wilson, "Motion-Pictures Move into the New Deal," *Literary Digest* (Jan. 6, 1934): 9.

Chapter 7

1. Sumner Welles, "Draft by Sumner Welles of a Statement on Pan-American Policy," 18; Pan American Union, *Bulletin* (1933): 761.
2. Raymond Moley, *The First New Deal*, 232.
3. Sumner Welles, *The Time for Decision*, 143, 149; Welles, "Draft by Sumner Welles," 18–20.
4. *New York Times*, Jan. 20, 1931.
5. Ibid., July 18, 1932; "The Nation Spends Millions on Travel," *Literary Digest* (Sept. 30, 1933): 38.
6. "The President Begins to Carry Out the Good-Neighbor Policy, Apr. 12, 1933," in Franklin D. Roosevelt, *Public Papers and Addresses*, 129–31.
7. "Business Looks at Roosevelt," *Business Week*, Mar. 1, 1933, 1–2.
8. "Louis M. Howe, Personal Secretary to the President, to Cordell Hull, Secretary of State," Nov. 9, 1933, in Nixon, ed., *Roosevelt and Foreign Affairs*, vol. 1, 477.
9. "White House Statement on the Conference of American States in Montevideo: A Practical Expression of the Good-Neighbor Policy," in Roosevelt, *Public Papers and Addresses*, 459–60.
10. Moley, *First New Deal*, 22–26, 32.
11. "Settling the War Debts with 'Patriotic Vacations'," *Literary Digest* (May 6, 1933): 35.
12. "Big Gain in Air Travel," *Literary Digest* (Dec. 16, 1933): 38; *Business Week*, July 28, 1934, 28; July 6, 1935, 31; Dec. 21, 1936, 30; Pan American Airways, *Annual Report*, 1934.
13. Bender, *Chosen Instrument*, 215–16.
14. Butler, *Amelia Earhart*, 256–66.
15. Ibid., 271.
16. Ibid., 280–82, 288.
17. *New York Times*, July 2 and 3, 1932.
18. W. B. Courtney, "Wings of the New Deal," *Colliers* (Feb. 17, 1934): 13.
19. Ibid.

20. Gabler, *Empire,* 316–17.
21. *Film Daily,* Mar. 4, 1933.
22. "A President after Hollywood's Heart," *Literary Digest* (Apr. 22, 1933): 13.
23. *Film Daily,* June 21, 1933.
24. Gabler, *Empire,* 316, 318.
25. *Radio Flash,* Aug. 12, Sept. 9 and 16, 1933.
26. "Movies and Radio Join Varied Brood of Blue Eagle," *News Week,* Dec. 9. 1933, 34.
27. *Film Daily,* Jan. 3, 1934.
28. Irwin F. Gellman, *Good Neighbor Diplomacy: United States Policies in Latin America, 1933–1945,* 108.
29. Albrecht von Gleich, *Germany and Latin America,* 12–15; *New York Times,* Aug. 6, 1933.
30. William L. Shirer, *The Rise and Fall of the Third Reich* (New York: Simon and Schuster, 1960), 202–203.
31. *New York Times,* Dec. 29, 1933.
32. Report for Special Committee of the U.S. Senate to Investigate Foreign and Domestic, Ocean and Air Mail Contracts, Giving the Evolution of the Investment and Business of the PAA Corporation [no date], Box 63, Pan American Airways Collection, Collection Number 341, Special Collections and Archives, University of Miami.
33. Wilson, "Motion-Pictures Move," 9.
34. Ibid.
35. H. Freeman Matthews to U.S. Secretary of State, dispatch 1942, Nov. 20, 1934, 837.4061-Motion Pictures/27, RG 59, DS/NA.
36. Louis A. Pérez Jr., *On Becoming Cuban: Identity, Nationality, and Culture* (Chapel Hill: University of North Carolina Press, 1999), 284, 289.
37. Jefferson Caffery to U.S. Secretary of State, dispatch 2846 and attachments, Mar. 6, 1935, 837.4061-Motion Pictures/28; U.S. Department of State to American Embassy, Havana, telegram, Mar. 9, 1935, 837.4061-Motion Pictures/29; Jefferson Caffery to U.S. Secretary of State, dispatch 2997, Mar. 30, 1935, 837.4061-Motion Pictures/32, RG 59, DS/NA.
38. Pérez, *Becoming Cuban,* 287.
39. *San Diego Sun,* Aug. 16 and Sept. 19, 1937.
40. "Inter-American Travel Is Urged," *Star,* July 8, 1938, in General Records of the U.S. Department of Commerce, Record Group 40, Subject Files of the Director, National and Inter-American Fairs, 1929–1946, Box 20, National Archives, Washington, D.C. (hereafter RG 40, DC/NA).
41. Laurence Duggan, "First Inter-American Travel Congress," Box 20, RG40, DC/NA.
42. See Frederick L. Herron to Sumner Welles, Nov. 1, 1937, and Nov. 1, 1938, 832.4061-Motion Pictures/49 and 64; William C. Burdett to U.S. Secretary of State, Feb. 6, 1939, 832.4061-Motion Pictures/70; Frederick L. Herron to Laurence Duggan, Feb. 15, 1939, 832.4061-Motion Pictures/71; Memorandum of Conversation, U.S. Department of State, June 27, 1940, 832.4061-Motion Pictures/191, RG 59,DS/NA.
43. James Rowe Jr., memorandum for the president, June 24, 1940; John Stein-

368 / NOTES TO PAGES 339–54

beck to the President, June 24, 1940; F.D.R. to PA, memo, June 25, 1940; John to Joe, letter, no date; in Papers as President, President's Personal File, Franklin D. Roosevelt Library.

44. Norman Armour to U.S. Secretary of State, dispatch 961, July 17, 1940, 835.4061-Motion Pictures/218, RG 59, DS/NA.

45. Joe D. Walstrom to Commercial Affairs, U.S. Department of State, "The Argentine Reaction to Certain American Films," Aug. 26, 1940, 835.4061-Motion Pictures/219, RG 59, DS/NA.

46. *History of the Office of the Coordinator of Inter-American Affairs* (Washington, D.C.: U.S. Government Printing Office, 1947), 69, 71.

47. "History of the Motion Picture Society of the Americas," fourth draft, Dec. 4, 1944, Records Relating to the Motion Picture Society of the Americas, Box 961, Records of the U.S. Department of Information, Motion Picture Division, Record Group 229, National Archives, Washington, D.C.

Epilogue

1. "Bids for the Travel Dollar," *Business Week,* Apr. 21, 1934, 28–29; *News-Week* July 6, 1932, 9–10; "Signs of Recovery in Shipping," *Literary Digest* (July 29, 1933): 32.

2. "Big Gain in Air Travel," *Literary Digest* (Dec. 16, 1933): 38; *Business Week,* July 28, 1934, 28; July 6, 1935, 31; Dec. 21, 1936, 30; Pan American Airways, *Annual Report,* 1934.

3. *New York Times,* May 20, 2001, Travel Section, 11.

4. Trevor H. B. Sofield and Fung Mei Sarah Li, "Tourism Development and Cultural Policies in China," *Annals of Tourism Research* (Apr., 1998): 369–70.

5. *New York Times Magazine,* May 20, 2001.

6. *New York Times,* June 17, 2001; *Financial Times,* Jan. 12–13, 2002.

7. *Los Angeles Times,* June 16, 2002.

8. *Financial Times,* Nov. 16, 2001.

9. *Los Angeles Times,* Oct. 5, 2001.

10. Ibid., Oct. 4, 2001; *New York Times,* Sept. 29, Oct. 7, Nov. 11 and 28, Dec. 16, 2001.

11. *USA Today,* Jan. 25, 2002.

12. *New York Times,* Apr. 13, 1997.

Bibliography

Books and Articles

Abel, Richard. *The Cine Goes to Town: French Cinema, 1896–1914.* Berkeley: University of California Press, 1998.

———. *The Red Rooster Scare: Making Cinema American, 1900–1910.* Berkeley: University of California Press, 1999.

Allen, Roy. *The Pan American Clipper: The History of Pan American's Flying-Boats, 1931 to 1946.* New York: Barnes and Noble Books, 2000.

Allwood, John. *The Great Exhibitions.* London: Studio Vista, 1977.

Aron, Cindy S. *Working at Play: A History of Vacations in the United States.* New York: Oxford University Press, 1999.

Bell, Elizabeth S. *Sisters of the Wind: Voices of Early Women Aviators.* Pasadena: Trilogy Books, 1994.

Bender, Marilyn, and Selig Altschul. *The Chosen Instrument: Pan Am, Juan Trippe, the Rise and Fall of an American Entrepreneur.* New York: Simon and Schuster, 1982.

Bilstein, Roger E. *Flight in America, 1900–1983: From the Wrights to the Astronauts.* Baltimore: Johns Hopkins University Press, 1984.

Birk, Dorothy Daniels. *The World Came to St. Louis: A Visit to the 1904 World's Fair.* St. Louis: Bethany Press, 1979.

Boardman, Andrea. *Destination Mexico: "A Foreign Land a Step Away," U.S. Tourism to Mexico, 1880s–1950s.* Dallas: Southern Methodist University, DeGolyer Library, 2001.

Bosworth, C. A. "Army Men Find Planes Useful at Frisco." *Aero* (January 28, 1911).

———. "Great Flying at the Golden Gate." *Aero* (February 4, 1911).

Brock, Horace. *More about Pan-Am.* Lunenberg, Vt.: Stinehour, 1980.

Burden, William A. M. *The Struggle for Airways in Latin America.* New York: Council on Foreign Relations, 1943.

Butler, Susan. *East to the Dawn: The Life of Amelia Earhart.* Reading, Mass.: Addison-Wesley, 1997.

Chanute, Octave. *Progress in Flying Machines.* Long Beach: Lorenz and Herweg, 1976. Facsimile of 1894 edition.

Chenea, Virgil E. "Skyways That Bind the Americas." *Scientific American* (December, 1932).

Cohen, Paula Marantz. *Silent Film and the Triumph of the American Myth.* New York: Oxford University Press, 1991.

Conkling, Alfred R. *Appleton's Guide to Mexico.* New York: D. Appleton, 1884.

Corn, Joseph J. *The Winged Gospel: America's Romance with Aviation, 1900–1950.* New York: Oxford University Press, 1983.

Corrigan, Douglas. *That's My Story.* New York: E. P. Dutton, 1938.

Crafton, Donald. *The Talkies: American Cinema's Transition to Sound, 1926–1931.* Vol. 4 of *The History of the American Cinema,* ed. Charles Harpole. New York: Charles Scribner's Sons, 1997.

Crouch, Tom D. "Engineers and the Airplane." In *The Wright Brothers, Heirs of Prometheus,* ed. Richard P. Hallion. Washington, D.C.: Smithsonian Institution Press, 1978.

———. *A Dream of Wings: Americans and the Airplane, 1875–1905.* New York: W. W. Norton, 1981.

———. *The Bishop's Boys: A Life of Wilbur and Orville Wright.* New York. W. W. Norton, 1989.

Daley, Robert. *An American Saga: Juan Trippe and His Pan Am Empire.* New York: Random House, 1980.

DeBauche, Leslie Midkoff. *Reel Patriotism: The Movies and World War I.* Madison: University of Wisconsin Press, 1997.

Demetz, Peter. *The Air Show at Brescia, 1909.* New York: Farrar, Straus and Giroux, 2002.

Dick, Harold G. *Graf Zeppelin and Hindenburg.* Washington, D.C.: Smithsonian Institution Press, 1985.

Douglas, Susan J. "Amateur Operators and American Broadcasting: Shaping the Future of Radio." In *Imagining Tomorrow: History Technology, and the American Future,* ed. Joseph J. Corn. Cambridge: MIT Press, 1986.

Erb, Cynthia. *Tracking King Kong.* Detroit: Wayne State University Press, 1998.

Farmer, James H. *Celluloid Wings.* Blue Ridge Summit, Penn.: Tab Books, 1984.

Friedlander, Mark P. Jr., and Gene Gurney. *Higher, Faster, and Farther.* New York: William Morrow, 1973.

Fritzsche, Peter. *A Nation of Fliers: German Aviation and the Popular Imagination.* Cambridge: Harvard University Press, 1992.

Fuller, Kathryn H. *At the Picture Show: Small-Town Audiences and the Creation of Movie Fan Culture.* Washington, D.C.: Smithsonian Institution Press, 1996.

Fulton, Albert R. *Motion Pictures: The Development of an Art.* Norman: University of Oklahoma Press, 1980.

Gabler, Neal. *An Empire of Their Own: How the Jews Invented Hollywood.* New York: Anchor Books/Doubleday, 1988.

Gellman, Irwin F. *Good Neighbor Diplomacy: United States Policies in Latin America, 1933–1945.* Baltimore: Johns Hopkins University Press, 1979.

Greenwood, James, and Maxine Greenwood. *Stunt Flying in the Movies.* Blue Ridge Summit, Penn.: TAB Books, 1982.

Gunning, Tom. *D. W. Griffith and the Origins of American Narrative Film.* Urbana: University of Illinois Press, 1991.

———. "The World as Object Lesson: Cinema Audiences, Visual Culture, and the St. Louis World's Fair, 1904." *Film History* 6, no. 4 (Winter, 1994): 422–41.

Gurney, Gene. *Flying Aces of World War I.* New York: Random House, 1965.

Hallion, Richard P. "Daniel and Harry Guggenheim and the Philanthropy of

Flight." In *Aviation's Golden Age: Portraits from the 1920s and 1930s,* ed. William M. Leary. Iowa City: University of Iowa Press, 1989.

Hassler, Dorothy K. "Aeroplanes, Then." *Flying* (December, 1953).

Hatfield, David Daniel. *Dominguez Air Meet.* Inglewood, Calif.: Northrop University Press, 1976.

Haver, Ronald. *David O. Selznick's Hollywood.* New York: A. A. Knopf, 1980.

Hoganson, Kristin. "Cosmopolitan Domesticity: Importing the American Dream, 1865–1920." *The American Historical Review* (February, 2002).

Jarvie, I. C. *Movies and Society.* New York: Basic Books, 1970.

Jeffreys-Junes, Rhodri. *Changing Differences: Women and the Shaping of American Foreign Policy, 1917–1994.* New Brunswick, N.J.: Rutgers University Press, 1995.

Jewell, Richard B. *The RKO Story.* New York: Arlington House, 1982.

Jowett, Garth. *Film, the Democratic Art.* Boston: Little, Brown, 1976.

Kasson, John F. *Amusing the Million: Coney Island at the Turn of the Century.* New York: Hill and Wang, 1978.

Kennedy, Joseph P., ed. *The Story of the Films.* Chicago: A. W. Shaw, 1927.

Kennedy, Thomas Hart. *An Introduction to the Economics of Air Transportation.* New York: Macmillan, 1924.

King, John. *Magical Reels: A History of Cinema in Latin America.* London: Verso, 1990.

Lee, David D. "Herbert Hoover and the Golden Age of Aviation." In *Aviation's Golden Age: Portraits from the 1920s and 1930s,* ed. William M. Leary. Iowa City: University of Iowa Press, 1989.

Lindbergh, Charles A. *The Spirit of St. Louis.* New York: Charles Scribner's Sons, 1953.

Lissitzyn, Oliver James. *International Air Transport and National Policy.* New York: Council on Foreign Relations, 1942.

Lord, Walter. *The Good Years: From 1900 to the First World War.* New York: Harper and Brothers, 1960.

Marquis, Alice G. *Hopes and Ashes: The Birth of Modern Times, 1929–1939.* New York: Free Press, 1986.

Maurer, Jean-Luc, and Arlette Zeigler. "Tourism and Indonesian Cultural Minorities." In *Tourism: Manufacturing the Exotic,* ed. Pierre Rosse. Copenhagen: International Work Group for Indigenous Affairs, 1988.

McFarland, Marvin W., ed. *The Papers of Wilbur and Orville Wright,* vol. 1. New York: McGraw-Hill, 1953.

Moley, Raymond. *The First New Deal.* New York: Harcourt, Brace and World, 1966.

Mucigrosso, Robert. *Celebrating the New World: Chicago's Columbian Exposition of 1893.* Chicago: Ivan R. Dee, 1993.

Nixon, Edgar B., ed. *Franklin D. Roosevelt and Foreign Affairs.* Cambridge: Harvard University Press, 1969.

O'Neill, Paul. *Barnstormers and Speed Kings.* Alexandria, Va.: Time-Life Books, 1981.

Paris, Michael, *From the Wright Brothers to "Top Gun": Aviation, Nationalism, and Popular Cinema.* Manchester: Manchester University Press, 1995.

Pendo, Stephen. *Aviation in the Cinema.* Metuchen, N.J.: Scarecrow Press, 1995.

Pomeroy, Earl S. *In Search of the Golden West: The Tourist in Western America.* New York: Alfred A. Knopf, 1957.

Prendergast, Curtis. *The First Aviators.* Alexandria, Va.: Time-Life Books, 1980.

Reich, David. *The Life of Nelson A. Rockefeller: Worlds to Conquer, 1908–1958.* New York: Doubleday, 1996.

Roemer, Michael. *Telling Stories: Post-Modernism and the Invalidation of Traditional Narrative.* Lanham, Md.: Roman and Littlefield, 1995.

Roosevelt, Franklin D. *The Public Papers and Addresses of Franklin D. Roosevelt,* vol. 2, comp. Samuel I. Rosenman. New York: Random House, 1938.

Roscoe, Theodore. *On the Seas and in the Skies: A History of the U.S. Navy's Air Power.* New York: Hawthorn Books, 1970.

Rosenberg, Emily S. *Spreading the American Dream: American Economic and Cultural Expansion, 1890–1945.* New York: Hill and Wang, 1982.

Roville, Gerard. "Ethnic Minorities and the Development of Tourism in the Valleys of North Pakistan." In *Tourism: Manufacturing the Exotic,* ed. Pierre Rosse. Copenhagen: International Work Group for Indigenous Affairs, 1988.

Rowe, Percy. *The Great Atlantic Air Race.* Toronto: McClelland and Stewart, 1977.

Rydell, Robert W. *All the World's a Fair: Visions of Empire at American International Expositions, 1876–1916.* Chicago: University of Chicago Press, 1984.

Schwartz, Rosalie. *Pleasure Island: Tourism and Temptation in Cuba.* Lincoln: University of Nebraska Press, 1997.

Selznick, David O. *Memos from David O. Selznick.* New York: Viking, 1972.

Sklar, Robert. *Movie-Made America: A Cultural History of the American Movies.* New York: Random House Vintage Books, 1976.

Slide, Anthony. *Early American Cinema.* Metuchen, N.J.: Scarecrow, Press, 1994.

Sobel, Robert. *RCA.* New York: Stein and Day, 1986.

Sofield, Trevor H. B., and Fung Mei Sarah Li. "Tourism Development and Cultural Policies in China." *Annals of Tourism Research* (April, 1998).

Stanley, Robert H. *The Celluloid Empire: A History of the American Movie Industry.* New York: Hastings House, 1978.

Taylor, Frank F. *To Hell with Paradise: A History of the Jamaican Tourist Industry.* Pittsburgh: University of Pittsburgh Press, 1993.

Thompson, Kristin. *Exporting Entertainment: America in the World Film Market 1907–1934.* London: British Film Institute, 1985.

Villard, Henry Serrano. *Contact! The Story of the Early Birds,* rev. ed. Washington, D.C.: Smithsonian Institution Press, 1987.

Von Gleich, Albrecht. *Germany and Latin America.* Santa Monica: Rand Corporation, 1968.

Wagenknecht, Edward. *The Movies in the Age of Innocence.* Norman: University of Oklahoma Press, 1962.

Wagner, William. *Ryan, the Aviator.* New York: McGraw-Hill, 1971.

Welles, Sumner. *The Time for Decision.* New York: Harper and Brothers, 1944.

———. "Draft by Sumner Welles of a Statement on Pan-American Policy." Vol. 1 of *Franklin D. Roosevelt and Foreign Affairs,* ed. Edgar B. Nixon. Cambridge: Harvard University Press, 1969.

Whitney, Cornelius Vanderbilt. *High Peaks.* Lexington: University Press of Kentucky, 1977.

Wohl, Robert. *A Passion for Wings: Aviation and the Western Imagination, 1908–1918.* New Haven: Yale University Press, 1994.

Woll, Allen L. *The Latin Image in American Film.* Los Angeles: UCLA Latin American Center Publication, 1977.

Wright, Hamilton. "With the Bird-Men at Los Angeles." *The World To-Day.* London: Published for the Movement for World Evangelization by Marshall, Morgan, and Scott, Ltd., n.d.

Wright, Wilbur. "Flying as a Sport." *Scientific American* (February 29, 1908).

Periodicals

Annals of Tourism Research
Business Week
Film Daily
Literary Digest
Los Angeles Times
Motion Picture Guide
New York Times
News-Week
Pan American Air Ways
Radio Flash
Scientific American
Time Magazine

Archives and Collections

Cooper, Merian C. Papers. L. Tom Perry Special Collections Library, Harold B. Lee Library, Brigham Young University.

Pan American Airways Collection. Special Collections and Archives. University of Miami.

RKO-Radio Pictures Script and Production Files. Special Collections. University of California, Los Angeles.

San Diego Aerospace Museum Archive.

U.S. Department of Commerce. General Records. Record Group 40. U.S. National Archives.

U.S. Department of Information. Records of Record Group 229. Records relating to the Motion Picture Society of the Americas. U.S. National Archives.

U.S. Department of State. General Records. Record Group 59. U.S. National Archives.

White, Francis. Papers. Herbert Hoover Presidential Library.

Index

Photos and illustrations are indicated with *italicized* page numbers.